Vice President of Editorial — Melissa Wagner
Director of Acquisitions — Mikaela Felty
Director of Book Development — Jocelynn Hessler
Production Manager — Mike Brehm
Cover Design — Jose Rosado

Published in the United States of America by
IGI Global Scientific Publishing
701 East Chocolate Avenue
Hershey, PA, 17033, USA
Tel: 717-533-8845 | Fax: 717-533-7115
Website: https://www.igi-global.com E-mail: cust@igi-global.com

Library of Congress Cataloging-in-Publication Data

LCCN: 2025044991 (CIP Data Pending)
ISBN13: 9798337374062
Isbn13Softcover: 9798337374079
EISBN13: 9798337374086

British Cataloguing in Publication Data
A Cataloguing in Publication record for this book is available from the British Library.

Security, Law, and Influence in the Age of Techno-Politics

Alp Cenk Arslan
Turkish National Police Academy, Turkey

Murat Tinas
Turkish National Police Academy, Turkey

IGI Global
Scientific Publishing
Publishing Tomorrow's Research Today

Table of Contents

Detailed Table of Contents

This chapter explores the weaponization of social media as a transformative force in national security, international relations, and domestic politics. By examining key case studies—such as Facebook's role in the 2016 U.S. elections, the politicized functions of X during the 2024 election cycle, TikTok's involvement in the Mahsa Amini protests, and information warfare during the Russia-Ukraine conflict—the chapter illustrates how algorithm-driven platforms reshape political discourse and public perception. The analysis frames these developments through the lens of algorithmic targeting, diminished state control, and platform privatization, emphasizing the blurred boundaries between civic engagement and strategic influence. The chapter proposes the "Algorithmic Shaping Theory" to describe how social media platforms systematically structure public consciousness and behavior, urging a reevaluation of governance, surveillance, and global digital policy frameworks.

This chapter critically examines the increasing use of Facial Recognition Technology (FRT) in EU border management and its implications for migrant communities, asylum seekers, and displaced persons. While FRT is often promoted as a tool for enhancing security and streamlining identity verification, its deployment raises significant concerns related to privacy violations, algorithmic bias, and systemic discrimination. This study explores these challenges through legal, ethical, and human rights lenses, offering an interdisciplinary analysis of biometric surveillance practices at borders. The chapter underscores the urgent need for robust regulatory frameworks, oversight mechanisms, and alternative, rights-based approaches to border security.

This chapter provides a comprehensive examination of the cybersecurity threats facing critical digital infrastructure systems in an era of rapid digital transformation. Focusing on three essential sectors—energy, water, and financial systems—the analysis reveals how cyber attackers exploit vulnerabilities in these infrastructures,

challenges. This situation highlights the urgent need for Bangladesh to enact laws that protect individuals from unjustified internet shutdowns.

Preface

We are living through a period of accelerated convergence between technology, security, and political power where algorithms write policies, data governs borders, and digital infrastructure forms the bedrock of both statecraft and civil life. As digital tools reshape governance, influence, and control, a new era of *techno-politics* emerges in which technological decisions are inextricably linked with legal frameworks, societal norms, and geopolitical strategies.

The goal of this edited volume is to explore this convergence through a multidisciplinary lens, combining perspectives from law, policing, intelligence, cyber governance, and international relations. Each chapter offers an in-depth case study or theoretical framework to understand how digital transformation is altering both the practice and the principles of governance, particularly in areas where human rights, security, and state power intersect.

What unites these diverse contributions is a central premise: *technology is not neutral*. From algorithms to infrastructure, from predictive policing to biometric surveillance, technological choices embed political values, legal assumptions, and institutional priorities. This book aims to provide policymakers, scholars, and practitioners with critical insights into how to navigate these techno-political waters.

CHAPTER OVERVIEW

Chapter 1: Techno-Politics and Data Protection Law

By Aurelie Banck

This opening chapter positions data protection as a cornerstone of techno-politics. Drawing on global regulatory trends such as the EU's GDPR and the rising push for data localization, Banck demonstrates how legal frameworks around personal data are used not only to protect privacy but also to assert geopolitical influence.

The chapter emphasizes the strategic role of data regulation in shaping international digital power dynamics.

Chapter 2: Policing with Algorithms: Sci-Fi Visions Meet Real-World Repercussions/Applications (APPRAISE)

By Sérgio Felgueiras and Sónia Morgado

Exploring the boundary between dystopian fiction and present-day policing, this chapter examines real-world AI law enforcement tools and the ethical concerns they raise. Focusing on the EU's APPRAISE project, the authors highlight the importance of transparency, bias mitigation, and human oversight in deploying AI responsibly within security agencies.

Chapter 3: OSINT in the Techno-Political Era: From Intelligence Collection to Exerting Influence

By Murat Tınas and Doğukan Tuncal

This chapter traces the evolution of Open Source Intelligence (OSINT) in the digital era. The authors argue that OSINT is no longer just a method of collection, but a strategic instrument for influence operations. Using the case of Russia's actions in Crimea and Ukraine, the chapter analyzes how state actors use OSINT to shape public narratives and geopolitical perception.

Chapter 4: A New Era of Predictive Risk Management: Building JA.I.Net Engine for Law Enforcement, Diplomacy and Healthcare

By Mihaela Meresi

Introducing a novel AI framework, JA.I.Net, this chapter fuses ancient cyclical models from Jyotisha with modern AI techniques to mitigate bias and enhance predictive accuracy in fields like law enforcement and healthcare. Meresi proposes a culturally integrated, ethically aligned approach to AI development, challenging the Western-centric paradigms that dominate current systems.

Chapter 5: Algorithmic Armaments: Social Media's Role in Information Warfare and Political Influence

By Efnan Gülşen Özkan

This chapter dissects the use of social media platforms as tools of information warfare and political manipulation. Drawing on recent case studies, including U.S.

and Iranian political unrest and the Russia-Ukraine conflict, Özkan develops the "Algorithmic Shaping Theory" to explain how algorithmic systems condition public behavior, challenging the foundations of democratic discourse and state sovereignty.

Chapter 6: The Impact of Facial Recognition Technology on Migrant Communities at EU Borders

By Gianina Anemona Radu

Radu offers a critical human rights perspective on the deployment of Facial Recognition Technology (FRT) at European borders. Through an interdisciplinary lens, this chapter examines how biometric surveillance disproportionately affects vulnerable populations, raising pressing legal and ethical concerns related to discrimination, oversight, and accountability.

Chapter 7: Protection of Critical Digital Infrastructure: Cyber Attacks and Threats to Energy, Water, and Financial Systems

By Yusuf Dinçel

Focusing on cybersecurity vulnerabilities in critical infrastructure sectors, Dinçel explores how increasing digitization has made essential systems more efficient—but also more fragile. The chapter discusses state and non-state cyber threats targeting energy, water, and financial services, and calls for robust protection strategies to ensure national resilience.

Chapter 8: Extremism in the Age of the Internet: The Rise of Algorithmic Radicalization

By Yağız Atay

Atay delves into the psychological and technological underpinnings of algorithm-driven radicalization. Framing it as a hybrid sociotechnical phenomenon, this chapter emphasizes the urgent need for regulatory, educational, and technological interventions to prevent the spread of extremism facilitated by content recommendation systems and echo chambers.

Chapter 9: Bangladesh Quota Reform Movement 2024: The Impact of Internet Shutdown on the ICT Sector

By Psychee Zaman, Md. Sanaullah, and Md. Ashrafuzzaman

Concluding the volume, this chapter examines the real-world consequences of government-imposed internet shutdowns, using the 2024 Bangladesh student protests as a case study. The authors detail the economic, social, and professional disruptions caused by digital blackouts, advocating for stronger legal protections against arbitrary shutdowns in democratic societies.

Together, the chapters in *Security, Law, and Influence in the Age of Techno-Politics* challenge readers to reconsider the foundational assumptions of governance, power, and security in the 21st century. The questions raised about accountability, surveillance, influence, and digital rights are technical, legal, and deeply political. We hope this book will serve as a vital resource for those navigating this complex terrain.

Alp Cenk Arslan & Murat Tınas
Turkish National Police Academy
September 2025

Chapter 1
Techno-Politics and Data Protection Law

Aurelie Banck
https://orcid.org/0009-0009-0060-0165
Paris Evry, France

ABSTRACT

Data and in particular personal data are everywhere and when technological transformations through IA deployment are rapidly redefining worldwide equilibrium of powers, data protection and privacy is a critical issue and a fundamental pillar of Technico politics. The increasing digitalization of private companies and public services raises urgent questions about sovereignty, surveillance and global inequalities. This article explores how data protection and privacy is at the core of political influence and is part of "Techno-Politics". From the "Brussels effect" of the GDPR to the requirement of data localization in some countries, we will expose how countries try to influence digital innovation and market through data protection regulations. It aims to raise awareness among policymakers, legal professionals, and the public about the importance of data protection within the context of Techno-Politics.

INTRODUCTION

In the digital age, data protection and privacy are no longer just technical or legal concerns — they are at the heart of *techno-politics*. Drawing on the work of Langdon Winner (1980) and Sheila Jasanoff (2004), this chapter defines *techno-politics* as the ways in which technological systems and infrastructures are deeply embedded in power relations, shaping and reflecting broader political and social struggles. From

DOI: 10.4018/979-8-3373-7406-2.ch001

this perspective, data flows, digital infrastructures, and regulatory frameworks are not neutral but actively co-produce new forms of governance, control, and resistance.

Winner's classic question, "Do artefacts have politics?" (1980) remains central today. From smart city infrastructures to AI algorithms, technologies configure who holds power, who benefits, and who is made vulnerable. Jasanoff (2004) expands this by showing how science and technology co-produce social orders and legal regimes. In this sense, techno-politics is not a niche debate but a framework to understand how data infrastructures — cloud systems, cross-border transfers, algorithmic surveillance — reflect and reshape sovereignty, rights, and power. Modern data protection law emerged in Europe partly as a response to the risks of authoritarian misuse of information systems. Today, it operates as both a rights guarantee and a market governance tool. The EU's General Data Protection Regulation (GDPR), the US's fragmented sectoral approach, and China's state-centered model show how different actors embed values and strategic goals in legal rules.

This chapter focuses on three contemporary techno-political tensions: the clash between cross-border data flows and national data sovereignty, the conflict between privacy rights and expanding state surveillance capabilities, and the growing asymmetry of power between nation-states and dominant digital platforms. These tensions are not abstract: they manifest in concrete events such as the European Court of Justice's *Schrems II* ruling (2020), which invalidated the EU–US Privacy Shield; national restrictions on TikTok and Huawei, reflecting concerns over data sovereignty and geopolitical rivalry; and ongoing enforcement actions against companies like Clearview AI for unlawful biometric surveillance. This analysis argues that robust data governance is a critical site where questions of autonomy, democracy, and sovereignty are being redefined. The goal is to demonstrate how contemporary data protection regimes — from the EU's GDPR and AI Act to China's Data Security Law and emerging US privacy legislation — illustrate competing models of techno-political power.

By combining conceptual clarity, theoretical grounding, and recent empirical cases, this chapter seeks to contribute to ongoing debates on how societies can govern technological transformation in ways that safeguard fundamental rights and democratic accountability.

This article is structured into three parts. The first part examines the current legal framework and regulations: in Europe, focusing on how the General Data Protection Regulation (GDPR) has propagated the "Brussels Effect" globally, un the United States and in China.

The sedond part explores how other regimes utilize data regulation as a means of power to extend their influence. Its illustrates conflict between cross-border data flows and national data sovereignty, frictions between individual privacy rights and state surveillance and the struggle between the regulatory reach of national governments and the global dominance of transnational digital platforms.

Finally, the last part analyses the outcomes in a globalized world, where disparities in data protection regulations and privacy standards lead to inequalities not only for individuals but also for companies.

Objective: This article aims to raise awareness among policymakers, legal professionals, and the public about the importance of data protection within the context of Techno-Politics.

1. LEGAL FRAMEWORK AND REGULATION

In this part, three regional contexts are examined: Europe, as the normative leader in data protection law; the United States, as the primary hub of digital innovation and home to major platforms such as Facebook, the broader GAFAM cluster, and OpenAI; and China, representing a state-centric model that combines technological advancement with strong sovereign oversight of data.

1.1 Europe

1.1.1 Data protection regulation in Europe – a long story short

Data protection in Europe has a long history. Since the Second World War and the persecution of individuals based on their political beliefs, religion, or sexual orientation, Europe—particularly France and Germany—and the defiance against public registers and their interconnexion in a time when Internet was experimental have strongly advocated for establishing data protection rules. This commitment became especially prominent in the 1970s. Looking back, the first data protection regulation was introduced in 1970 at the regional level by the German state of Hesse[1]. The first national-level regulation followed in 1971, enacted by Sweden[2]. In France, data protection legislation was adopted in 1978 after a public scandal.

Initially, this comprehensive framework was designed to protect individuals from state authorities. The main driver behind its adoption was a government project aiming to interconnect public databases using a single identifier. As more national data protection laws emerged across Europe, the European Commission grew concerned about the impact of fragmented legal frameworks. At the time, the Commission's primary objective was to establish a single market in which goods and services could move freely — recognizing that data plays a supporting role in this exchange. Consequently, any barriers to the free flow of data were seen as potential obstacles to commercial trade. Regulation was, even then, a fundamental aspect of the business environment.

That's why in 1990 the Commission of European Communities[3] proposed to adopt a data protection framework at European level. In the explanatory statement, the project clearly stated that

> *« the difference in levels of protection of privacy in relation to the processing of personal data afforded in the Member States may prevent the transmission of such data from the territory of one Member State to that of another Member State; (…) this difference may therefore constitute an obstacle to the pursuit of a number of economic activities at Community level, distort competition and impede authorities in the discharge of their responsibilities under Community law ».*

1.1.2 Directive 95/46/EC: First Steps Toward Harmonization

After five years of discussion, the Directive 95/46/EC of the European Parliament and of the Council of 24 October 1995 on the protection of individuals with regard to the processing of personal data and the free movement of such data (Directive 95/46/EC of the European Parliament and of the Council of 24 October 1995 on the protection of individuals with regard to the processing of personal data and on the free movement of such data. (1995). *Official Journal of the European Communities*, L 281, 31–50.https://eur-lex.europa.eu/legal-content/EN/TXT/?uri =celex%3A31995L0046) was enacted by European institutions. As all Directive which is a text of minimum harmonisation, the text needed to be transposed in each Member States to be included in the national framework. Like all directives—being instruments of minimum harmonization contrary to regulation which a directly applicable in all Members States—it required transposition into the national laws of each Member State to become effective domestically. As a result, despite the existence of a European-level framework, data protection across Europe remained fragmented. This led to distortions of competition and created legal complexity for market players operating within the European Union (EU). As an example, France decided to submit some processing activities (based on their level of risks) to prior authorisation of the French Data Protection Authority (DPA)– the Commission National de l'Informatique et des Libertés – when the same processing in another European country was subject to a simple prior record to the national DPA. Beyond that, the 2000s were marked by the rise of the Internet, the widespread adoption of personal computers (from just 213 computers connected to the Internet in 1981 to over 300 million users by 2001 (Sandywell, 2006), and the emergence of new services and players. The threat to personal data was no longer primarily its concentration in public hands, but rather its widespread dissemination across a rapidly expanding digital landscape. As Barry Sandywell pointed out, the risks associated with technology have been "democratized" alongside its widespread adoption. This situation leaded to a new paradigm which implied to review European data protection rules.

1.1.3 General Data Protection Regulation (GDPR): a new area

The European Commission announced its intention to adopt a new framework in 2010 (European Commission. (2010). The first draft of the General Data Protection Regulation (GDPR) was published in 2012, and the regulation was formally adopted in 2016, with a two-year transition period to allow public and private entities time to comply. Like many digital regulations, the GDPR was the subject of intense debate among Member States and stakeholders—over 4,000 amendments were proposed in the European Parliament—and lobbying from major tech companies was particularly strong in attempts to influence its provisions.

As a result, the final text of the GDPR represents a compromise. It includes around 50 provisions where Member States are allowed to introduce national specificities, provided they notify the European Commission before adoption. The original aim of the Commission was to strengthen individual rights by ensuring the consistent application of data protection rules, increasing transparency for data subjects, and enhancing individuals' control over their personal data. However, as with the previous directive, one of the core objectives remained the facilitation of the internal market and the free flow of data. It was also this principle that led the Commission to switch legal instruments—from a directive, which requires national transposition, to a regulation, which is directly applicable across all Member States.

Beyond that change, and from a broader perspective, the main difference between the GDPR and the previous legal framework is the introduction of a cross-cutting principle of accountability. Organizations subject to the regulation must be able to demonstrate at any time that they are in compliance with the regulation. The administrative burden of recording processing activities with the Data Protection Authority (DPA) was reduced, marking a shift from an ex-ante to an ex-post regulatory approach—where the DPA is now more focused on enforcement and remediation.

As a result, infringements of the regulation could be "subject to administrative fine up to 20 000 000 million euros or in the case of an undertaking, up to 4% of the total worldwide annual turnover of the preceding financial year, whichever is higher» (European Union. (2016). *General Data Protection Regulation (GDPR), Regulation (EU) 2016/679 of the European Parliament and of the Council of 27 April 2016 on the protection of natural persons with regard to the processing of personal data and on the free movement of such data, and repealing Directive 95/46/ EC*, Article 83(4). *Official Journal of the European Union*, L 119, 1–88). Additionally, Member States are required to authorize non-profit bodies, organizations, or associations that are properly constituted and active in the field of data protection to lodge complaints on behalf of individuals and to request compensation in front of civil jurisdictions. These entities can exercise individuals' rights, lodge complaint and seek compensation, thereby enabling collective action to improve the redress available to individuals in cases of harm caused by data breaches and infringements.

This comprehensive framework has rapidly shaped data protection laws in numerous jurisdictions worldwide. The question remains: how did this come to be? By using legal means.

1.1.4 "Brussels effet", how European data protection rules became an international framework

The GDPR's standards and comprehensive approach to data protection law in Europe have significantly shaped, and continue to shape, global data protection norms. As the world's largest consumer market, Europe has solidified this influence through three key legal instruments—extraterritoriality, sub-processing and contractual obligations, and data transfer mechanisms—all of which had their roots in the earlier directive

1.1.4.1 Extraterritorial Effect

The GDPR is applicable to companies, legal and natural person which are established within Europe. Its scope of applicability is determined not by the data subject's citizenship or residency, but by the location of the data processing entity. Consequently, an American citizen staying in Paris would be afforded the protections of the GDPR when their personal data is processed by a hotel or any other organization operating within the EU. In order to ensure a level playing field within the European market and to subject entities not established within the EU to the same regulatory obligations, the GDPR was endowed with extraterritorial effect. Article 3(2) stipulates that the Regulation applies to « *the processing of personal data of data subjects who are in the Union by a controller or processor not established in the Union, where the processing activities are related to the offering of goods or services, irrespective of whether payment by the data subject is required, to such data subjects in the Union; or the monitoring of their behaviour as far as their behaviour takes place within the Union.* » This second basis for applicability is commonly referred to as the targeting criterion. It ensures that non-European entities processing the personal data of individuals located within the EU are subject to the same regulatory framework as EU-based actors. Data Protection Authorities (DPAs) have already enforced the GDPR against non-EU companies—most notably against Clearview AI, a facial recognition firm, which was fined by both the French and Italian DPAs for collecting images of individuals from online sources without adequate transparency or lawful basis. Granting a regulation extraterritorial effect is, in practice, one of the most effective mechanisms for extending its scope. It compels foreign companies to comply with the regulation as a condition for accessing the European market. A second, more subtle mechanism involves leveraging the value chain by requiring entities—such as distributors or contractors—to impose upon their suppliers the same regulatory obligations to which they themselves are subject.

1.1.4.2 Value-Chain Enforcement

Article 28 of the GDPR specifies that, 'Where processing is to be carried out on behalf of a controller, the controller shall use only processors providing sufficient guarantees to implement appropriate technical and organisational measures in such a manner that processing will meet the requirements of this Regulation and ensure the protection of the rights of the data subject.' In this regard, the outsourcing of data processing activities must not serve as a means to circumvent or diminish the level of protection afforded to personal data by the data controller. Consequently, Article 28(3) of the GDPR mandates that processing by a processor be governed by a contract or other legal act under Union or Member State law. This legal instrument must contain a range of specific provisions, foremost among them the obligation for the processor to act exclusively on the documented instructions of the controller, to apply security measures compliant with the GDPR, to report data breaches to the controller and to demonstrate its compliance. These requirements apply regardless of the processor's geographical location, including when the processor is established outside the European Union. Moreover, Article 28(4) stipulates that, 'Where a processor engages another processor for carrying out specific processing activities on behalf of the controller, the same data protection obligations as set out in the contract or other legal act between the controller and the processor, as referred to in paragraph 3, shall be imposed on that other processor by way of a contract or other legal act under Union or Member State law.' In this way, the GDPR ensures that its obligations cascade throughout the entire value chain. These requirements multiplicate the number of companies having to apply European data protection rules and are shaping global privacy landscape through contractual measures.

Outsourcing the processing of personal data to a supplier must not be used as a means to weaken the level of protection afforded under the GDPR, nor should the transfer of such data to a third country serve to circumvent these safeguards.

1.1.4.3 Data Transfers Mechanisms

The GDPR establishes a secure space for the exchange of personal data within Europe. This 'data protection area' extends beyond the boundaries of the European Union, encompassing the entire European Economic Area (EEA), and thereby applies to a total of 30 countries. Countries outside the European Economic Area are designated as 'third countries,' and transfers of personal data to these jurisdictions are subject to specific restrictions and conditions. The underlying objective is to extend the GDPR's sphere of protection through either multilateral or bilateral mechanisms.

The analysis will cover the mechanisms for international data transfers under the GDPR, such as adequacy decisions, standard contractual clauses, and binding corporate rules. It will assess the impact of these mechanisms on global data flows and the challenges they present.

The "Brussels Effect" refers to the European Union's (EU) unique ability to set global standards through its regulations, even beyond its own borders. This effect occurs because the EU is one of the largest and most lucrative consumer markets in the world, with stringent regulatory standards and strong enforcement mechanisms. As a result, multinational companies often find it more efficient and cost-effective to comply with EU regulations globally, rather than maintaining different standards for different markets. The concept of the "Brussels Effect" was coined by Professor Anu Bradford of Columbia Law School. She introduced the term in 2012, and later published a comprehensive book on the topic: *The Brussels Effect: How the European Union Rules the World (*Bradford, Anu, "The Brussels Effect: How the European Union Rules the World" (2020). *Faculty Books*. 232). GDPR is a key example of this phenomenon, clearly demonstrating how EU can influence market without coercion or formal international agreement.

As a result of the Brussels Effect, the number of data protection regulations around the world has grown significantly over the past decade. In 2010, there were only 56 such regulations globally. By 2020, this number had nearly doubled to 106. Today, more than 160 jurisdictions (DLA Piper. (n.d.). have adopted data protection laws. However, these laws vary in their level of maturity—some are well-developed and closely aligned with comprehensive frameworks like the EU's General Data Protection Regulation (GDPR), while others are still in the early stages of implementation and enforcement. In addition to data protection, the European Union actively pursues the regulation of the entire data economy via a range of complementary legal frameworks.

1.4.4 Beyond GDPR: regulations of digital economy as a whole

Beyond the GDPR, several other legislative and policy initiatives illustrate the EU's broader and long-term commitment to fostering data-driven innovation within a regulated and ethical framework.

- **Digital Single Market Strategy**: Launched in 2015, this strategy aims to tear down regulatory walls and move from 28 national digital markets to a single one. By harmonizing digital regulations across member states, the EU seeks to reduce fragmentation and barriers to cross-border digital activity, enabling businesses to scale faster and citizens to access services uniformly across Europe. The Strategy encompasses areas like e-commerce, geo-blocking, online content, VAT modernization, and cybersecurity, creating an integrated environment conducive to innovation.

- **Digital Services Act (DSA)** (European Union. (2022). *Regulation (EU) 2022/2065 of the European Parliament and of the Council of 19 October 2022 on a Single Market for Digital Services (Digital Services Act) and amending Directive 2000/31/EC*. Official Journal of the European Union, L 277, 1–102. https://eur-lex.europa.eu/legal-content/EN/TXT/?uri=CELEX%3A32022R2065) **and Digital Markets Act (DMA)** (European Union. (2022). *Regulation (EU) 2022/1925 of the European Parliament and of the Council of 14 September 2022 on contestable and fair markets in the digital sector (Digital Markets Act) and amending Directives (EU) 2019/1937 and (EU) 2020/1828*. Official Journal of the European Union, L 265, 1–66. https://eur-lex.europa.eu/legal-content/EN/TXT/?uri=CELEX%3A32022R1925): These landmark regulations, adopted in 2022, represent a comprehensive overhaul of the rules governing digital platforms. The DSA seeks to enhance accountability, transparency, and user protections in online environments, particularly by regulating illegal content and disinformation. The DMA targets the anti-competitive behaviors of "gatekeeper" platforms, promoting contestability and fairness in digital markets. Together, these acts aim to ensure that innovation is not stifled by monopolistic practices, thereby enabling a more dynamic and competitive digital ecosystem.
- **Data Governance Act (DGA)** (European Union. (2022). *Regulation (EU) 2022/868 of the European Parliament and of the Council of 30 May 2022 on European data governance (Data Governance Act) and amending Regulation (EU) 2018/1724*. Official Journal of the European Union, L 152, 1–44. https://eur-lex.europa.eu/legal-content/EN/TXT/?uri=CELEX%3A32022R0868) **and Data Act** (European Union. (2024). *Regulation (EU) 2023/2854 of the European Parliament and of the Council of 13 December 2023 on harmonised rules on fair access to and use of data (Data Act)*. Official Journal of the European Union, L 2023/2854, 1–64. https://eur-lex.europa.eu/legal-content/EN/TXT/?uri=CELEX%3A32023R2854): Adopted to address emerging challenges around data availability and interoperability, these regulations promote the reuse of public-sector data, the creation of common European data spaces, and the establishment of trusted data-sharing intermediaries. The DGA facilitates voluntary data sharing across sectors and borders, encouraging innovative uses of data while preserving trust. The Data Act complements this by enhancing data portability and ensuring fair access to indus-

trial data, empowering businesses, especially SMEs, to harness data-driven opportunities.

- **Artificial Intelligence Act (AIA)** (European Parliament and Council of the European Union. (2024). *Regulation (EU) 2024/1689 of the European Parliament and of the Council on artificial intelligence (Artificial Intelligence Act)*. Official Journal of the European Union. https://eur-lex.europa.eu/legal-content/EN/TXT/?uri=CELEX%3A32024R1689): Proposed in 2021 and still undergoing legislative negotiation, the AIA introduces a risk-based framework for the development and deployment of AI systems. High-risk AI applications—such as those used in critical infrastructure, education, or law enforcement—will be subject to stringent requirements, while minimal-risk applications face lighter obligations. By fostering trustworthy AI, the EU seeks to stimulate innovation in a manner that aligns with its core values of human dignity, democracy, and the rule of law.

These legislative instruments collectively aim to create a robust, inclusive, and sustainable digital ecosystem founded on the twin pillars of rights protection and economic resilience. By embedding ethical considerations directly into the digital economy, the EU aspires not merely to regulate the digital transition but to actively shape it according to a vision of responsible innovation that serves society as a whole. This vision stands in contrast to the regulatory stance adopted by the United States, another leading actor in the global digital market.

1.2 The United States

1.2.1 Market-Led Innovation with Emerging Regulatory Trends: Historical Context and Policy Orientation

In contrast to the European Union, the United States has historically prioritized economic freedom, technological advancement, and entrepreneurial dynamism over the establishment of a comprehensive, unified data protection regime. The American legal tradition strongly favors a sectoral approach to privacy and data regulation, whereby protections emerge from a patchwork of industry-specific statutes, common law torts, and consumer protection doctrines rather than through a centralized framework. This decentralized system reflects broader constitutional values emphasizing freedom of speech, free market competition, and limited government intervention in private enterprise.

Key federal statutes exemplify this sectoral model:

- Health Insurance Portability and Accountability Act (HIPAA): Enacted in 1996, HIPAA establishes national standards for the protection of sensitive patient health information. It applies to healthcare providers, insurers, and clearinghouses, imposing strict requirements on the handling of medical records.
- Gramm-Leach-Bliley Act (GLBA): Passed in 1999, the GLBA regulates the collection, disclosure, and safeguarding of consumers' financial information by financial institutions. It mandates transparency through privacy notices and requires institutions to implement safeguards to protect customer data.
- Children's Online Privacy Protection Act (COPPA): Introduced in 1998, COPPA governs the online collection of personal information from children under the age of 13. It requires verifiable parental consent and places limitations on the types of data that can be collected.

Despite these sector-specific protections, the absence of an overarching federal privacy law has led to a regulatory landscape that is highly fragmented and reactive rather than cohesive and anticipatory. Gaps between sectoral statutes often leave large categories of personal data unprotected, and inconsistent requirements across industries and jurisdictions create compliance challenges for businesses operating at scale.

Moreover, this sectoral approach has proven ill-suited to addressing the complexities of the modern data economy, where personal data flows seamlessly across sectors, borders, and technological platforms. The proliferation of big data analytics, machine learning, and behavioral advertising has exposed significant regulatory blind spots, resulting in high-profile data breaches, widespread public mistrust, and calls for systemic reform.

State-level initiatives—such as the California Consumer Privacy Act California Consumer Privacy Act ((CCPA), Cal. Civ. Code § 1798.100 et seq. (2018)) and its successor, the California Privacy Rights Act (California Privacy Rights Act (CPRA), California Proposition 24 (2020)) —have partially filled the void, demonstrating a growing appetite for stronger privacy protections. Nonetheless, the lack of federal uniformity risks creating a "patchwork quilt" of privacy laws that may ultimately hinder innovation by imposing conflicting obligations on interstate commerce.

Calls for a comprehensive federal privacy law have intensified in recent years, with bipartisan legislative proposals such as the American Data Privacy Protection Act (ADPPA) seeking to establish baseline standards. However, political disagreements over issues such as preemption of state laws and the scope of private rights of action have thus far impeded progress.

The United States' continued reliance on a sectoral, reactive model stands in stark contrast to the European Union's proactive, rights-based approach, highlighting fundamental differences in regulatory philosophy and cultural attitudes toward privacy, innovation, and the role of government in the digital economy.

1.2.2 State-Level Initiatives and Federal Proposals

In the absence of a comprehensive federal privacy framework, individual U.S. states have increasingly taken the lead in establishing their own data protection regimes. These state-level initiatives have significantly reshaped the American privacy landscape, introducing varied but often robust models for safeguarding personal information.

- **California Consumer Privacy Act (CCPA)** and **California Privacy Rights Act (CPRA)**: California has been at the forefront of state-level privacy reform. The CCPA, enacted in 2018, provides consumers with unprecedented rights regarding their personal data, including the right to access, delete, and opt-out of the sale of personal information. The CPRA, approved by voters in 2020, strengthens and expands the CCPA by creating the California Privacy Protection Agency (CPPA), granting consumers new rights such as the right to correct inaccurate data and to limit the use of sensitive personal information. California's framework has become a de facto model for privacy legislation across the United States.
- **Virginia Consumer Data Protection Act (VCDPA)** (Va. Code Ann. § 59.1-575 et seq. (2021): Enacted in 2021, Virginia's VCDPA establishes consumer rights similar to those found in the GDPR, such as the rights to access, correct, delete, and obtain a copy of personal data. It also imposes obligations on data controllers and processors to conduct data protection assessments for high-risk processing activities. Unlike the CCPA, the VCDPA incorporates a more business-friendly approach, with fewer private rights of action.
- **Colorado Privacy Act (CPA)** (Colo. Rev. Stat. § 6-1-1301 et seq. (2021)): Passed in 2021, the CPA mirrors many aspects of both the CCPA and VCDPA, including consumer rights and requirements for data protection assessments. It introduces nuanced obligations regarding transparency, purpose specification, and secondary use limitations, and it empowers the Colorado Attorney General to promulgate rules ensuring compliance.

Beyond these, several other states, including Utah, Connecticut, and Oregon, have passed or are considering similar comprehensive privacy laws, further diversifying the U.S. data protection landscape.

At the federal level, legislative proposals such as the **American Data Privacy Protection Act (ADPPA)** represent serious attempts to establish harmonized national standards. The ADPPA, introduced with bipartisan support, seeks to balance consumer rights with business interests by imposing data minimization obligations, strengthening transparency requirements, and granting individuals greater control over their data. Notably, it proposes preemption of state laws and limited private rights of action—two issues that have historically been stumbling blocks in federal privacy negotiations.

Despite growing momentum, significant political obstacles remain. Debates persist over the extent to which federal legislation should preempt stricter state laws like the CCPA/CPRA, and whether individuals should have the right to sue companies for privacy violations. Moreover, concerns about enforcement mechanisms, regulatory oversight, and the balance between innovation and protection continue to complicate consensus-building efforts.

In the absence of comprehensive federal legislation, the trend toward state-led privacy regulation is likely to accelerate, further increasing regulatory complexity for businesses operating across multiple jurisdictions. The evolving patchwork of laws underscores the urgent need for coherent national privacy standards that provide robust protections while fostering innovation and economic growth.

1.2.3 Impacts on Innovation

The sectoral and market-driven approach to data protection in the United States has had profound implications for innovation, technological development, and competitive dynamics both domestically and globally. On one hand, the relatively permissive regulatory environment has historically enabled American companies to pursue rapid innovation with minimal compliance constraints. On the other hand, emerging regulatory fragmentation and growing public distrust in data practices are increasingly challenging the sustainability of this model.

Rapid Innovation and Market Dynamism

The absence of a comprehensive federal data protection framework has allowed American technology companies to experiment freely with novel business models centered around the collection, analysis, and monetization of personal data. The "move fast and break things" ethos, particularly prevalent among Silicon Valley firms, thrived in an environment where regulatory barriers were minimal and innovation cycles could proceed with few legal encumbrances. This permissive environment facilitated the meteoric rise of platform giants such as Google, Facebook (Meta), Amazon, and Apple, whose business models leverage extensive personal data collection to offer free or low-cost digital services.

Access to vast amounts of consumer data without stringent restrictions has been a critical driver of advancements in targeted advertising, personalized content delivery, and behavioral analytics. It has also underpinned significant progress in emerging technologies such as artificial intelligence, predictive analytics, and Internet of Things (IoT) applications. For much of the 21st century, the U.S. maintained a global competitive advantage by fostering an ecosystem that rewarded speed, scalability, and data-driven innovation.

Fragmentation and Rising Compliance Costs

However, the sectoral nature of U.S. privacy regulation has begun to introduce substantial complexity for businesses. As multiple states enact divergent privacy laws — with California, Virginia, Colorado, and others establishing distinct regulatory regimes — companies operating nationally must navigate a labyrinth of overlapping and sometimes conflicting obligations. This patchwork imposes increased compliance costs, legal uncertainty, and operational burdens, particularly for small and medium-sized enterprises (SMEs) and startups that lack the resources of large multinationals.

Moreover, the absence of federal preemption has complicated efforts to develop uniform privacy standards, leading to fears that a "race to the top" among states could result in excessively stringent requirements that stifle innovation. For many businesses, the need to adapt to an evolving mosaic of state-level laws mirrors the very compliance challenges that U.S. critics once cited against the GDPR.

Erosion of Consumer Trust

Another critical impact on innovation stems from the erosion of consumer trust. High-profile incidents — such as the Equifax data breach, the misuse of Facebook data by Cambridge Analytica, and repeated revelations of widespread surveillance practices — have severely undermined public confidence in the ability of companies and institutions to safeguard personal information.

Surveys consistently indicate that a majority of Americans feel they have little to no control over the data collected about them and that companies are not transparent about their practices. This growing mistrust poses significant risks to the long-term viability of data-driven innovation models, as consumer skepticism may lead to reduced willingness to share information, increased use of privacy-enhancing tools, and stronger demands for regulatory intervention.

Trust, once lost, is difficult to rebuild — and in a digital economy increasingly reliant on voluntary data sharing, trust is a critical enabler of sustainable innovation.

Chilling Effects and Defensive Innovation

In response to the heightened regulatory uncertainty and public scrutiny, some firms have adopted defensive innovation strategies, emphasizing compliance over creativity. Rather than exploring bold new uses of data, companies may prioritize minimizing legal risks, resulting in more conservative product development approaches. This chilling effect, although less pronounced than under GDPR regimes, is nonetheless beginning to reshape the American innovation landscape.

Large, resource-rich firms are better positioned to adapt to the evolving regulatory environment, while smaller innovators may struggle to navigate the complexities, leading to market consolidation and reduced diversity in technological solutions. In this sense, the same dynamics observed in Europe regarding SMEs' challenges are beginning to materialize in the U.S. context as well.

Opportunities for Competitive Differentiation

Despite these challenges, emerging privacy regulations also present opportunities for innovation and competitive differentiation. Companies that proactively adopt privacy-by-design principles, enhance transparency, and empower users with greater control over their data may be able to position themselves as market leaders in the new digital trust economy.

There is growing consumer demand for products and services that prioritize ethical data practices, and companies that respond effectively can tap into this demand. Privacy-focused firms such as DuckDuckGo (in search engines) and Signal (in messaging) illustrate how building trust can serve as a powerful differentiator.

Moreover, innovation in privacy-enhancing technologies (PETs), decentralized identity solutions, and secure data sharing platforms is a rapidly growing field, offering new avenues for entrepreneurial activity and technological leadership.

The U.S. approach to data protection has historically enabled extraordinary innovation by minimizing regulatory barriers. Yet, without a coherent and forward-looking federal privacy framework, the risks of fragmentation, compliance burdens, trust erosion, and defensive innovation are mounting.

At this critical juncture, policymakers, businesses, and civil society must collaboratively reimagine a model of innovation that integrates robust privacy protections as an enabler — rather than an impediment — to technological progress. Failing to do so could jeopardize America's long-standing leadership in the digital economy and cede the initiative to jurisdictions that succeed in building more trusted, resilient digital ecosystems.

Following the discussion of Europe and the United States, it is essential to assess a third major player in the global data protection landscape: China.

1.3 China: State-Led Innovation and Data Sovereignty

China's data protection strategy is profoundly shaped by its dual ambitions: consolidating state power and accelerating digital innovation to achieve global technological leadership. The Chinese government regards data as a "national strategic resource," essential both for driving economic modernization and for maintaining internal political stability. Consequently, China's regulatory framework reflects a synthesis of promoting innovation while simultaneously exerting robust state control over data flows.

1.3.1 Strategic Framework

China has established a comprehensive and evolving legal framework that governs cybersecurity, data security, and personal information protection. The three cornerstone statutes in this architecture are:

- **Cybersecurity Law** (Cybersecurity Law of the People's Republic of China) **(2017)**: This law laid the foundational requirements for network security, critical information infrastructure protection, and data localization. It introduced the notion of "network sovereignty," asserting the state's paramount role in overseeing all information infrastructure within its borders.
- **Data Security Law (DSL)** (Data Security Law of the People's Republic of China, 2021): The DSL expands regulatory oversight to all data activities, emphasizing the classification and hierarchical management of data based on its importance to national security, the economy, and public interests. It imposes stringent obligations on companies to implement data protection mechanisms and conduct regular risk assessments.
- **Personal Information Protection Law (PIPL) (2021)**: Often described as China's equivalent to the GDPR, the PIPL establishes comprehensive rights for individuals over their personal data and imposes extensive obligations on data handlers. However, notable differences include broader exceptions for state access and significant emphasis on "personal information processors'" duties.

Together, these laws create a sophisticated framework that is extraterritorial in scope, applying to entities outside China if they process Chinese citizens' data.

1.3.2 Data Localization and Cross-Border Transfers

A defining feature of China's data governance model is its rigorous data localization requirements. Companies deemed critical information infrastructure operators must store all personal and important data within China. Cross-border data transfers are permissible only after undergoing government-conducted security assessments, particularly if the data involves sensitive sectors like finance, transportation, or telecommunications.

This localization policy serves multiple strategic purposes: preserving national security, facilitating government surveillance capabilities, and enhancing economic self-sufficiency by ensuring that data—often called "the new oil"—remains under domestic control.

The restrictive environment surrounding data transfers has presented challenges for multinational corporations operating in China, raising compliance costs, creating operational barriers, and complicating participation in global data ecosystems.

1.3.3 Impacts on Innovation

China's distinctive approach to data governance has simultaneously enabled remarkable technological innovation and raised serious concerns about digital authoritarianism.

Technological Advancement and Global Competitiveness

China's digital economy has experienced explosive growth under this regulatory regime. Companies like Alibaba, Tencent, ByteDance, and Huawei have leveraged the vast domestic market, abundant data resources, and state-backed industrial policies to pioneer advancements in e-commerce, fintech, artificial intelligence, and telecommunications. Massive datasets collected under relatively permissive domestic surveillance norms have fueled AI training at an unprecedented scale, positioning China as a global leader in AI research and applications.

Government-led initiatives such as **"Made in China 2025"** and the **"Next Generation Artificial Intelligence Development Plan"** illustrate the state's strategic vision to dominate future high-tech industries. Significant investments in research and development, coupled with relaxed data-sharing rules between companies and public authorities, have accelerated the deployment of innovative technologies.

Innovation Under Constraints

Nonetheless, China's model presents innovation trade-offs. The emphasis on state control introduces risks of stifling open scientific inquiry, limiting information flow, and deterring international collaboration. Strict content regulation, censorship, and government intervention in corporate affairs (e.g., actions against tech giants like Ant Group) can discourage risk-taking and creative entrepreneurship.

Moreover, China's data governance framework has contributed to "digital decoupling" between China and Western economies. Diverging standards on privacy, cybersecurity, and information governance have led to geopolitical tensions, supply chain fragmentation, and restricted market access for Chinese and foreign firms alike.

Global Influence and "Digital Silk Road"

Beyond its borders, China is actively exporting its digital governance model through initiatives like the **"Digital Silk Road,"** part of the broader Belt and Road Initiative (BRI). By promoting Chinese standards for data management, smart cities, surveillance technologies, and 5G infrastructure in partner countries, China seeks to extend its influence over global digital norms and infrastructure development.

While these efforts offer emerging economies new technological options, they also raise concerns about the diffusion of authoritarian digital practices, including surveillance, censorship, and limited privacy protections.

1.4 Comparative Analysis

Table 1. Comparative Analysis

Criteria	European Union	United States	China
Regulatory Philosophy	Rights-based, trust-building	Market-driven, sectoral	State-centered, sovereignty-driven
Legal Framework	Comprehensive (GDPR, DSA, DMA, AIA)	Fragmented (HIPAA, GLBA, CCPA, CPRA)	Comprehensive but state-prioritized (PIPL, DSL)
Impact on Innovation	Trust as innovation catalyst; burden on SMEs	Rapid innovation; trust erosion risks	Rapid innovation; censorship concerns
Global Influence	High (Brussels Effect)	High (Big Tech dominance)	Rising (Digital Silk Road)

The divergent approaches of the EU, US, and China to data governance reflect their distinct social contracts, economic priorities, and political structures. While the EU champions trust and rights, the US prioritizes market dynamism, and China emphasizes state control.

Once the regulatory perspectives of Europe, the United States, and China have been discussed, we will explore concrete case studies demonstrating how data protection regimes have triggered conflicts among states, market players, and contrasting visions for governing data.

2. CONTEMPORARY CASES STUDIES

To avoid excessive abstraction, this section anchors the techno-political analysis in specific, recent developments. These cases demonstrate how legal frameworks, corporate strategies, and state interests intersect to shape the global governance of data. As discussed, the European Union has sought to influence data protection regulation on a large scale by governing cross-border data transfers. Personal data circulates throughout global value chains, and a primary objective of European regulators is to ensure that the personal data of individuals within Europe enjoys the same level of protection regardless of where it is processed. This objective has given rise to significant legal cases, most notably *Schrems II*.

2.1 Schrems II and Transatlantic Data Flows

The *Schrems II* ruling (2020) by the European Court of Justice (ECJ) invalidated the EU–US Privacy Shield framework, which had previously enabled over 5,000 companies to transfer personal data legally from the EU to the US. The decision was driven by concerns that US surveillance laws — particularly Section 702 of the FISA Amendments Act and Executive Order 12333 — failed to provide EU citizens with adequate legal remedies or safeguards comparable to the GDPR's guarantees. This landmark ruling forced multinational companies, from technology giants to small and medium-sized enterprises (SMEs), to urgently re-assess their data transfer mechanisms. Many organisations pivoted to Standard Contractual Clauses (SCCs) as an alternative, but the ECJ emphasised that these too require "case-by-case" assessments and the implementation of supplementary measures if the destination country cannot ensure an equivalent level of data protection.

Schrems II demonstrates how European courts function as techno-political gate-keepers, asserting EU privacy norms extraterritorially and influencing the global governance of digital flows. The ruling exemplifies the capacity of legal instruments to reconfigure cross-border data trade while simultaneously upholding fundamental rights. However, it also introduces significant legal and operational uncertainty for companies engaged in transatlantic data exchanges, compelling firms to allocate additional resources to compliance and risk mitigation. Moreover, the decision has intensified diplomatic and economic tensions between the European Union and the United States, prompting protracted negotiations for a successor framework and sparking debates about digital sovereignty, regulatory divergence, and the balance between national security and individual privacy.

In this context, *Schrems II* is not merely a legal precedent but a manifestation of a broader techno-political struggle over the territorial reach of data protection standards in an increasingly interconnected world. It highlights the contested nature of global digital governance and the pivotal role of courts, civil society actors, and data protection authorities in shaping the evolving landscape of cross-border data flows. As such, it serves as a critical case for understanding how legal contestation and judicial oversight can recalibrate the power dynamics between states, corporations, and individuals in the digital age.

Another emblematic example of how tensions between technological innovation, legal regulation, and fundamental rights unfold is the case of Clearview AI, which highlights the complex challenges posed by facial recognition technologies and the large-scale collection of biometric data."

2.2 Clearview AI and Biometric Surveillance

Another emblematic example of how tensions between technological innovation, legal regulation, and fundamental rights unfold is the case of Clearview AI, which highlights the complex challenges posed by facial recognition technologies and the large-scale collection of biometric data. Clearview AI, a US-based company, built a vast database by scraping billions of images from publicly accessible websites and social media platforms without the explicit consent of the individuals depicted. Its powerful facial recognition tool has been marketed to law enforcement agencies and private actors worldwide, raising profound concerns about privacy, mass surveillance, and the erosion of anonymity in public spaces.

European data protection authorities have responded forcefully to Clearview's practices, arguing that they violate core principles of the General Data Protection Regulation (GDPR), such as purpose limitation, transparency, and lawful consent. Several national regulators, including those in France, Italy, and the United Kingdom, have issued orders demanding that Clearview cease processing data relating to person within EU and delete any data already collected. These actions illustrate the extraterritorial reach of European data protection norms and the challenges of enforcing privacy rights against companies operating in jurisdictions with weaker or divergent regulatory standards.

The Clearview AI case thus underscores how emerging surveillance technologies can clash with established legal safeguards, placing regulators in the position of having to balance innovation and security interests against the protection of individual rights. Moreover, it reveals the practical difficulties of ensuring effective enforcement when data collection practices are global, opaque, and technologically sophisticated. Like *Schrems II*, this case exemplifies how legal and regulatory interventions can reshape corporate practices and push the global governance of data towards greater accountability—while also sparking debates about digital sovereignty, technological limits, and the normative boundaries of acceptable data use.

While the Clearview AI case foregrounds the tensions around biometric surveillance and consent, the controversies surrounding TikTok illustrate how geopolitical concerns, platform governance, and questions of national security intersect with data protection in the context of a globally popular social media platform."

2.3 TikTok, Data Sovereignty, and Platform Governance

The Chinese-owned app TikTok became a focal point in global debates over data sovereignty and national security. Between 2020 and 2024, the US, India, and several EU member states took steps to ban or restrict TikTok on government devices — citing risks that user data could be accessed by the Chinese state under China's National Intelligence Law.

India's 2020 ban on TikTok and dozens of other Chinese apps, justified on grounds of data security and digital sovereignty, affected hundreds of millions of users and triggered trade tensions. In the US, attempts under the Trump administration to force TikTok's sale to a domestic company foreshadowed ongoing discussions under the Biden administration about national security reviews and possible bans.

TikTok's case illustrates how techno-politics extends beyond privacy to encompass geopolitics, industrial policy, and platform governance. It demonstrates that data infrastructures can become tools of statecraft, trade leverage, and ideological contestation — and shows how states may invoke security narratives to restrict foreign digital influence.

The preceding case studies demonstrate that conflicts over data protection regulations are not limited to abstract legal principles but play out in tangible disputes between states, corporations, and regulatory bodies. However, while advanced economies such as the European Union, the United States, and China actively shape global data governance through robust legal frameworks and enforcement, large parts of the world remain on the margins of this techno-political landscape. It is therefore crucial to examine how these asymmetries create and reinforce global inequalities in data protection and digital access. The next section turns to this dimension, highlighting how regulatory gaps, uneven enforcement capacities, and structural dependencies contribute to a widening digital divide.

3. GLOBAL INEQUALITIES IN DATA PROTECTION AND DIGITAL ACCESS

The global landscape of data protection is characterized not only by regulatory diversity but also by profound inequalities. Differences in regulatory capacities, technological infrastructures, and political will across regions have exacerbated existing socio-economic divides. In an interconnected world where data flows transcend national boundaries, disparities in data protection frameworks create new forms of digital inequality, undermining human rights, limiting economic opportunities, and entrenching geopolitical imbalances.

This section explores the multifaceted dimensions of global inequalities in data protection, focusing on the digital divide, the economic ramifications of regulatory disparities, and their broader implications for global innovation and social justice.

3.1 The Digital Divide and Data Protection

Traditionally, the "digital divide" referred to unequal access to internet connectivity and digital technologies. Today, it increasingly encompasses disparities in data protection, digital literacy, and control over personal information. Individuals in regions with weak or non-existent data protection frameworks are disproportionately vulnerable to exploitation, surveillance, and exclusion from the benefits of the digital economy.

While the European Union, parts of North America, and some Asian economies have robust privacy laws, many low- and middle-income countries (LMICs) still lack comprehensive data governance frameworks. As a result, billions of people navigate the digital landscape without meaningful protections or recourse against abuses.

3.1.1 Understanding the Digital Divide: Data Protection as a New Dimension of Inequality

Robust data protection frameworks are essential for ensuring that individuals can safely participate in the digital economy. However, many low- and middle-income countries (LMICs) lack comprehensive data protection laws. As of 2024, over 40% of UN member states had either weak or non-existent data protection regulations.

This regulatory gap leaves vulnerable populations exposed to exploitative practices, including:

- Unconsented data harvesting
- Algorithmic discrimination
- Identity theft and financial fraud

Moreover, the absence of legal recourse exacerbates power asymmetries between global technology firms and individuals in the Global South.

3.1.2 Structural Causes of Regulatory Gaps

Several interrelated structural factors contribute to the persistence of regulatory gaps in data protection across different regions of the world, particularly in developing economies.

Institutional Capacity Deficits: Many countries lack the institutional foundations necessary to draft, implement, and enforce comprehensive data protection laws. Regulatory bodies often suffer from underfunding, insufficient staffing, and a lack of technical expertise needed to keep pace with the rapid evolution of digital technologies. Without strong data protection authorities capable of independent oversight and effective enforcement, even well-drafted laws can fail in practice.

Economic Priorities and Resource Constraints: In low- and middle-income countries, economic priorities often focus on immediate development needs such as poverty alleviation, healthcare, infrastructure, and education. As a result, issues related to digital rights and privacy may be perceived as secondary concerns, leading to delays in legislative initiatives or weak regulatory frameworks that favor economic growth over individual rights.

Geopolitical and Trade Pressures: Developing countries frequently face external pressures from powerful economic actors and multinational corporations that seek minimal regulatory restrictions on data exploitation. In some cases, international trade agreements may prioritize the liberalization of data flows without sufficient safeguards for privacy and data protection, limiting the policy space available for emerging economies to craft robust data governance regimes.

Technological Dependence: Reliance on foreign technology providers for digital infrastructure and services can also limit regulatory autonomy. Countries dependent on imported technologies may be reluctant to impose strict data protection requirements for fear of disrupting critical services or alienating key partners. This technological dependence creates a cycle where external norms and business models are imported alongside infrastructure, often without adequate local adaptation or scrutiny.

Legal Transplantation Without Localization: When countries adopt data protection laws modeled on foreign frameworks like the GDPR without adapting them to local legal traditions, socio-economic conditions, and enforcement capacities, the resulting regulations can be ineffective or counterproductive. Legal transplantation without meaningful localization can create compliance burdens that local businesses are ill-equipped to meet, or produce laws that are poorly enforced and quickly eroded.

Lack of Public Awareness and Civic Advocacy: In many regions, public understanding of data privacy issues remains limited. Without strong civic advocacy and informed citizen demand for rights-respecting data governance, political incentives to prioritize data protection are weakened. Grassroots movements, civil society organizations, and independent media play crucial roles in pushing for stronger protections, but their effectiveness varies widely across different political and cultural contexts.

Addressing these structural causes requires a comprehensive, context-sensitive approach that combines international support with local capacity-building efforts. It is essential to recognize that robust data protection frameworks are not luxury goods for wealthy nations, but essential foundations for democratic governance, economic resilience, and human dignity in the digital age.

3.2 Economic Implications of Data Protection Inequalities

3.2.1 Barriers to Digital Trade

Divergent data protection standards act as non-tariff barriers to digital trade. Companies face increased compliance costs when operating across jurisdictions with inconsistent rules, deterring investment in less regulated markets.

For LMICs, this dynamic can:

- Limit access to global digital markets
- Reduce attractiveness to foreign investors
- Impede local digital entrepreneurship

Divergent data protection standards act as non-tariff barriers to digital trade. Countries with strong data protection regimes often impose restrictions on data transfers to jurisdictions deemed to have inadequate safeguards. This creates significant barriers for businesses operating across borders, particularly for SMEs in developing countries that cannot easily navigate complex compliance requirements.

The absence of harmonized frameworks impedes participation in the global digital economy, limits foreign direct investment, and restricts opportunities for technological collaboration.

3.2.2 Exploitative Data Practices

In the absence of strong data protection laws, multinational corporations often engage in "data colonialism"—extracting valuable personal and behavioral data from populations without adequate compensation or benefit-sharing.

Examples include:

- Targeted advertising exploiting personal vulnerabilities
- Data-driven political manipulation
- Surveillance capitalism models prioritizing profit over privacy

Such practices entrench economic inequalities, as value derived from data flows disproportionately to actors in highly regulated, wealthy jurisdictions. Such practices reinforce systemic disadvantages, making it harder for developing economies to build homegrown digital industries and achieve data sovereignty.

3.3 Innovation and Capacity Disparities

3.3.1 Innovation in the Absence of Regulation

Strong data rights can foster trust and innovation by creating environments where individuals feel safe sharing information. However, the uneven global distribution of privacy protections results in a concentration of innovation within jurisdictions that have both robust data laws and the technical ecosystems to support advanced research and development.

Countries without effective data governance structures risk being relegated to the periphery of the digital economy—as mere consumers of imported technologies rather than creators of new digital solutions.

3.3.2 Capacity Constraints

Developing countries often face significant capacity challenges:

- Lack of trained data protection officers
- Weak enforcement institutions
- Insufficient judicial expertise on data rights

The lack of robust data protection frameworks and limited opportunities for digital innovation in developing economies contribute significantly to the phenomenon of "brain drain," where skilled individuals, particularly in technology-related fields, migrate to jurisdictions that offer better career prospects, stronger legal protections, and more vibrant innovation ecosystems. This movement of talent has profound implications not only for the individuals involved but also for their home countries, which lose critical human capital needed to drive domestic innovation and build resilient digital economies.

Brain drain exacerbates technological dependence by depriving developing nations of the skilled workforce required to build indigenous tech sectors, conduct advanced research, and implement sophisticated regulatory regimes. As a result, these countries become increasingly reliant on imported technologies, platforms, and digital infrastructures developed elsewhere—often with little regard for local needs, cultures, or interests.

The dependency extends beyond technology consumption to critical areas such as cybersecurity, digital financial services, and e-governance. In many cases, developing countries must adopt foreign solutions without the capacity to audit, customize, or control these systems fully, raising serious concerns about digital sovereignty, privacy risks, and economic resilience.

Moreover, technological dependence can reinforce structural inequalities within the global economy. Countries unable to develop their digital industries remain trapped in low-value segments of global value chains, exporting raw materials and labor while importing high-value digital goods and services. This dynamic mirrors historical patterns of economic colonialism, where control over critical infrastructure and knowledge flows remains concentrated in the hands of a few technologically advanced nations.

Addressing brain drain and technological dependence requires a multifaceted strategy that includes:

- **Investing in Education and Research**: Expanding access to high-quality STEM education, supporting local research institutions, and promoting entrepreneurship are essential to building robust domestic innovation ecosystems.
- **Strengthening Data Protection Frameworks**: Ensuring that individuals' rights are protected and that data governance practices align with international best practices can make countries more attractive to digital talent and investment.
- **Creating Incentives for Return Migration**: Programs that encourage diaspora communities to return, invest, or collaborate with their home countries can help reverse brain drain and foster knowledge transfer.
- **Promoting South-South Cooperation**: Collaborative efforts among developing countries can facilitate technology transfer, build regional innovation hubs, and reduce dependency on dominant digital powers.

Ultimately, fostering homegrown technological capacity and retaining skilled talent are critical to achieving true digital sovereignty, equitable participation in the global digital economy, and sustainable, inclusive development.

These constraints hinder both the protection of individual rights and the development of competitive digital industries.

3.4 Policy Responses and Global Initiatives

3.4.1 International Cooperation

International cooperation is a critical pillar in addressing the global disparities in data protection regimes. Recognizing the transnational nature of data flows and digital services, various multilateral and regional institutions have initiated frameworks and agreements to encourage the development and harmonization of privacy standards worldwide. These efforts seek to balance the free movement of information with the imperative to protect personal data, thereby fostering trust and equity in the global digital economy.

Notable examples of international initiatives include:

- **Convention 108+**[4]: As the only legally binding international treaty dedicated to data protection, the modernized Council of Europe Convention 108+ plays a foundational role in global privacy governance. It emphasizes accountability, transparency, and the rights of individuals in both public and private sector data processing. Its accessibility to non-European states reflects its aspiration to become a universal reference for personal data protection.
- **OECD Privacy Guidelines**[5]: These guidelines offer a flexible yet principled approach to privacy protection that promotes cross-border data flows while ensuring that privacy safeguards are upheld. The guidelines introduce concepts such as purpose specification, data minimization, and individual participation, which have influenced the development of privacy laws in diverse jurisdictions.
- **African Union's Malabo Convention**[6]: The Convention on Cyber Security and Personal Data Protection, adopted in 2014, is a landmark regional instrument for African countries. It aims to strengthen cyber resilience while establishing a harmonized framework for data protection, including the creation of national data protection authorities and the recognition of data subjects' rights.

Despite these advances, the global uptake of such frameworks remains uneven. Many states have yet to ratify or fully implement the standards outlined in these instruments, often due to capacity constraints, competing national priorities, or political hesitancy. Furthermore, enforcement mechanisms tend to be weak or nonexistent, reducing the practical impact of these agreements.

To enhance the effectiveness of international cooperation, future initiatives should focus on:

- **Strengthening monitoring and accountability mechanisms** to ensure compliance and meaningful enforcement.
- **Providing technical and financial assistance** to support implementation, particularly in low-income countries.
- **Facilitating multistakeholder dialogue** that includes governments, civil society, the private sector, and academia.
- **Building bridges between regional frameworks** to enhance interoperability without imposing a one-size-fits-all model.

Ultimately, robust international cooperation grounded in mutual respect, capacity sharing, and human rights alignment is essential for building a fairer and more inclusive global data protection ecosystem.

3.4.2 Capacity Building

International organizations and leading economies must prioritize capacity building to bridge global data protection divides. Effective strategies include:

- Providing technical assistance for legislative drafting and regulatory enforcement.
- Facilitating knowledge-sharing platforms for best practices.
- Funding education programs in data governance, cybersecurity, and digital rights.

Capacity building should empower local institutions, respecting cultural contexts while adhering to universal human rights principles.

3.4.3 Interoperability and Technology Transfer

Rather than enforcing a singular model, efforts should focus on promoting interoperability between different data protection frameworks. Initiatives such as the OECD Privacy Guidelines, Convention 108+, and regional instruments like the African Union's Malabo Convention provide models for flexible, rights-respecting frameworks that support cross-border data flows.

Interoperability helps prevent digital fragmentation while respecting national sovereignty and diversity.

Encouraging technology transfer can help developing countries leapfrog to modern data protection infrastructures. This includes:

- Open-source data protection tools

- Privacy-enhancing technologies (PETs)
- Training in ethical AI and data governance

Best practices from the EU's GDPR implementation offer valuable lessons but must be adapted to local contexts to ensure relevance and sustainability.

3.5 Ethical Considerations

3.5.1 Digital Sovereignty vs. Digital Imperalism

Efforts to strengthen global data protection must avoid replicating patterns of digital imperialism, where dominant actors impose their data governance frameworks on less powerful regions without meaningful consultation or respect for local contexts. True digital sovereignty is not merely about maintaining territorial control over data; it is about empowering countries and communities to define and enforce data governance structures that align with their societal values, cultural traditions, and development goals, while remaining consistent with universal human rights principles.

The tension between digital sovereignty and global interoperability must be carefully managed. Excessive data nationalism risks fragmenting the global internet into isolated "data islands," undermining innovation and cross-border collaboration. Conversely, unchecked digital imperialism can erode national autonomy, marginalize local voices, and exacerbate global inequalities.

Achieving a balanced model requires inclusive global dialogue that respects diversity while upholding fundamental rights to privacy, freedom of expression, and equitable access to information.

3.5.2 Avoiding Regulatory Imperialism

In the global effort to develop coherent standards for data protection, it is essential to avoid the trap of regulatory imperialism—where one dominant jurisdiction, such as the European Union with its GDPR, sets a model that other countries are expected to follow uncritically. While the EU framework has had a positive influence on raising global awareness and promoting stronger privacy rights, the imposition of a single model without adaptation to local contexts can undermine national sovereignty, legal traditions, and socio-cultural values.

Effective data protection does not require uniformity, but rather interoperability. Legal frameworks should be designed to allow for contextualization, taking into account diverse legal systems, economic conditions, technological readiness, and governance capacities. Flexibility ensures that regulations are both enforceable and relevant in their specific environments.

Moreover, the development of global data protection norms must be inclusive and participatory. It is vital to involve countries from all regions—particularly those in the Global South—in shaping these standards. Their perspectives, priorities, and constraints must be considered to build trust, legitimacy, and long-term effectiveness.

By prioritizing cooperation over imposition, the international community can work toward data protection systems that are globally coherent but locally grounded—ensuring privacy and trust while respecting diversity in approach and implementation.

3.5.3 Promoting Human-Centric Data Governance

Ultimately, data governance frameworks should prioritize human dignity, autonomy, and equity over purely economic considerations.

To create a digital environment that truly serves humanity, human rights must be integrated by design into all stages of technological development and policy-making. This approach requires moving beyond reactive compliance measures towards proactive embedding of rights considerations in:

- System architecture and technical standards.
- Business models and corporate strategies.
- National legislation and international agreements.

Human rights impact assessments, participatory design processes, and transparent accountability mechanisms should become standard practices across sectors. Embedding human rights by design strengthens resilience against abuses, builds public trust, and ensures that technological innovation advances human dignity rather than undermining it.

CONCLUSION

Emerging Technologies

The rise of artificial intelligence (AI), biometric surveillance, blockchain technologies, quantum computing, and algorithmic decision-making processes introduces profound new risks that threaten to exacerbate existing digital inequalities. Unregulated AI systems, for instance, risk perpetuating biases and discrimination against marginalized populations due to their reliance on historical datasets that reflect societal inequalities. Similarly, biometric surveillance technologies, if deployed without sufficient oversight, can enable unprecedented levels of control over vulnerable communities, undermining democratic governance and civil liberties.

The widespread use of facial recognition technology and predictive policing algorithms without comprehensive ethical guidelines disproportionately targets historically disadvantaged groups, amplifying systemic biases. Furthermore, the advent of quantum computing threatens to undermine current cryptographic protections, exposing personal data to new vulnerabilities and increasing the urgency for developing quantum-resistant security protocols.

In this rapidly evolving technological environment, regulatory innovation must remain proactive, adaptable, and inclusive. Failing to anticipate the implications of emerging technologies could result in a future where data inequalities not only persist but become further entrenched through technological reinforcement.

Building a Human Centric Global Digital Order

The establishment of a human-centric global digital order is an urgent imperative for safeguarding dignity, autonomy, and equity in the digital age. This vision demands the creation of international frameworks that prioritize individuals' rights over mere economic efficiencies or geopolitical dominance.

Building such an order requires:

- Strengthened Multilateral Institutions: Organizations like the United Nations, International Telecommunication Union (ITU), and the World Trade Organization (WTO) must be empowered and reformed to address the governance of global data flows and digital rights, ensuring that policy decisions are inclusive, transparent, and equitable.
- Global Digital Compacts: Proposals for global digital compacts should include enforceable commitments to human rights standards in data governance, the ethical use of AI, and universal access to digital infrastructure and education.
- Multi-Stakeholder Dialogues: Governments, private sector actors, academia, civil society, and indigenous communities must collaborate in shaping norms, regulations, and standards to ensure that diverse perspectives are represented.

A human-centric digital future is predicated on embedding fairness, accountability, transparency, and respect for human dignity at the core of technological innovation.

Rethinking Data Ownership and Empowerment

An additional dimension of addressing future challenges involves fundamentally rethinking concepts of data ownership. Currently, individuals often have little meaningful control over the data they generate, which is typically owned and monetized by corporate entities.

Emerging models propose shifting toward frameworks of data stewardship or data trusts, wherein individuals collectively govern their data through intermediaries committed to prioritizing their rights and interests. Such models could democratize access to data-driven benefits while safeguarding privacy and autonomy.

Decentralized technologies, including blockchain-based identity management systems, present potential pathways for empowering individuals to retain ownership and control over their digital selves. However, these solutions require careful design to avoid creating new forms of exclusion or complexity.

Global inequalities in data protection represent both a profound challenge and a critical opportunity. Without concerted action, disparities will deepen, entrenching economic, social, and political divides. However, with inclusive, collaborative efforts, it is possible to build a more equitable digital future.

Policymakers, international organizations, private sector actors, and civil society must work together to:

- Strengthen institutional capacities
- Foster global cooperation
- Promote ethical, human-centric data governance

Only by addressing these challenges can we ensure that the digital revolution benefits all humanity, rather than exacerbating existing inequalities.

As the digital age reshapes the foundations of the global economy, politics, and society, data protection and privacy have emerged as central pillars of a just and inclusive technological future. The governance of personal data is no longer a niche legal concern but a defining feature of techno-political power in the 21st century. This analysis has illustrated how different regulatory models—European, American, and Chinese—reflect broader societal values and political priorities, and how these frameworks shape global innovation trajectories.

The European Union's rights-based approach to data governance has positioned trust and accountability as enablers of innovation. In contrast, the United States' sectoral and market-driven strategy has historically favored rapid technological progress, often at the expense of comprehensive privacy protections. China's state-centric model, combining innovation with assertive control, highlights how data can be leveraged not only for economic development but also for strategic and ideological influence.

Beyond these models, the global picture remains starkly uneven. Deep disparities in data protection capacities, legal frameworks, and technological infrastructure leave many countries—particularly in the Global South—exposed to exploitation, dependent on foreign technologies, and excluded from shaping the norms that govern their digital futures. The persistence of these inequalities challenges the ideal of a truly global, inclusive, and rights-respecting digital order.

Addressing these challenges requires a multidimensional strategy. Strengthening institutional capacities, promoting interoperability among privacy frameworks, fostering ethical innovation, and embedding human rights by design into all layers of governance are essential. Efforts must also be made to reverse brain drain, support local innovation ecosystems, and empower communities to participate in shaping data governance policies that reflect their values.

Ultimately, building a human-centric global digital order demands a bold reimagining of how we govern data, technology, and innovation. It calls for co-operation across borders, sectors, and cultures to ensure that the digital revolution enhances—not undermines—human dignity, equity, and democracy. In the age of techno-politics, our collective choices today will define the freedoms, opportunities, and safeguards of generations to come.

This chapter has argued that data protection and privacy must be understood through the lens of *techno-politics* — as contested sites where infrastructures, legal norms, and power relations intersect. Building on insights from Science and Technology Studies, the analysis has shown that technologies like AI systems, biometric surveillance tools, and cross-border data networks are never politically neutral. Instead, they are shaped by — and actively shape — struggles over individual autonomy, national sovereignty, and democratic accountability.

Recent developments illustrate this vividly: the *Schrems II* judgment has redefined the legal boundaries of transatlantic data flows; countries such as India, China, and the US are adopting new localization and cybersecurity laws to assert digital sovereignty; and enforcement actions against firms like Clearview AI reveal the urgent need to protect citizens against intrusive surveillance practices. Meanwhile, the EU's proposed AI Act signals a new frontier in regulating algorithmic decision-making to align technological innovation with fundamental rights.

These cases highlight a central tension: how to balance the free flow of data, global digital trade, and innovation with the imperative to safeguard privacy and human dignity. As states, firms, and transnational platforms compete to set the rules of the digital economy, new forms of governance are emerging — but so too are new risks of fragmentation, digital inequality, and regulatory capture.

To navigate these challenges, policymakers, scholars, and citizens must treat data governance not as a narrow legal issue but as a critical pillar of modern democracy. Embedding robust privacy protections, promoting accountability for powerful platforms, and defending the digital autonomy of individuals and communities will be essential to building a human-centric digital order.

Ultimately, techno-politics reminds us that the infrastructures and standards we build today will define the freedoms and constraints of tomorrow's digital societies. This makes the question of who shapes data protection — and for whose benefit — one of the defining political questions of our time.

REFERENCES

Bradford, A. (2020). *The Brussels Effect: How the European Union Rules the World.* Oxford University Press. DOI: 10.1093/oso/9780190088583.001.0001

California Consumer Privacy Act (CCPA), Cal. Civ. Code § 1798.100 et seq. (2018).

California Privacy Rights Act (CPRA), California Proposition 24 (2020).

Charter of Fundamental Rights of the European Union, 2000/C 364/01. (2000). *Official Journal of the European Communities*, C 364, 1–22.

Colorado Privacy Act (CPA), Colo. Rev. Stat. § 6-1-1301 et seq. (2021).

Commission Nationale de l'Informatique et des Libertés (CNIL). (n.d.). *1970–2021: la protection des données essaime le monde*. LINC. Retrieved June 29, 2025, from https://linc.cnil.fr/1970-2021-la-protection-des-donnees-essaime-le-monde

Convention 108+, Council of Europe Modernised Convention for the Protection of Individuals with regard to Processing of Personal Data. (2018). Council of Europe.

Council of Europe. (1981). *Convention for the Protection of Individuals with regard to Automatic Processing of Personal Data* (ETS No. 108). Strasbourg: Council of Europe.

Cybersecurity Law of the People's Republic of China. (2017).

Data Security Law of the People's Republic of China. (2021).

Directive 95/46/EC of the European Parliament and of the Council of 24 October 1995 on the protection of individuals with regard to the processing of personal data and on the free movement of such data. (1995). *Official Journal of the European Communities*, L 281, 31–50.

European Commission. (2010). *Communication from the Commission to the European Parliament, the Council, the Economic and Social Committee and the Committee of the Regions: A comprehensive approach on personal data protection in the European Union* (COM(2010) 609 final). Brussels: European Commission: https://eur-lex.europa.eu/legal-content/EN/TXT/?uri=CELEX%3A52010DC0609

European Union. (2022). *Regulation (EU) 2022/1925 of the European Parliament and of the Council of 14 September 2022 on contestable and fair markets in the digital sector (Digital Markets Act) and amending Directives (EU) 2019/1937 and (EU) 2020/1828.* Official Journal of the European Union, L 265, 1–66. https://eur-lex.europa.eu/legal-content/EN/TXT/?uri=CELEX%3A32022R1925

European Union. (2022). *Regulation (EU) 2022/2065 of the European Parliament and of the Council of 19 October 2022 on a Single Market for Digital Services (Digital Services Act) and amending Directive 2000/31/EC*. Official Journal of the European Union, L 277, 1–102. https://eur-lex.europa.eu/legal-content/EN/TXT/?uri=CELEX%3A32022R2065

European Union. (2022). *Regulation (EU) 2022/868 of the European Parliament and of the Council of 30 May 2022 on European data governance (Data Governance Act) and amending Regulation (EU) 2018/1724*. Official Journal of the European Union, L 152, 1–44. https://eur-lex.europa.eu/legal-content/EN/TXT/?uri=CELEX%3A32022R0868

European Union. (2024). *Regulation (EU) 2023/2854 of the European Parliament and of the Council of 13 December 2023 on harmonised rules on fair access to and use of data (Data Act)*. Official Journal of the European Union, L 2023/2854, 1–64. https://eur-lex.europa.eu/legal-content/EN/TXT/?uri=CELEX%3A32023R2854

General Data Protection Regulation (GDPR), Regulation (EU) 2016/679 of the European Parliament and of the Council of 27 April 2016 on the protection of natural persons with regard to the processing of personal data and on the free movement of such data, and repealing Directive 95/46/EC. (2016). *Official Journal of the European Union*, L 119, 1–88.

Jasanoff, S. (2004). The idiom of co-production. In *States of knowledge* (pp. 1–12). Routledge. DOI: 10.4324/9780203413845-6

OECD Guidelines on the Protection of Privacy and Transborder Flows of Personal Data. (2013). Organisation for Economic Co-operation and Development.

Personal Information Protection Law of the People's Republic of China. (2021).

Piper, D. L. A. (n.d.). *Data protection laws of the world*. DLA Piper. Retrieved June 29, 2025, from https://www.dlapiperdataprotection.com

Sandywell, B. (2006). Monsters in cyberspace: Cyberphobia and cultural panic in the information age. *Information Communication and Society*, *9*(1), 39–61. DOI: 10.1080/13691180500519407

Virginia Consumer Data Protection Act (VCDPA), Va. Code Ann. § 59.1-575 et seq. (2021).

Winner, L. (1980). Do artifacts have politics? *Daedalus*, *109*(1), 121–136.

ENDNOTES

1 In Germany, data protection regulation is of the competency of the regional state.

2 It entered into force in 1973.

3 Today the European Commission

4 Convention 108+, Council of Europe Modernised Convention for the Protection of Individuals with regard to Processing of Personal Data. (2018). Strasbourg: Council of Europe.

5 OECD Guidelines on the Protection of Privacy and Transborder Flows of Personal Data. (2013). Organisation for Economic Co-operation and Development.

6 African Union Convention on Cyber Security and Personal Data Protection (Malabo Convention). (2014).

Chapter 2
Policing with Algorithms: Sci-Fi Visions Meet Real-World Repercussions/Applications (APPRAISE)

Sérgio Felgueiras
https://orcid.org/0000-0001-6885-7439
ISCPSI, Portugal

Sónia M. A. Morgado
https://orcid.org/0000-0002-7036-5174
ISCPSI, Portugal

ABSTRACT

Science fiction depicts AI policing dramatically (e.g., Minority Report, Black Mirror), raising concerns about bias and control. In contrast, Europe's reality, like the APPRAISE project, is more measured, focusing on responsible AI development in law enforcement. Real-world AI tools, such as data analysis, predictive policing, facial recognition, and biometric sensors, enhance efficiency but bring challenges: algorithmic bias, privacy issues, and accountability questions. The future isn't a dystopia but depends on responsible implementation, requiring transparency, regulations (like the EU AI Act), and human oversight. EU projects like APPRAISE prioritize ethical development, bias mitigation, transparency, and accountability. Approaching AI cautiously and ethically allows harnessing its potential for a safer, fairer future, avoiding unchecked AI from fiction.

DOI: 10.4018/979-8-3373-7406-2.ch002

INTRODUCTION

Science fiction paints a vivid picture of AI-powered policing, from "Minority Report's" pre-crime units to "Black Mirror's" pervasive surveillance (e.g., Nosedive episode). Fictional depictions such as Minority Report (Spielberg, 2002) present a futuristic world where predictive policing enables law enforcement to arrest individuals before crimes occur, while Black Mirror – Nosedive (Jones, 2016) imagines a society ruled by surveillance and algorithmic control. On the other hand, Person of Interest (Nolan et al., 2011-2016) reveals crime sustained by an algorithm from a social security number. The God's Eye, from the franchise Fast and Furious (Wan, 2015), introduces technology capable of "God's Eye" with the capacity to track anyone, anywhere in the world, in real-time using facial recognition. While these portrayals raise valid concerns about algorithmic bias and societal control, European reality is more measured. Although these cautionary tales of surveillance and predictive policing exaggerate the capabilities and dangers of AI, they resonate with growing real-world concerns surrounding the ethical use of AI in law enforcement, particularly regarding bias, privacy, and accountability (Morgado, 2017; Morgado & Felgueiras, 2021).

The digital transformation of public security systems has ushered in a new era for law enforcement, characterized by the integration of advanced technologies — most notably Artificial Intelligence (AI). Law enforcement agencies worldwide are employing AI-driven solutions to enhance crime forecasting, allocate resources more effectively, and support forensic investigations (Gerbrandy & Zweers, 2019). However, such advancements inevitably raise questions about ethical boundaries and potential infringements on civil liberties (Barfield, 2020). For example, while predictive analytics can allocate police patrols more effectively, it may also entrench historical biases in policing data (Lum & Isaac, 2016). Consequently, lawmakers and stakeholders are pressed to develop regulations that strike a balance between technological innovation and the protection of individual rights (European Commission, 2021a).

In the European context, two key legislative instruments shape the discourse on AI in policing: the proposed EU AI Act (European Commission, 2021a) and Regulation (EU) 2024/1689 (European Parliament & Council, 2024). Both instruments emphasize ethical considerations and robust data protection standards, reflecting a growing consensus that AI must be deployed in a manner consistent with the Charter of Fundamental Rights of the European Union (European Union Agency for Fundamental Rights, 2018). This chapter critically examines the practical applications of AI in policing, outlines the legal and ethical frameworks guiding these technologies, analyzes key challenges, and offers strategic recommendations for practitioners and policymakers.

Yet, despite increasing clarity in policy instruments, the on-the-ground realities of implementing AI solutions can be highly variable. Police forces differ in terms of budget, training, and operational priorities, leading to inconsistencies in how AI tools are selected and deployed. This divergence underscores the need for universally accepted standards, transparency, and mechanisms to ensure accountability (Lum & Isaac, 2016). Without such alignment, the technology may inadvertently exacerbate systemic issues rather than resolve them. Furthermore, the effectiveness of regulatory instruments like the AI Act hinges on overcoming significant political and institutional hurdles at the Member State level. Translating legislative intent into practical, harmonized oversight across the EU remains a complex challenge, often hindered by divergent national priorities and administrative capacities.

Moreover, the public perception of AI in policing remains mixed. On the one hand, citizens expect law enforcement agencies to adopt modern tools to combat sophisticated criminal networks; on the other hand, there is growing apprehension about surveillance overreach and data misuse (Barfield, 2020). Addressing these concerns requires a concerted effort from policymakers, civil society, and law enforcement agencies to engage in open dialogue, ensuring that the adoption of AI technologies is neither opaque nor divorced from public scrutiny.

Initiatives like the APPRAISE project emphasize the responsible development of AI tools for law enforcement. As Europe navigates these concerns, the European Union's AI Act (European Parliament, 2023) and projects such as APPRAISE (APPRAISE, 2024; Morgado et al., 2024) emphasize ethical development and deployment. These initiatives focus on transparency, minimizing bias, and ensuring accountability in the use of AI tools (Morgado & Felgueiras, 2021; Morgado, 2023). In this context, initiatives such as the APPRAISE project emerge as key examples of how Europe is striving to harness the benefits of AI for law enforcement while addressing the associated risks because it involves and reinforces privacy because the foundation of it is determined by Social, Ethical, Legal, and Privacy (SELP) (APPRAISE, 2021; Morgado et al., 2024a). APPRAISE brought together 27 organizations from nine European countries to develop a comprehensive security framework that enhances cyber, physical, and public safety through a proactive, integrated, and risk-focused approach.

The global landscape shows varying levels of AI adoption in law enforcement, with countries like the United States and China pioneering the use of surveillance systems and predictive policing tools (Morgado & Felgueiras, 2022; Peterson & Hoffman, 2022). China, for instance, has implemented comprehensive AI surveillance systems, including facial recognition technologies, on a scale unparalleled in the West, often raising concerns about state control and privacy violations (Aho & Duffield, 2020; Mugari & Obioha, 2021). In the U.S., AI has been used for crime analysis and predictive policing, but studies have highlighted cases where these tools reinforce racial biases, leading to disproportionately high targeting of minority groups (Gallon, 2023; Limantė, 2024). Europe, however, has adopted a more cautious and measured approach. The European Union has taken proactive steps to regulate AI's integration into law enforcement through frameworks like the General Data Protection Regulation (GDPR) and the proposed AI Act (European Parliament, 2023), which is intended to govern high-risk AI applications, including those used in public safety (Gille et al., 2024; Mazur, 2023). Central to this regulatory approach is the belief that AI must be developed responsibly, ensuring that technological advancements do not undermine fundamental human rights or democratic principles (Donahoe & Metzger, 2019; Morgado & Felgueiras, 2021).

While AI presents undeniable opportunities for enhancing law enforcement, such as increasing efficiency, improving response times, and optimizing resource allocation, there is a prevailing tension between technological optimism and ethical caution. Proponents of AI in policing argue that advanced algorithms can offer unprecedented insights, enabling law enforcement agencies to make data-driven decisions that could potentially reduce crime rates and improve public safety because it allows a better understanding and a diagnosis within a proactive model (Morgado & Felgueiras, 2021; Morgado et al., 2024b). However, ethical caution is warranted.

This perspective is due to answer the following question: How can the European Union effectively balance the potential benefits of artificial intelligence (AI) in law enforcement with the risks of bias, privacy infringements, and lack of accountability?

This chapter aims to explore AI's role in European law enforcement, with a particular focus on the risks of bias, privacy infringements, and the challenge of ensuring accountability. We will analyze the real-world applications of AI, such as data analysis, predictive policing, and facial recognition, and examine their ethical and practical implications. Furthermore, the chapter will critically assess the effectiveness of the APPRAISE project in mitigating these risks, considering whether it can provide a model for ethical AI use in law enforcement globally. By examining the intersection of science fiction's dystopian warnings and real-world AI applications, we seek to provide an in-depth understanding of how Europe is navigating this rapidly evolving landscape. The discussion will also contextualize the potential for AI to serve as a force for good, promoting public safety without compromising civil liberties, if robust ethical and legal frameworks guide it.

Having established the context and the core tension, the following section delves into the specific AI applications currently being employed in policing and their inherent.

CURRENT AI APPLICATIONS IN POLICING

AI technologies have found various applications in law enforcement, from data analysis to biometric (psychological or behaviour) recognition (Dagar & Kumar, 2020; Roksandić et al., 2022). These innovations are significantly transforming traditional policing methods by enhancing efficiency, enabling data-driven decisions, and providing powerful tools for crime prevention and detection. However, these advancements also raise concerns about bias, privacy, and accountability. This section provides a deeper analysis of how AI technologies are currently deployed in law enforcement and explores the potential benefits and ethical concerns associated with these applications.

AI has gained traction in several domains of law enforcement, transforming how police gather intelligence, analyze evidence, and interact with communities. Each application area interfaces with existing regulations in distinct ways, demanding careful scrutiny of risks and benefits. While AI systems promise heightened efficiency and precision, they also carry the potential for unintended consequences, such as the entrenchment of biases or violations of privacy.

Additionally, law enforcement agencies must grapple with the challenge of integrating AI technologies into traditional policing practices. Incorporating AI tools often necessitates infrastructure upgrades, specialized training, and inter-agency coordination. These operational demands are compounded by legal constraints, which require authorities to comply with robust data protection standards and demonstrate that any infringement of rights is strictly necessary and proportionate (European Parliament & Council, 2024). Consequently, effective AI deployment calls for a holistic approach that balances technical feasibility with ethical and legal imperatives.

Predictive Policing

AI in policing frequently involves data analysis. This approach is one of the most widely adopted AI technologies in law enforcement (Brayne, 2017; Rademacher, 2020). Through machine learning algorithms, AI systems can process massive datasets and identify patterns that would be impossible or time-consuming for human officers to discern. In practice, this often means sorting through crime reports, surveillance footage, and even social media activity to detect trends that point to criminal activity. This form of data analysis is particularly valuable in high-crime urban environments, where large amounts of data must be quickly assessed to make informed policing decisions (Afzal & Panagiotopoulos, 2024).

Predictive policing utilizes historical crime data—often drawn from sources like 911 call logs, arrest records, and community reports—to forecast future crime hotspots (Berk, 2021; Perry et al., 2013). In the European Union, such data often intersect with large-scale databases regulated under the Interoperability Framework of Regulation (EU) 2024/1689, which aims to streamline information sharing while maintaining strict data protection safeguards. Although predictive analytics can improve the efficiency of patrols, the risk of over-policing in specific neighbourhoods remains a serious concern (Lum & Isaac, 2016). Policymakers and law enforcement agencies must ensure these tools comply with the EU AI Act's provisions on high-risk systems, particularly regarding transparency, data quality, and human oversight (European Commission, 2021a).

By identifying patterns in crime occurrences, AI can suggest where crimes are likely to happen, guiding law enforcement on where to patrol or deploy resources. The concept of predictive policing closely mirrors the system portrayed in The Minority Report (Spielberg, 2002), where AI is used to prevent crimes before they occur, though the real-world application is far less invasive and speculative. Also, it is exemplified in shows like Person of Interest (Nolan et al., 2011-2016), which aids in investigative work, uncovering patterns that might otherwise go unnoticed. Predictive policing algorithms are another key application, analyzing crime data to predict high-risk areas and optimize patrol allocation. The concept is reminiscent of The Wire's (Simon et al., 2002–2008) portrayal of data-informed crime prevention but raises concerns about over-policing of specific communities if not implemented responsibly (Almasoud & Idowu, 2025; Udoh, 2020).

A second layer of complexity arises from the diversity of data sources feeding predictive models. If the underlying datasets are skewed or incomplete, the system may produce unreliable forecasts, inadvertently directing more policing resources to areas already suffering from over-policing (Lum & Isaac, 2016). This situation can create a feedback loop in which certain communities are disproportionately subjected to police scrutiny, eroding trust and community relations. From a technical standpoint, this feedback loop is a classic case of dataset drift, where the model's predictions influence the data-gathering process, leading to a self-reinforcing and increasingly skewed dataset that is difficult to correct. Socially, this erosion of trust can manifest as decreased citizen cooperation in reporting crimes and providing witness testimony, paradoxically undermining the very goal of improving public safety. To mitigate this risk, law enforcement agencies should regularly audit their datasets, employ diverse data inputs, and involve external experts in evaluating predictive model performance.

Furthermore, predictive policing algorithms can struggle to account for the broader social determinants of crime, such as economic disparities, educational opportunities, and community health. These socio-economic factors often lie beyond the immediate purview of policing agencies but significantly influence crime patterns (Perry et al., 2013; Morgado, 2013). A narrow focus on static crime data risks oversimplifying complex social issues, potentially leading to short-term gains but longer-term detriments in community well-being and trust in law enforcement.

However, the risks of predictive policing are significant. One of the primary concerns is the potential for over-policing in communities that are already heavily monitored due to historical crime patterns (Olaoye, 2024). In a scenario where data from marginalized communities is disproportionately represented in crime datasets, predictive policing systems may direct law enforcement agencies to focus more resources on those areas, perpetuating cycles of surveillance and enforcement (Cossette-Lefebvre & Maclure, 2023; Richardson et al., 2019; Selbst, 2017; Rothstein et al., 2022). This reality not only risks reinforcing existing biases but also undermines trust between law enforcement and the public (Malek, 2022). In the United States, the COMPAS tool has demonstrated how predictive policing models can lead to biased outcomes (Washington, 2019). Studies showed that COMPAS disproportionately classified African-American defendants as high-risk for recidivism, even when their actual likelihood of reoffending was low (Berk, 2021). Such examples underscore the importance of critically examining how data is used and ensuring that AI models do not simply replicate historical inequalities. In fact, AI systems trained on biased data can perpetuate existing social inequalities. Research suggests that predictive policing models, if not carefully designed, can reinforce racial profiling and the disproportionate targeting of marginalized communities (Richardson, 2021; Ziosi & Pruss, 2024), much like the discriminatory parole algorithms depicted in Orange is the New Black (Kohan et al., 2013-2019). For AI policing tools to serve the public fairly, significant efforts are required to ensure algorithmic transparency and to prevent bias from entering AI training datasets (Bagaric et al., 2022).

In Europe, projects like APPRAISE emphasize the importance of scrutinizing the datasets that feed AI systems. APPRAISE seeks to mitigate bias by ensuring that data used in predictive policing models is not only accurate but also reflective of broader societal dynamics, such as the socio-economic context of crime (Morgado, 2013; Morgado & Felgueiras, 2021). This holistic approach helps ensure that AI is used to address the root causes of crime rather than reinforce problematic policing practices (Van Brakel, 2020). This method aligns with the principles of problem-oriented policing (Goldstein, 1990), which focuses on addressing the root causes of crime rather than merely reacting to incidents. By integrating AI, policing can shift from a reactive cycle (Stevens, 2001) to a proactive approach that enhances control over police work, much like POP's collaborative, preventive strategies. This practice conveys a cognitive comprehension of predictive policing or at least a technological solution that is very close to predictive policing (Söderholm, 2023), which might not compromise human rights or ethical principles if it is grounded in risk assessment algorithms (Castets-Renard, 2021) or assumptions like the ones provided by APPRAISE.

Facial Recognition and Biometrics

Facial recognition technology is one of the most controversial AI applications in law enforcement. By comparing faces captured on surveillance cameras to images in police databases, facial recognition systems enable law enforcement to identify suspects, missing persons, or persons of interest in real-time (Stacy, 2017). This technology can dramatically increase the efficiency of police operations, especially in crowded public spaces such as airports, train stations, and significant events where manual identification would be time-consuming and error-prone (Helbing et al., 2015), by enabling real-time identification of individuals, helping locate crimes or missing persons. For instance, the portrayal of facial recognition in Terminator 2: Judgment Day (Cameron, 1991) mirrors the actual implementation in various European security operations.

Facial recognition technology has become a prominent tool for real-time surveillance and suspect identification (European Commission, 2021b). Under Regulation (EU) 2024/1689, cross-border data exchanges involving biometric information face heightened scrutiny, given the sensitivity of such data. Additionally, the AI Act categorizes facial recognition as high-risk, mandating strict compliance measures such as documentation of datasets, bias mitigation, and human oversight (European Commission, 2021a). Research has shown that facial recognition algorithms can misidentify people of colour and women at higher rates (Buolamwini & Gebru, 2018), raising ethical and legal questions about discrimination and due process.

However, increased reliance on these technologies raises privacy and accuracy concerns and prompts the need for strong ethical and legal frameworks to prevent misuse (Smith & Miller, 2022). Facial recognition technology is less accurate when identifying people of color and women, raising concerns about algorithmic bias (Leslie, 2020; Perkowitz, 2021; Schuetz, 2021). It has been reported that some facial recognition algorithms had false favourable rates that were up to 10 times higher for people of African and Asian descent compared to those of European descent (Wehril et al., 2022). This disparity could lead to wrongful arrests or misidentification, exacerbating tensions between law enforcement and minority communities. Legally, the use of a tool with known, significant disparities in accuracy raises profound questions regarding the right to a fair trial and the principle of equality before the law, as enshrined in Articles 20 and 21 of the Charter of Fundamental Rights. Evidence derived from such a flawed system could be subject to legal challenges, potentially rendering entire investigations inadmissible in court and creating significant legal liability for police agencies. A key concern is the potential for mass surveillance when facial recognition tools are deployed in public spaces without robust oversight. Civil liberties groups argue that continuous monitoring can generate a chilling effect, discouraging citizens from lawful assembly or free expression (Barfield, 2020). In this context, an overreliance on automated identification systems may fundamentally alter the dynamic between police forces and the communities they serve, instilling fear rather than fostering cooperation.

The GDPR in Europe has imposed strict regulations on the use of facial recognition, requiring law enforcement agencies to justify its use and ensure that any data collected complies with privacy protections. While these regulations offer strong safeguards, concerns remain about the long-term implications of widespread biometric surveillance. Critics argue that even if facial recognition is implemented with the best intentions, it could pave the way for a surveillance state where citizens' movements are constantly monitored (Catlett et al., 2023), as depicted in dystopian media such as Black Mirror (Bridges & Armstrong, 2011 -).

In response to these concerns, some jurisdictions have implemented moratoriums or outright bans on the use of facial recognition by law enforcement (Buolamwini & Gebru, 2018). These legislative responses aim to safeguard civil rights while policymakers refine legal frameworks that account for technological risks. Law enforcement agencies wishing to employ facial recognition must, therefore, ensure that they meet all transparency requirements, conduct independent impact assessments, and develop protocols that allow individuals to challenge potential misidentifications.

In contrast, biometric tools beyond facial recognition, such as iris scans and fingerprinting, are increasingly reliable and widely accepted forms of AI application in law enforcement. These tools have been used to improve security measures at border checkpoints and in criminal investigations, where accurate identification is critical. Biometric sensors enable police to quickly verify identities, reduce fraudulent activities, and track criminal movements across borders (Lynch, 2020). However, the ethical use of biometrics requires clear guidelines to ensure that these technologies are not misused. The risk of overreach becomes apparent when biometric data is collected without consent or used for purposes beyond law enforcement (Migliorini, 2023; Smith & Miller, 2021). Europe's regulatory frameworks, including the GDPR and the AI Act, emphasize the need for transparency and accountability in the use of biometric technologies to prevent potential abuses and ensure that individual rights are not compromised.

Data Mining and Cross-Matching

Data mining tools enable law enforcement agencies to crossmatch data from various sources, including immigration, vehicle registration, and criminal databases (Brayne, 2020). Regulation (EU) 2024/1689 supports such interoperability but imposes clear guidelines for data handling and privacy protection (European Parliament & Council, 2024). Violations of these guidelines can lead to breaches of the Charter of Fundamental Rights, especially around privacy and non-discrimination

(European Union Agency for Fundamental Rights, 2018). Hence, agencies must conduct impact assessments to ensure that cross-matching processes do not infringe on individual rights.

Another dimension is the sheer volume of data that can be aggregated and analyzed in real-time. Big data analytics enable the rapid identification of suspect patterns or correlations, potentially giving law enforcement unprecedented capabilities (Brayne, 2020). However, the indiscriminate or overly broad use of such tools raises concerns about dragging innocent individuals into police databases or inadvertently outing vulnerable populations, such as undocumented migrants.

Moreover, data mining practices intersect with broader questions about who controls the data and under what conditions. Police forces must carefully vet third-party vendors, ensure data quality, and maintain robust security measures to prevent breaches. A single vulnerability in a cross-matching system could compromise sensitive personal information, leading to public backlash and diminished trust in law enforcement.

Forensic Analysis

In forensic investigations, AI-assisted applications—such as automated DNA matching, fingerprint analysis, or audio-video enhancements—can accelerate the identification of suspects and the processing of evidence (Dudek et al., 2023; Geradts & Franke, 2023; Zangana et al., 2025). The EU AI Act recognizes these as potentially high-risk domains where accuracy and human review are paramount (European Commission, 2021a). Failure to meet established standards could invalidate evidence in court and undermine the fairness of trials. As such, stringent audit trails, validation protocols, and calibration processes are necessary to align with both scientific best practices and EU regulations.

Yet the rapid evolution of AI-powered forensic tools can outpace judicial understanding and legislative updates. Courts may grapple with interpreting the reliability of novel algorithms that have not undergone lengthy peer review (Dudek et al., 2023; Geradts & Franke, 2023; Zangana et al., 2025). This procedure can lead to inconsistent rulings, leaving law enforcement agencies in a legal grey area when employing advanced forensic methods.

Additionally, forensic AI applications can risk creating a veneer of infallibility. When algorithms produce results with minimal human intervention, judges and jurors might overestimate the reliability of such findings (European Commission, 2021a). Proper training and guidelines are, therefore, critical to ensure that forensic examiners, attorneys, and the judiciary are aware of the limitations inherent in AI-assisted evidence analysis. Understanding these diverse applications is crucial for appreciating the complex legal and ethical frameworks within which AI in policing must operate.

LEGAL AND ETHICAL FRAMEWORKS

AI-driven policing initiatives operate within a complex web of legal and ethical considerations designed to safeguard fundamental rights. These frameworks not only clarify the obligations of law enforcement agencies but also delineate the rights of individuals who may be affected by AI systems.

Crucially, European legislation aims to strike a proportional balance: enabling legitimate law enforcement objectives while preventing the infringement of personal liberties. The interplay between the AI Act and Regulation (EU) 2024/1689 illustrates how lawmakers are attempting to align new technological capabilities with longstanding principles of necessity, proportionality, and accountability (European Commission, 2021a; European Parliament & Council, 2024). The resulting legal landscape is continually evolving, requiring ongoing adaptation by both policymakers and police departments.

EU AI Act

The proposed EU AI Act is the cornerstone of Europe's approach to regulating AI. Systems deemed high-risk—such as those used by law enforcement—must meet robust requirements, including transparency and human oversight (European Commission, 2021a). Non-compliance can trigger heavy penalties, reinforcing the need for police forces to embed regulatory compliance into their technological procurement and operational protocols. Furthermore, the Act demands a risk-based approach, obliging developers and users of AI to assess and mitigate potential harms meticulously.

In addition, the Act stipulates mandatory conformity assessments, user training requirements, and post-market monitoring obligations for high-risk AI systems. These measures aim to minimize the risk of harmful outcomes while ensuring that AI developers and deployers remain accountable throughout the product lifecycle (European Commission, 2021a). For law enforcement, this translates into a heightened responsibility to document the data sources, training methods, and decision-making processes underlying AI-driven tools.

Finally, the EU AI Act underscores the importance of fostering public trust. By mandating audit trails and transparent labelling of high-risk systems, the Act encourages a culture of scrutiny and openness. Law enforcement agencies that fail to adhere to these principles risk both legal repercussions and reputational damage, potentially undermining community trust in AI-enabled policing strategies. However, a key challenge for the AI Act's effectiveness will be its enforcement across the 27 Member States. The creation and funding of competent national supervisory authorities with sufficient technical expertise to audit complex AI systems remain a significant policy and logistical hurdle. Without robust and consistent enforcement, the Act risks becoming a 'paper tiger,' with its requirements only weakly implemented at the operational level.

Regulation (EU) 2024/1689

Regulation (EU) 2024/1689 complements the AI Act by enhancing interoperability among databases such as the Schengen Information System (SIS), Eurodac, and the Visa Information System (VIS) (European Parliament & Council, 2024). It also tightens safeguards for personal data, reflecting the EU's enduring commitment to privacy, as enshrined in the General Data Protection Regulation (GDPR) (European Commission, 2019). Under this Regulation, data sharing must be strictly necessary and proportionate to law enforcement objectives, thereby constraining broad or indiscriminate use of AI.

Another key feature of Regulation (EU) 2024/1689 is the emphasis on data quality and accuracy. Inaccurate or outdated entries in shared databases can lead to wrongful identification or unjustified surveillance measures, eroding public confidence in AI-based law enforcement (European Parliament & Council, 2024). By mandating regular reviews and corrections, the Regulation attempts to mitigate such risks, although the effectiveness of these measures depends significantly on consistent implementation across Member States.

Moreover, the Regulation intersects with the principle of data minimization, a core tenet of EU data protection laws. Police forces must justify the scope and duration of data retention, ensuring that information is not held indefinitely or repurposed for unrelated activities. This approach underscores a fundamental tension between the desire for comprehensive intelligence capabilities and the imperative to respect individual privacy rights.

Charter of Fundamental Rights of the European Union

All AI applications in policing must align with the Charter of Fundamental Rights, which underscores the right to privacy (Article 7), data protection (Article 8), non-discrimination (Article 21), and access to justice (Article 47) (European Union Agency for Fundamental Rights, 2018). Accordingly, AI systems should be designed and deployed to respect human dignity and protect vulnerable populations from potential harm (Doshi-Velez & Kim, 2017). This strong legal foundation guides courts, policymakers, and law enforcement agencies in scrutinizing whether specific AI deployments comply with fundamental rights.

In practice, aligning AI policing tools with the Charter requires a systematic approach to impact assessments and oversight. Authorities must not only anticipate the potential negative externalities of AI but also engage with community stakeholders to address concerns about discrimination or privacy violations (European Union Agency for Fundamental Rights, 2018). Failure to do so can lead to legal challenges, public backlash, and diminished trust in law enforcement institutions.

Furthermore, the Charter's emphasis on transparency and accountability has direct implications for AI governance. The principle of fair trial (Article 47) implies that individuals subject to algorithmic scrutiny should have an opportunity to understand the basis of accusations or suspicions. This system necessitates interpretable AI models, thorough documentation, and avenues for legal redress, all of which complicate the deployment of opaque or proprietary algorithms. Navigating these complex legal and ethical considerations is paramount, but it also brings to light significant challenges that must be addressed for responsible AI implementation in policing.

KEY CHALLENGES

Although AI holds transformative potential for modern policing, its adoption is fraught with challenges that extend beyond mere technical hurdles. Issues such as algorithmic bias, lack of transparency, and governance complexities can hinder both the efficacy of AI tools and the legitimacy of law enforcement.

Addressing these challenges requires a multi-stakeholder approach that includes legislators, technology developers, civil society, and frontline police officers. Without broad collaboration, well-intentioned regulatory frameworks may fail to translate into tangible protections, leaving gaps in oversight and accountability.

Bias and Discrimination

A central challenge in AI-driven policing is algorithmic bias. AI models learn from historical datasets that may contain discriminatory patterns, leading to over-policing of specific communities (Buolamwini & Gebru, 2018). Such biases conflict with the EU's commitment to equality and non-discrimination, as codified in primary and secondary legislation. Police forces must, therefore, conduct rigorous bias audits and consider adopting diverse training data or alternative modelling approaches (Lum & Isaac, 2016).

Compounding the issue is the difficulty of detecting subtle forms of bias. Even seemingly neutral datasets can encode discriminatory elements, such as differential arrest rates influenced by past policing practices. This process can manifest as a pernicious cycle, where AI systems perpetuate historical injustices under the guise of objective data analysis (Buolamwini & Gebru, 2018). Technically, this challenge goes beyond simply cleaning data; it involves the very definition of 'fairness,' for which multiple, often mutually exclusive, mathematical definitions exist (e.g., demographic parity, equalized odds). Socially, the choice of which fairness metric to prioritize is not a technical decision but an ethical and political one, requiring broad societal debate that is often absent from the procurement and deployment process of these technologies. A critical step involves transparent documentation of data sources and the creation of "checkpoints" at which bias can be systematically identified.

Efforts to mitigate bias must also acknowledge that discrimination is not merely a technical flaw but a societal one. Collaborative partnerships with community organizations, advocacy groups, and academic researchers can help law enforcement agencies better understand the socio-historical context of the data they employ. This broader perspective is essential for developing AI-driven tools that genuinely serve the public good rather than replicate structural inequalities.

Lack of Transparency

The "black box" nature of specific AI algorithms makes it difficult for officers, defendants, or courts to scrutinize how decisions are reached (Doshi-Velez & Kim, 2017). A lack of transparency can undermine the legitimacy of policing actions and hamper legal redress for individuals who believe they have been unfairly targeted. The EU AI Act mandates explainability measures for high-risk systems, although the exact technical requirements remain an evolving area of policy (European Commission, 2021a).

In law enforcement contexts, opacity exacerbates power imbalances. Defendants may struggle to challenge evidence generated by AI if they cannot access or interpret the underlying algorithms (Doshi-Velez & Kim, 2017). Similarly, police officers themselves may rely on AI outputs without fully understanding the data inputs or model assumptions, thereby hindering responsible usage. This opacity is often compounded by the commercial interests of private vendors who claim intellectual property rights over their algorithms. This creates a fundamental conflict between public accountability and private profit, making it difficult for public bodies to conduct independent audits or for defendants to meaningfully challenge the algorithmic evidence presented against them. Achieving meaningful transparency requires user-friendly interfaces, detailed documentation, and the involvement of multidisciplinary teams who can interpret algorithmic outputs.

Furthermore, transparency is not solely a matter of technical disclosure. It also entails proactive communication with the public about how and why specific AI tools are employed, as well as the potential risks and safeguards (European Commission, 2021a). This openness can foster public trust and allow for more informed dialogue on the scope and limits of AI in policing. However, transparency efforts must be balanced against genuine security concerns, ensuring that criminals do not exploit detailed knowledge of law enforcement tactics.

Overreliance on Automation

Technological tools are meant to assist, not supplant, human judgment. However, an uncritical reliance on AI may erode professional discretion and ethical decision-making within law enforcement agencies (Brayne, 2020). Officers may treat algorithmic outputs as infallible, overlooking a context that a machine learning model cannot capture. Training and strict guidelines are necessary to ensure that the final decision always involves a human officer with the authority to override automated recommendations.

This risk of "automation bias" can be particularly acute in high-stress situations, where officers may default to AI guidance under time pressure (Brayne, 2020). In such scenarios, failing to apply critical thinking can lead to wrongful arrests or the overlooking of alternative investigative avenues. Structured protocols that delineate the roles of AI outputs versus human judgment can mitigate these dangers, but only if strong institutional cultures back them.

Additionally, overreliance can diminish the skills and situational awareness of officers who become too dependent on automated systems for routine tasks. This de-skilling effect not only compromises the agility of law enforcement but also poses a risk if AI systems fail or produce errors. A balanced approach that combines the efficiency of AI with the nuance of human expertise is imperative for practical and ethical policing.

Cross-Border Data Governance

One of the central goals of Regulation (EU) 2024/1689 is to harmonize data exchange among Member States. Yet divergences in local implementation can create loopholes and inconsistencies, particularly concerning data protection, oversight mechanisms, and technical compatibility (European Parliament & Council, 2024). Addressing these discrepancies is crucial for building mutual trust among Member States and upholding the uniform application of EU law.

Moreover, cross-border investigations often involve multiple agencies, each with its own protocols and data systems. Ensuring interoperability without compromising privacy or data integrity is a delicate balancing act (European Union Agency for Fundamental Rights, 2018). Conflicts can arise over issues like data retention periods, permissible uses of shared information, or the standards for verifying an individual's identity across multiple databases.

As transnational crimes like terrorism, human trafficking, and cybercrime become more sophisticated, robust cross-border cooperation is increasingly indispensable. Yet inconsistent or fragmented approaches to AI-enabled policing tools risk creating "weak links" that can be exploited by criminal networks. Harmonized regulations, joint training initiatives, and continuous dialogue between Member States are essential to realize the full benefits of cross-border AI data-sharing.

One of the most pressing issues with AI in policing is accountability. When AI systems make mistakes—whether they misidentify a suspect or incorrectly predict criminal activity—determining responsibility becomes complex. Human oversight remains critical to ensure that AI complements human judgment rather than replacing it. Clear guidelines must establish how law enforcement agencies address errors made by AI tools to avoid undue harm. Despite significant technological progress leading to the discovery and resolution of numerous mysteries, contemporary society, particularly for some, exhibits a paradoxical cognitive landscape. This circumstance is characterized by fragmented understanding, constrained thinking limited to a finite set of symbols, and abbreviated communication. Consequently, interpersonal experiences become fleeting and superficial, often dissolving before meaningful connections can develop (Dinušová, 2024). Addressing these multifaceted challenges necessitates a proactive and strategic approach, leading us to explore key recommendations for the responsible implementation of AI in policing.

APPRAISE PROJECT AND RESPONSIBLE AI IMPLEMENTATION

The European Union's AI Act and initiatives like the APPRAISE project are designed to ensure that AI in policing is developed and implemented ethically (Morgado et al., 2023). APPRAISE emphasizes transparency, accountability, and bias reduction, offering a framework for responsible AI deployment in law enforcement. APPRAISE and related projects such as FENIX and AI4Cities have developed ethical guidelines for the use of AI in law enforcement, including efforts to address algorithmic biases and ensure the transparency of AI-powered policing tools (Morgado et al., 2021). The APPRAISE project, spearheaded by the European Union, is designed to ensure that AI tools used by law enforcement agencies are ethical, transparent, and accountable (Morgado et al., 2024). APPRAISE focuses on creating a balanced approach where AI technologies are developed with attention to fairness and bias mitigation, privacy protection, and human oversight. The project's core objective is to establish an ethical framework that guides the development of

AI tools to prevent the mistakes seen in other global contexts, such as algorithmic racial profiling in the United States and reinforcing the right to privacy (Berk, 2021; Kavoliūnaitė-Ragauskienė, 2024; Washington, 2019). APPRAISE also ensures compliance with the AI Act's rigorous standards by fostering interdisciplinary collaboration between technologists, legal experts, law enforcement agencies, and civil society organizations (Morgado et al., 2024a).

In the context of combating terrorism, especially against soft targets such as public venues or critical infrastructure, APPRAISE works to mitigate these risks by enhancing surveillance, predictive analytics, and decision-support tools in a transparent, accountable manner. This focus on safeguarding human rights while improving AI's capacity for threat detection draws inspiration from science fiction's recurring theme of balancing technological advancement with ethical governance. By integrating human oversight and ethical reviews into its AI systems, APPRAISE seeks to prevent the kinds of uncontrolled AI deployments that are often warned against in science fiction. Moreover, the project highlights the growing need for advanced AI in counter-terrorism operations, where quick decisions are crucial, but accuracy and ethical responsibility cannot be compromised. This strategy is particularly relevant for predictive policing and monitoring public spaces to detect potential terrorist threats before they occur. In these scenarios, APPRAISE's approach mirrors the ethical dilemmas posed in science fiction, emphasizing the dangers of allowing AI systems too much autonomy in decision-making processes without proper human oversight. While the framework developed by APPRAISE is a significant step forward, its ultimate success will depend on the ability to translate these ethical principles into measurable outcomes. Future analysis should focus on evidence from the project's pilot implementations, examining key performance indicators related to bias reduction, transparency in practice, and the actual impact on both crime rates and community trust. It is crucial to assess whether the project's human-in-the-loop model can be effectively maintained under the high-pressure, resource-constrained conditions of real-world policing. For instance, in works like Minority Report (Spielberg, 2002), where predictive crime prevention leads to ethical violations, the APPRAISE project ensures that human rights are protected by mandating human intervention at critical decision points.

The APPRAISE project draws an intriguing parallel to science fiction in its efforts to combat terrorism against soft targets, emphasizing the importance of responsible AI deployment in areas where public safety is paramount. In much of science fiction, the dangers of unchecked AI are vividly portrayed, where automated systems can turn against human interests or compromise ethical standards, especially when dealing with vulnerable populations or critical infrastructures. APPRAISE uses this narrative as a cautionary framework, ensuring that its AI tools are carefully monitored and controlled to prevent similar dystopian outcomes while maximizing its potential benefits for European societies.

In this way, APPRAISE aligns with broader EU initiatives and projects like NoBIAS (NoBIAS, 2024), which aims to understand, mitigate, and account for biases in AI systems. These projects collectively ensure that the use of AI in sensitive areas such as counterterrorism is not only efficient but also fair, transparent, and accountable. The intersection of AI with ethical policing tools directly addresses the vulnerabilities of soft targets to terrorist attacks, applying sophisticated technology to both detect and prevent such threats while ensuring that these tools are used responsibly. In fact, it can be stated that it is a holistic way to rethink policing with a built-in democratic algorithm (Van Brakel, 2020).

RECOMMENDATIONS

Bridging the gap between ambitious regulatory frameworks and operational realities requires clear, actionable strategies. The following recommendations aim to reinforce legal compliance, ethical standards, and effectiveness in AI-enabled policing.

Implementation of these recommendations will vary depending on national contexts, agency resources, and legislative nuances. Nonetheless, they offer a blueprint that can help shape a coherent, rights-based approach to AI in law enforcement.

Independent Oversight Bodies

Establishing specialized, independent oversight bodies—both at national and EU levels—can ensure that law enforcement agencies align their AI practices with legal and ethical standards (Gerbrandy & Zweers, 2019). These bodies would oversee impact assessments, monitor compliance, and investigate complaints related to AI use.

Beyond mere compliance monitoring, these oversight entities should have the authority to conduct unannounced audits, issue binding recommendations, and impose sanctions for misconduct. By maintaining a balance between guidance and enforcement, they can cultivate a culture of accountability and continuous improvement. Such bodies could also facilitate knowledge exchange across jurisdictions, helping to standardize AI practices while accounting for regional variations. A significant political challenge, however, will be ensuring these bodies are truly independent and adequately resourced. Their effectiveness could be undermined if they are susceptible to political pressure or lack the budget and technical expertise to meaningfully challenge the decisions of law enforcement agencies and powerful technology vendors.

Furthermore, these independent institutions can serve as a liaison between the public and law enforcement, offering a forum where grievances can be heard and resolved. Citizen engagement and stakeholder consultations can increase the legitimacy of AI-driven l policing as communities gain a sense of ownership and input into how surveillance and data analysis tools are deployed.

Human-in-the-Loop Decision Making

Critical decisions, especially those involving potential infringements on fundamental rights, should involve authorized human officers rather than fully automated systems (Elluri et al., 2025; Perry et al., 2013). This principle is integral to the EU AI Act's stipulation that high-risk applications require meaningful human oversight (European Commission, 2021a). Police departments could, for instance, implement a mandatory review process where humans validate or reject algorithmic recommendations.

A structured approach to human oversight may include multi-tiered review panels, where experts in technology, ethics, and law assess the outputs of AI tools before final decisions are made. Such panels can offer checks and balances, ensuring that data-driven insights are contextualized by local knowledge and ethical considerations. Additionally, embedding transparency in these decision chains—such as logging each stage of the review—enhances accountability.

Equally vital is the need for training officers and supervisors in effectively interpreting algorithmic advice. Without appropriate understanding and caution, the human-in-the-loop could become a mere "rubber stamp," inadvertently endorsing flawed AI outputs. Ongoing education, simulations, and scenario-based exercises can foster a robust decision-making culture where AI is a tool, not the ultimate arbiter.

Training and Education

Continuous training programs that cover the technical, legal, and ethical dimensions of AI are essential. Officers and analysts should be able to interpret algorithmic outputs, identify potential biases, and understand the relevant provisions of the EU AI Act and Regulation (EU) 2024/1689 (Dudek et al., 2023; Geradts & Franke, 2023; Zangana et al., 2025). Such training fosters a culture of accountability and fosters a deeper understanding of the interplay between technology and civil rights.

Curricula should extend beyond mere system operation to include broader discussions on civil liberties, anti-discrimination laws, and data protection principles. This holistic approach can help officers recognize when AI-driven insights conflict with core policing values or public expectations. Involving external stakeholders, such as academic experts or civil society groups, can further enrich these programs by providing alternative perspectives.

Moreover, training should not be a one-time event. As AI tools evolve, periodic refresher courses and advanced modules can keep personnel abreast of new functionalities and regulatory changes. Such an iterative training model ensures that law enforcement stays adaptive, continuously refining its approach to align with emerging best practices and legislative developments.

Transparent Procurement and Public Engagement

Ensuring transparency in AI procurement processes helps manage public perceptions and promotes trust (Barfield, 2020). Police agencies can publish details about the vendors, technology capabilities, and results of pre-deployment impact assessments. Public forums and town halls might also allow community members to voice concerns, thereby strengthening democratic oversight of new policing technologies.

Beyond transparency, public engagement can serve as a feedback mechanism for identifying unforeseen consequences. Citizens can offer insights into local community dynamics that may not be apparent to technology vendors or national-level policymakers. Structured dialogues, open workshops, and inclusive consultations can thus refine AI deployment strategies to serve diverse populations better.

Yet, transparency efforts can face resistance from commercial interests, as vendors may seek to protect proprietary algorithms. Striking a balance between corporate confidentiality and public accountability is essential. Negotiating contractual clauses that permit a degree of algorithmic audibility without compromising trade secrets can create a middle ground that meets both ethical and commercial concerns.

Enhanced EU Coordination

Reinforcing collaboration among Member States is necessary to address the cross-border nature of modern criminal activities and data flows (European Commission, 2021b). Forums and working groups could be established to harmonize best practices, share lessons learned, and fine-tune the implementation of EU-wide regulations like Regulation (EU) 2024/1689. This approach is key to maintaining consistent standards for data protection and accountability throughout the EU.

Enhanced coordination could include the creation of joint training academies or exchange programs, where officers from different Member States learn about AI tools, legal frameworks, and cultural considerations in policing. Such initiatives would help foster mutual trust and facilitate rapid, effective joint operations in cross-border cases (European Parliament & Council, 2024). Additionally, integrated data-sharing platforms, built on uniform standards, could drastically reduce delays and communication gaps.

Nevertheless, achieving harmonization is a gradual process. Varying political climates, budget constraints, and social attitudes toward surveillance can impede swift alignment across the EU. A flexible but persistent strategy—supported by EU-level funding and legislative incentives—can accelerate the adoption of uniform protocols while respecting national sovereignties and local policing priorities.

Continuous Evaluation and Adaptation

The field of AI is rapidly evolving, and its applications in policing will undoubtedly change over time. Therefore, it is essential to establish mechanisms for the continuous evaluation of AI tools deployed by law enforcement agencies. This process includes regular audits of algorithmic performance, assessment of their impact on different communities, and evaluation of their compliance with evolving legal and ethical standards. Such evaluations should inform adaptive strategies, allowing police forces to refine their use of AI, update training programs, and engage in ongoing dialogue with technology developers and civil society to address new challenges as they emerge.

Promoting Public Trust and Accountability Mechanisms

Building and maintaining public trust is paramount for the successful and ethical integration of AI into policing. Beyond transparency in procurement, this requires clear communication with the public about how AI tools are used, the safeguards in place, and the avenues for redress if errors or harm occur. Establishing accessible and effective accountability mechanisms, such as independent review boards and clear procedures for challenging algorithmic decisions, can empower citizens and reinforce the legitimacy of AI-assisted policing. Proactive public engagement and education initiatives can also help demystify AI technologies and foster a more informed and trustful relationship between law enforcement and the communities they serve. These recommendations underscore the importance of a structured and ethically grounded approach to AI adoption in policing contexts.

CONCLUSION

Artificial Intelligence holds great promise for modern policing, offering new ways to address complex security challenges, improve efficiency, and optimize resource allocation. Nonetheless, the technology's potential must be matched by strong legal safeguards, rigorous ethical commitments, and institutional checks and balances (European Union Agency for Fundamental Rights, 2018). The EU's regulatory efforts—exemplified by the AI Act and Regulation (EU) 2024/1689—reflect an evolving framework that seeks to promote both innovation and respect for fundamental rights. To realize AI's full benefits, law enforcement agencies need to engage in continuous monitoring, periodic audits, and adaptive training. As technology evolves, so too must our understanding of its implications for democratic governance, civil liberties, and the rule of law.

The future of AI in policing is not the dystopian vision portrayed in science fiction but rather one that depends on responsible development, ethical guidelines, and human oversight. Initiatives like APPRAISE demonstrate Europe's commitment to ensuring that AI is developed responsibly for law enforcement and that it serves society fairly and ethically. Although AI can boost policing efficiency and effectiveness, significant challenges remain, particularly concerning bias, privacy, and accountability. Through transparency, Regulation, and ethical foresight, AI can be integrated into law enforcement in ways that enhance security without compromising individual freedoms. As AI continues to evolve, it is crucial to remain vigilant of its potential pitfalls and ensure that technology serves humanity rather than controlling it.

Drawing from the analysis, the future of AI in policing in Europe, as exemplified by initiatives like APPRAISE, is shaping a reality grounded in responsible development, ethical frameworks, and human oversight—a measured contrast to the unchecked, often dystopian, AI depicted in science fiction.

Moreover, the future of AI in policing will inevitably expand beyond current applications, touching areas like drone surveillance, crowd analytics, and deepfake detection. Policymakers and practitioners should remain vigilant, updating regulations and best practices to address new technological frontiers. Fostering collaboration with tech developers, civil society, and legal experts will be vital in shaping a policing landscape that remains accountable, and rights oriented.

Ultimately, a people-centered approach—grounded in transparency, inclusivity, and deep respect for human dignity—must guide the deployment of AI in policing. By embedding these values into institutional frameworks and daily operations, law enforcement agencies can harness AI's transformative power while upholding the principles of justice that form the bedrock of democratic societies.

REFERENCES

Afzal, M., & Panagiotopoulos, P. (2024). Data in Policing: An Integrative Review. *International Journal of Public Administration*, *48*(7), 411–430. DOI: 10.1080/01900692.2024.2360586

Aho, B., & Duffield, R. (2020). Beyond surveillance capitalism: Privacy, regulation and big data in Europe and China. *Economy and Society*, *49*(2), 187–212. DOI: 10.1080/03085147.2019.1690275

Almasoud, A. S., & Idowu, J. A. (2025). Algorithmic fairness in predictive policing. *AI and Ethics*, *5*(3), 2323–2337. DOI: 10.1007/s43681-024-00541-3

APPRAISE. (2021). fAcilitating Public & Private secuRity operAtors to mitigate terrorIsm Scenarios against soft targEts – APPRAISE: the future for preventing and providing security for soft targets. https://appraise-h2020.eu

Bagaric, M., Svilar, J., Bull, M., Hunter, D., & Stobbs, N. (2022). The solution to the pervasive bias and discrimination in the criminal justice system: Transparent and fair Artificial Intelligence. *The American Criminal Law Review*, *59*(1), 95–148. https://ssrn.com/abstract=3795911

Berk, R. A. (2021). Artificial intelligence, predictive policing, and risk assessment for law enforcement. *Annual Review of Criminology*, *4*(1), 209–237. DOI: 10.1146/annurev-criminol-051520-012342

Brayne, S. (2017). Big data surveillance: The case of policing. *American Sociological Review*, *82*(5), 977–1008. DOI: 10.1177/0003122417725865 PMID: 38322733

Brayne, S. (2020). *Predict and surveil: Data, policing, and the future of criminal justice*. Oxford University Press. DOI: 10.1093/oso/9780190684099.001.0001

Brooker, C., Bridges, W., & Armstrong, J. (2011 -). Black mirror [TV series]. Zeppotron Productions; House of Tomorrow Productions; Broke & Bones Productions.

Buolamwini, J., & Gebru, T. (2018). Gender Shades: Intersectional Accuracy Disparities in Commercial Gender Classification. *Proceedings of the 1st Conference on Fairness, Accountability and Transparency*, 77–91.

Cameron, J. (1991). Terminator 2: Judgment day [Movie]. Carolco Pictures, Pacific Western Productions, Lightstorm Entertainment, Le Studio Canal+; TriStar Pictures.

Castets-Renard, C. (2021). Human Rights and Algorithmic Impact Assessment for Predictive Policing Constitutional Challenges in the Algorithmic Society, Cambridge University Press, Forthcoming, Available at SSRN: https://ssrn.com/abstract=3890283

Catlett, C., Portugali, J., & Venkatakrishnan, V. (2023). Privacy and trust in artificially intelligent cities. In Portugali, J. (Ed.), *The Crisis of Democracy in the Age of Cities* (pp. 167–183). Edward Elgar Publishing. DOI: 10.4337/9781803923055.00018

Cossette-Lefebvre, H., & Maclure, J. (2023). AI's fairness problem: Understanding wrongful discrimination in the context of automated decision-making. *AI and Ethics, 3*(4), 1255–1269. DOI: 10.1007/s43681-022-00233-w

Dinušová, D. (2024). *Dôveryhodnosť Policajného zboru v perspektívach filozofie a etiky (The Credibility of Police Force in Philosophical and Ethical Perspectives).* Academy of the Police Force in Bratislava.

Donahoe, E., & Metzger, M. M. (2019). Artificial intelligence and human rights. *Journal of Democracy, 30*(2), 115–126. DOI: 10.1353/jod.2019.0029

Doshi-Velez, F., & Kim, F. (2017). Towards a rigorousscience of interpretable machine learning. arXiv preprint arXiv:1702.08608.

Dudek, A., Dąbek, A., Zborowska, I., & Lichosik, J. (2023). Integrating artificial intelligence in forensic science. *E-methodology, 10*(10), 15–28. DOI: 10.15503/emet2023.15.28

Elluri, L., Mandalapu, V., Vyas, P., & Roy, N. (2025). Recent advancements in machine learning for cybercrime prediction. *Journal of Computer Information Systems, 65*(2), 249–263. DOI: 10.1080/08874417.2023.2270457

European Commission. (2021a). Proposal for a Regulation of the European Parliament and of the Council Laying Down Harmonised Rules on Artificial Intelligence (Artificial Intelligence Act) and Amending Certain Union Legislative Acts. COM(2021) 206 final.

European Commission. (2021b). Communication from the Commission to the European Parliament, the Council, the European Economic and Social Committee and the Committee of the Regions on the European strategy for data. COM(2020) 66 final.

European Commission. (2019). Regulation (EU) 2016/679 of the European Parliament and of the Council of 27 April 2016 on the protection of natural persons with regard to the processing of personal data and on the free movement of such data, and repealing Directive 95/46/EC (General Data Protection Regulation). Official Journal of the European Union, L 119, 4.5.2016, p. 1–88.

European Parliament. (2023). EU AI Act: first regulation on artificial intelligence. https://www.europarl.europa.eu/topics/en/article/20230601STO93804/eu-ai-act-first-regulation-on-artificial-intelligenceEuropean

European Union Agency for Fundamental Rights. (2018). *Fundamental rights implications of the future development of AI systems in policing*. Publications Office of the European Union.

Geradts, Z., & Franke, K. (Eds.). (2023). *Artificial Intelligence (AI) in Forensic Sciences*. Wiley.

Gerbrandy, A., & Zweers, K. (2019). Artificial intelligence and law enforcement: Impacts on legal certainty and fundamental rights. Research Paper, Vrije Universiteit Amsterdam.

Gille, M., Tropmann-Frick, M., & Schomacker, T. (2024). Balancing public interest, fundamental rights, and innovation: The EU's governance model for non-high-risk AI systems. *Internet Policy Review*, *13*(3). Advance online publication. DOI: 10.14763/2024.3.1797

Goldstein, H. (1990). *Problem-oriented policing*. McGraw Hill.

Helbing, D., Brockmann, D., Chadefaux, T., Donnay, K., Blanke, U., Woolley-Meza, O., Moussaid, M., Johansson, A., Krause, J., Schutte, S., & Perc, M. (2015). Saving human lives: What complexity science and information systems can contribute. *Journal of Statistical Physics*, *158*(3), 735–781. DOI: 10.1007/s10955-014-1024-9 PMID: 26074625

Jones, R., Schur, M., & Brooker, C. (Writer) & Wright, J. (Director) (2016, 21 de Outubro). Nosedive (Series 3, Episode 1) [TV series episode]. In C. Brooker, B. Reisz, & A. Jones (Executive Ptoducers), Black Mirror. Zeppotron Productions; House of Tomorrow Productions; Broke & Bones Productions.

Kavoliūnaitė-Ragauskienė, E. (2024). Right to Privacy and Data Protection Concerns Raised by the Development and Usage of Face Recognition Technologies in the European Union. *Journal of Human Rights Practice*, *16*(2), 658–674. DOI: 10.1093/jhuman/huad065

Kohan, J., Hess, S., & Hermann (Executive Producers) (2013-2019). Orange is the new black [TV series]. Lionsgate Television; Titled.

Leslie, D. (2020). Understanding bias in facial recognition technologies. arXiv preprint arXiv:2010.07023. https://doi.org//arXiv.2010.07023DOI: 10.48550

Limantė, A. (2024). Bias in facial recognition technologies used by law enforcement: Understanding the causes and searching for a way out. *Nordic Journal of Human Rights*, *42*(2), 115–134. DOI: 10.1080/18918131.2023.2277581

Lum, K., & Isaac, W. (2016). To predict and serve? *Significance*, *13*(5), 14–19. DOI: 10.1111/j.1740-9713.2016.00960.x

Lynch, J. (2020). Face off: Law enforcement use of face recognition technology. Available at *SSRN* 3909038. DOI: 10.2139/ssrn.3909038

Malek, M. A. (2022). Criminal courts' artificial intelligence: The way it reinforces bias and discrimination. *AI and Ethics*, *2*(1), 233–245. DOI: 10.1007/s43681-022-00137-9

Mazur, J. (2023). Artificial Intelligence vs Data Protection: How the GDPR Can Help to Develop a Precautionary Regulatory Approach to AI? In Kornilakis, A., Nouskalis, G., Pergantis, V., & Tzimas, T. (Eds.), *Artificial Intelligence and Normative Challenges. Law, Governance and Technology Series* (Vol. 59, pp. 215–233). Springer., DOI: 10.1007/978-3-031-41081-9_12

Migliorini, S. (2023). Biometric harm. Law. *Technology & Humans*, *5*(2), 238–251. DOI: 10.5204/lthj.2830

Morgado, S. M. A. (2013). Crime and socio-economic context: A framework approach. In Z. V. Sovreski, M. Mokryš, Š. Badura, A., Lieskovský (Eds.), Proceedings in Advanced Research in Scientific Areas (ARSA 2013), (pp. 139 – 142.). Slovakia: EDIS - Publishing Institution of the University of Zilina.

Morgado, S. M. A. (2023). Inteligência artificial e metamorfose dos paradigmas: Economia na era da transformação. Congresso Nacional da Ordem dos Economistas – Portugal e os Desafios do Presente: O papel dos Economistas e Gestores.https://www.ordemeconomistas.pt/xportalv3/file/XEOCM_Documento/74260936/file/S%C3%B3nia%20Aniceto%20Morgado.pdf

Morgado, S. M. A., Carvalho, M., & Felgueiras, S. (2024b). Diagnosis model for detection of e-threats against soft-targets. In A. Rocha, H. Adeli, G., Dzemyda, F., Moreira, and V. Colla (eds). Information Systems and Technologies. WorldCIST 2023. Lecture Notes in Networks and Systems, vol 800 (pp. 249–262). Springer, Cham. DOI: 10.1007/978-3-031-45645-9_24

Morgado, S. M. A., & Felgueiras, S. (2021). Big data in policing: Profiling, patterns, and out of the box thinking. In Rocha, A., Adeli, H., Dzemyda, G., Moreira, F., & Ramalho Correia, A. M. (Eds.), *Trends and Applications in Information Systems and Technologies. WorldCIST 2021. Advances in Intelligent Systems and Computing* (Vol. 1365, pp. 217–226). Springer., DOI: 10.1007/978-3-030-72657-7_21

Morgado, S. M. A., & Felgueiras, S. (2022). Technological policing: Big data versus real data. Politeia. *Revista Portuguesa de Ciências Policiais*, (XIX), 139–151. DOI: 10.57776/hkcb-br21

Morgado, S. M. A., Nabais, T., & Felgueiras, S. (2024a). Unveiling the project fAcilitating Public & Private secuRity operAtors to mitigate terrorIsm Scenarios against soft targEts – APPRAISE: the future for preventing and providing security for soft targets. In R. N. A. Fernandes, & P. Machado (Coord.). 40 anos das Ciências Policiais em Portugal (pp. 277-285), ICPOL.

Mugari, I., & Obioha, E. E. (2021). Predictive policing and crime control in the United States of America and Europe: Trends in a decade of research and the future of predictive policing. *Social Sciences (Basel, Switzerland)*, *10*(6), 1–14. DOI: 10.3390/socsci10060234

NoBias. (2024). NoBIAS: Artificial Intelligence without Bias. https://nobias-project.eu

Nolan, J., Plageman, G., Abrams, J. J., Thé, D., & Fisher, C. (Executive Producers). (2011-2016). Person of interest [TV series]. Killer Films; Bad Robot; Bonanza Productions; Warner Bros. Television.

Olaoye, F., & Egon, A. (2024). Predictive policing and crime prevention. https://easychair.org/publications/preprint/lQ2r/open

Parliament and Council. (2024). Regulation (EU) 2024/1689 of the European Parliament and of the Council of 13 June 2024 establishing the interoperability between information systems in the area of justice and home affairs and amending Regulations (EU) 2018/1726, (EU) 2019/816 and (EU) 2019/818. Official Journal of the European Union, L, 2024/1689, 13.6.2024.

Perkowitz, S. (2021). The bias in the machine: Facial recognition technology and racial disparities. https://mit-serc.pubpub.org/pub/bias-in-machine/release/1?readingCollection=34db8026

Perry, W. L., McInnis, B., Price, A. R., Smith, S., & Hollywood, J. S. (2013). *Predictive policing: The role of crime forecasting in law enforcement operations*. RAND Corporation. DOI: 10.7249/RR233

Peterson, D., & Hoffman, S. (2022). *Geopolitical implications of AI and digital surveillance adoption*. Brookings Institution.

Rademacher, T. (2020). Artificial intelligence and law enforcement. In Wischmeyer, T., & Rademacher, T. (Eds.), *Regulating Artificial Intelligence* (pp. 225–254). Springer., DOI: 10.1007/978-3-030-32361-5_10

Richardson, R. (2021). Racial segregation and the data-driven society: How our failure to reckon with root causes perpetuates separate and unequal realities. *Berkeley Technology Law Journal*, *36*(3), 1051. DOI: 10.15779/Z38PN8XG3V

Richardson, R., Schultz, J. M., & Crawford, K. (2019). Dirty data, bad predictions: How civil rights violations impact police data, predictive policing systems, and justice. *NYUL Rev. Online*, *94*, 15.

Roksandić, S., Protrka, N., & Engelhart, M. (2022, May). Trustworthy Artificial Intelligence and its use by Law Enforcement Authorities: where do we stand? In 2022 45th Jubilee International Convention on Information, Communication and Electronic Technology (MIPRO) (pp. 1225-1232). IEEE. Opatija, Croatia. DOI: 10.23919/MIPRO55190.2022.9803606

Schuetz, P. N. (2021). Fly in the Face of Bias: Algorithmic Bias in Law Enforcement's Facial Recognition Technology and the Need for an Adaptive Legal Framework. *Minnesota Journal of Law & Inequality*, *39*(1), 221–254. DOI: 10.24926/25730037.626

Selbst, A. D. (2017). Disparate Impact in Big Data Policing. *SSRN*, *52*(1), 109–195. DOI: 10.2139/ssrn.2819182

Simon, D., Colesberry, R. F., & Noble, N. K. (Executive Producers). (2002-2008). The wire [TV series]. Blown Deadline Productions, HBO Entertainment. HBO.

Smith, M., & Miller, S. (2021). *Biometric identification, law and ethics*. Springer Nature. DOI: 10.1007/978-3-030-90256-8

Smith, M., & Miller, S. (2022). The ethical application of biometric facial recognition technology. *AI & Society*, *37*(1), 167–175. DOI: 10.1007/s00146-021-01199-9 PMID: 33867693

Söderholm, S. (2023). Fundamental rights control when implementing predictive policing–a European perspective. *Peking University Law Journal*, *11*(1), 91–104. DOI: 10.1080/20517483.2023.2223850

Spielberg, S. (2002). Minory report [Movie]. 20th Century Fox, Dreamworks Pictures, Amblin Entertainment, Blue Tulip Productions; 20th Century Fox.

Stacy, E. (2017). *Human and algorithm facial recognition performance: Face in a crowd.* University of Technology Sydney.

Stevens, J. (2001, April 24-25). Defining intelligence-led policing. [Paper presented]. 2nd World Investigation of Crime Conference, Durban, South Africa.

Udoh, E. S. (2020, September). Is the data fair? An assessment of the data quality of algorithmic policing systems. In *Proceedings of the 13th International Conference on Theory and Practice of Electronic Governance* (pp. 1-7). DOI: 10.1145/3428502.3428503

Van Brakel, R. (2020). Rethinking predictive policing: Towards a holistic framework of democratic algorithmic surveillance. In Schuilenbur, M., & Peeters, R. (Eds.), *The Algorithmic Society* (pp. 104–118). Routledge. DOI: 10.4324/9780429261404-9

Wan, J. (2015). Fast and furious 7 [Movie]. MRC, Original Film, One Race Films, China Film Co., Ltd.; Universal Pictures.

Washington, A. L. (2019). How to argue with an algorithm: Lessons from the COMPAS ProPublica Debate. The Colorado Technology Law Journal, 17(1), 1-37. https://ssrn.com/abstract=3357874

Zangana, H. M., Omar, M., & Mohammed, D. (2025). Introduction to Artificial Intelligence in Cybersecurity and Forensic Science. In Omar, M., Zangana, H. M., & Mohammed, D. (Eds.), *Integrating Artificial Intelligence in Cybersecurity and Forensic Practices* (pp. 1–24). IGI Global Scientific Publishing., DOI: 10.4018/979-8-3373-0588-2.ch001

Ziosi, M., & Pruss, D. (2024, June). Evidence of what, for whom? The socially contested role of algorithmic bias in a predictive policing tool. In The 2024 ACM Conference on Fairness, Accountability, and Transparency (pp. 1596-1608). DOI: 10.1145/3630106.3658991

Chapter 3
OSINT in the Techno-Political Era:
From Intelligence Collection to Exerting Influence

Murat Tınas
https://orcid.org/0000-0001-5844-0808
Turkish National Police Academy, Turkey

Doğukan Tuncal
https://orcid.org/0000-0001-9299-4425
Turkish National Police Academy, Turkey

ABSTRACT

This study investigates the impact of technological developments on the processes and effectiveness of open-source intelligence (OSINT) in the techno-political era. The research question guiding this study is: "How have advanced technological developments influenced OSINT processes and its overall effectiveness?". The core hypothesis posits that the expansion of collection capabilities through technological advancements has significantly increased OSINT's efficiency as a collection method, however, these advancements have also transformed OSINT from a collection mechanism into an instrument of influence within the intelligence theory. As a result, OSINT today is not only a discipline of collection but has also become means of shaping narratives, perceptions, and strategic influence from an intersubjective perspective. To empirically validate this hypothesis, the study adopts a qualitative research design and conducts a case study analysis of the Russian Federation's (RF) OSINT activities during the annexation of Crimea in 2014 and the full-scale invasion of Ukraine in 2022.

DOI: 10.4018/979-8-3373-7406-2.ch003

1. INTRODUCTION

In the 21st century, the unprecedented acceleration of technological innovation has not only altered the contours of economic production and social relations but has also introduced a novel techno-political environment. This emergent environment does not merely consist of new instruments or digital infrastructures; rather, it constitutes a profound transformation in the way political authority, governance, and strategic behavior are practiced and contested. Technologies such as artificial intelligence (AI), big data analytics, and machine learning no longer function as neutral instruments of today's conjuncture but have become integral components of the political sphere—actively shaping and influencing discourses, decision-making processes, and power relations.

As this techno-political atmosphere evolves, its ramifications extend far beyond the economic and social domains, reaching deeply into the realms of national security and intelligence. The intelligence sector, which historically operated under the principles of secrecy, selectivity, and hierarchical control of information, now faces the challenges and opportunities posed by a landscape characterized by hyper-connectivity, information saturation, and algorithmic governance. In this context, open-source intelligence (OSINT)—once considered supplementary to clandestine collection techniques—has emerged as both a central and contentious domain within the intelligence cycle.

Unlike clandestine forms of intelligence collection that grounds on secrecy and restricted access, OSINT derives its value from openly available sources, including social media, news outlets, satellite imagery, academic publications, grey literature, and public databases. Traditionally, its role within the intelligence community has been viewed through a procedural lens: OSINT served as an auxiliary method of information gathering, often at the preliminary, descriptive or corroborative stages of analysis. However, this procedural conceptual framing is increasingly inadequate in capturing the full scope of OSINT's current and potential utility, as its capabilities have significantly expanded with the technological advancements of recent decades.

In this context, in light of the research question "How has the techno-political era affected the qualities of OSINT activities from the perspective of intelligence theory?", this study argues, as its main hypothesis, that the nature of OSINT is undergoing a transformative shift in the techno-political era by incorporating the function of influencing besides the function of understanding—one that is not merely methodological but also ontological. The integration of advanced technologies into OSINT processes—and thereby the acquisition of the capacity to access an unprecedented volume of individuals—has fundamentally transformed both the methods of open-source data collection and the ways in which such data can be utilized to exert influence. In terms of understanding, big data, use of AI, natural language processing, sentiment analysis, and real-time geospatial tracking have drastically increased the volume, speed, and granularity of open-source data collection. In terms of exerting influence, the use of emerging technologies—combined with the capacity to reach vast numbers of individuals—has altered perceptions of OSINT implementation, transforming it into an instrument of influence as well. As a result, OSINT and its surrounding environment have undergone not only a methodological but also an ontological transformation, also representing a shift in the role OSINT plays within the broader intelligence architecture.

From the perspective of exerting influence, as OSINT increasingly conforms to the logic of algorithmic processing and digital dissemination, it no longer merely serves as an instrument of collection, but rather emerges as an active component of strategic narrative construction and perception management—thus aligning with core functions traditionally associated with psychological operations. In environments where hybrid threats, information warfare, and psychological operations dominate contemporary conflict landscapes, together with the increasing technological capacities, the boundaries between collection and operations start to blur. OSINT, by virtue of its open and publicly visible character, now serves as both a mirror and a speaker: reflecting societal tensions and amplifying specific discourses to shape adversarial behavior, domestic attitudes, international alignments, and even contributes to the tactical-level operations too.

In addressing the aforementioned research question and operationalizing the main hypothesis, this study adopts a qualitative research design, applying case study method. The RF invasion of Crimea in 2014 and then Ukraine in 2022 provides a critical case through which OSINT's evolving nature can be empirically observed. During the conflict, OSINT emerged not only as a means of intelligence collection but also as a central component of strategic influence. These cases present through the lens of four structural factors—mass digitization, participatory media, algorithmic curation, and technological scalability— that OSINT has evolved into an instrument of strategic influence in the techno-political era, by not only supporting intelligence collection but actively participates in shaping perceptions, legitimizing narratives, and conducting psychological operations in contested information environments. This dual use of OSINT—both as a mechanism for factual verification and a tool for influence—highlights its evolution from a supplementary intelligence source to a dynamic instrument of warfare. Thus, this study aims to contribute to both the literature and practical field by revealing the structural transformation occurring in the qualities of OSINT activities.

2. LITERATURE REVIEW AND METHODOLOGY

Understanding the role of OSINT within intelligence theory—as well as the ontological transformation it is currently undergoing, as proposed in this study—necessitates a comprehensive review of the existing literature and a critical appraisal of how OSINT has been conceptualized therein. In this context, the current section will begin with a brief discussion on the conceptualization of intelligence—kept deliberately concise given that it is not the primary focus of the study. Subsequently, through an in-depth literature review, the prevailing conceptualizations and perceptions of OSINT will be identified, thereby clarifying the study's intended contribution to both academic discourse and practical implementation.

Intelligence theory fundamentally progresses along two main trajectories. The first, initiated by Kent and later advanced by thinkers such as Lowenthal, Gill and Phythian—despite the nuances among them—conceptualizes intelligence as a triadic structure: a form of knowledge, the institutional framework that produces this knowledge, and the process, namely the intelligence cycle (Kent 1949; Lowenthal 2008; Gill and Phythian 2018). The second group of scholars led by Warner, while not outright rejecting this conceptualization, argues that intelligence is essentially a covert state activity carried out to understand and to influence foreign actors (2002, p. 21). Undoubtedly, the element of influence—explicitly absent in the first school's framework—constitutes the foundational pillar of the Warner's perspective, offering a more functional and explanatory lens particularly regarding the processual nature of intelligence. In this context, a literature review examining how these schools approach OSINT will contribute significantly to a deeper understanding of the contemporary nature and function of open-source intelligence.

This military doctrine defines OSINT as intelligence derived from the systematic exploitation of publicly available information to support traditional decision-making processes, particularly within the context of unified land operations. In the field manuel prepared by US Army, the emphasis is placed on OSINT's supporting role in intelligence preparation of the battlefield (IPB), situational awareness, and corroboration of classified sources, with procedural guidance for collection, validation, and dissemination (Department of the Army 2012, pp. 1.1 - 1.5). In another military approach, OSINT has been framed as a tactical enabler for Special Operations Forces, primarily valued for its low-cost, low-risk contribution to pre-mission planning and situational awareness (Steele 2004, pp. 1-3). In the more recent publication of US Army named as Open Source Intelligence Analyst Manual, OSINT is framed as a legally bounded, passive support discipline intended to complement classified intelligence sources through techniques such as metadata analysis and deep web research (US Army 2016).

Wiil argues that OSINT serves primarily as a support mechanism in counter-terrorism, particularly through the detection of networks and the analysis of online activity via computational techniques (2011, pp. 159-171). From the cybercrime perspective, in the edited study by Tayebi, Glässer, and Skillicorn, it is argued that OSINT has significant utility in detecting cybercrime through social media analytics, with emphasis on machine learning, metadata analysis, and behavioral inference (2020). In the edited book by Hobbs, Moran, and Salisbury, it is argued that OSINT has evolved into a mature discipline contributing to situational awareness, network analysis, and digital trace interpretation, particularly through SOCMINT and big data integration (2014). However, the volume still treats OSINT as a complementary component within all-source intelligence and does not address its transformation into a strategic actor in terms of influence function.

Bean (2011) argues that OSINT's development has been shaped less by its technical affordances and more by institutional discourse, bureaucratic negotiation, and the post-9/11 reorganization of the U.S. intelligence community. Drawing on organizational and communication theory, he examines how open-source information was legitimized through public-private partnerships and democratic accountability narratives (pp. 23-57). However, the analysis centers on institutional integration and transparency, leaving OSINT's transformation into a tool of algorithmic influence and strategic perception management largely unexamined.

From a different perspective, Huang argues that OSINT serves as a highly effective forensic instrument in post-incident investigations, particularly through the use of social media data, biometrics, and visual recognition to identify participants in the January 6 Capitol riots (2021, pp. 142-445). Similarly, Appel remarks that OSINT functions primarily as a digital investigative tool used for vetting, profiling, and threat assessment, particularly within law enforcement and corporate security contexts (2011, pp. 3-40).

In the report published by I-Intelligence, it is argued in the foreword that OSINT functions as a highly practical and technical discipline, with an extensive emphasis on tools for data collection, verification, and profiling across platforms such as social media and the dark web (Bielska et al. 2020, pp. 3-14). From a more operational perspective, Holden-Rhodes argues that OSINT provides a pragmatic and effective intelligence capability for counter-narcotics operations, emphasizing its utility in inter-agency coordination and strategic forecasting through modeling data (1997, pp. 9-24). Focusing on the collection and analysis methods in OSINT, Hoffman argues that OSINT is best understood as a structured and technically rigorous process for investigative purposes, particularly in cybersecurity, law enforcement, and personal profiling (2019, pp. 21-32). Hassan and Hijazi explain that OSINT serves primarily as a tactical and technical method for online investigations, focusing on surface, deep, and dark web data extraction, as well as metadata analysis and digital privacy (2018, pp. 1-19).

As one of the most comprehensive approaches, NATO frames OSINT as a foundational component of all-source intelligence, emphasizing its utility in strategic awareness, coalition interoperability, and early warning systems (2002, pp. 2-55). While the work institutionalizes OSINT within NATO and PfP structures, however, even it does not address its transformation into an autonomous instrument of influence, nor does it explore its algorithmic or psychological applications.

Baker conceptualizes OSINT as a practical investigative methodology that integrates AI, big data, and NLP to enhance digital profiling, infrastructure mapping, and social media analysis. As seen, he touches upon the technological features of today's OSINT configuration in a correct manner, however, the study does not engage with ontological transformation of OSINT into a strategic tool of influence, remaining focused on its operational and technical applications with technological advancements (2023, pp. 3-22). In a similar vein, Palacín conceptualizes OSINT as a technical enabler for data-driven threat intelligence and adversary tracking by focusing on its infrastructure, toolkits, and procedural rigor (2021, p. 17).

In terms of the published articles and dissertations on the nature of OSINT, Slater conceptualizes SOCMINT, as a sub-discipline of OSINT and a structured investigative tool for combating human trafficking, emphasizing metadata extraction, forensic validation, and early detection (2023, pp. 10-18).

In her study focusing on the technological developments in OSINT techniques, Gioti examines the integration of AI into OSINT for enhancing cyber threat intelligence, emphasizing automation, anomaly detection, and geospatial analysis (2023, pp. 32-54). While technically comprehensive and touching upon the impact of technological advancements on OSINT praxeology, the study does not conceptualize OSINT as an instrument of influence or narrative construction, leaving its ontological transformation unaddressed. On the other hand, Perez (2024) offers a detailed conceptual taxonomy of OSINT definitions, addressing jurisdictional, definitional, and methodological inconsistencies. Despite acknowledging technological shifts, the article does not deal with theorizing OSINT's transformation in today's world.

In a more technical study, Dale develops a deep learning-based OSINT pipeline for real-time cybersecurity threat detection via Twitter data (2023, pp. 5-29). While methodologically advanced and reveals the capacity of today's OSINT practice with recent technological advancements, the study lacks the understanding of how all these techno-advancements shapes and transforms the qualities of OSINT conceptually. Similar with the previous study, Browne, Abedin, and Chowdhury conduct a systematic review of 163 studies utilizing AI techniques—such as SVM, CNN, and LSTM—in OSINT applications (2024, 2912-2924).

In terms of the less technical approach of the intelligence scholars, Lowenthal conceptualizes OSINT as a collection discipline within the broader intelligence cycle, describing it as one of several sources that support national security decision-making (2008, pp. 182-183). Gill and Phythian similarly conceptualize OSINT as a supplementary component within the broader intelligence collection framework, emphasizing its relevance in the digital era (2018, pp. 131-132).

As evidenced by the comprehensive literature review presented above, the existing academic discourse on OSINT—largely shaped by practical experience to date—tends to position OSINT within the "process" component of the triadic conceptualization of intelligence, referring to what is commonly understood in practice as the intelligence cycle. Accordingly, OSINT is typically treated as a supplementary collection activity, primarily serving the function of understanding. However, within the framework advanced by the Warner's perception —which conceives of intelligence not only as understanding but also as an instrument of influence—there exists no study that systematically analyzes, positions, or debates OSINT. This study seeks to address that clear gap by situating OSINT within the Warner's conceptual framework, thereby advancing the argument that OSINT functions not only as a means of collection but also as a tool of influence.

3. THE ONTOLOGICAL TRANSFORMATION IN THE NATURE OF OSINT

In the techno-political era, the convergence of technological infrastructures with political practice has not only altered the ways of governance and conflict but has also profoundly reshaped the architecture of intelligence itself. The shift is not merely one of instrumentality—introducing new tools or accelerating existing processes—but a structural transformation in how intelligence is conceptualized, produced, and operationalized. Within this context, OSINT, once described as a supplementary and epistemic role in intelligence cycle, has undergone a deep ontological transformation. This transformation is catalyzed by developments that are inherently techno-political: they emerge at the intersection of computational affordances, digital platforms, and strategic communication imperatives. As OSINT becomes increasingly integrated with algorithmic visibility, artificial intelligence, and platform-driven public discourse, it no longer simply reflects the world but participates in shaping it. The following subsections identify and elaborate on the six structural developments that have rendered this transformation both possible and irreversible.

The first structural shift underpinning OSINT's transformation lies in the mass digitization of textual, visual, and geospatial data. From the early 1990s onward, state institutions, think tanks, academic databases, and media archives began systematically digitizing repositories of knowledge. Public access to documents previously confined to physical shelves dramatically increased. This process, while initially seen as a democratizing movement in the information age, also laid the groundwork for intelligence actors to exploit vast, open information systems. OSINT's traditional limitation—lack of depth or timeliness compared to classified sources—was partly mitigated by this development. At this stage, however, OSINT remained a supplementary observational tool, used mainly for corroboration or contextual enrichment. Yet, the seeds of ontological shift were planted: intelligence could now emerge from visibility, not just secrecy.

The second phase of transformation was marked by the rise of participatory web technologies, especially social media platforms after 2004. The Web 2.0 era did not simply expand the volume of data—it restructured the nature of data production. Users became sensors, commentators, and agents of narrative, creating digital footprints that could be mapped, analyzed, and predicted. The intelligence value of this participatory data far exceeded that of traditional open sources. OSINT actors began to extract not only facts but also emotional trends, political sentiments, and behavioral indicators from this data stream. In essence, the information environment itself became dynamic and reactive—OSINT was no longer a window into external events, but a way to engage with the event-making process. This reflexive dynamic marked the beginning of OSINT's shift from being a descriptive instrument to a generative one.

A pivotal driver of OSINT's ontological shift lies in the rise of algorithmically curated platforms. In the post-2010 digital landscape, platforms such as YouTube, TikTok, X (formerly Twitter), and Facebook do not merely host information—they curate it. Through opaque algorithms, they determine what becomes visible, credible, or viral. This "logic of visibility" transforms the intelligence environment itself: influence is no longer exerted through access control (as in the Cold War model) but through algorithmic amplification. OSINT actors increasingly operate within this logic, not merely interpreting content but strategically shaping what will be seen, by whom, and when. This grants OSINT a new operational capacity: narrative modulation via platform dynamics. In this sense, the ontological condition of OSINT shifts from supplementary to substantial.

Technological scalability has played a critical role in OSINT's transformation. The incorporation of AI—particularly natural language processing, image recognition, sentiment analysis, and predictive analytics—into OSINT workflows has allowed for real-time processing of vast, heterogeneous data. The traditional intelligence-cycle bottlenecks (human analysts, translation delays, verification hurdles) are increasingly bypassed by machine-augmented OSINT. In this context, OSINT not only collects and verifies but anticipates and predicts. Target audience analysis, psychographic segmentation, and network mapping now allow OSINT practitioners to identify narrative vulnerabilities, manipulate digital attention, and even simulate potential reactions. This predictive capability reframes OSINT not as an "input" to intelligence but as a semi-autonomous actor in shaping operational reality.

Table 1. The Ontological Transformation of OSINT in the Techno-Political Era

The Ontological Transformation of OSINT in the Techno-Political Era		
	Traditional OSINT (Pre-Techno-Political Era)	**Transformed OSINT (Techno-Political Era)**
Function	Collection discipline and contextual understanding	Narrative production and strategic influence
Epistemological Role	Descriptive and corroborative	Generative and performative
Temporal Scope	Post-event analysis (reactive)	Real-time engagement and prediction (proactive)
Audience	Limited to internal intelligence consumers	Public, adversaries, allies, global media
Visibility Logic	Passive transparency	Algorithmic curation and platform visibility
Narrative Position	Observes and decodes narratives	Creates, reframes, and circulates narratives
Strategic Function	Supplementary	Instrument of Psychological Operations

(Generated by the authors)

As can be seen from Table 1 presented above, these structural shifts have enabled OSINT to transcend its traditional epistemic function—centered on collection and analyzing grounded on the function of understanding—and to incorporate a new, influence-driven dimension: the ability to reconstruct, reframe, and re-disseminate information in ways that shape perception and behavior. In this sense, OSINT now operates not merely as a mirror that reflects reality, but as a filter and amplifier that produces strategically subjective versions of truth. As algorithmic visibility and participatory media facilitate access to unprecedentedly large and diverse audiences, OSINT is increasingly capable of functioning as a component of psychological warfare, operations and propaganda—not only mapping target populations but also engaging them through tailored and emotionally charged messaging, and selective amplification. This dual role—understanding through information acquisition and influencing through narrative dissemination—represents the ontological transformation at the heart of this study. OSINT, in the techno-political era, is no longer limited to observing the battlefield; it enters the battlefield as a cognitive actor. In this context, the case study analyses presented below will contribute to the confirmation of the aforementioned hypothesis inherent to this study.

3.1. Case Study Analysis: Russian Federation's Targeted Activities During the Invasion of Crimea in 2014 and Ukraine in 2022

In order to empirically assess the validity of the central hypothesis proposed in this study—that OSINT in the techno-political era has undergone an ontological transformation by incorporating the function of influence alongside its traditional function of understanding—it is methodologically necessary to analyze for scientific confirmation how this transformation becomes visible in concrete cases. Specifically, the integration of advanced technologies such as AI, big data analytics, and algorithmic visibility into OSINT processes suggests a profound structural shift in its role within the intelligence architecture. However, to evaluate whether this theoretical proposition holds under real-world conditions, this section deals with a systematic case-based analysis. The selected cases will be examined through the lens of the structural developments previously identified—namely mass digitization, participatory media, algorithmic curation, AI-enabled prediction, and the resulting duality of epistemic and influence functions. Through this analytical framework, the presence and operationalization of these techno-political transformations within each case can be identified and mapped. This approach not only allows for the tracing of OSINT's functional evolution in practice but also provides empirical grounding for the ontological claims advanced by this study. Ultimately, the objective is to determine the extent to which OSINT's influence-exerting capacity—enabled by techno-political transformation—is not merely possible in theory, but observable and measurable in contemporary phenomena.

In response to the evolving global conjuncture and in alignment with the imperatives of the techno-political era, the RF's has enacted a series of institutional restructurings aimed at enhancing its capacity to exert influence. Among these, a particularly salient example—aligned with the hypothesis of this study—is the Internet Research Agency (IRA), which epitomizes Russia's strategic use of OSINT-based methodologies not merely for epistemic purposes, but as an instrument of influence embedded within the techno-political domain.

Established in St. Petersburg in 2013 and reportedly linked to the Kremlin, the IRA functions as a proxy actor designed to manipulate Western public opinion, exacerbate social and political polarization, delegitimize credible media institutions, erode public trust in democratic norms, and interfere in the domestic political processes of targeted states (Hoch, 2020; Bail et al., 2020).

In pursuit of these objectives, the IRA operates by generating and disseminating content via fictitious personas across social media platforms, strategically orchestrating digital interactions to amplify its narratives. Its targeted engagement with relatively niche yet influenceable online communities—such as those on Tumblr—

demonstrates its operational proficiency in constructing trust-based digital ecosystems before injecting politically charged content, thus underscoring its capacity within the realm of influence operations (Hoch, 2020).

A particularly illustrative case is the IRA's systematic targeting of African-American communities during the 2016 U.S. presidential election. Through coordinated Twitter campaigns disseminating negative narratives about Hillary Clinton, the agency exploited contentious sociopolitical issues such as police brutality, racial injustice, immigration, and gun control. These campaigns, which generated over 57,000 tweets, not only shaped digital discourse but also translated into offline mobilization by interacting with American users and facilitating real-world protests and public demonstrations (Bail et al., 2020).

Such cases constitute concrete reflections of the function of OSINT-driven influence, posited in this study's hypothesis, wherein open-source methodologies are no longer confined to intelligence collection but serve as tools for narrative reproduction and strategic persuasion. Within this framework, the RF emerges as a key actor in the techno-political arena—one that has developed instruments aimed at the reproduction of information. However, to fully comprehend the evolution of these instruments from tools of understanding to mechanisms of influence, one must examine the operational modalities deployed during RF's annexation of Crimea in 2014 and the full-scale invasion of Ukraine in 2022.

3.1.1. Russian Federation's Influence Focused OSINT Activities during the Invasion of Crimea in 2014

In 2014, during the occupation of Crimea and the subsequent operations, the RF employed OSINT activities—and the domains hosting such activities—not merely for the purpose of acquiring information and understanding unfolding processes, but also with the intent of generating influence in service of its own political and military interests.

First, RF aimed at controlling and directing the information environment and the domain that OSINT activities operated within. To do so, Ukrainian TV channels such as 5th Channel, 1+1, and Crimea-24 were shut down and replaced with Russian state media like Russia-1. Disinformation accusing Ukrainian forces of attacking civilians in Donbas were spread in open sources including social media, and further expanded Russian influence in Luhansk and Donetsk (Markovets, Buchyn, Kovalchuk, and Basyuk, 2023, pp. 9-14). OSINT-derived insights also fueled targeted psychological operations, such as direct messages sent to Ukrainian soldiers urging them to surrender by asserting they were abandoned by their own government (Markovets, Buchyn, Kovalchuk, and Basyuk, 2023, pp. 9-14).

In line with its broader information-psychological operations strategy during the 2014 Crimea operation, the RF utilized a narrative that operates in the OSINT domain, shaping to manufacture perceptions of humanitarian crisis and defection, thereby legitimizing its intervention. RF state media, particularly TASS, repeatedly reported that hundreds of ethnic Russian-speaking refugees were fleeing Ukraine to seek asylum in Russia due to alleged brutality by Ukrainian forces. These narratives were disseminated with inflated figures—such as 245,000 asylum seekers—and were accompanied by misleading visual content, including footage taken from the Ukrainian-Polish border falsely presented as the Ukrainian-Russian crossing (TASS, 2014a; TASS 2014b; TASS 2014c). Here again, by using and distorting an open source environment which was formerly benefited for extracting information and understanding the course of actions, RF aimed at shaping the both reality and narrative in order to influence interests.

In parallel, OSINT originated operations extended into the military domain, with open source outlets like Izvestiya falsely claiming that the Ukrainian Navy's flagship Hetman Sahaydachniy had defected to Russia. Such claims, published in open source environments which are usually used by different governmental and non-governmental actors, such as ministries of foreign affairs or individuals that is likely to be affected by such exposure, sought to erode confidence in Ukrainian sovereignty and military cohesion. These operations were also supported by various organized online influence campaigns. One of the very significant cases is the "LLC - Internet Research Case" which is one of the most obvious cases in which Kremlin benefited from troll farms operating in OSINT environment. In this case, the St. Petersburg-based LLC Internet Research, a company widely known for hiring paid personnel to operate fake social media personas across multiple languages and platforms. In 21 October 2014, job postings from this organization openly sought candidates with English proficiency and analytical skills to produce content aligned with designated political narratives. These operatives, sometimes numbering in the hundreds, were tasked not only with amplifying pro-Kremlin discourse, but also with discrediting the Ukrainian government, Western institutions, and opposition movements, both in domestic suchlike Runet and international media ecosystems (Jaitner and Mattson, 2015, pp. 43-44).

As seen, the various influence operations conducted by the RF—particularly through the Internet Research Agency (IRA) and its information-psychological interventions during the 2014 Crimea operation and afterwards—offer an empirical manifestation of OSINT's ontological transformation, as theorized in this study. First, the mass digitization of textual and visual materials enabled the Kremlin to access, manipulate, and disseminate narratives across open platforms, utilizing open-source visual content (e.g., border footage) to construct distorted humanitarian crises, thus illustrating how digitized visibility becomes an instrument of strategic storytelling.

Second, the rise of participatory media—exemplified by the IRA's exploitation of social platforms—facilitated the incorporation of politically charged narratives into trust-based digital ecosystems, where users themselves became agents of data circulation and amplification. Third, these campaigns operated within the logic of algorithmic curation, targeting niche communities and leveraging platform algorithms to amplify divisive content and suppress alternative discourses, thereby manipulating digital attention through controlled visibility. Lastly, the deployment of technologically scalable tools, such as sentiment analysis and psychographic targeting by paid operatives within troll farms (e.g., the LLC Internet Research case), reveals a shift in OSINT's function from passive information retrieval to predictive and persuasive engagement. Altogether, these cases validate the claim that OSINT—restructured by techno-political infrastructures—now operates as a generative force of influence, not merely a descriptive tool of understanding.

3.1.2. Russian Federation's Influence Focused OSINT Activities during the Occupation of Ukraine in 2022

Given the course after the RF invaded Ukraine in 2022 is evaluated, it is possible to observe similar patterns. In the aftermath of RF's invasion of Ukraine in 2022, the RF significantly expanded its use of social media as a tool of psychological operations. The structural transformation of OSINT into an influence agent through mass digitization is exemplified by RF's creation of over 100 Telegram channels in newly occupied Ukrainian regions during the early weeks of the 2022 invasion (Atlantic Council 2024, p. 3). These channels operated as surrogate local media outlets, broadcasting curated messages from pro-Russian actors and recycling digitized Kremlin narratives. Unlike traditional media warfare, these channels leveraged mass-digitized ideological content—repackaged Russian symbols, state media reports, and fabricated local news—to simulate informational sovereignty (Atlantic Council 2024, pp. 5-7). The OSINT apparatus here functioned not to observe or analyze, but to actively shape public consciousness in contested territories. By digitizing and projecting a virtual political order, OSINT became a tool of narrative occupation.

In September 2022 and May 2023, Russian Telegram milbloggers (military bloggers) such as Rybar, Dva Mayora, and Wargonzo published over 6,000 posts within days of Ukraine's Kharkiv counteroffensive and the Belgorod incursion. These channels provided real-time updates, battlefield maps, video footage, and emotional analysis, which were widely reposted across Telegram and picked up by Russian news outlets (Atlantic Council 2024, pp. 16–18). This reflects a fundamental shift in OSINT: information is no longer gathered by institutions from external sources—it is co-produced by citizen-actors or intelligence-actos embedded within the system. The milbloggers did not merely describe the war; they interpreted it, and stirred nationalist sentiment.

From 2021 to 2023, RIA Novosti's Telegram channel grew to nearly 30 billion annual views, SolovyovLive reached 20 billion, and Readovka achieved a 91-fold increase in engagement (Atlantic Council 2024, pp. 9-13). This surge occurred not because of traditional credibility, but due to strategic cross-posting and amplification by algorithmically entangled pro-Kremlin networks. These media accounts reposted and reshared one another's content systematically, creating a curated visibility loop that privileged pro-Russian narratives across Telegram. The channels also suppressed alternative interpretations by overwhelming users with volume and visibility which is a significant influence example by denying the popularization of alternative narratives. Here, OSINT operations leveraged platform architecture—ranking algorithms, virality patterns, and repost logic—not merely to inform, but to manipulate the information environment.

The structural transformation of OSINT through technological scalability which refers to the capacity of OSINT to use AI and automated tools to process vast data in real time, enabling predictive analysis and strategic influence at scale, was clearly demonstrated by the activities of Russian hacktivist communities on Telegram, which showed distinct surges in coordinated posting activity in advance of high-profile cyberattacks targeting Ukraine (Atlantic Council 2024, p. 26). These pre-attack spikes did not merely reflect activist enthusiasm or spontaneous mobilization; they were indicators of a technologically enhanced OSINT infrastructure operating as an anticipatory instrument of psychological influence. These Telegram channels leveraged platform-level affordances and computational capabilities—such as automated post scheduling, sentiment-saturated language, visual meme generation, and rapid cross-post amplification—allowing them to disseminate targeted disinformation at scale and in real time (Atlantic Council 2024, p. 26). Prior to cyber incidents, the channels repeatedly amplified emotionally provocative narratives (e.g., fabricated bioweapons labs in Ukraine or anti-Polish conspiracies), often accompanied by emotionally charged imagery and keywords optimized for virality (Atlantic Council 2024, p. 26). This case illustrates the core function of technological scalability: OSINT actors were able to process and deploy massive volumes of tailored content with minimal latency, targeting specific audiences with predictive intent. These campaigns were designed not only to prepare the narrative environment for subsequent cyberattacks, but also to manipulate public perception, disorient attribution efforts, and provoke mistrust toward enemy governments and institutions.

Given all these activities of RF, the post-2022 information landscape clearly demonstrates how all four structural factors—mass digitization, participatory media, algorithmic curation, and technological scalability—have converged to transform OSINT from a passive and supplementary intelligence collection discipline into an active instrument of influence. Rather than merely collecting from the relevant domain, OSINT now shapes both the domain and the information within: it constructs narrative legitimacy in conflict zones, fuels emotionally resonant discourse through participatory actors, manipulates visibility through algorithmic ecosystems, and anticipates adversarial behavior through scalable, AI-enhanced operations. In this techno-political paradigm, OSINT no longer reflects strategic realities—it contributes to their production, namely serving as a significant instrument for the influence function of intelligence.

CONCLUSION

As previously described, this study has premised that the nature of OSINT has undergone a fundamental ontological transformation in the techno-political era. Far from being a mere supplementary tool for collection phase the intelligence cycle, OSINT now operates as a strategic instrument of influence, since mass digitization, participatory media, algorithmic curation, and technological scalability transformed it to do so. Empirical evidence from the RF's OSINT-focused operations during the 2014 annexation of Crimea and the 2022 full-scale invasion of Ukraine reveals that OSINT is no longer confined to reflecting events or environments, or to provide the basis for efforts to understand. Instead, it actively constructs perception, amplifies selected narratives, and anticipates behavioral outcomes in contested information spaces, which basically constitutes the function of influence in intelligence theory. In this new paradigm, OSINT has evolved into a hybrid actor—simultaneously epistemic and performative—reshaping the very dynamics of intelligence and psychological operations in modern conflict theaters.

Consequently, the findings of this study compel a rethinking of intelligence theory and frameworks surrounding OSINT. The traditional division between intelligence collection and influence operations has been increasingly blurred, giving rise to a new operational logic in which open-source visibility is not only observed but engineered. As OSINT continues to integrate with AI-driven analytics and algorithmic dissemination, its capacity to shape cognitive environments will likely intensify. With its growing integration into AI-driven analytics and algorithmically governed dissemination mechanisms, OSINT now functions within a continuum where data acquisition and influence projection are no longer sequential but simultaneous. This convergence calls for a revised analytical framework that reflects the dual ontological status of OSINT as both an intelligence input and an operational output in contemporary intelligence architecture.

REFERENCES

Appel, E. J. (2011). *Internet searches for vetting, investigations, and open-source intelligence*. CRC Press.

Atlantic Council. (2024). *Russian Telegram in 2024: A growing ecosystem for propaganda and information operations*. Atlantic Council's Digital Forensic Research Lab.

Bail, C. A., Guay, B., Maloney, E., Combs, A., Hillygus, D. S., Merhout, F., Freelon, D., & Volfovsky, A. (2020). Assessing the Russian Internet Research Agency's impact on the political attitudes and behaviors of American Twitter users in late 2017. *Proceedings of the National Academy of Sciences of the United States of America*, *117*(1), 243–250. DOI: 10.1073/pnas.1906420116 PMID: 31767743

Baker, R. L. (2023). *Deep dive: Exploring the real-world value of open source intelligence*. Wiley.

Bean, H. (2011). *No more secrets: Open source information and the reshaping of U.S. intelligence*. Praeger Security International. DOI: 10.5040/9798400691799

Bielska, A., Stępień, M., Terefenko, M., & Węgrzyn, P. (2020). *Open source intelligence tools and resources handbook*. I-Intelligence.

Bordes Perez, A. (2024). What is really open source intelligence? A conceptual analysis of the different notions of OSINT. *Romanian Intelligence Studies Review*, *1*(31), 51–74.

Browne, T. O., Abedin, M., & Chowdhury, M. J. M. (2024). A systematic review on research utilising artificial intelligence for open source intelligence (OSINT) applications. *International Journal of Information Security*, *23*(4), 2911–2938. DOI: 10.1007/s10207-024-00868-2

Dale, D. S. (2023). *Open source intelligence for cybersecurity events via Twitter data* (Master's thesis, California State University, San Bernardino). ProQuest Dissertations Publishing.

Department of the Army. (2012). *Open-source intelligence (ATP 2-22.9)*. Headquarters, Department of the Army. https://irp.fas.org/doddir/army/atp2-22-9.pdf

Gill, P., & Phythian, M. (2018). *Intelligence in an insecure world* (3rd ed.). Polity Press.

Gioti, A. (2023). Advancements in open source intelligence techniques and the role of artificial intelligence in cyber threat intelligence (Master's thesis). University of the Aegean.

Hassan, N. A., & Hijazi, R. (2018). *Open source intelligence methods and tools: A practical guide to online intelligence*. Apress. DOI: 10.1007/978-1-4842-3213-2

Hobbs, C., Moran, M., & Salisbury, D. (Eds.). (2014). *Open source intelligence in the twenty-first century: New approaches and opportunities*. Palgrave Macmillan. DOI: 10.1057/9781137353320

Hoch, N. (2020). Russian Internet Research Agency disinformation activities on Tumblr: Identity, privacy, and ambivalence. *Media, War & Conflict, 13*(3), 309–326.

Hoffman, M. (2019). *Open source (OSINT) intelligence gathering and analysis (SANS SEC487 Coursebook)*. SANS Institute.

Holden-Rhodes, J. F. (1997). *Sharing the secrets: Open source intelligence and the war on drugs*. Praeger.

Huang, D. F. (2021). *Nowhere to hide: Open source intelligence gathering*. DFH Press.

Jaitner, M., & Mattsson, P. A. (2015). "Russian information warfare of 2014". In M. Maybaum, A.-M. Osula, and L. Lindström (Eds.), *7th International Conference on Cyber Conflict: Architectures in Cyberspace,* pp. 39–51. NATO CCD COE Publications.

Kent, S. (1949). *Strategic Intelligence for American World Policy*. Princeton University Press.

Lowenthal, M. M. (2008). *Intelligence: From secrets to policy* (4th ed.). CQ Press.

Markovets, O., Buchyn, M., Kovalchuk, A., & Basyuk, T. (2023). Russian information-psychological special operations in Ukraine and peculiarities of system design for their countermeasures. *Proceedings of the 2nd International Workshop on Social Communication and Information Activity in Digital Humanities (SCIA 2023)*, 3564, pp. 87–104.

NATO. (2002). NATO open source intelligence reader.

Palacín, V. (2021). *Practical threat intelligence and data-driven threat hunting: A hands-on guide to threat hunting with the ATT&CK™ framework and open source tools*. Packt Publishing.

Slater, A. P. (2023). Social media intelligence (SOCMINT) investigative framework as a human trafficking deterrent tool (Master's thesis). American Military University.

Steele, R. D. (2004). *Special Operations Forces Open Source Intelligence (OSINT) handbook*. OSS Inc.

TASS. (2014a). *Number of requests for asylum by Ukrainians doubles in Krasnodar region* [Число обращений граждан Украины в ФМС в Краснодарском крае увеличилось на 100%]. *TASS Russian News Agency*, 26 March. http://itar-tass.com/obschestvo/1075504

TASS. (2014b). *Ukrainians request temporary asylum in Novgorod* [Граждане Украины просят временное убежище в Новгородской области]. *TASS Russian News Agency*, 26 March. http://itar-tass.com/spb-news/1076617

TASS. (2014c). *FMS: Over 245k Ukrainians ask for asylum in Russia* [ФМС: за временным убежищем в РФ обратились более 245 тыс. граждан Украины]. *TASS Russian News Agency*, 4 December. http://itar-tass.com/obschestvo/1616949

Tayebi, M. A., Glässer, U., & Skillicorn, D. B. (Eds.). (2020). *Open source intelligence and cyber crime: Social media analytics*. Springer. U.S. Army. 2016. Open source intelligence (OSINT) Analyst Manual. DOI: 10.1007/978-3-030-41251-7

Warner, M. (2002). Wanted: A Definition of "Intelligence". *Studies in Intelligence*, *46*(3), 15–22.

Wiil, U. K. (Ed.). (2011). *Counterterrorism and open source intelligence*. Springer., DOI: 10.1007/978-3-7091-0388-3

Chapter 4
A New Era of Predictive Risk Management:
Building JA.I.Net Engine for Law Enforcement, Diplomacy, and Healthcare

Mihaela Meresi
https://orcid.org/0009-0005-4692-6911
Independent Researcher, Belgium

ABSTRACT

AI-driven predictive systems (e.g., COMPAS, PredPol) suffer from bias and rigidity due to reliance on static historical data, overlooking psychological and temporal human dynamics. This paper introduces JA.I.Net Engine, a hybrid framework integrating Jyotisha – an ancient science of time and behaviour - with AI to overcome these limitations. Jyotisha's cyclical models decode latent mental states and risk phases, while AI contributes computational precision. Together, they enable context-aware, bias-mitigated predictions for law enforcement, diplomacy and healthcare. We propose a Translational Systems Science approach that bridges Jyotisha's epistemologies with quantum and exascale computing. JA.I.Net achieves 12× efficiency in synthetic data generation (30 mins vs. 10 hours) and reduces memory use by 99%, validating the viability of culturally grounded AI. Its human-centric design addresses potential ethical gaps in predictive policing, offering a scalable template for harmonising ancient wisdom with emerging technologies to preempt harm, without perpetuating systemic inequities.

DOI: 10.4018/979-8-3373-7406-2.ch004

INTRODUCTION

In the digital age, predictive risk management systems have become central to law enforcement, cybersecurity and national security. Artificial intelligence (AI), big data analytics and machine learning have transformed methodologies by addressing vast datasets to uncover patterns and forecast events. Systems like PredPol and COMPAS exemplify these advancements, using historical data to identify crime hotspots and assess recidivism risks. Yet while these tools offer impressive computational power, their dependence on past trends and static data often limits their ability to capture the full complexity of human behaviour.

Critics have noted that many AI-based models operate as opaque "black boxes," frequently reinforcing systemic biases due to their reliance on historical datasets. For example, COMPAS has been widely criticised for disproportionately flagging Black defendants (Argwin et. al. 2016) as high-risk, while PredPol's deployment in the UK has raised concerns over racial discrimination (Sankin, Mattu, 2023). Similarly, Chicago's Strategic Subject List (SSL) designed to predict individuals at risk of involvement in violent incidents, has drawn criticism for perpetuating bias and lacking transparency (Tucek, 2015). Platforms such as HunchLab, which aggregate diverse data sources - from historical crime records to weather patterns and social media signals - aim to forecast criminal activity but still fall short in capturing the full spectrum of human motivations, intentions and behaviours (Ferguson, 2017, Richardson et.al. 2019). These limitations underscore the need for alternative frameworks that can measurably enhance predictive accuracy while addressing ethical concerns.

An unconventional yet promising approach emerges in Jyotisha, an ancient system of knowledge, recognised as "the sixth limb of Vedanga" - the auxiliary, practice-oriented disciplines that support the core theory of the Veda. Rooted in the study of time (Kāla) and human behaviour, Jyotisha offers insights that diverge significantly from linear, static data-dependent models. Rather than relying solely on empirical records, it emphasises the cyclical and rhythmic nature of time, presenting a structured framework for interpreting how natural energies - particularly the dynamics of time and space - correlate with both individual and collective behavioural patterns.

The integration of Jyotisha with modern AI creates a compelling and innovative synergy. While AI excels at processing and analysing massive volumes of quantitative data, it often overlooks the subtle psychological, emotional and temporal factors that shape human action. Jyotisha addresses this gap by offering a dynamic, time-sensitive perspective capable of identifying latent risk periods and psychological predispositions. In law enforcement, for example, aligning Jyotisha insights with predictive policing models could enable agencies to recognise periods when individuals or communities are most vulnerable to behavioural shifts. In international diplomacy, the application of Jyotisha may enhance negotiations and conflict resolution by pinpointing optimal times for diplomatic engagement. Similarly, in healthcare, this hybrid approach could forecast periods of heightened vulnerability, allowing for proactive interventions that are more precisely tailored to individual psychological needs.

Despite scepticism within some modern scientific circles, the strength of Jyotisha lies in its complementary nature. It enriches AI-driven models by adding a cyclical, psychologically informed dimension to risk assessment. This integration bridges the gap between computational precision and the complexities of human behaviour, fostering more ethical, inclusive and context-aware pattern recognition and decision-making processes. Combining AI's data-driven power with Jyotisha's time-centered insights offers a transformative paradigm for predictive risk management. Decision-makers in law enforcement, diplomacy, healthcare and beyond can develop strategies that are not only more accurate but also more attuned to the intricate realities of human existence.

This author does not limit scientific analysis of criminal behaviour to those individuals merely "in conflict with the law" (Bonta and Andrews, 2023). Instead, she advances a broader, clinically grounded understanding of crime as a manifestation of distinct psychological states that lead - whether intentionally or unintentionally - to the infliction of pain, loss, or destruction upon others or oneself, with or without an awareness of potential reward. Criminal conduct, from this perspective, is understood as a clinically manageable destructive behavioural expression of an underlying imbalance: a deviation from human health, both individual and collective.

A critical reassessment of contemporary legal systems reveals their frequent misalignment with principles of human dignity and collective evolution. Despite nominal progress, many jurisdictions perpetuate harm through the codification of exploitative practices - including but not limited to institutionalised prostitution, coercive marital norms – including against children - and the commodification of human biological material. Such legal frameworks often exacerbate systemic inequities, as evidenced by the persistent global prevalence of extreme poverty (World Bank, 2022), modern slavery (ILO, 2022) and socially sanctioned disenfranchisement. This reality necessitates moving beyond positivist legal definitions of crime - which often conflate legality with morality - toward a clinically and ecologically grounded paradigm. Inspired by holistic frameworks, behaviour might be assessed through dual lenses: psychosocial vitality and systemic health metrics, offering a more nuanced understanding of harm beyond statutory compliance.

The persistent challenge of bridging theoretical research and real-world problem-solving in complex sociotechnical systems finds compelling resolution in Rouse's (2011) Translational Systems Science (TSS) framework. This approach proves particularly salient for interdisciplinary work integrating Jyotisha's epistemological structures with computational criminology, as it accounts for emergent behaviours arising from dynamic interactions among human cognition, technological systems and environmental factors - phenomena irreducible to reductionist analysis. The TSS paradigm mirrors this study's navigation of "wicked problems" like urban crime prevention, where conventional disciplinary boundaries obstruct ethical, culturally-attuned solutions. By framing Jyotisha-AI integration as a bidirectional translational process, the research transcends mere technical application: the machine learning refines models while field-tested criminal pattern analysis informs algorithmic development.

The imperative to connect scholarly discovery with tangible societal impact finds compelling articulation in Woolf's (2008) seminal delineation of translational research. His conceptualisation of the "bench-to-bedside" continuum (originally developed in medical contexts but profoundly relevant to computational social science) underscores the critical gaps this research seeks to bridge between Jyotisha's theoretical constructs and applied tools in predictive criminology. The persistent "know-do gap" he identifies in traditional research paradigms mirrors the current disconnect between cultural knowledge systems like Jyotisha and contemporary crime prevention methodologies – a chasm this study deliberately confronts. By adopting Woolf's lens, the research gains conceptual scaffolding to navigate the complex pathway from algorithmic discoveries in individualised analysis to their ethical deployment in public safety interventions, while maintaining scientific rigor throughout the translation process. His emphasis on measuring real-world impact rather than mere theoretical novelty aligns precisely with this project's commitment to developing culturally-informed predictive models that ultimately reduce violent crime incidence through early, non-stigmatising interventions.

In the clinical and integrative context, criminal psychology is best understood as the study of true deviance from health - not merely as social nonconformity, but as a pathological condition. It concerns behaviours and mental states that culminate in the degradation or destruction of life, whether directed outward or inward. This perspective acknowledges varying degrees of gravity, both in the nature of the behaviour and in its consequences. Ethical considerations in analysing and addressing such pathologies must transcend cultural relativism. They must serve the fundamental imperatives of humanity: self-preservation, species evolution and the sustained promotion of human well-being. These priorities must guide ethical frameworks governing interventions and treatments. The welfare and evolution of humankind, in harmonious alignment with verifiable natural laws, must remain the central objective -unbounded by the limitations of cultural or historical specifics. Prevailing legal definitions of criminal behaviour are, in this respect, profoundly inadequate. They offer neither reliable diagnostic tools nor effective guidance for therapeutic intervention. At best, they reflect society's contemporary perception of deviant behaviour and prescribe punitive responses rooted in retribution rather than rehabilitation. Incarceration, isolation and capital punishment persist as blunt instruments of control, more focused on the spectacle of punishment than on addressing the underlying disharmony afflicting the individual and the collective.

Moral definitions of criminal behaviour fare no better when they remain confined within the normative structures of specific societies or religious traditions. Behaviour considered immoral and illegal in one cultural context may be both legally and morally endorsed in another. For example, the legal concept of the "age of consent" varies widely across cultures, reflecting divergent legal and moral standards concerning children, often without explicit consideration for long-term health and well-being. Practices such as forced child marriage, condemned in many societies as a violation of human rights, remain religiously and culturally approved norms in others. Similarly, prostitution -recognised as a legal profession in some Western European countries - remains punishable by imprisonment or even death in other parts of the world. These stark variations underscore the limitations of moral frameworks that are tethered to local customs, temporal values and the parochial ethics of nation-states or religious institutions.

Social definitions of crime acquire added complexity where customary norms persist beneath modern legal frameworks. Across Europe, ancient social codes covertly govern behaviour, frequently contradicting contemporary statutes and religious edicts. This dissonance manifests in enduring racial and religious discrimination, domestic violence against vulnerable groups, child marriage practices, and even tacitly sanctioned human trafficking—where local authorities often facilitate prostitution and slavery despite legal prohibitions. Such contradictions reveal the tenacity of informal power structures that subvert progressive legal reforms. These parallel legal systems - state-sanctioned and customary, overt and covert -generate profound systemic instability. The resulting collectivisation of criminality accelerates societal degradation, manifesting through economic collapse, environmental devastation, entrenched poverty and escalating factional violence. As these conditions intensify, they erode the state's foundational legitimacy, ultimately nullifying any consensus on objective legal authority. This juridical vacuum fosters a self-perpetuating cycle where lawlessness begets institutional failure and institutional failure normalises pervasive criminality.

While legal, moral and social definitions each offer insights into the phenomena of crime, they remain ultimately constrained by their respective psychologies and historical contexts. Only the clinical definition - one that rigorously investigates the causality of behaviour beyond ideological or cultural distortion - has the potential to illuminate the true nature of criminality. A clinically grounded approach, informed by demonstrable science, is the only viable path forward in understanding, diagnosing, predicting and ultimately treating and preventing criminal behaviour. It is within such a framework that the hopes articulated by Dr. James Bonta and Dr. D.A. Andrews may be realised: "If PCC (Psychology of Criminal Conduct) has something of value to offer, it should be able to assist in predicting who will and will not commit crimes in the future and suggest deliberate interventions that will reduce future crime." (Bonta, J., Andrews, D. A. 2023).

Nevertheless, the classical definitions of criminal behaviour articulated by authors such as Mannheim (1965) - multi-factorial causation, Ullmann & Krasner (1976) - learning theory, or Jessor & Jessor (1977) - problem behaviour theory, while valuable in theory, have proven elusive in practice, difficult to apply and ultimately insufficient as frameworks for addressing the root causes of criminal conduct. The state of global society in 2025 - marked by systemic corruption, criminality, war, disease, hunger, exploitation and extreme poverty - offers undeniable evidence of their shortcomings. A fundamental oversight persists at the core of these classical theories: the failure to account for the deeper, often hidden, causes of criminal and highly destructive human behaviour.

The broad classification of crime as "antisocial behaviour" is inadequate. From a clinical perspective, criminal behaviour frequently includes self-directed harm and internalised pathology that may not manifest as overtly antisocial or anti-legal conduct. The scope of clinical victimology demonstrates that the harm experienced by victims is not always reflected in public acts of antisocial behaviour. Consider the example of an army officer who is celebrated in public but secretly abuses his family. Such individuals may never face legal consequences, as their victims are too fearful to come forward. They may not violate the moral codes of their professional and religious milieu, where such abuse may be normalised as part of private life. Yet clinically, the pattern of spousal rape and child abuse through domestic psychological terror constitutes a severe and measurable pathology, with extensive consequences for the perpetrators, victims and societies at large.

The discrepancy amongst legal framework, public perception and clinical reality underscores a critical flaw in understanding of criminal behaviour. Many classical criminologists, predominantly men working within narrow cultural paradigms, formulated definitions that reflect their own societal blind spots. In doing so, they omitted significant dimensions of criminality whether knowingly or unconsciously. The challenge today is not merely to critique these limitations but to move beyond them, toward solid, scientifically valid frameworks that integrate comprehensive, predictive knowledge systems with modern technology.

This chapter proposes a radical rethinking of criminal psychology and risk assessment through the integration of Jyotisha—the ancient Vedic science of light, time, and causality—with contemporary and emerging AI and quantum-based technologies. Far from being obscure or unscientific, Jyotisha presents a comprehensive model of human behaviour grounded in observable and verifiable natural patterns, including psycho-physiological and psycho-functional architectures. Its predictive precision, when combined with the advanced data-processing capacities of machine learning algorithms, opens a new frontier in risk assessment, predictive intervention, and the proactive prevention of large-scale threats such as terrorism, the destruction of critical infrastructure, or mass violence. Within this context, the future of criminal psychology may lie in an integrated, human-centric model—one that transcends disciplinary silos and embraces both ancient wisdom and cutting-edge technology in the service of human survival, evolution, and societal well-being.

THE LIMITATIONS OF MODERN PREDICTIVE MODELS

Predictive risk management models powered by AI have increasingly been adopted in law enforcement, promising to revolutionise crime prevention. However, the operational realities of predictive policing, as meticulously documented by Perry et al. (2013), highlight ongoing challenges, including algorithmic bias and community distrust, particularly evident in their case studies from Los Angeles and Santa Cruz. Perry et al.'s findings (e.g., that even highly accurate forecasts become ineffective when officers do not trust or understand them) take on renewed significance in the context of this work. Here, the cultural specifics that might raise concerns among positivist criminologists could, conversely, serve as an advantage in communities where Western crime models are perceived as alien or even oppressive. Nonetheless, their cautionary notes about "over-reliance on pattern detection without human oversight" remain deeply relevant. They underscore the importance of ensuring that Stage 2 pattern-matching algorithms in this model are equipped with safeguards to prevent self-fulfilling prophecies, just as Perry et al. recommend for conventional systems. Moreover, their observation that predictive tools alter police workflows implies that Jyotisha-informed models would require specialised training to prevent misapplication. This challenge is compounded by the need to translate Jyotisha's symbolic and cyclical correlations into actionable police strategies without resorting to cultural reductionism.

This tension between innovation and implementation mirrors Perry et al.'s core paradox: predictive policing's greatest strength - its ability to uncover hidden patterns - becomes its greatest liability when institutions misinterpret probabilistic outputs as deterministic certainties. This research faces that paradox doubly, requiring not only the translation of statistical risk scores into operational protocols but also the intercultural mediation of Jyotisha's symbolic logic into evidentiary and mathematical standards acceptable within legal frameworks. Perry's recommendation to "embed social scientists in police units" to mitigate algorithmic misuse suggests an even more critical role for Jyotisha scholars in this model, not merely as data contributors, but as co-interpreters of AI-generated patterns. In this light, the combinatorial complexity of the 53.7 million synthetic charts (the Stage 1 data set) may function not as a technical burden but as a protective feature: by producing probabilities too nuanced for reductive enforcement responses, the system may inherently resist the kind of oversimplification that Perry et al. caution against in mainstream predictive policing..

Chainey and Ratcliffe's (2013) foundational work on crime mapping acquires new interpretive layers when viewed through Jyotisha's lens. Where traditional GIS crime analysis relies on physical terrain features and urban infrastructure (their "risk terrain modelling"), this research introduces a parallel topography: the 53.7 million potential Graha-Bhava configurations effectively create a cosmographic crime atlas, where additional alignments correlate with spatio-temporal crime patterns in ways conventional geography cannot capture. This synthesis addresses a core limitation Chainey and Ratcliffe identify in standard crime mapping - their inability to account for temporally dynamic risk factors. Their emphasis on "environmental backcloths" for criminal behaviour finds an unexpected counterpart in JA.I.Net model's capacity to treat personal charts as personalised risk landscapes, potentially revealing how individuals interact with physical spaces differently, based on natural psycho-pre-dispositions. However, their caution against "cartographic determinism" remains relevant: AI-derived Jyotisha crime patterns must undergo the same rigorous ground-truthing applied in conventional hotspot analyses, ensuring that mathematical correlations do not override the socio-economic realities and contextual human factors of policing. Chainey and Ratcliffe's documented challenges with "crime displacement" in spatially targeted policing (where intervention in one hot spot merely shifts activity elsewhere) could be mitigated by JA.I.Net model's ability to identify individual-specific risk geographies independent of physical locations. A perpetrator with strong G1,4,8 influences in B8, for instance, will exhibit specific mobility patterns that defy conventional terrain analysis. The integration of Jyotisha-derived predictions with standard GIS tools would create what might be termed "K-Risk terrain modelling" - where police patrol routes account for both the JA.I.Net profiles of high-risk individuals and the physical spaces where their patterns suggest heightened vulnerability to criminal behaviour. Such synthesis would operationalise Chainey and Ratcliffe's unrealised vision of spatio-temporal crime mapping, while demanding new protocols to prevent personal data from being misread as geographic fatalism.

The paradigm-shifting work of Bowers, Johnson, and Pease (2004) on prospective hot-spotting - which reoriented crime mapping from reactive analysis to predictive modelling - finds an unexpected but theoretically fertile counterpart in Jyotisha-based approach. Their demonstration that crime clusters exhibit near-repeat patterns (where incidents spatially and temporally "echo" initial events) inadvertently highlights the limitations of purely environmental criminology: by focusing exclusively on physical geography, such models neglect the personal risk geographies that Jyotisha's 53.7 million configurations might reveal. Where their pioneering algorithm identifies "what places are vulnerable" based on past offenses, JA.I.Net framework asks a more radical question: "which individuals are predisposed to make any (given) place vulnerable?" This complementarity becomes especially important when considering their finding that 50% of repeat victimisations occur within 1 month of initial incidents: such temporal regularity aligns strikingly with Jyotisha's emphasis on time calculation (Panchanga, Calendars, Muhurta) and identification of specific triggers for behavioural shifts. Yet the caution against over-reliance on mechanistic predictions remains essential: any model's risk factors would require the human-mediated interpretation, ensuring that mathematical probabilities don't degenerate into deterministic stigmatisation. This synthesis suggests a hybrid policing framework where environmental hot-spotting and biographical risk profiling (JA.I.Net contribution) interact dynamically. Bowers et al.'s finding that "risk diffuses spatially but decays temporally" can be enhanced through JA.I.Net's dynamic chart analysis. Unlike static criminal records, Jyotisha charts function as evolving personal risk matrices, identifying individuals whose natural configurations may prolong risk timelines, revealing chronic predispositions invisible to environmental models alone. Their successful field trials in Merseyside, where prospective mapping reduced burglaries by 33%, imply that integrating Jyotisha-derived alerts could further enhance prevention efficacy.

Tools such as COMPAS and PredPol exemplify certain advancements in predictive politicking by using historical data to identify crime hotspots, forecast criminal activity and assess recidivism risks. These systems offer enhanced data-driven decision-making, yet their heavy reliance on historical trends introduces significant limitations that undermine their overall effectiveness and ethical deployment. One major drawback of these AI-driven models is the inherent algorithmic bias stemming from their dependence on historical datasets. In regions with a legacy of over-policing marginalised communities, such models tend to perpetuate existing disparities. For instance, PredPol has been observed to systematically concentrate police presence in low-income, predominantly Black and Hispanic neighbourhoods, thereby reinforcing cycles of surveillance and criminalisation. Similarly, COMPAS has been criticised for overestimating recidivism risk among Black defendants while underestimating it for White defendants, raising profound concerns about racial discrimination. These biases are compounded by the opaque nature of many AI models, which operate as "black boxes" with little transparency regarding their decision-making processes. In October 2023, The Markup published an analysis revealing that predictive policing algorithms used by certain law enforcement agencies, such as Geolitica's software (formerly known as PredPol), demonstrated alarmingly low accuracy rates. An examination of 23.631 predictions generated between February and December 2018 for the Plainfield Police Department in New Jersey indicated that fewer than 100 predictions accurately aligned with reported crimes, resulting in a success rate of less than 1%. This startling statistic highlights not only the technological limitations of these systems but also their failure to adapt to the dynamic and multifaceted nature of human behaviour.

AI models in predictive risk management struggle with a fundamental lack of psychological insight. Human behaviour is shaped by a complex interplay of emotions, motivations, elements of imagination, intentions and environmental influences, factors that quantitative analysis alone cannot fully capture. AI systems excel at identifying statistical patterns within large datasets, yet they are often unable to account for qualitative dimensions such as personal transformations or rehabilitation potential throughout shifting psychological states. Consequently, individuals may be flagged as high-risk based solely on prior offenses or demographic factors, while critical variables are overlooked. A similar challenge exists in the realm of diplomacy, where AI models rely on historical political data, economic indicators and geopolitical trends to forecast international stability. These models frequently fail to account for sudden shifts in public sentiment, cultural transformations or unique leadership qualities that can dramatically alter political landscapes. As a result, AI predictions were often inaccurate in forecasting major geopolitical upheavals, calling into question their reliability in high-stakes diplomatic scenarios.

Machine learning algorithms, by design, extrapolate future events based on correlations identified in past data. However, human behaviour and political environments are fluid, and unprecedented events can rapidly render historical trends obsolete. The COVID-19 pandemic, for example, dramatically disrupted established patterns in crime, governance and diplomacy, exposing the vulnerabilities of AI models that were unprepared for such deviations. These shortcomings suggest that while AI-driven predictive models provide valuable quantitative insights, they are ill-equipped to capture the full complexity of human behaviour and societal change. To overcome these limitations, we can integrate alternative knowledge systems that offer deeper insights into behavioural patterns, psychological dynamics and time-based influences.

HISTORICAL FRAMEWORK FOR PREDICTIVE ANALYSIS

Ancient texts such as the Surya Siddhanta reveal sophisticated understandings of astronomy and mathematics that have influenced the intellectual traditions of Islamic, Hindu, Hellenistic and European cultures. The legacy of Vedic mathematics - including concepts like zero, decimal notation, and infinite series - has profoundly shaped modern computational and algorithmic thought. This cross-cultural synthesis demonstrates that Jyotisha is not an isolated relic of antiquity but an integral part of a broader intellectual tradition that continues to inform contemporary approaches to prediction, decision-making and risk management.

Despite the advances in AI and machine learning for forecasting human behaviour and anticipating risks, predictive tools remain limited by their reliance on static data. This dependence often reinforces existing biases and fails to capture the full complexity of human nature, emotion, intention and socio-cultural dynamics. As a result, debates on fairness, justice and ethical responsibility have intensified, especially when these models are applied to high-stakes areas like criminal justice, mental health or international relations. There is a pressing need for alternative frameworks that complement and enrich data-driven approaches, offering a deeper understanding of human behaviour. One promising alternative is Jyotisha, a core component of the Vedic tradition that transcends simple prognostication. It is a sophisticated synthesis of behavioural science, psychology and advanced studies of time. Rather than reducing human experience to deterministic predictions, Jyotisha offers a nuanced framework for understanding the cyclical nature of life and the interconnectedness of individual actions and environment. Central to this approach is the belief that the microcosm of personal existence mirrors the macrocosm, allowing practitioners to chart an individual's unique journey through time by identifying latent strengths and vulnerabilities.

Historically, Jyotisha has occupied a prominent position among the six Vedangas – auxiliary, practical disciplines that underpin the study of the Vedas, the ancient sacred texts of Vedic civilisation. Its practice, which dates back thousands of years to the Vedic period (circa 15.000 – 3.500 BCE), has evolved far beyond the Sanskrit translation of "the science of light." Jyotisha is fundamentally engaged with understanding the dynamic interplay amongst natural energies in specific spaces perimeters of life, in space and time (Yugas, Dashas, Antar-Dashas). Moreover, it seeks to elucidate how these factors influence both human behaviour and terrestrial events, revealing the underlying forces that govern existence by mapping the complex interrelations among space-environmental, temporal and behavioural variables.

Jyotisha has three major branches: (1) Samhita – the science of natural phenomena causing a wide, collective impact: weather, earthquakes, political affairs etc; (2) Ganita – the astronomical and mathematical foundation of Jyotisha dealing with calculations, time keeping, calendar systems, Panchanga etc. - key texts include the Bija Ganita, Surya Siddhanta, Lilavati, Aryabhatiya etc.) and (3) Hora - predictive branch of Jyotisha dealing with what we call, today, foresight or risk assessment - Brihat Parashara Hora Shastra, Brihat Jataka, Phaladipika, Saravali etc.).

Samhita sub-division often overlaps with Nimitta Shastra (omenology) and Muhurta (electional calculations based on Panchanga, for timing events/ planning). It sometimes overlaps with fields like Ayurveda, which also originates from the Atharva Veda, though the medical texts themselves (e.g., Sushruta Samhita, Charaka Samhita) are not part of Jyotisha proper. Bhrigu Samhita is an outstanding exception, dealing with the entirety of human collective. Legend has it that Sage Bhrigu, through divine vision (divya drishti) and deep meditation, compiled charts and predictions for millions of individuals, categorised by pattern positions. Some scholars say that these charts were written on palm leaves, and only specific individuals were meant to access them in each age/era/yuga. Hypothetically, to reconstruct Bhrigu Samhita, with the technological capabilities of our era, it would mean to quantify/ translate in our current, scientific understanding, the full spectrum of human patterns, for the entire species of our planet.

A detailed examination of Jyotisha's core components further clarifies its approach. The concept of psychological archetypes – patterns - is central to the system. The influence of each Graha is determined by its specific position within an individual's interactions with other space- time indicators. The notion of "Bhava" delineates the various space-time perimeters or domains of human existence, encompassing a wide spectrum of quantifiable elements, from the physical body and family dynamics to broader societal engagements and career trajectories, thereby offering a mapped trajectory of life's journey and highlighting potential strengths and challenges across different stages of development.

Integral to the Jyotisha framework is its sophisticated understanding of time, clearly manifested in the concept of Dasha s, which delineate distinct periods marked by specific influences. Such temporal segmentation not only provides a predictive mechanism for events but also captures the psychological and emotional undercurrents that accompany these transitions. The concept of Gochara - representing the real-time movement of the Grahas as they interact with the fixed positions of an individual - signals shifts in psychological states and guides individuals through critical junctures. Panchanga furnishes a detailed framework for discerning inherent qualities of temporal sections, thereby aligning actions with planning. In doing so, it highlights the broader applicability of Jyotisha beyond individual prognostication, extending its relevance to collective decision-making processes.

The potential integration of Jyotisha into modern risk management frameworks is particularly compelling. In the realm of law enforcement, the psychological insights derived from Jyotisha, such as the identification of individual predispositions and behavioural cycles, could serve to complement and refine the statistical predictions generated by AI systems, thereby mitigating the risk of algorithmic bias. Similarly, in international diplomacy, where the interplay of cultural, emotional and psychological factors exerts a decisive influence, the cyclical insights provided by Jyotisha can inform strategies that are both nuanced and contextually sensitive. This synthesis of ancient wisdom with modern technology thus opens a promising avenue toward risk management strategies that are as ethically sound as they are analytically robust. A thorough understanding of Jyotisha and its modern applications necessitates an exploration of its historical underpinnings and the expansive intellectual traditions from which it emerged. Vedic knowledge represents a corpus of wisdom once embedded in a much broader, interconnected intellectual tradition that spanned multiple ancient civilisations. While India ultimately became the primary repository for the Vedic corpus, substantial evidence suggests that its foundational principles including cosmology, mathematics, linguistics and metaphysics were integral to a shared global heritage. This is particularly evident in the astronomical and mathematical traditions documented in Vedic texts. For instance, the precision of Vedic timekeeping, as illustrated in works such as the Surya Siddhanta, reflects an advanced understanding of temporal cycles, eclipses and the precessional motion of the Earth. These insights not only parallel but also complement the calendrical systems developed by Mesopotamian, Egyptian, and Mesoamerican civilisations, underscoring a collective pursuit of astronomical accuracy that transcended cultural boundaries.

The false dichotomy between indigenous and scientific knowledge systems – a divide that has long constrained interdisciplinary innovation – finds its definitive critique in Agrawal's (1995) seminal work. His deconstruction of the epistemic boundaries separating "traditional" and "modern" knowledge resonates profoundly with this study's integration of Jyotisha's astrological frameworks with computational criminology. Where others might see irreconcilable differences between ancient Jyotisha and contemporary predictive algorithms, Agrawal's lens reveals a fertile middle ground: this methodology neither reduces Jyotisha to mere folkloric curiosity nor imposes scientific reductivism on its holistic logic. Instead, the research exemplifies a vision of "hybrid knowledge spaces" – where the systematic observation embedded in Jyotisha's 53.7 million possible charts meets the pattern-recognition capacities of machine learning on equal epistemic footing. This approach deliberately circumvents what Agrawal identifies as the "extractive" model of indigenous knowledge appropriation, instead fostering a bidirectional exchange where computational methods validate Jyotisha's predictive claims while the system's cultural integrity informs ethical AI deployment. The resulting synthesis embodies the commonly known opinion that all knowledge systems operate through rules of evidence and verification, whether those rules manifest through natural elements or statistical significance thresholds. This epistemological parity fundamentally reshapes how predictive tools might be received by both law enforcement and source communities. Where traditional criminology often imposes external analytical frameworks, Agrawal's paradigm supports the idea that Jyotisha-derived models could achieve greater stakeholder trust through their embedded cultural logic – particularly when identifying at-risk youth. The 53.7 million charts' combinatorial complexity, far from being a computational hurdle, becomes an asset when framed as a parallel to modern "big data" approaches. Such alignment of knowledge systems may prove essential when transitioning from pattern detection (Stage 1) to intervention design (Stage 2), as it provides shared conceptual scaffolding for policymakers accustomed to quantitative analytics and communities protective of traditional wisdom.

The refinement of mathematical thought within Vedic texts reveal a high degree of sophistication in areas such as trigonometry and spherical calculations, suggesting that the mathematical principles they enshrine may have been developed through intercultural exchange. Moreover, the analytical structure of Sanskrit, as systematised in Panini's Ashtadhyayi, stands as one of the earliest formal grammatical systems. Its rigorous approach to language bears a remarkable resemblance to later developments including modern field of computational linguistics. The historical interactions among Persia, India and Greece, especially during the Achaemenid and Hellenistic periods, lend support to the notion that Vedic linguistic structures significantly influenced broader intellectual trajectories, beyond the Indian subcontinent. The work of Pingala in the 3rd century BCE, for instance, introduced binary number concepts within the context of Sanskrit prosody. Later mathematicians, including Aryabhata and Brahmagupta, developed iterative methods for computing trigonometric values and solving complex equations. Figures like Bhaskara II and Madhava of Sangamagrama further refined these approaches, devising algorithms that anticipated innovations in calculus and infinite series. This intellectual lineage - from the early insights of Vedic thought to the algorithmic frameworks of later cultures - demonstrates the lasting impact of ancient methodologies on modern scientific thought.

The mathematical innovations of Vedic scholars have had a lasting impact on global intellectual history, particularly through their subsequent integration into other scientific traditions. Foundational concepts such as zero, decimal notation and infinite series became mathematical frameworks of this world's cultures, such as the commonly referred "Arabic numerals" and computational techniques. The seminal contributions of scholars like Al-Khwarizmi, whose treatises on algebra and algorithms laid the groundwork for modern computational methods, are a testament to the enduring legacy of these ancient discoveries/ innovations. In this manner, the intellectual heritage of Vedic mathematics not only enriched its immediate cultural context but also played a pivotal role in shaping the evolution of global scientific thought.

The term "algebra" comes from Al-Khwarizmi's treatise Al-Jabr ( ) - transl. "completion" or "rejoining" - and subsequently the term "algorithm" emerged. His systematic methods for solving mathematical problems laid the groundwork for modern computational techniques. His pioneering work in algebra, which introduced step-by-step procedures for resolving equations, was profoundly influenced by earlier Vedic mathematical principles. Subsequent figures such as Al-Kindi and Ibn al-Haytham further refined these methods, applying structured, sequential approaches across fields as varied as cryptography, optics, and physics. This intellectual continuity illustrates how ancient Vedic algorithmic reasoning underpins many of the sophisticated computational methodologies that are integral to contemporary scientific inquiry.

Philosophically, Vedic thought is marked by a profound reverence for the cyclical nature of time, a perspective that resonates with diverse wisdom traditions worldwide. The Vedic model of cyclic time, which is central to Jyotisha, finds echoes in ancient Greek, Mayan and Daoist philosophies. The conception that human existence unfolds in repetitive cycles, marked by phases of growth, transformation and renewal, serves as a unifying theme that links disparate cultural narratives. Such philosophical commonalities underscore the view that the quest to understand the fundamental nature of existence is a shared human effort that transcends regional and temporal boundaries.

While significant intellectual losses occurred in regions such as Alexandria, Babylon and Egypt as a result of warfare, conquest or shifts in dominant cultural paradigms, relatively continuous scholarly traditions ensured the survival and transmission of its ancient wisdom. The enduring oral traditions, meticulous preservation of sacred texts and establishment of rigorous academic institutions all contributed to the resilience of Vedic thought. In this light, Vedic wisdom should be viewed not as an isolated cultural artefact but as a vital component of a broader global intellectual heritage, one that has evolved through centuries of intercultural dialogue and exchange. This historical continuum, which situates Jyotisha within the wider context of Vedic knowledge, provides a foundation for appreciating its modern relevance. By bridging the gap between ancient epistemologies and modern scientific inquiry, Jyotisha invites a re-evaluation of the assumptions underlying current predictive models, paving the way for methodologies that are more comprehensive and more attuned to the complex interplay of true factors that shape human experience. Such an integration is emblematic of a broader trend toward recognising that true predictive accuracy may only be achieved by synthesising and, most importantly, testing and validating diverse epistemological traditions.

During the Islamic Golden Age, between the 8th and 14th centuries, scholars such as Al-Kindi, Jabir ibn Hayyan, Muhammad ibn Musa al-Khwarizmi, Hunayn ibn Ishaq and others played pivotal roles in assimilating and advancing diverse intellectual legacies. Under the Abbasid Caliphate (circa 750–1258), a vigorous translation movement, centered in Baghdad's House of Wisdom (Bayt al-Hikma) sought to integrate knowledge from Persian, Sanskrit, Syriac, Greek, and other languages. Vedic texts on astronomy, medicine and philosophy were translated into Arabic, enriching the world's scholarly corpus with treatises on calendrical science, advanced mathematics, astronomical observations, and medical practices. This cross-cultural synthesis attests to the enduring legacy of ancient wisdom and its power to inform and transform successive intellectual traditions. During this period, the emergence of algorithmic thought established a direct lineage between ancient Vedic scholarship and later Islamic and European achievements.

Among the luminaries of the Islamic Golden Age was Mariam al-Ijliya, also known as al-Asturlabi, a pioneering scientist and skilled artisan renowned for her construction and refinement of sophisticated astronomical instruments known as astrolabes. Her achievements highlight the often underrepresented role of women in the scientific endeavours of the medieval Islamic world and underscore the collaborative and cumulative nature of humanity's pursuit of knowledge. Active during the 10th century in Aleppo, under the patronage of Sayf al-Dawla - renowned as the most prominent member of the Hamdanid dynasty and the founder of the Emirate of Aleppo - Mariam al-Ijliya contributed significantly to the advancement of astronomical instrumentation. She refined and constructed intricate devices that enabled precise calculations of time, celestial phenomena and geographic orientation, thereby facilitating both terrestrial navigation and astronomical observation. The precision engineering inherent in Mariam's astrolabes laid an essential foundation for the subsequent development of mechanical clocks, automata and calculating devices in both the Islamic world and medieval Europe. Her legacy directly informed the technological advancements that characterised the Age of Exploration, where instruments derived from the astrolabe played a critical role in enabling global maritime navigation. Astrolabes, as complex models of the celestial sphere, were multifaceted devices that served a wide range of functions. They enabled the measurement of time during day and night by calculating the positions of stars and planets and they facilitated the determination of latitude, thereby supporting navigation. Astrolabes were used in surveying and triangulation to measure heights and distances, contributing to the early practices of geodesy and cartography. They further assisted in predicting the future positions of celestial bodies, informing calendrical systems and other astrological calculations. The construction and use of astrolabes involved sophisticated mathematical principles, including spherical trigonometry and geometry - particularly the application of stereographic projection, a method by which the three-dimensional celestial sphere is mapped onto a two-dimensional plane. This mathematical technique remains foundational in modern cartography, astronomy and computer graphics. Moreover, the operation of an astrolabe required a series of procedural steps that reflect an early form of algorithmic thinking, wherein sequential calculations were employed to solve complex problems. Astrolabes may be viewed as analog precursors to modern computational devices, processing intricate astronomical data through mechanical manipulation. The mathematical and conceptual frameworks underlying these instruments not only exemplify the advanced state of medieval scientific knowledge but also prefigure algorithmic processes that would later inform the fields of computer science and automation.

The early Vedic tradition of observational astronomy highlights a sophisticated array of astronomical instruments rooted in Vedic cosmology. These instruments, both conceptual and monumental in scale, were designed for precise observation of celestial phenomena, serving as analog computers for timekeeping, calendrical regulation and event prediction. Among the most significant was the Samrat Yantra, known as the "supreme instrument" or "king of instruments" - a massive equinoctial sundial with triangular gnomon aligned with the Earth's axis - casting a shadow on carefully graduated quadrants. This allowed for the precise measurement of local time to within seconds and accurate readings of celestial bodies' declination, altitude and azimuth. Its function parallels the earlier Shanku Yantra (gnomon) used during the Vedic period, though in a more refined and grander form. Other important instruments include the Jaya Prakash Yantra, an architectural embodiment of celestial mapping systems found in texts like the Surya Siddhanta and Panchasiddhantika; the Rama Yantra, complementing the Jaya Prakash by facilitating similar measurements through large circular walls and pillars, evolving the principles of the Chakra and Dhanur Yantras into precise observational tools; the Narivalaya Yantra, crucial for Panchanga construction, providing accurate solar data for determining tithi (lunar day), nakshatra (stellar mansion/ constellation) and other temporal divisions; the Kapala Yantra, a bowl-shaped instrument for determining the Sun's altitude and time, essential for tracking diurnal motion and aligning ritual and calendrical events; and the Misra Yantra, a composite instrument that integrates multiple celestial functions, blending Vedic principles with later Islamic and Hellenistic influences, marking the pinnacle of Indian astronomical instrumentation.

The question of whether science can truly be multicultural, posed provocatively by Sandra Harding (1998), finds a compelling test case in this research's fusion of Jyotisha's frameworks with computational criminology. Harding's critique of Western science's presumed universality underscores the radical potential of this methodology: rather than treating Jyotisha as a static "traditional" system to be validated (or dismissed) by dominant empirical paradigms, this approach enacts what Harding terms "strong objectivity"- centering marginalised knowledge systems as coequal foundations for scientific inquiry. Her analysis of how Eurocentric biases distort even well-intentioned research resonates deeply with this project's ethical safeguards, particularly in ensuring that predictive algorithms derived from Jyotisha avoid reproducing the racialised profiling endemic to conventional criminological models. By treating Jyotisha's 53.7 million combinatorial possibilities not as anthropological curiosities but as a legitimate alternative rationality for pattern recognition, this vision is treating science as a tool for human emancipation rather than domination. Such epistemological reorientation carries profound implications for stakeholder engagement. Harding's view on "situated knowledges" suggests that the credibility of JA.I.Net – type predictions may depend less on statistical metrics alone than on their interpretive fidelity to Jyotisha's native ontological and highly ethical commitments - a consideration critical when presenting findings to communities protective of ethics – through various religions or deontology. The 53.7 million charts, in this light, become more than a dataset; they represent an epistemic negotiation between computational scalability and cultural authenticity. Traditional practitioners must see machine learning not as a colonial imposition but as an amplificatory tool for their own knowledge system.

The integration of Jyotisha with contemporary risk management paradigms thus emerges both as a novel interdisciplinary endeavour and as a natural extension of a long-standing tradition of inquiry that has continually sought to reconcile empirical observation with metaphysical insight. By bridging the deep, cyclical insights of ancient Vedic wisdom with the data-centric precision of modern AI, it becomes possible to formulate predictive models that more accurately reflect the intricate tapestry of human existence. In practical terms, incorporating Jyotisha into predictive risk management could enable law enforcement agencies to anticipate shifts in criminal behaviour by considering nuanced psychological predispositions and cyclical life patterns. Likewise, in international diplomacy, the cyclical insights derived from Jyotisha could inform the timing of negotiations and policy decisions by supplementing quantitative analyses with an understanding of the underlying dynamics.

Challenges of contemporary predictive risk management are not solely technological but also epistemological. Current AI models are constrained by their inability to capture the dynamic, evolving nature of human behaviour, a quality that ancient systems like Jyotisha have long sought to address. By adopting an integrative approach that draws on both ancient wisdom and modern scientific inquiry, it is possible to construct predictive frameworks that are robust, adaptable, and capable of navigating the complexities of an interconnected world.

The study of Jyotisha and its integration with modern predictive models invites a re-evaluation of how knowledge is conceptualised, preserved and transmitted across cultures and epochs. Far from being a relic of a bygone era, Jyotisha represents a rich, multidimensional scientific system that offers enduring insights into the nature of time, behaviour and human experience. Its resources show its capacity to inform contemporary debates on risk, ethics and governance. Such a synthesis of historical wisdom and contemporary capabilities offers a promising avenue for addressing the multifaceted challenges of our era, paving the way for ethical, effective and context-aware decision-making in law enforcement, healthcare, governance and diplomacy. The dialogue between ancient Jyotisha and modern AI-driven methodologies reveals a profound opportunity to reimagine the foundations of predictive risk management. This integrated perspective not only enriches our conceptualisation of risk but also challenges us to reframe the relationship between technology and humanity in ways that are both healing and ethically sound.

THE AI-JYOTISHA HYBRID MODEL (JA.I.NET): TRANSLATIONAL DATA SCIENCE AND A NEW APPROACH TO RISK ASSESSMENT

The contemporary landscape of risk assessment is undergoing a profound transformation as recent models, predominantly anchored in AI and machine learning, struggle to encapsulate the multifaceted nature of human behaviour. In fields as varied as law enforcement, international diplomacy and healthcare, predictive systems that rely exclusively on historical datasets are deficient in addressing the subtleties of psychological and cultural dynamics. These limitations are most evident in scenarios where human decision-making, shaped by deeply personal and context-specific factors, cannot be fully apprehended by algorithms that prioritise quantifiable trends over qualitative nuances. In light of these challenges, the integration of the ancient Vedic system of Jyotisha with modern AI presents a compelling alternative. This synthesis of traditional wisdom and contemporary technology promises not only to overcome the inherent biases of data-dependent models but also to enhance risk assessment frameworks by incorporating temporal, emotional, intentional and cognitive dimensions.

Foundational Vedic archetypes from such as Kaal Purush (KP), which posits a universal anatomical and behavioural template, and the Manus, who establish primordial ethical and social orders, represent enduring psycho-structural blueprints. The KP standard model not only maps physiological and anatomical features across the twelve Bhavas (life domains), but also reflects psychological tendencies, cognitive proclivities and potential behavioural trajectories. Each Bhava corresponds to a sector of experience, encoding both anatomical correlates and psychosocial functionalities.

Incorporating this human-model architecture into machine learning environments offers an opportunity to recover and operationalise previously inaccessible insights about human nature. By correlating structured behavioural data with Jyotisha-based templates, researchers in criminology, psychiatry and broader fields of psychopathology can refine their ability to identify destructive causalities, optimise prevention strategies and enhance rehabilitation and reintegration protocols.

The first machine-based implementation of this paradigm (JA.I.Net1) will be built on a foundational 53M Dataset (Mereşi, 2025, p.24), representing all valid permutations of 9 distinct elements (Grahas, G1–G9) distributed across 12 unique life domains (Bhavas, B1–B12). This model adheres to the following Jyotisha-informed structural rules: each Bhava can contain multiple Grahas; G8 must be positioned in direct opposition to G9 and never within the same Bhava - resulting in only 6 valid pairs: (B1, B7), (B2, B8), (B3, B9), (B4, B10), (B5, B11), and (B6, B12); G4 must remain proximal to G1, either within the same Bhava or in an adjacent one, producing 36 valid placements for G4, given 12 possibilities for G1; all nine Grahas must be used exactly once; some Bhavas may remain empty. The total number of valid configurations, then, is calculated as: 6 (G8+G9) × 36 (G1+G4) × 12^5 (remaining permutations) = 6 × 36 × 248. 832 = 53.747.712.

The computational challenges inherent in generating 53.7 million synthetic charts under constrained combinatorial conditions reveal a striking dichotomy between brute-force and optimised algorithmic approaches. A naïve implementation in Python, blindly evaluating every possible permutation while ignoring inherent mathematical symmetries and parallel processing capabilities, languishes for approximately ten hours while using over 100 GB of memory. Through systematic optimisation, this computational process can be further improved, to later serve scalability and non-dependence on historical data: by exploiting the inherent rotational symmetry of the Bhava cycle and enforcing mirror symmetry constraints on Graha positions, the problem space collapses from 53.7 million permutations to 4.47 million base cases. When this mathematical insight combines with parallel processing across eight CPU cores, the transformation proves remarkable - computation time plummets to just thirty minutes while memory requirements shrink below 1 GB. This twelve-fold performance improvement demonstrates how algorithmic elegance can overcome raw computational demands, enabling large-scale cultural pattern analysis without requiring specialised high-performance infrastructure, at least in the first stage of building the engine (JA.I.Net1) and primary validation. However, as complexity scales exponentially in later phases, particularly when integrating real-time predictions or multivariate temporal models, emerging technologies such as exascale computing offer new frontiers. With their capacity to simulate vast combinatorial spaces and model intricate interdependencies at near-instantaneous speeds, exascale systems present a compelling infrastructure for pushing JA.I.Net5-6 beyond current computational horizons. Exascale systems will allow real-time generation and analysis of billions of permutations, unlocking granularity for large scale applications (e.g. cultural trend modelling) or hyper-parametric simulations in ethno-mathematics. Such scalability would also mitigate memory bottlenecks entirely, as distributed architectures could handle the problem's residual combinatorial complexity with trivial overhead.

Similarly, quantum computing introduces a paradigm shift. Its potential for exploiting quantum parallelism and entanglement-based correlations may render entire classes of these combinatorial constraints solvable in radically different ways, especially those that remain intractable even under classical symmetry reduction.

Quantum annealing (e.g., D-Wave) or gate-based systems (e.g., IBM Qiskit) could theoretically exploit superposition and entanglement to evaluate all permutations simultaneously, reducing the divisional chart (varga) problem to a single energy-minimisation step. While fault-tolerant quantum hardware remains years away, hybrid quantum-classical algorithms (e.g., QAOA) could soon accelerate symmetry detection in problems like the Bhava cycle, potentially collapsing the solution space exponentially faster than classical methods.

The implications ripple across multiple disciplines: beyond its immediate application in criminal psychology analytics, JA.I.Net methodology offers a template for quantifying traditional knowledge systems through computational frameworks. It clearly bridges the world of ethno-mathematics with cutting-edge AI, while providing a case study in how algorithmic refinement can render massive combinatorial problems tractable. Future work could explore hybrid classical-quantum pipelines or exascale deployments to further democratise access to cultural pattern analysis, ensuring that even the most constrained communities can leverage HPC-grade insights without infrastructure barriers. The approach particularly shines in predictive modelling scenarios requiring constrained dataset generation, proving that ancient mathematics, cultural heritage preservation, HPC and Quantum can indeed find common ground through thoughtful algorithmic design.

Based on the 53M dataset, the top 5% of configurations (about 2.7 million) will indicate high-risk behavioural patterns, forming the primary focus for forensic psychology, predictive criminology and the development of advanced analytical tools. An additional 15% (about 8 million) reflect medium-risk potential, bringing the total core research subset to about 20% (some 10.7 million combinations). With the integration of Nakshatra granulation (Stage 2) and further application of Dasha-based temporal markers and Varga overlays, the model gains the capacity to detect latent or emerging risks with greater precision. The remaining 80% (some 43 million micro-profiles) while low-risk from a criminological perspective, hold significant potential for cross-disciplinary applications — such as early-stage medical diagnostics in paediatry, ophthalmology, oncology, neurology, psychiatry, hematologic disorders, metabolic and bone diseases, inflammatory and autoimmune diseases, structural and developmental disorders, genetic and rare diseases etc.

Jyotisha's inherent complexity, with non-linear, hierarchical dependencies makes it ideally suited to neural computation. Rule-based systems often fail to detect such embedded, multi-dimensional patterns; neural models, by contrast, excel at discovering latent relationships, subtle markers, and emergent behavioural constellations. Neural models are capable of learning and improving continuously; the more data we provide - Jataka charts, case studies, and behavioural profiles - the more accurate and insightful these systems become. A well-trained network, drawing on this architecture, can model probabilistic behavioural risks, including tendencies toward sadism, violence, serial rape/ murder or disassociation. These insights can trigger early warning mechanisms, predict periods of heightened vulnerability and adapt dynamically to new data.

With iterative refinement, the AI-Jyotisha hybrid system can serve as both a predictive and diagnostic tool, offering valuable intervention indicators not only in criminology but across wider, multidisciplinary domains of mental health, education and public policy. This synthesis does more than bridge ancient wisdom and computational innovation, it establishes a new frontier in translational data science. Here, sacred cosmology informs empirical inquiry and machine intelligence serves the timeless pursuit of understanding human behaviour.

AI-driven models are adept at identifying statistical correlations and patterns within vast troves of data, yet they are inherently limited in their capacity to interpret the internal states, latent desires, intentions and cyclical transformations that shape human actions. In contrast, Jyotisha offers a system of pattern recognition and behavioural analysis that has evolved over millennia. Its foundational principles rest on the belief that the positions and movements of natural energies, starting with the moment of an individual's birth, have a profound influence on their psychological makeup, motivations, intentional patterns and life trajectory. Jyotisha provides insights that extend far beyond the mere prediction of future events. The integration of Jyotisha with modern AI is not simply a juxtaposition of disparate methodologies but rather a harmonisation of complementary paradigms. The system of Grahas in Jyotisha can be viewed as analogous to the psychological archetypes proposed by Carl Jung. Grahas, such as *Chandra* (G2) - associated with emotions and subconscious patterns - mirror Jung's concept of the *anima*, reflecting the unconscious forces that shape human behaviour. Similarly, the influence of *Rahu* (G8), associated with ambition and unconventional behaviour, resonates with the Jungian shadow, representing those hidden and often unacknowledged facets of personality that can precipitate both creativity and self-destructive tendencies. Through this lens, Jyotisha does not merely offer deterministic predictions; it provides a diagnostic tool that can reveal the interplay of internal psychological forces in a manner that is both symbolic and empirically resonant with contemporary behavioural science.

Jyotisha's cyclical understanding of time presents another significant advantage over static, data-bound AI models. The concept of Dasha offers a dynamic model for understanding the evolution of human behaviour over time. Much like longitudinal studies in modern psychology that track changes in behaviour and personality across the lifespan, Dashas delineate periods marked by varying degrees of risk, transformation, or stability. An individual experiencing a Rahu Dasha may undergo phases of heightened ambition and potential instability, while a Chandra Dasha might signal a period characterised by emotional sensitivity and introspection. Moreover, the notion of Gochara, which captures the real-time movement of Grahas and their interactions with an individual's pattern, provides a granular view of how external events can trigger internal psychological shifts. This dynamic interplay between fixed natal influences and the fluidity of temporal cycles affords a predictive depth that is absent in conventional AI approaches.

Such a hybrid model is not without its challenges, one of the most significant hurdles being the modern perception of Jyotisha itself. Often dismissed as purely mystical or esoteric, it is frequently relegated to the realm of superstition rather than being recognised as a sophisticated system that employs mathematical tools, enabling experimentation and validation when integrated with other scientific disciplines and empirical observations. Overcoming this perception requires not only rigorous empirical validation in controlled laboratory environments, but also a concerted effort to bridge the epistemological gap between ancient wisdom and contemporary scientific paradigms. To this end, interdisciplinary research must be undertaken to establish robust methodologies that effectively translate the qualitative insights of Jyotisha into quantifiable metrics compatible with AI systems. Such efforts should involve developing standardised frameworks for interpreting research data in a translational context.

A critical challenge is the integration of two fundamentally different paradigms, one rooted in the empirical methodologies of modern data science and the other in the symbolic and cyclical logic of ancient Vedic thought. The process of harmonising these disparate approaches needs the development of hybrid algorithms capable of processing both quantitative data and qualitative, temporally dynamic variables. This task is compounded by the inherent complexity of human behaviour, which resists simplistic categorisation and demands a multifaceted analytical approach. Moreover, the ethical implications of such integration must be carefully considered, particularly in contexts where predictive models directly influence public policy, human rights and individual liberties. Ensuring that the hybrid model operates in a manner that is both transparent and just is paramount, as any perceived or actual biases could have far-reaching consequences for marginalised communities and vulnerable populations.

Modern data science increasingly employs modular architectures, where components like data ingestion, processing, analysis and visualisation operate independently yet interconnect seamlessly. This modularity supports scalability and flexibility in handling diverse datasets, while common data formats, protocols and ontologies enable disparate systems to exchange and interpret data consistently. Initiatives such as the FAIR Data (Findable, Accessible, Interoperable, and Reusable) principles further standardise data management practices on an international scale. Additionally, Application Programming Interfaces (APIs), open-source platforms and cloud-based environments (e.g. AWS, Azure, Google Cloud) provide robust, standardised tools that enhance interoperability and reproducibility. Collaborative tools such as Jupyter notebooks and containerisation technologies like Docker foster interdisciplinary teamwork, allowing experts from various fields to integrate their data and models effectively. This collaborative, translational approach is critical for a first pilot project, as it enables the rich, symbolic language of Jyotisha to be translated into quantifiable metrics. By merging Jyotisha's qualitative insights with the statistical and computational techniques of modern AI, we can create more comprehensive and actionable risk assessment models.

Translational data science is essentially the bridge between raw, often qualitative research data and the quantitative models that drive modern AI systems. Traditional Jyotisha contains rich symbolic and qualitative insights, such as descriptions of temporal items, environmental influences, cyclical patterns and psycho-behavioural archetypes. Translational data science involves converting these qualitative insights into quantifiable research data. This could mean coding textual descriptions into numerical values, developing scales for interpreting the strength formulae and/or timing of environmental influences, using statistical methods to summarise historical observations documented in Jyotisha texts. Once the Jyotisha-derived research data are quantified, they are standardised using common data formats and protocols. This standardisation ensures that the data are interoperable with other datasets and can be seamlessly integrated into modern analytics frameworks. In many fields, initiatives like FAIR (Findable, Accessible, Interoperable, and Reusable) help guarantee that the *meta*data meet these standards. In this context, AI primarily refers to the use of machine learning algorithms that can process large volumes of data to uncover patterns, make predictions and support empirical observations and decision-making concerning model validation. The quantified Jyotisha data - now part of a larger dataset - can be fed into dedicated machine learning models.

Practically, researchers will employ supervised machine learning techniques to train models using historical Jyotisha data alongside known outcomes (such as past events and risk factors). Over time, as the model receives feedback from its predictions, it adjusts its parameters not only to improve accuracy but also to scale for specialised applications. In this framework, AI is not merely a tool for powerful analytics; it is an advanced system that leverages statistical methods and machine learning to analyse complex, multidimensional research data. Its strength lies in its ability to integrate qualitative Jyotisha insights with modern empirical datasets to produce nuanced predictions. By synthesising the temporal and psychological dimensions of Jyotisha with data-driven approaches, AI can uncover trends, patterns and risk factors that would remain hidden using conventional methods alone.

The potential of the AI-Jyotisha hybrid model (JA.I.Net) extends beyond immediate applications. At its core, this approach challenges the prevailing notion that technological progress must displace traditional knowledge systems. Instead, it suggests that reconciling ancient wisdom with modern scientific inquiry can lead to more nuanced, ethical, and effective predictive frameworks. The hybrid model represents a paradigm shift in risk assessment, acknowledging that data, no matter how precise, cannot capture the full scope of human experience without insights from millennia-old knowledge systems. This synthesis of Jyotisha with AI-driven methodologies invites a broader re-examination of knowledge itself, showing that wisdom is not solely the domain of modern science but an evolving tapestry woven from diverse cultural and intellectual traditions.

Despite its potential, a key challenge is empirically validating Jyotisha's principles within a modern scientific framework. Integrating qualitative insights with quantitative data requires rigorous interdisciplinary methods that can withstand scrutiny from both technologists and Jyotisha scholars. Studies must not only test the predictive power of Jyotisha-informed variables but also establish their relevance in a statistically robust and contextually sensitive way. Merging these paradigms calls for rethinking the assumptions underpinning risk models. The hybrid approach requires a flexible framework that accommodates both the deterministic logic of machine learning and the symbolic insights of ancient wisdom. This demands the development of tools and methodologies to bridge these domains, ensuring the resulting model is coherent, comprehensive, and actionable.

Ethical considerations are paramount in implementing the new model. As predictive systems increasingly shape public policy and individual outcomes, it is crucial that they operate transparently and justly. The integration must avoid cultural appropriation or misinterpretation of Jyotisha's principles. Safeguards must be in place to prevent the hybrid model from perpetuating biases or creating new forms of discrimination.

The promise of the AI-Jyotisha hybrid model lies in its ability to enhance predictive accuracy while challenging us to reconsider the artificial boundaries between past, present and future sciences of risk assessment. This model has the potential to revolutionise how we predict and manage risks in an interconnected world. As societies navigate challenges in diplomatic cooperation, technological advancement and shifting cultural landscapes, integrating diverse epistemological frameworks becomes not only advantageous but essential. The proposed model serves as a testament to the enduring relevance of ancient wisdom in the modern era, reminding us that human knowledge is an evolving process, shaped by collective insights across time and space and committed to advancing the well-being of humanity.

PRACTICAL APPLICATIONS OF THE JA.I.NET MODEL

In the realm of law enforcement and predictive policing, integrating Jyotisha offers a promising solution to the shortcomings of models that rely solely on historical crime data. Current systems often overlook the subtle psychological currents and cyclical tendencies that underline criminal behaviour, resulting in predictions that are both impersonal and inherently biased. By incorporating Jyotisha's insights into an individual's psychological profile and cyclical predispositions, law enforcement agencies and policymakers can develop more tailored and dynamic intervention strategies. This approach enables the identification of critical periods during which individuals or groups are statistically more prone to risk-taking behaviours or violent outbursts, thereby allowing for pre-emptive measures that are both humane and effective. Blending Jyotisha's principles with modern predictive analytics not only enhances our understanding of the psychological dynamics at play but also paves the way for more personalised, ethical, and context-aware interventions. Imagine a metropolitan police department seeking to enhance its predictive policing capabilities. Models relying solely on historical crime data may successfully identify statistical hotspots and recurring patterns, yet they often overlook the underlying psychological drivers and the potential for rehabilitation in criminal behaviour. By integrating Jyotisha's cyclical analysis into its predictive framework, the department could pinpoint periods when specific individuals or communities are more vulnerable to criminal impulses due to particular psychological states. This additional layer of insight would enable law enforcement to deploy resources more judiciously, shifting from reactive responses to proactive, preventive measures informed by a deeper understanding of human behaviour.

Similarly, in the realm of diplomacy and international relations, the fusion of AI with Jyotisha provides a novel framework for understanding geopolitical dynamics. International negotiations, alliances and conflicts are influenced not only by quantifiable economic and political indicators but also by the less tangible dimensions of cultural sentiment and emotional resonance. By applying Jyotisha's temporal analysis, policymakers can better identify optimal periods for diplomatic engagement, informed by the collective psychological state of a nation or region as shaped by both historical cycles and contemporary emotional currents. This integrative approach yields a more holistic assessment of risk, one that is attuned to both empirical data and the subtler forces that drive international affairs. Timing, a critical factor in the success of diplomatic initiatives, is central to Jyotisha's methodology. Its study of Panchanga ("the five arms of time") provide critical insights for planning negotiations or peace-building efforts. By aligning key diplomatic actions with appropriate periods, leaders can avoid the pitfalls of poorly timed decisions that have historically escalated tensions or led to geopolitical instability. This refined temporal awareness, when integrated with traditional diplomatic analysis, offers a strategic advantage. It enables decision-makers to navigate the intricate landscape of international relations with greater respect and precision, ensuring that diplomatic initiatives are both context-aware and optimally timed for win-win outcomes.

The healthcare sector, particularly in mental health, stands to gain immensely from an AI-Jyotisha hybrid model. Modern healthcare recognises that early detection and proactive intervention are essential to mitigate mental health crises and reduce recidivism among vulnerable individuals. While current AI systems excel at identifying statistical correlations within clinical data, they often overlook the psychological and temporal factors that serve as early indicators of distress. Integrating Jyotisha's framework into healthcare enables practitioners to anticipate periods of heightened vulnerability. For example, an individual undergoing a specific Dasha (personal era) may temporarily experience increased stress or impulsivity, signalling a critical window during which tailored therapeutic interventions could pre-empt a crisis. This fusion not only enhances the precision of risk assessments but also fosters a proactive and compassionate approach to mental healthcare. Beyond individual care, Jyotisha's ability to discern collective patterns offers healthcare providers valuable insights for managing broader public health challenges. Practitioners can develop more personalised intervention plans, optimise resource allocation and ultimately reduce public health costs.

In the field of intelligence, the hybrid AI-Jyotisha model can significantly enhance early warning systems and threat assessments. Traditional intelligence analysis relies on vast datasets, from geospatial imagery to social media signals and historical political trends, to identify emerging risks, yet it often misses the cyclical and psychological under-currents that drive human behaviour and geopolitical shifts. By incorporating Jyotisha's cyclical analysis, intelligence agencies gain deeper insights into the timing and nature of emerging threats. For example, Jyotisha's insights on environmental indicators and their impact on national sentiment and leadership tendencies serve as qualitative complements to quantitative data. When translated into measurable variables through translational data science, these indicators can feed machine learning algorithms designed to detect subtle anomalies such as the rising influence of foreign ideologies, unauthorised foreign-based social engineering and other internal or external threats to national security. This fusion enables intelligence analysts to refine their models and anticipate potential disruptions before they manifest, resulting in a more robust, context-aware intelligence framework that identifies risks early and adapts to the evolving dynamics of global affairs in an efficient and effective manner.

Protection of critical infrastructures such as energy grids, transportation networks, food and water systems, communication networks etc. is another promising application for the hybrid model. These systems face physical threats (e.g. natural disasters, terrorist attacks) and human-induced disruptions (e.g. sabotage, cyber-attacks). Traditional monitoring relies on real-time sensor data, historical incident reports and retrospective risk assessments to identify vulnerabilities. However, such systems often overlook the complex interplay among environmental factors, human behaviour, temporal items and the cyclical nature of socio-economic trends that can precipitate failures. Integrating Jyotisha's temporal-qualitative insights into the predictive framework enables a more nuanced risk assessment. For example, by analysing Jyotisha-derived patterns alongside sensor data, operators will be able to pinpoint periods when critical infrastructure is more susceptible to stress or failure. Imagine an energy grid: beyond routine metrics, the hybrid model could detect subtle shifts in environmental and human conditions that historically coincide with increased equipment failures, power outages, natural or made-made disasters. This information can trigger preemptive maintenance, enhanced security, efficient resource allocation and targeted cybersecurity measures.

In the field of criminology and victimology, the conceptual framework of Jyotisha finds striking parallels with contemporary theories in behavioural psychology and data analytics. Its notion of Grahas resonates with modern interpretations of psychological archetypes, as evidenced in the works of Jung and Freud, underscoring the profound influence of unconscious forces on human behaviour. Much like Freud's exploration of the unconscious, which revealed how repressed desires and unresolved conflicts drive our actions, Jyotisha posits that the Grahas represent elemental forces subtly shaping our psyche and life experiences. Furthermore, just as Piaget's theory of child development delineates distinct stages in cognitive growth, illustrating how innate predispositions interact with environmental stimuli to foster development, Jyotisha's cyclical framework and successive Dashas (personal eras of development) map out different phases in an individual's whole life. Each Dasha corresponds to specific patterns of behaviour evolution, echoing the stage-wise progression observed by Piaget. In addition, Jyotisha offers ethically controversial (yet scientifically verifiable) insights into individual longevity, health patterns – not only mental but also anatomic and functional - and more. Modern criminology and forensic psychology, like Jyotisha, aim to reveal the hidden forces that shape human behaviour. For instance, Cesare Lombroso - the founder of the Italian school of criminology and modern criminal anthropology - pioneered the idea that criminal behaviour can be linked to inherent, biological factors (biological determinism). This concept finds a parallel in Jyotisha, particularly in its D40–D45 formula, which offers a clear framework for investigating inherited traits/ patterns from biological parents. Enrico Ferri, a student of Lombroso, later argued that crime was not solely the result of biological predispositions. He introduced the term "criminal sociology" which viewed crime as the product of interactions between the individual and their environment. By expanding criminology beyond biology, Ferri paved the way for a multidisciplinary approach. He also emphasised the concept of "social defence," arguing that the purpose of punishment and criminal justice was not moral retribution, but rather the protection of society and the prevention of crime. Ferri advocated for rehabilitation, education, and preventive measures in place of harsh punishments.

Today, authors such as Robert Hare and Adrian Raine delve into the neuropsychological and personality dimensions that predispose individuals to antisocial or criminal behaviour. Hare's research on psychopathy, for example, highlights underlying "emotional deficits" and "impulsivity" that can trigger destructive actions, complementing – without knowing - how Jyotisha signals the exact periods of heightened risk. Similarly, Raine's studies in neuro-criminology reveal that structural and functional anomalies in the brain can predispose individuals to criminal tendencies, echoing Jyotisha's notion that certain physical imprints and space-time influences predispose behaviour beyond what is immediately observable. The emphasis is on identifying and understanding deep-seated, often hidden factors that drive behaviour. This shared perspective underscores the potential of integrating Jyotisha with modern forensic insights to create a more comprehensive framework for predicting and managing risk.

The integration of Jyotisha into contemporary risk management frameworks represents more than an enhancement of technological capacity; it signifies a fundamental rethinking of how we conceptualise and predict human behaviour. By synthesising the empirical rigor of modern data analytics with the revolutionary insights of Jyotisha, we can develop predictive models that are both more precise and more humane. This synthesis recognises that human beings are not static entities defined solely by past behaviours, but dynamic, non-linear, and heterogeneous individuals whose trajectories are shaped by both individual psychological forces and external environmental rhythms. In the context of predictive policing, this approach offers the promise of *a priori* rehabilitation, identifying non-linear pathways for early intervention that can gently guide individuals toward change before they commit a crime, thereby fostering preventive education and personal growth.

The dialogue between ancient Jyotisha and modern AI-driven methodologies challenges us to transcend traditional paradigms, reframe the relationship between technology and humanity and develop risk management strategies that are as context-aware as they are analytically robust. Such an approach promises to foster informed, compassionate and effective decision-making in an increasingly complex and interconnected world.

ETHICAL CONSIDERATIONS AND CHALLENGES

Although the model promises enhanced decision-making capabilities and improved safety, it also introduces risks related to bias, privacy, discrimination and potential overreach. AI-driven systems, particularly those used in predictive policing, have been shown to reinforce historical inequities. Tools such as COMPAS and PredPol rely on historical crime data, which can result in disproportionate targeting of minority communities and economically disadvantaged areas. The inherent limitations of these models arise from their dependence on past patterns, thereby perpetuating existing biases and obscuring the nuances of individual behaviour. By contrast, Jyotisha offers a framework based on the analysis of psychological archetypes and cyclical behavioural patterns rather than solely on demographic or historical data. This approach seeks to interpret latent tendencies and personal motivations, mitigating bias by focusing on individualised, temporally relevant insights.

The ethical application of Jyotisha is not without its challenges. There exists the risk that its principles could be misinterpreted or manipulated to reinforce stereotypes, leading to discriminatory practices. Therefore, any integration of Jyotisha into predictive systems must be accompanied by rigorous oversight and transparency, to prevent misuse. Mechanisms for accountability and ethical governance are essential to ensure that the insights provided by both AI and Jyotisha are applied in ways that respect individual rights and promote social justice.

Privacy concerns also loom large in the deployment of predictive risk management technologies. AI systems often require extensive data collection, which can lead to invasive surveillance practices and the erosion of civil liberties. The collection and analysis of data regarding individuals' behaviours, locations and interactions pose significant challenges to maintaining confidentiality and autonomy. Although Jyotisha relies on a more limited set of personal information and less intrusive indicators, its use in governance could still facilitate predictive profiling if not properly regulated. The protection of individual privacy, therefore, demands robust data anonymisation practices, transparent data management and clear consent protocols. One notable advantage of Jyotisha over conventional AI models is its inherent interpretability. AI systems frequently operate as opaque "black boxes," where the rationale behind a given prediction is difficult to ascertain. This opacity can undermine public trust and hinder efforts to rectify errors or biases. Jyotisha, by contrast, operates within a well-defined conceptual framework that delineates how predictions are derived. This transparency offers a clearer understanding of the decision-making process and also opens multiple avenues for non-invasive, non-punitive and low-cost interventions. In contexts such as criminal justice, such an approach may enable more rehabilitative strategies that focus on addressing underlying behavioural issues rather than merely administering punitive measures.

Integrating the strengths of Jyotisha with the computational prowess of AI holds the potential to create a hybrid model that balances predictive accuracy with ethical oversight. Such a system can identify high-risk periods for intervention without resorting to blanket, static data-driven judgments that overlook individual circumstances. This hybrid approach will require transparency in the underlying algorithms and robust accountability mechanisms to guard against misuse for surveillance or political repression. The potential misuse of predictive technologies in surveillance and political control represents one of the most significant ethical risks. The deployment of AI-based systems has already led to practices that raise concerns about social control and the infringement of civil liberties. The integration of Jyotisha does not eliminate these dangers; rather, it introduces new ethical complexities if its insights into psychological tendencies are exploited for coercive purposes. Preventing such abuses necessitates not only technological safeguards but also comprehensive regulatory and legislative frameworks. These measures should mandate transparency, ensure that methodologies are fully disclosed and guarantee that individuals have their rights protected.

The fusion of AI and Jyotisha in predictive risk management offers promising avenues for more accurate and empathetic decision-making. Ethical considerations must guide every stage of development and implementation. Transparency, accountability and robust privacy protections must be integral to this hybrid model. Only by embedding these principles can we hope to harness the true benefits of both ancient wisdom and modern technology, promoting equitable outcomes.

QUANTUM SUPPORT IN HYBRID MODELLING

The integration of quantum computing heralds a transformative shift in predictive risk management, enabling the capture of non-linear dynamics, interdependencies and "uncertainty" inherent in human behaviour and societal trends. While classical AI models operate on deterministic, linear algorithms and rely on historical datasets, they often fall short in accounting for the cyclical, probabilistic nature of human experience that Jyotisha seeks to elucidate. Quantum computing, with its abilities rooted in superposition and entanglement, offers an elegant solution to these limitations by processing multiple possibilities simultaneously and embracing "uncertainty" as an intrinsic component of prediction.

At the heart of this hybrid model is the contrast between classical and quantum approaches to probability. AI systems typically employ Bayesian probability, basing predictions on fixed datasets. In contrast, quantum probability recognises "uncertainty" and the "wave-like" behaviour of information, aligning naturally with Jyotisha's advanced probabilistic forecasts that depend on dynamic environmental and temporal-qualitative states. By incorporating quantum principles, an AI-Jyotisha hybrid can transcend linear/ uni-directional causality, effectively modelling the complex, multi-directional, multi-temporal, cyclical interactions that govern human behaviour. One of the key advantages of quantum computing, in this context, is its capacity for superposition, which enables computational states to exist in multiple configurations simultaneously. Jyotisha, similarly, considers numerous natural influences at once. Quantum-enhanced AI can maintain and evaluate these overlapping influences, leading to more precise predictions by capturing the full spectrum of interdependent variables. Furthermore, quantum entanglement - the phenomenon in which particles remain connected regardless of distance - mirrors Jyotisha's premise that environmental movements exert interconnected, far-reaching effects on human consciousness, psychology, behaviour and societal events. By leveraging entanglement, our hybrid model can establish deeper correlations among environmental patterns and human behavioural outcomes, thereby enriching the predictive framework.

Quantum machine learning (QML) further refines this approach. Modern machine learning often encounters difficulties in handling hidden variables and complex interdependencies, challenges that are central to understanding the subtleties of natural influences. QML, with its enhanced capacity to process vast, probabilistic datasets, can integrate Jyotisha's combinatorial logic with quantum algorithms. This synergy provides a nuanced understanding of individual psychological tendencies, intentions, decision-making patterns and long-term behavioural shifts, thus offering a more personalised and adaptable model for predictive risk management.

In practical applications such as predictive criminology, the integration of quantum-enhanced AI with Jyotisha promises to revolutionise crime forecasting tools and law enforcement training in advanced capabilities. By incorporating the cyclical insights from Jyotisha and processing them through quantum algorithms, the hybrid system can forecast the likelihood of criminal activities and identify critical time windows during which these behaviours are more likely to manifest. This approach enables agencies to deploy more targeted and timely interventions, reducing over-policing and mitigating systemic biases. In international relations, diplomatic initiatives can be timed with greater precision, increasing the probability of successful outcomes. Similarly, in healthcare, particularly within mental health and preventive medicine, integrating quantum AI with Jyotisha's time-based diagnostics offers the promise of personalised treatment regimens. By processing biological rhythms, environmental factors and environmental data concurrently, healthcare providers could forecast periods of vulnerability and intervene pre-emptively to enhance patient outcomes.

Furthermore, quantum computing's contribution to Panchanga-based time tools and Ayurvedic diagnostics cannot be understated. The Panchanga benefits from quantum parallelism in processing complex, overlapping time cycles. This capability allows for more accurate predictions of physiological and psychological states, while Ayurveda's emphasis on time cycles in health can be fine-tuned by quantum machine learning to optimise treatment protocols.

In 2025, quantum computing remains an emerging technology, and developing robust computational frameworks that integrate ancient cyclical theories with modern algorithms requires dedicated effort, interdisciplinary collaboration and continued innovation. Equally critical is the establishment of rigorous ethical guidelines to ensure these powerful predictive tools are deployed responsibly, safeguarding individual rights and preventing overreach.

The fusion of quantum principles, AI's data-driven analysis and Jyotisha's cyclical capabilities paves the way for a new era in predictive risk management. This integrated model holds the promise of transcending traditional limitations by embracing complexity, uncertainty and non-linearity, thereby offering a more holistic, context-aware, and ethically sound framework for understanding and predicting human behaviour in an increasingly interconnected world.

POLICY RECOMMENDATIONS: TRUST AND ACCOUNTABILITY

In light of the convergence of AI, quantum computing and Jyotisha in predictive risk management, robust regulatory oversight is essential to ensure responsible implementation. These integrated systems promise significant improvements in sectors such as law enforcement, protection of critical infrastructure, healthcare, governance, global diplomacy. However, without comprehensive policy frameworks, they risk exacerbating issues like bias, privacy violations and overreach. A foundational measure is the establishment of rigorous oversight mechanisms. Hybrid predictive tools should undergo regular audits and independent evaluations by interdisciplinary teams comprising Vedic scholars (who are also advanced ethicists[1]), data scientists, AI experts, legal professionals. Such reviews will assess the accuracy, fairness and ethical implications of predictions, ensuring that forecasts derive from legitimate, true factors rather than arbitrary correlations. In critical areas like national security, law enforcement and healthcare, publicly accessible accountability reports would detail the usage, impact and safeguards of these systems, fostering public trust and sufficient transparency. It is equally vital to delineate clear limitations on the application of these models. For instance, in law enforcement, predictive tools should be confined to high-risk scenarios such as terrorist threats to critical infrastructure, human trafficking, organised crime, and must never serve as the sole basis for punitive actions. Instead, they should function as trusted advisory instruments within broader investigative frameworks. In non-security contexts like workplace assessments or psychological evaluations, the principle of informed consent must prevail, ensuring that individuals are fully aware of how their data is used and have the right to opt out without facing discrimination or negative repercussions.

Furthermore, strict legislative measures must be implemented to prevent the weaponisation of these hybrid models for political repression against civilians. It is imperative that these technologies are not exploited to target free activists, journalists or other free groups under the guise of public security. Transparency in decision-making processes and mandatory governmental oversight in the deployment of these systems are critical to mitigating potential abuses. Such safeguards will help ensure that this integration remains a tool for enhancing societal well-being rather than reinforcing oppressive control.

The incorporation of quantum-enhanced AI introduces additional layers of complexity. Quantum computing amplifies the analytical power of predictive models, however, these advanced capabilities also heighten ethical concerns, necessitating a regulatory framework that addresses both traditional issues—such as algorithmic bias—and emerging challenges unique to quantum technologies. Policymakers must collaborate closely with experts across disciplines to develop guidelines that are both rigorous and adaptable, ensuring that technological advancements do not compromise ethical standards.

CONCLUSION

This chapter has explored the transformative potential of integrating artificial intelligence with Jyotisha - and further enhanced by quantum computing - to forge a hybrid model (JA.I.Net) for predictive risk management that is both comprehensive and ethically grounded. The hybrid model addresses the inherent limitations of current risk assessment methods. This synthesis not only improves predictive accuracy across sectors such as law enforcement, healthcare, diplomacy and critical infrastructure protection but also offers a more nuanced understanding of the complex interplay of psychological, environmental and temporal factors that influence human actions. A central advantage of this integrated approach is its ability to mitigate the biases that often plague conventional AI-driven models.

By shifting the focus toward personalised analysis of behavioural predispositions and time-sensitive risk factors, the hybrid model paves the way for more equitable and context-aware interventions. The progressive infusion of quantum computing into this framework offers significant enhancements in handling non-linearity and uncertainty. Quantum superposition and entanglement enable the simultaneous processing of multiple interdependent variables, thereby capturing the intricate, cyclical influences that Jyotisha identifies. This quantum-enhanced layer not only refines pattern recognition but also aligns closely with the probabilistic nature of Jyotisha's predictions, which view human behaviour as a dynamic interplay of fluctuating forces rather than fixed outcomes. Consequently, the integration of quantum concepts ensures that the hybrid model remains adaptable and robust in the face of complex, real-world scenarios.

Policy considerations and ethical safeguards are essential to the successful deployment of these integrated technologies. As demonstrated in earlier sections, rigorous oversight mechanisms, interdisciplinary collaboration and clear regulatory frameworks are imperative to prevent misuse, protect individual rights and ensure transparency. Whether applied in national security, international diplomacy, or public health, the hybrid model must operate within well-defined ethical boundaries. The convergence of ancient wisdom and modern technology in this hybrid model invites a reimagining of predictive risk management, moving society beyond the constraints of linear, data-centric models, improving the human-centric precision of predictive analytics and decision-making. Through interdisciplinary research, the integration of AI, quantum and Jyotisha can catalyse the development of predictive tools that are more cost-effective, more socially just and more contextually aware. As we look into the future, the challenge will be to harness these complementary methodologies responsibly, ensuring that the benefits of enhanced predictive accuracy are realised while upholding the fundamental values of fairness, privacy and human dignity.

FUTURE DIRECTIONS: RESEARCH, DEVELOPMENT & INNOVATION

The Future research in this domain must prioritise advancing the Technology Readiness Level (TRL) of AI-Jyotisha hybrid models (JA.I.Net1-9) to empirically validate their predictive capabilities within contemporary risk management contexts. Integrating AI's robust data processing with Jyotisha's deep, cyclical insights, and further enhanced by quantum computing capabilities, offers a transformative approach to forecasting human behaviour. Realising this promise requires a concerted effort to refine models through interdisciplinary research, technological innovation and rigorous ethical oversight. One of the foremost priorities is the empirical validation of Jyotisha's predictive frameworks when integrated with modern AI algorithms. Large-scale studies are needed to assess the accuracy and reliability of formulae in real-world scenarios, spanning sectors such as law enforcement and mental health. Such studies will enable systematic evaluations of whether the models can reduce bias, enhance pattern recognition and provide more context-sensitive predictions than current AI systems. Pilot programs in controlled environments, ranging from corporate risk assessments to geopolitical forecasting, are essential for gathering data on performance and identifying practical challenges early in the development process.

Interdisciplinary collaboration lies at the heart of these advancements. Bringing together Jyotisha scholars, social scientists, data scientists, AI researchers, quantum computing experts, legal professionals, will be vital for developing refined hybrid models. This collaborative approach will not only facilitate the technical integration of ancient cyclical frameworks with modern machine learning but will also ensure that the resulting models adhere to ethical best practices. By blending diverse perspectives, researchers can create predictive systems that respect cultural contexts, maintain transparency, and foster public trust.

Innovation will further play a pivotal role in optimisation: AI algorithms need to be adapted to incorporate the time-sensitive, psychological patterns inherent in Jyotisha, while quantum computing offers the potential to process complex, non-linear interactions among variables. The refinement of quantum machine learning, in particular, promises to enhance the system's ability to handle multiple inter-dependent factors simultaneously, resulting in more nuanced forecasts of human behaviour. This integration will enable models to move beyond static, historical data and incorporate dynamic, future-oriented insights, thereby improving the accuracy of risk assessments in rapidly evolving contexts.

Policymakers will develop national and international standards that govern the responsible use of these technologies, ensuring that they will enhance public welfare. International cooperation in science is key to ensuring the long-term success of these new tools. As AI-Jyotisha models become more prevalent across borders, a unified set of protocols and guidelines may be essential to maintain consistency in ethical implementation. Training programs designed for policymakers, practitioners and the general public will help demystify the underlying principles and global benefits. An informed stakeholder community will support the ethical deployment of these systems and advocate for policies that balance innovation with individual rights and societal values, while respecting diverse cultural perspectives.

REFERENCES

Agrawal, A. (1995). Dismantling the divide between indigenous and scientific knowledge. *Development and Change.*

Bonta, J., & Andrews, D. A. (2023). *The Psychology of Criminal Conduct.*

Bowers, K. J., Johnson, S. D., & Pease, K. (2004). Prospective hot-spotting: The future of crime mapping? *British Journal of Criminology.*

Chainey, S., & Ratcliffe, J. (2013). *GIS and crime mapping* (2nd ed.). Wiley.

Ferguson, A G (2017) The rise of big data policing: Surveillance, race, and the future of law enforcement NYU Press

Harding, S (1998) Is science multicultural? Postcolonialisms, feminisms, and epistemologies Indiana University Press

International Labour Organisation. (2022) Global Estimates of Modern Slavery: Forced Labour and Forced Marriage https://www.ilo.org/publications/major-publications/global-estimates-modern-slavery-forced-labour-and-forced-marriage

Meresi, M. (2025). *Pattern recognition models, neural networks and machine learning for risk assessment: Building JA.I.Net.1 engine & scalable applications, predictive criminology, Amazon.com.* KDP.

Panini (1897) The Ashtadhyayi (S C Vasu, Trans) Benares, Panini Office

Perry, W L, McInnis, B, Price, C C, Smith, S C, & Hollywood, J S (2013) Predictive policing: The role of crime forecasting in law enforcement operations RAND Corporation

Richardson, R., Schultz, J., & Crawford, K. (2019) Dirty data, bad predictions: How civil rights violations impact police data, predictive policing systems, and justice. New York University Law Review https://nyulawreview.org/wp-content/uploads/2019/04/NYULawReview-94-Richardson_etal-FIN.pdf

Rouse, W B (2011) Translational systems science: From discovery to application Wiley

Sankin, A., & Mattu, S. (2023) Predictive Policing Software Terrible At Predicting Crimes https://themarkup.org/prediction-bias/2023/10/02/predictive-policing-software-terrible-at-predicting-crimes

Tucek, A. (2015) Constraining Big Brother: The Legal Deficiencies Surrounding Chicago's Use of the Strategic Subject List https://legal-forum.uchicago.edu/print-archive/constraining-big-brother-legal-deficiencies-surrounding-chicagos-use-strategic

Woolf, S. H. (2008). The meaning of translational research and why it matters. *Journal of the American Medical Association*, *299*(2), 211–213.

ADDITIONAL READING

Angwin, J, Larson, J, Mattu, S, Kirchner, L, & ProPublica (2016) Machine Bias: There's Software Used across the Country to Predict Future Criminals And It's Biased against Blacks. https://www.propublica.org/article/machine-bias-risk-assessments-in-criminal-sentencing

Aufrecht, T (1891) Catalogus catalogorum

Ballabh, R. (Ed.). (1980). *Surya-Siddhanta Astronomical and Mathematical Texts Series No I Lucknow University.*

Carleton, B, Cunningham, B, & Thorkildsen, Z (2020, October) The use of predictive analytics in policing Bureau of Justice Assistance, US Department of Justice

Raman, B. V. (1947). *Three hundred important combinations Bangalore*. Raman Publications.

Varahamihira, S. (1919) Brihat Jataka (English Trans) Bangalore

ENDNOTES

1 In Volume 1, Shloka 5-8 of the Brihat Parashara Hora Shastra, it is stated that Jyotisha should not be imparted to those with unethical inclinations. This passage underscores that the knowledge of Jyotisha is considered sacred and is intended only for individuals of pure character and moral integrity: "*(...) only good will follow the teaching of this science to the disciples who are peacefully inclined, who honour the preceptors and elders, who speak only truth and who are God-fearing. Woeful for ever doubtlessly will it be to impart knowledge of this science to an unwilling student, to a heterodox and to a crafty person.*"

Chapter 5

Algorithmic Armaments: Social Media's Role in Information Warfare and Political Influence

Efnan Gülşen Özkan
https://orcid.org/0009-0004-3792-2313
Turkish National Police Academy, Turkey

ABSTRACT

This chapter explores the weaponization of social media as a transformative force in national security, international relations, and domestic politics. By examining key case studies—such as Facebook's role in the 2016 U.S. elections, the politicized functions of X during the 2024 election cycle, TikTok's involvement in the Mahsa Amini protests, and information warfare during the Russia-Ukraine conflict—the chapter illustrates how algorithm-driven platforms reshape political discourse and public perception. The analysis frames these developments through the lens of algorithmic targeting, diminished state control, and platform privatization, emphasizing the blurred boundaries between civic engagement and strategic influence. The chapter proposes the "Algorithmic Shaping Theory" to describe how social media platforms systematically structure public consciousness and behavior, urging a reevaluation of governance, surveillance, and global digital policy frameworks.

INTRODUCTION

> *"What we're building here is a machine that makes decisions for you. And you're just an input." Ex Machina (2014)*

The digital age has emerged as a significant era in which increasing competition within geopolitical power dynamics and the redefinition of strategies have become prominent. While the communication innovations brought by the digital

DOI: 10.4018/979-8-3373-7406-2.ch005

age—particularly social media platforms—initially appear to have positive qualities for society, they have in fact become critically important for international power balances, national security, and domestic political processes (Tucker et al., 2017). The redefinition of these power dynamics and strategies has introduced complex challenges and scenarios for national security, international relations, and domestic politics. Social media platforms are the most widely accepted and used innovations within communication technologies for society (Van Dijck et al., 2018). The primary reason for the deep penetration of these platforms into individuals' and societies' lives lies in their algorithms. These algorithms are developed based on psychological principles and human behavior—sometimes even targeting hormonal responses—making them deeply embedded and indispensable communication channels (Zuboff, 2019; Andrejevic, 2020). As social media becomes an integral part of daily life and personal spaces, it has also opened up new avenues of use in areas such as intelligence, national security, and international relations (Tucker et al., 2017). This emergence has led to new geopolitical power dynamics, necessitating novel strategies and generating diverse scenarios (Bradshaw & Howard, 2019). This study examines the complex relationship between social media algorithms and techno-political strategies in the digital age, focusing on how digital platforms shape narratives, influence perceptions, and impact public opinion.

The rise of platforms such as Facebook, Twitter (now rebranded as X), TikTok, and Instagram has brought about a revolutionary shift from the communication era to the information age, offering instantaneous, borderless interaction and communication opportunities. These platforms democratized content production by allowing individuals and societies to express their views to global audiences without the need for gatekeeping (Van Dijck et al., 2018). However, this democratization is dual-sided: while it empowers grassroots activities and fosters global connectivity, it simultaneously creates opportunities for various actors—such as non-state organizations, private companies, and foreign governments—to manipulate information and exert control over perception management (Freelon et al., 2022). This study illustrates the critical role of social media platforms and their algorithms in both internal and external political dynamics, national security, and interventions by private companies through real-world examples. The core reason behind algorithms' pivotal role lies in their focus on the individual rather than the society and their bottom-up approach to influence (Pariser, 2011; Gillespie, 2018). Since individuals lack traditional gatekeepers, they can be easily targeted and influenced, with their perceptions shaped more effortlessly. The personalized experience offered by social media algorithms places individuals in a stream they believe is shaped by their own preferences and interests, reminiscent of Plato's cave where prisoners perceive shadows on the wall as reality. However, this personalized flow is strategically directed toward collective goals. By targeting individuals first, the ultimate goal becomes the formation and direction of public opinion.

Algorithmic governance has become a central element in the transformative landscape of social media and communication. Algorithms play a pivotal role in curating content, utilizing complex mathematical models to analyze user behaviors and attitudes. This personalization enhances user engagement but also raises concerns about the formation of echo chambers, where individuals are predominantly exposed to information that reinforces their existing beliefs. Such environments can intensify societal polarization and diminish exposure to diverse perspectives (Kitchens, Johnson & Gray, 2020). The pervasive integration of social media algorithms into daily life extends beyond individual experiences, influencing geopolitical power dynamics. The dominance of private companies over these platforms poses challenges to national and international power structures, particularly for states. In response, governments have increasingly collaborated with private entities, sometimes providing support or funding to navigate this new strategic landscape (Bradshaw & Howard, 2019). A notable example is the 2024 rebranding of Twitter to X, which introduced operational changes that complicated the techno-political environment. Under new ownership, allegations emerged that X's algorithmic settings favored certain political narratives during the 2024 U.S. Presidential elections, potentially suppressing alternative viewpoints. Analyses suggested that these changes amplified specific narratives while marginalizing others, highlighting the significant influence of platform governance and algorithmic design on public opinion and democratic processes. The owner of X, Elon Musk, reportedly used the platform to promote his personal political views, including support for pro-Trump propaganda. This case underscores the critical role of social media platforms and their algorithms in shaping political discourse and influencing democratic outcomes.

The examples discussed are recent and underscore the techno-political context of this study. The intersection of social media algorithms with geopolitical strategies signifies a profound paradigm shift in international relations and national security processes. The capacity of these platforms to influence public attitudes and behaviors, mobilize action, and disseminate information—accurate or otherwise—necessitates a reevaluation of traditional security paradigms. Addressing the complexities and challenges posed by the weaponization of social media requires a multidisciplinary approach, incorporating insights from political science, international relations, information technology, management information systems, and intelligence studies. Policymakers, decision-makers, and technology companies must collaborate to establish robust mechanisms that safeguard democratic institutions and maintain international stability in the digital age (Zuboff, 2019; Cinelli et al., 2021).

THEORETICAL FRAMEWORK: ALGORITHMS, PERCEPTION, AND DATA SOVEREIGNTY

"How do you wake up from the Matrix when you don't know you're in the Matrix?" - Tristan Harris, The Social Dilemma (Former Design Ethicist at Google)

In the digital age, algorithms occupy a central position in the dissemination and consumption of information—whether accurate or false. When examined through a techno-political lens, algorithms profoundly influence public perception and power relations, producing dramatically different outcomes depending on their application. This section theoretically explores the foundations of algorithmic governance, focusing on how algorithms shape political discourse, reinforce biases and judgments, and influence democratic processes at both national and international levels. Drawing from fields such as platform capitalism, data sovereignty, and political communication, this chapter aims to demonstrate the wide-ranging effects of algorithmic systems on contemporary digital society. Algorithmic governance refers to the regulation and management of societal communication—particularly the distribution of information—through complex mathematical models. Social media platforms use such algorithms to select content for users, personalize experiences, and prioritize information flows. These systems rank and filter content based on users' preferences and behavioral patterns. While this process enhances engagement, time spent on platforms, and exposure, it also introduces risks such as reduced transparency, limited accountability, and increased susceptibility to manipulation (Zuboff, 2019; Helbing et al., 2021).

Initially developed to rank content in search engines or organize news feeds, algorithms now serve as tools for shaping perception, guiding power dynamics, and filtering or suppressing discourse. To understand the sociopolitical impact of digital technologies, one must first grasp the operational logic and structural mechanisms of algorithms. This requires moving beyond theoretical understanding to also address their technical functioning and behavioral or psychological impacts. At their core, algorithms consist of input, process, and output. On social media platforms, user-generated data and interactions—clicks, likes, shares, comments, and time spent—serve as inputs. These are then processed by machine learning algorithms and statistical models that analyze patterns to predict what content a user is likely to engage with next. Based on this prediction, the system generates a ranked output of content, creating a feedback loop where the resulting data becomes the new input. This potentially infinite loop is primarily fueled by user data. Figure 1 illustrates this process.

Figure 1. Feedback loop

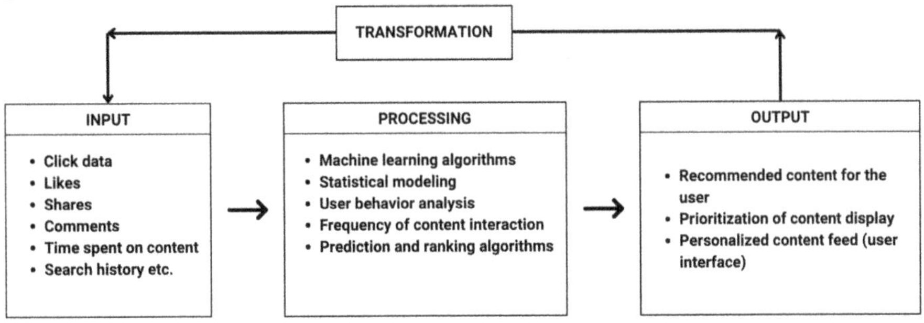

Figure 1 has been created by the author.

These algorithmic systems do more than personalize content—they also detect similarities among users, implementing techniques such as *collaborative filtering* to recommend content based on the behaviors of similar users. This leads to phenomena such as *echo chambers* and *filter bubbles*, which are discussed in more detail later. There are three primary technical models widely used in social media platforms: collaborative filtering, which makes recommendations based on similar user behavior; content-based filtering, which recommends items similar to those a user has interacted with previously; and hybrid models, which combine the strengths of both for higher accuracy (Ribeiro et al., 2020). These models effectively enclose users within algorithmic cages, exposing them to sociological and psychological manipulation. This manipulation—along with the ability to shape public perception—is of considerable interest to state and non-state actors alike. From a techno-political perspective, social media platforms and their algorithms are becoming increasingly pivotal in the reshaping of global power dynamics.

What makes algorithmic steering so powerful is the lack of transparency—users are unaware of the criteria determining the content they see. Platforms increasingly rely on deep learning models such as Convolutional Neural Networks (CNNs) for visual data, Recurrent Neural Networks (RNNs) and transformers for natural language processing. These models are trained on terabytes of data and continuously optimized through user interaction. Due to their complexity, even developers often do not fully understand their inner workings, a phenomenon known as epistemic opacity (Burrell, 2016). This asymmetry in knowledge creates a new form of power imbalance. Of particular concern to policymakers is the use of reinforcement learning, wherein algorithms learn from the outcomes they generate and adjust to maximize long-term engagement or profit. As user preferences are repeatedly reinforced, exposure to opposing or diverse views declines, forming echo chambers and filter bubbles. People are increasingly exposed only to information that confirms their existing beliefs, leading to ideological polarization (Cinelli et al., 2021). Research shows that hyperactive users—those with high interaction levels—can disproportionately shape public discourse. Algorithms may interpret the behaviors of these small but active groups as representative of broader trends, thereby distorting public opinion. Content that evokes strong emotions like anger, fear, or moral disgust is more likely to be prioritized by algorithms due to its higher engagement potential (Brady et al., 2021). These processes are not purely technical; they are embedded within the logic of platform capitalism. Social media platforms monetize attention by analyzing and processing user data to personalize content and target advertising. Users' behaviors are treated as a form of digital labor, and the users themselves become commodified. The data collected is repackaged as behavioral surplus and sold in secondary markets (Zuboff, 2019). Algorithms thereby redefine visibility, access to information, and even the production of value. From a data sovereignty perspective, this raises critical concerns regarding user control and consent.

Ultimately, in the techno-political context, algorithms do not merely curate content—they determine which messages, narratives, and discourses gain prominence. Politically charged content with high emotional impact and viral potential is more likely to be amplified. Advertising algorithms on platforms like Facebook and Google may even tailor exposure based on inferred political orientation, ethnicity, or gender, leading to micro-targeting strategies that reinforce existing beliefs rather than persuading undecided voters. This can result in algorithmic exclusion, where some views are highly visible while others are drowned in digital silence. Therefore, algorithms must no longer be seen as neutral technological tools. They are active agents in shaping perception, attention, and visibility. They not only determine what we see, but how we see it. Understanding algorithms is no longer merely a technical skill; it is a democratic necessity. Only through a multidisciplinary approach and effective regulation can we restore individual and societal autonomy in the face of these invisible systems of control.

THE TRANSFORMATION OF SOCIAL MEDIA PLATFORMS: FROM SUBJECTS TO ACTORS

"The medium is the message." – Marshall McLuhan (Media Theorist, Understanding Media)

Social media platforms represent a revolutionary means and source of communication in the digital age. Unlike traditional media, these digital environments have evolved into not only communication channels but also prominent actors in the production and circulation of influence and information. Their role has expanded far beyond facilitating social interaction to exerting global influence and shaping public opinion. As these platforms gain increasing political and economic power, their influence extends deeper into social structures, international relations, and even national security contexts. The fact that such critical influence can be achieved with minimal regulatory scrutiny is one of the key factors behind their unchecked growth. This section analyzes the transformation of social media platforms from communicative subjects to powerful agents capable of restructuring the public sphere.

From Twitter to X: Privatization and the Restriction of Public Interest

The acquisition of Twitter by Elon Musk and its subsequent rebranding as "X" exemplifies the transformation of social media platforms from communication tools into political and economic power actors. This transformation became highly visible during the 2024 U.S. presidential election, in which Musk played an influential role in shaping political discourse through the platform. Under Musk's leadership, the platform began to act as a tool for reshaping the socio-political landscape, moving away from serving the public good toward prioritizing private and political interests. Public utility has increasingly been substituted by commercial incentives, transforming users from participants into products. This reflects a broader trend where the platform evolves from being a passive subject to an active agent that uses user-generated content to further political, economic, and security agendas. A critical concern here is the absence of ethical frameworks and accountability mechanisms. Algorithmic systems devoid of normative human values determine the content users encounter. Furthermore, the collection of user data—once framed as benign analytics—has become a deeply contested issue, as this data is now used for political profiling and behavioral manipulation. Elon Musk reportedly donated approximately $259 million to various Super PACs supporting Donald Trump during the 2024 U.S. election campaign (Reuters, 2024). Notably, the America PAC received the largest share of this amount, while RBG PAC received $20 million, funding messages likening Trump's abortion stance to that of liberal icon Ruth Bader Ginsburg (The Guardian, 2024). Simultaneously, X's algorithms were allegedly adjusted to boost pro-Trump content, intensifying concerns over algorithmic bias. Additionally, the platform was reportedly used to disseminate announcements from federal agencies, blurring the lines between private ownership and public communication infrastructure (Napoli, 2019). These developments illustrate how platforms like X no longer serve merely as conduits for speech but act as political agents with the power to manipulate information flows, compromise electoral integrity, and undermine democratic norms (Balkin, 2018; Zuboff, 2019). The exploitation of user data for political targeting brings forward urgent ethical and legal questions regarding surveillance capitalism, privacy, and the erosion of civic trust.

Musk's ownership highlights the rising influence of private capital in shaping the digital public sphere. The consolidation of such influence into the hands of a single actor—backed by powerful algorithms—calls for a reassessment of platform governance, ownership structures, and democratic safeguards. Upholding principles such as transparency, accountability, and neutrality is critical for ensuring that these platforms contribute positively to the public interest.

Meta/Facebook: From Social Network to Electoral Engineering

One of the most evident examples of the transformation social media platforms have undergone, and the impact they have had on individuals and society, is the Facebook platform (now Meta). Initially developed as a platform to sustain social relationships between individuals in the digital arena, Facebook allowed users to reconnect with elementary school friends, share personal statuses (relationships, status, work, etc.), and engage in social interactions. Over time, however, through the development of algorithms and data-driven targeting systems, the platform evolved from a simple social network into a powerful force capable of shaping political processes and impacting society at large. One of the critical turning points in this transformation was the 2016 U.S. Presidential Elections. Facebook's relationship with the data analysis company Cambridge Analytica came to public attention, revealing that user data was collected without consent and used in political campaigns (Tufekci, 2018). Cambridge Analytica accessed data from about 87 million Facebook users through personality tests conducted on the platform in an effort to predict their personality traits. The collected and analyzed data were used to model individuals' political inclinations and engage in manipulative perception campaigns via micro-targeting (Hinds, Williams & Joinson, 2020). This pivotal event demonstrated that social media platforms are not just tools of communication brought about by technology, but rather political actors that can shape public opinion. Meta tracks user interactions and personal data, analyzing every detail from content preferences to engagement durations, and, based on this data, presents personalized advertisements and news feeds. This process not only enabled political figures and parties to directly reach voters, but also gave rise to an algorithm with the potential to shape individuals' political preferences (Huq, 2024). The recognition of this power raised certain threats and questions. Facebook's algorithmic systems analyze users' past behaviors to highlight similar content, thereby creating echo chambers and filter bubbles (Pariser, 2011). This leads to individuals encountering only content that aligns with their views, weakening the democratic information environment. The Cambridge Analytica scandal revealed the lack of transparency in Facebook's data collection and usage practices, leading to intense ethical and legal criticisms (Cohen, 2019). In the aftermath, data protection regulations were implemented, particularly in the European Union, and awareness regarding users' data privacy increased (Bradshaw et al., 2019). The European Union's General Data Protection Regulation (GDPR) is one example of such measures, which became more effectively enforced after this incident. The use of algorithmic power, as seen in this case, not only threatens individual privacy but also the legitimacy of democratic processes. Platforms like Meta, whose algorithms can be manipulated by political actors, are now a political issue closely tied to national security, public opinion, democratic values, and power dynamics, rather than a mere technological concern (Van Dijck, 2013).

TikTok: The New Paradigm of Mass Mobilization through Algorithmic Guidance

Among the most recent social media platforms of the digital age and currently one of the most viral, TikTok has transcended its role as a social media platform. Through its algorithmic structure, TikTok has become a digital power actor capable of shaping public opinion, setting agendas, and triggering social movements. Unlike traditional mass communication platforms, TikTok's algorithm works based on hyper-personalization techniques derived from an individual's interaction history. The content shown to a user is determined by viewing time, user-producer interactions, sharing tendencies, and metadata analysis (Munger, 2021). This process, known as "algorithmic steering," directs users toward certain content, paving the way for them to adopt specific viewpoints without their awareness (Binns, 2018). TikTok's "For You Page" (FYP) algorithm not only increases the viral potential of produced content but also develops the nature of digital activism patterns (Gillespie, 2018). Users constantly exposed to similar views are more likely to encounter echo chambers and confirmation bias, increasing polarization within the public sphere (Tufekci, 2015). This creates a manipulation mechanism with complex calculations that can also self-learn. The effect of TikTok on mass mobilization has been clearly observed in various protest movements. The democracy protests in Hong Kong, the women's rights protests in Iran following the death of Mahsa Amini, and awareness content related to the Black Lives Matter movement demonstrate the platform's role in converting digital participation into societal and physical activism (Morozov, 2018; Walsh, 2024). In this context, TikTok can be regarded as not just a content production and sharing tool, but also as a catalyst for "cyber-social mobilization". However, this mobilization potential also offers strategic intervention opportunities for states and private interest groups. Since TikTok is owned by the Chinese company ByteDance, there is a possibility that user data could be shared with the Chinese government under China's Cybersecurity Law, which has been considered a "national security threat" by Western states, especially the United States (Huq, 2024). In this context, the platform is categorized as a "hybrid threat" on both technical and normative levels (Pomerantsev, 2019).

TikTok's vast data corpus, when combined with AI-based content personalization and steering algorithms, creates an unpredictable space for power use by external actors. Concepts such as information warfare, perception operations, and cognitive conflict are now applied not only in state-centric security strategies but also in digital processes conducted through platforms like TikTok. Especially in the information age, certain ideological messages or disinformation content becoming more visible through algorithms marks the beginning of a new era in shaping and even creating public opinion. TikTok, therefore, has become a hybrid actor in the field of digital geopolitics, characterized by both opportunities and risks in transnational and cross-border information struggles (Fuchs, 2020). The lack of transparency in its algorithmic infrastructure transforms the platform into a strategic tool for intelligence gathering, social engineering, and psychological operations (psyops) (Andrejevic, 2019). In an environment where the content users are exposed to is shaped by AI decisions, traditional media literacy may not be sufficient. This makes "algorithmic literacy" and "digital awareness" increasingly important concepts (Binns, 2018). Thus, TikTok has evolved into a multi-dimensional phenomenon at the center of global digital competition. It is no longer just a tool for entertainment or content production, but has become a platform that should be analyzed at geopolitical, psychological, and techno-political levels (Gerbaudo, 2024). From a techno-political perspective, the manipulation of masses can now be achieved not only through ideological discourse but also through algorithmic constructions. This reality indicates that social media platforms like TikTok will play a decisive role in shaping new generations of security understandings in the digital age (Huq, 2024).

Complex Relationships Between States and Platforms

From a techno-political perspective in the digital age, the concept of national sovereignty has expanded beyond physical borders. Sovereignty is now also processed through data sovereignty, digital assets, and ownership of algorithms (Binns, 2018). As the concept of sovereignty takes on new definitions, it has also become dependent on the control of digital infrastructures, data flows, and algorithmic systems. Social media platforms, which represent a critical point in this transformation, stand as hybrid actors confronting national governments' regulatory capacities. States wish to regulate these platforms for reasons such as national security, social order, and data sovereignty; on the other hand, platforms resist these regulatory efforts to preserve their commercial and cultural influence and protect their profits (Van Dijck, 2013). In this context, regulations like the European Union's Digital Services Act

(DSA) aim to make platforms more accountable in areas such as content moderation, transparency principles, and user safety (Bradshaw et al., 2019). The law introduces new obligations regarding algorithmic responsibility, the removal of illegal content, combating disinformation, and protecting personal data. The pressure exerted by the United States on TikTok is shaped by concerns regarding the ownership of digital infrastructure and the geopolitical competition with China, focusing on issues such as data nationalism and strategic dependency (Pomerantsev, 2019). In both cases, states are positioning platforms not only as commercial but also as strategic actors and developing intervention mechanisms (Morozov, 2018). The relationship between states and platforms is not merely one of conflict. As highlighted in reports by the OECD, many states actively use social media platforms for public communication, crisis management, the promotion of public policies, and even the digitalization of governance processes (Gerbaudo, 2024). This example demonstrates that there is a model of asymmetric yet interdependent collaboration between states and social media platforms. For instance, in times of crisis (such as during a pandemic, natural disasters, or wars), social media has become an indispensable information channel for official government communication (Tufekci, 2017).

On the other hand, social media platforms are also venues for cross-border communication, public diplomacy, cyber influence operations, and perception management. Analyses published in ISSJournal show that digital platforms are used by foreign policy actors to both manage domestic public opinion and influence foreign public opinion (Morozov, 2018). Accordingly, social media has become an algorithmic weapon not only for non-state actors but also for states. The struggle is now centered around fundamental concepts such as digital sovereignty, algorithmic governance, data nationalism, and information security (Fuchs, 2020). The strategies of platforms to evade state control and the efforts of states to re-establish their authority over the digital realm have become one of the most critical political issues of the digital age. In the future, how this tension evolves will directly affect the boundaries of the digital public sphere and the future of the internet (Van Dijck, 2013).

CASE STUDIES I – ELECTION MANIPULATIONS AND THE ENCROACHMENT OF THE DEMOCRATIC SPACE

-*"People believe what they see, and what they see is what we tell them." Wag the Dog (1997)*

In the techno-political landscape of the digital age, the concept of geopolitics has undergone a significant transformation, particularly in election processes. Social media platforms have moved beyond being mere spaces for individual interaction and have become important tools for mass manipulation and public opinion formation. This transformation has had a significant impact on the shaping of democratic processes and societal participation, with the digital battlefield now being a key site for election manipulation wars. This section will examine the role of social media platforms in election manipulations and assess the impact of these manipulations on democratic participation.

Facebook and the 2016 US Elections: Cambridge Analytica, Targeting Algorithms, Fake News

The 2016 US Presidential Elections marked a pivotal moment for digital election engineering and social media algorithm-driven manipulation. The Cambridge Analytica scandal became one of the most notable examples of how personal data could be used for economic and political interests in the digital world. Cambridge Analytica illegally harvested Facebook users' personal data and used it to target political propaganda. (Hinds, Williams & Joinson, 2020). Along with the collection of personal interaction and communication data, algorithms enabled the presentation of highly detailed, personalized, and subconscious content to individual users. Targeting algorithms were developed to analyze users' interests, emotional states, behaviors, and attitudes on social media platforms and deliver the most appropriate messages to them. (Gerbaudo, 2024) The critical point here is that these messages are no longer guided solely by economic and commercial concerns but also by political agendas. (Tufekci, 2017) Such algorithms have the ability to deliver content personalized to a degree previously impossible with traditional media outlets. What distinguishes the algorithms used by social media platforms from traditional media is that individuals do not have any gatekeeper to protect them from such content. (Gerbaudo, 2024) While traditional media outlets are regulated by institutions, organizations, state bodies, and laws, social media platforms are not subject to sufficient authority. (Van Dijck, 2013) This gap creates the dangerous consequence of direct access to and influence over individuals. (Tufekci, 2017)

In addition to these issues, fake news has become one of the biggest problems on Facebook. Unverified stories spread rapidly through algorithms, overshadowing accurate information. The spread of false or misleading news harmed the election process and eroded public trust. (Pariser, 2011) These manipulative propaganda games, particularly targeting specific demographic groups such as Black and Hispanic voters, aimed to prevent them from participating in the election. (Morozov, 2018) This situation demonstrates how digital environments can undermine healthy public participation in democracies. Facebook, while taking steps to combat these manipulations, created a situation that questioned the platform's reliability and transparency due to the nature of algorithms and the rapid spread of such manipulations. (Van Dijck, 2013) The involvement of social media platforms in political processes should not be exemplified by only one platform. Twitter, now known as X, one of the oldest social media platforms, underwent a transformation when it was bought by Elon Musk, who also serves as an advisor to the US President Donald Trump's informal Government Efficiency Department (DOGE), for $44 billion in 2022. During this process, some employees were laid off, and policies on hate speech, misinformation, and user verification were updated, leading to the rebranding of Twitter as X. (Tufekci, 2015) In this process, significant changes were made to the platform's content moderation policies. These changes led to the rapid spread of misinformation and the rise of bot networks. The spread of misinformation, coupled with the dynamics of bot networks, raised concerns about the upcoming election process. Furthermore, Elon Musk's partisan stance further intensified these concerns. Musk donated a total of $259 million to Donald Trump's campaign during the 2024 elections. Of this donation, $239 million was funneled through the America PAC he established, with the remaining $20 million directed to the RBG PAC. Musk's political involvement extended beyond financial donations, as he participated in campaign rallies with Trump and used X to increase Trump's visibility. After Trump's election as President, Musk led a task force aiming to reduce government spending and regulation, further strengthening his ties with Trump. Musk's partisan stance and his ability to direct algorithms on the platform sparked debates about the potential spread of false information and manipulative content influencing voters' decisions. His emphasis on freedom of speech created challenges in fulfilling the platform's responsibility to moderate content, which eroded trust in democratic processes (Dawsey, Dou & Siddiqui, 2024; The Guardian 2024).

Points Where Democratic Participation Is Replaced by Behavioral Engineering

Social media platforms, initially perceived as tools to enhance democratic participation for political parties and voters, have over time evolved into powerful instruments in the field of behavioral engineering (Tufekci, 2015). States or non-state actors have begun to utilize these platforms to manipulate voters and shape perceptions (Bradshaw & Howard, 2017). Algorithms and targeting strategies are potent enough to steer voters toward specific behaviors and thought patterns (Gillespie, 2018). This process has led not only to manipulations during elections but also to a weakening of democratic participation in society at large (Tufekci, 2015). Social media platforms possess the power to shape the thoughts and behaviors of their users (Van Dijck, 2013). For instance, platforms influence voters not only with personalized content that captures their interests but also with content that emotionally and behaviorally manipulates them (Zuboff, 2019). Behavioral engineering can extend beyond elections to influence how users act in their daily lives and respond to certain content.

By analyzing viewing durations, interactions, and comments, these platforms can shape individuals' free will through algorithms and platform mechanisms (Gillespie, 2018). While the concept of democracy is built upon free thought and participation, such manipulations can lead to the erosion of democratic processes (Tufekci, 2015). The role of social media platforms in elections of international significance stands as one of the most prominent examples demonstrating the impact of the digital world on democratic processes (Bradshaw & Howard, 2017). Facebook's manipulation during the 2016 elections and Twitter's (now X) creation of democratic distrust during the 2024 elections illustrate how behavioral engineering affects democracy and reveal the complexity and effectiveness of the power struggle in the digital realm (Hinds, Williams & Joinson, 2020). In this context, it is evident that social media platforms are not merely spaces for individual expression. They have also become tools for societal and political influence (Tufekci, 2015). Consequently, the process in which democratic participation is replaced by behavioral engineering poses a growing threat in future elections, especially with the advancing momentum of artificial intelligence and algorithms (Zuboff, 2019).

CASE STUDIES II – NEW TOOLS OF PROTEST AND RESISTANCE

"If you want to control the people, control what they see and hear." – The X-Files (1993–2018)

Social media platforms are also closely related to the fields of security and intelligence (Bradshaw & Howard, 2017). Particularly when examined from a techno-political perspective, social media platforms have recently emerged as highly effective tools not only for political campaigns and election manipulations but also for societal protests, resistance movements, and certain activities (Tufekci, 2015). These platforms, which contribute to the rapid transformation of protests into mass movements, have become digital spaces where individuals can make their voices heard and drive societal change (Tufekci, 2015). This section will examine the potential and role of TikTok's advanced content algorithm in certain social movements

TikTok, Algorithms, and the Mahsa Amini Protests: Visual Protest, Viral Memory, and Digital Social Movements

In 2022, the death of Mahsa Amini, who was detained by Iran's "morality police," sparked a significant social protest movement not only within Iran but also globally. One of the most influential platforms supporting the digital visibility and worldwide dissemination of these protests was TikTok, a social media platform based on short video sharing. In this context, TikTok transcended its role as merely a video content sharing platform, becoming a digital public sphere where social movements took shape, gained visibility, and generated resistance. TikTok's sophisticated and complex "For You Page" (FYP) algorithm prioritizes content based on users' interests, interactions, and behaviors on the platform. This prioritization algorithm analyzes extensive user data, including time spent on videos, speed of likes, and comment reading activities, to provide a highly personalized content stream. During the Mahsa Amini protests, this advanced algorithmic structure played a significant role in making protest videos go viral (Walsh, 2024). These protest videos were not solely informational; the algorithms also engaged users through aesthetic and emotional narratives, creating a global "algorithmic collective memory" (Gensburger & Clavert, 2024). This algorithmic collective memory is continually updated and recirculated through the digital reproduction of protest images, chants, bodies, and rituals. This process can be described in social media terms as becoming "viral content." For instance, following the virality of Mahsa Amini protest content on TikTok, actions such as women cutting their hair, removing headscarves, or footage of security forces' harsh interventions became symbolic activities where individual experiences transformed into collective resistance through TikTok (Arafat & Khamis, 2025). In this context, the platform evolved into an effective space for feminist digital activism and visual protest. These digital spaces, particularly where women became subjects, disrupted traditional patriarchal representations and produced alternative public narratives (Arafat & Khamis, 2025).

While TikTok's advanced algorithms played a significant role in enhancing the visibility of protests, they also faced structural issues such as content censorship and algorithmic control. During the Mahsa Amini protests, it was alleged that TikTok's content algorithm prioritized certain protest content while simultaneously suppressing specific protest and propaganda content, especially in regions with strong state repression (Walsh, 2024). This indicates that the platform's algorithms are subject to techno-political decisions regarding which content remains in circulation or is more prominently displayed. TikTok's content management is primarily conducted through automated systems, user reports, and relatively opaque content filtering rules. Findings suggesting that some videos were removed or their visibility reduced under pressure from the Iranian government highlight the tension between digital freedom of expression and state repression (Walsh, 20244). The censorship applied not only involves the removal of content but also its algorithmic suppression, thereby attempting to weaken the digital protest memory. Simultaneously, the Mahsa Amini protests revealed state efforts to control social media platforms. The Iranian government restricted access to platforms like TikTok and Instagram to prevent and control the spread of protests, developed measures against VPN usage, and targeted digital content creators. Such interventions demonstrate that digital public spheres are vulnerable to state control. This should not be considered unique to Iran. Globally, many states are developing legal frameworks to regulate and control social media platform content. Practices such as China's strict censorship policies, India's data localization requirements for platforms, and Turkey's regulations mandating digital platforms to establish local representation illustrate the increasing influence of states over the digital realm. In this framework, TikTok can be seen as a dual-edged arena of power: on one hand, providing visibility to social movements, and on the other, becoming a digital world that states can use as a tool to suppress these movements.

CASE STUDY III – WAR AND PERCEPTION: THE DIGITAL BATTLEFIELD

"What is real? How do you define real?" – The Matrix (1999)

The nature of warfare has undergone a significant transformation with the rise of the digital age and its accompanying technologies. Parallel to traditional battlefields, there now exists a domain of conflict shaped by information, perception, and digital media: the digital battlefield. Notably, the recent Russia-Ukraine War has emerged not only as a conventional military conflict but also as a prominent example of an information war conducted through social media, algorithms, content creation, and intelligence operations. This section examines the struggles over perception management, propaganda practices, and disinformation strategies shaped through social media platforms.

Social Media and Information Warfare: Digital Platforms as Arenas of Propaganda

The Russia-Ukraine War stands out as one of the most striking examples of propaganda activities conducted in digital media. Both sides have utilized social media not merely as tools for disseminating information and announcements but also as weapons of psychological warfare and perception management. The study identifies social media as an effective tool for producing disinformation, spreading manipulative content, and directing mass psychology.

From the early stages of the Russia-Ukraine War, both Russia and Ukraine have actively used platforms like TikTok, Telegram, and X. Russia has particularly produced content through specific troll groups on Telegram, while Ukraine has effectively utilized visual-focused platforms (TikTok, Instagram) to showcase the tragic aspects of the war, document human rights violations globally, and garner international support. TikTok's content structure (short videos) possesses the potential to rapidly disseminate war visuals to users. Through hashtags like #StandWithUkraine and

#DonbasWar, war moments, amateur footage, and audiovisual montages have been conveyed to the international public. However, the same algorithm has also facilitated the spread of disinformation-based content. For instance, some images shared on TikTok during the early stages of the war were later revealed to be from different time periods or even different geographical locations. TikTok's For You Page (FYP) algorithm enhances the visibility of video content with high engagement, making the rapid spread of emotionally charged videos inevitable. This situation encourages propaganda mechanisms to produce content based on emotional manipulation (Bösch, & Divon, 2024; Astuti, Attaymini, & Dewi, 2022).

Throughout the war, the following manipulation and perception strategies have been observed on social media platforms like X and Telegram:

- Deepfake videos: Fake videos claiming that Zelensky had surrendered to Russia were disseminated (Chemerys, 2023).
- Troll armies: Coordinated accounts labeled Putin as a “charismatic leader” and Zelensky as a “comedian,” shaping public perception (Moreno Rubio, 2022).
- Symbolic hashtags: Russia's “#Uraa” call reinforced feelings of national belonging and nationalism by referencing past wars (Astuti, Attaymini, & Dewi, 2022).
- Manipulated heroism content: Both sides produced videos glorifying their soldiers (Astuti, Attaymini, & Dewi, 2022).

These examples demonstrate, within Foucault's discourse analysis framework, that power is produced not only physically but also at the narrative level (Foucault, 1975). Every piece of content produced in the digital environment constructs a new realm of truth. In the post-truth era, public opinions based on emotions rather than information are easily formed by algorithms. In this context, the information literacy skills of social media users determine how war content is internalized. Propaganda should be viewed not only as the creation of fake information and disinformative content but also as an activity that directs individuals toward specific political attitudes in an emotional and symbolic context. Therefore, the digital literacy skills of social media users hold strategic importance, especially during critical periods (wars, disasters, etc.).

Furthermore, social media platforms have become suitable not only for information warfare but also for conventional military warfare. Platforms like Telegram, focused on communication, have facilitated the sharing of frontline movements, coordination of military support, and logistical information through established chat groups. Social media platforms are no longer merely in the “background” or “influencers” of war but have become powerful weapons directly involved in warfare. The Russia-Ukraine War has revealed a hybrid type of warfare where new-generation media is used not only as a communication and interaction-focused entertainment center but also as a direct battlefield. Platforms like TikTok, X, and Telegram occupy a critical position in information wars, reproducing visibility, truth, and spheres of influence regarding the war through content flow algorithms (Alyukov, Kunilovskaya & Semenov, 2023).

ALGORITHMIC SHAPING THEORY

"What will happen to society, politics and daily life when non-conscious but highly intelligent algorithms know us better than we know ourselves?" (Harari, Homo Deus: A brief history of tomorrow, 2016)

The rise of the digital age has brought with it the development of the concept of techno-politics, and understanding this concept more clearly is now of paramount importance. Its presence in areas such as intelligence, national security, and geopolitics is not only significant but must now be understood and developed. The most important area where technology has found its place in politics is the use of social media platforms. Social media platforms and digital spaces have evolved into a significant structure that shapes individual behaviors, societal structures, thoughts, and even political processes (Zuboff, 2019). Most of these structures are driven and shaped by algorithms that, at some point, are no longer understood by users or even developers, and are complex and advanced (Pasquale, 2015). Algorithmic shaping operates by collecting and analyzing data in a deductive awareness toward collective public opinion after processing individual actions. Algorithms on social media platforms create a vast area of influence, from managing societal norms to generating massive data from the individual interaction and communication preferences of many people through platforms that provide innocent communication and interaction (Tufekci, 2015). Algorithms determine what content flow users will see within the app, what advertisements and content they will be exposed to, and whom they will interact with, offering prioritized scenarios that include such recommendations (Gillespie, 2014). This complex process, which initially aimed at personalizing a flow by processing data on individual preferences at the start of the platforms, has gradually started to be used to shape societal consciousness and behaviors (Beer, 2017).

Shaping theory argues that there is a structure that targets not only individual behaviors but also societal thought structures and attitudes. Since reaching large masses of society at this speed is incredibly difficult in normal and physical conditions, this method has become a powerful tool due to the ease of reaching individuals (Fuchs, 2017). In today's information age, as mentioned above, we are not only experiencing conventional wars. Information warfare has created a turning point in terms of national security, power politics, and intelligence (Rid, 2020). Information warfare, using soft powers, is a war method that affects the masses, determining victories and defeats without using hard power (Nye, 2004). When discussing information warfare, we must not ignore the formation and dissemination power of information in the digital age. In this context, it is clear that knowledge is the most important weapon. The way that social media platforms process user data as a weapon can be more easily understood with Figure 2.

Figure 2. Weaponization of user data

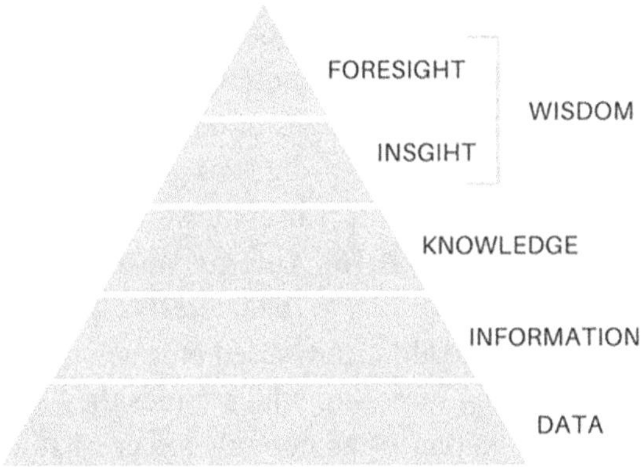

Extended by the author based on Ackoff's (1989) DIKW Pyramid model and in light of the analyses and interpretations made by Rowley (2007).

By starting with the data pyramid seen in Figure 2, the massive data piles obtained from users on social media platforms first turn into meaningful information and then into processable knowledge (Rowley, 2007). In this information age, where knowledge and data are considered the greatest power, the ammunition of social media platforms is quite vast (Van Dijck, 2014). However, it is not enough just to obtain knowledge and data. These data must be analyzed, and insights must be created, after which foresight formed by the insights will be the most critical point in shifting power balances in the techno-political context (Andrejevic, 2013). The wisdom part is created by these insights and foresights. In the information age, social media platforms have reached this power through complex algorithms, thanks to machine learning algorithms and complex computations that can generate trillions of diverse user scenarios, using their predictions in the most advantageous way (Kitchin, 2014). In this context, it is clear, as discussed at the beginning of the paper, that they do not merely aim for commercial and economic interests. The fact that algorithms have so much control over the masses, knowing and analyzing users better than users themselves, makes it easier for them to shape perceptions and change thoughts (Eubanks, 2018). Shaping theory also argues that individuals' perceptions are shaped by those who are in power in various domains like political, psychological, geopolitical, and economic fields, whether it is a person, company, institution, or organization (Foucault, 1975). In this sense, digital platforms have become an important actor in reshaping societal dynamics rather than just focusing on individuals (Couldry & Mejias, 2019).

The more a user is directed to certain types of content on a social media platform, the more they will consume that type of content, and as individuals continue to consume the same content, this consumption will reflect in the general perception of society (Pariser, 2011). Algorithms can have a determining effect on societal norms and values, because as users are continuously exposed to certain types of content, these contents start to settle in the societal consciousness (Bucher, 2018).

The idea that algorithms were initially neutral and only aimed at processing data was a common view during the early stages of digital platforms, but over time, it has become clear that this view is collapsing (Pasquale, 2015). Today, algorithms do not just process data; they also direct users towards specific thoughts, behaviors, and actions (Mittelstadt et al., 2016). This guidance brings about the idea that such direction can be shaped according to the interests of the platform owners and administrators. For example, the algorithms used on a news site provide users with specific types of news, thereby imposing which topics they should have thoughts about (Napoli, 2019). Such guidance can not only affect what users are exposed to but also how they think. On social media platforms, users generally only encounter content that agrees with their own views, leading to the polarization of opinions and the narrowing of societal perceptions (Sunstein, 2018). Moreover, preference production is also an important function of algorithms. Algorithms present options to users, often shaped by their previous actions and preferences, without the user's awareness (Zuboff, 2019). This process restricts the users' decision-making abilities and may push them to consume more and interact more. As a result, algorithms not only suggest content but also have the power to direct and shape the thoughts and attitudes of users (Gillespie, 2014). This creates a significant barrier to individuals' free will and reveals the societal-level impacts of algorithmic shaping (Eubanks, 2018).

Building on the example of news websites, it can be said that agenda-setting is one of the most powerful features of algorithms (McCombs, 2004). Social media platforms and digital spaces have the power to influence users' thoughts and attitudes on societal issues and topics in the agenda (Van Dijck & Poell, 2013). When content related to an event in the agenda spreads quickly, it creates an impact on societal consciousness and shapes how people think about that event (Chadwick, 2017). The responses given by users through algorithms lead them to interact with other users who have similar views and reactions. Opinion polarization and exposure to the same views are thus achieved (Sunstein, 2018). The reinforcement of a particular view is an effect caused by the algorithms on social media platforms. In this regard, filtering is another powerful strategy of algorithms. This strategy can prevent certain types of content from being seen by users, or suppress them to the point of invisibility (Binns et al., 2018). For example, content containing misinformation or disinformation on a platform may be filtered out by algorithms, hiding it from users. However, this filtering also leads to the exclusion of certain ideas and perspectives. This situation may increase societal polarization and obstruct democratic discussions (Helberger et al., 2020).

In conclusion, algorithmic shaping theory presents an important conceptual framework showing that digital platforms have become powerful tools for shaping not only individual behaviors but also societal views and behaviors. Algorithms do not merely affect individual behavior; they shape societal norms, values, and ideologies (Zuboff, 2019). The collapse of algorithmic neutrality demonstrates the increasing influence of algorithms, which are used by digital platforms for strategic purposes (Pasquale, 2015). Visibility, agenda-setting, and filtering have become key tools in shaping the power dynamics of platforms. This situation helps us understand in-depth how algorithms can limit individuals' free will and their societal-level effects (Couldry & Mejias, 2019).

CONCLUSION

As inspired by Zygmunt Bauman's thoughts on digital surveillance, it can be said: Modern power "wanted to be seen"; digital power, however, "wants to see" (Lyon, 2010).

As we approach the second quarter of the 21st century, with digital technologies permeating nearly every aspect of human life, traditional understandings of power and sovereignty are undergoing a significant transformation (Castells, 2015). At the core of this transformation are digital platforms and spaces equipped with multi-layered and complex algorithms, such as social media platforms, content-sharing applications, search engines, and digital advertising systems. Although these platforms were initially created as communication tools, they have evolved into powerful actors on the world stage that function in information production, perception management, and societal perception shaping (Van Dijck, 2013).

Understanding the multifaceted effects of these digital platforms on modern social structures, their regulatory needs, and the nature of emerging digital power is crucial in the digital age (Binns, 2018). Digital platforms and their algorithms, through big data analytics, can predict, direct, and even shape user behaviors (Greene, Martens, & Shmueli, 2022). This indicates the emergence of a new form of power that extends beyond the traditional centralized state structure (Benkler, 2016). Digital power arises not only from economic and commercial strength but also from information regimes built on data, the capacity to manipulate user behaviors, and the ability to shape and direct public opinion (Tufekci, 2015). This type of power aligns with Michel Foucault's conceptualization of biopolitics (Foucault, 2008). Digital platforms collect the most intimate data about individuals' daily lives, viewing them as manageable, monitorable, and directable subjects (Zuboff, 2019). This process transforms users from passive consumers into active data producers while simultaneously subjecting them to algorithmic domination (Andrejevic, 2014). The notion that social media users are seen not as individuals but as products by platforms is strikingly presented in Netflix's documentary "The Social Dilemma" with the statement, "If you don't pay for the product, you are the product" (Orlowski, 2020). Additionally, Edward Tufte's remark in the same documentary, "There are only two industries that call their customers 'users': illegal drugs and software," highlights the ruthlessness of sectors emerging with the acceleration of the digital age (Tufte, 2006).

Consequently, digital platforms can be said to hold hegemonic power over information as both producers and distributors of information (Bennett, 2017). On the other hand, Jürgen Habermas's concept of the "public sphere" represents a democratic space where individuals freely express and acquire opinions, constructing common sense (Habermas, 1989). However, the near-monopolization and privatization of this space by social media platforms have led to a significant transformation in the structure of the public sphere (Fuchs, 2017). Discussions in public, political, economic, and other areas now occur on privately owned platforms, whose algorithmic structures determine which voices are heard and which are suppressed (Couldry & Hepp, 2017). This new digital public sphere creates new sources of problems for both states and citizens (Gillespie, 2018). Notably, social movements where digital media played an active role, such as the Mahsa Amini protests and the George Floyd protests in the USA, have demonstrated that digital spaces can function not only as areas of interaction and discussion but also as spaces for organization and resistance (Tufekci, 2017). However, this also raises concerns about the potential for digital companies to directly or indirectly intervene in political processes and situations. For instance, a US-based platform collecting data from social media users in Europe or content censorship practices in China bring into question the jurisdiction of local laws over global digital actors. In this context, the European Union's Digital Services Act (DSA) and General Data Protection Regulation (GDPR) are considered significant steps toward protecting digital sovereignty. Nevertheless, the global applicability of these regulations remains a serious question (Bennett & Raab, 2017). The US's more free-market-based approach leaves the responsibilities of digital platforms to voluntary declarations, potentially rendering regulations ineffective (Floridi, 2020). Countries like China and Russia, on the other hand, are constructing a different authoritarian digital sovereignty model by bringing platforms under direct state control (Zeng, Stevens & Chen, 2017).

Current national and international legal systems struggle to keep pace with the rapid nature of social media platforms and digital spaces (Binns, 2018). Many countries lack adequate legal frameworks in areas such as disinformation, data breaches, content manipulation, cyberbullying, and cyber fraud (Tambini, 2017). This situation threatens both the protection of individual rights and societal security (Gillespie, 2018). Therefore, a multi-actor governance structure has become necessary for the supervision of digital platforms (Seattle University, n.d.). A transparent, inclusive, and accountable digital governance model should be adopted, involving states, the private sector, academia, civil society organizations (CSOs), and international organizations (Couldry & Hepp, 2017). Such a model should be structured to ensure both the protection of digital rights and the fulfillment of platforms' responsibilities toward individuals and societies. The automation of decisions by algorithms regarding what individuals see, think, and even feel leads to the confinement of individuals within content bubbles and echo chambers, weakening democratic debate and increasing societal polarization (Zuboff, 2019). Therefore, the transparency and auditability of algorithms are of great importance. Algorithms are not merely commercial tools but also social engineering systems with public consequences. In this context, the concept of "algorithmic accountability" should be placed at the center of digital public policies (Caplan et al., 2018). Digital platforms should operate not only for economic gain and revenue maximization but also with the responsibility of creating societal benefits and preventing disinformation (Greene, Martens, & Shmueli, 2022). Digital public interest can be achieved by platforms preventing disinformation, combating hate speech, respecting privacy rights, and promoting democratic participation (Floridi, 2020).

In addition to their socio-cultural impacts, digital platforms also have geopolitical consequences (Tufekci, 2017). The Russia-Ukraine War has shown how applications like TikTok and Telegram are used in information warfare (Pomerantsev, 2019). Similarly, the facilitation of information dissemination by social media platforms during the Mahsa Amini protests in Iran indicates the emergence of a new form of opposition where physical protests are digitalized (Howard, 2020). The progression of physical protests originating from digital discourses becoming more significant makes it difficult for states to predict (Tufekci, 2017). This suggests that digital platforms should be examined with sensitivity concerning national security concepts (Bennett, 2017). These examples demonstrate that digital platforms have now become "geopolitical actors" (Fuchs, 2017). As the control of information through digital platforms increases, so does the nature of warfare and resistance. Information warfare has merged with cyber warfare, replacing traditional military strategies with algorithmic guidance.

This study shows that digital platforms are no longer just communication tools in today's society; they have become complex actors with constructive, destructive, and regulatory effects on political, economic, and social orders (Van Dijck, 2013). Digital power is producing a new form of hegemony based on data and algorithms; transforming the concept of the public sphere into a digital public sphere, and reshaping individual freedoms and rights (Fuchs, 2017). Therefore, for the future of the digital world, a comprehensive, multi-actor, and ethics-based governance model is needed (Gillespie, 2018). Approaches like transparency and ethics-based governance, though advocated by social media platforms, still leave the potential for the abuse of power (Zuboff, 2019). Thus, a digital social contract, one that balances national sovereignty with global digital reality and prioritizes the public good over private interests, has become one of the most critical requirements of the digital age.

ACKNOWLEDGMENT

This work employed AI tools (ChatGPT-4o) to improve writing quality and clarity. All analyses and interpretations are solely the responsibility of the author.

REFERENCES

Alyukov, M., Kunilovskaya, M., & Semenov, A. (2023). Wartime Media Monitor (WarMM-2022): A Study of Information Manipulation on Russian Social Media during the Russia-Ukraine War. Proceedings of the 7th Joint SIGHUM Workshop on Computational Linguistics for Cultural Heritage, Social Sciences, Humanities and Literature. DOI: 10.18653/v1/2023.latechclfl-1.17

Andrejevic, M. (2013). *Infoglut: How too much information is changing the way we think and know*. Routledge. DOI: 10.4324/9780203075319

Andrejevic, M. (2014). Surveillance and alienation in the online economy. *Surveillance & Society, 12*(3), 381–393.

Andrejevic, M. (2019). *Automated media*. Routledge. DOI: 10.4324/9780429242595

Arafat, R., & Khamis, S. (2025). Unveiling the online dynamics influencing the success and virality of TikTok social movements: A case study on pro and anti hijab feminist activism. *Media, War & Conflict, 18*(2), 251–272. Advance online publication. DOI: 10.1177/17506352241308152

Astuti, Y. D., Attaymini, R., & Dewi, M. S. R. (2022). Digital media and war: Social media as a propaganda tool for the Russia-Ukraine conflict in the post-truth era.

Balkin, J. M. (2018). Free speech in the algorithmic society: Big data, private governance, and new school speech regulation. *U.C. Davis Law Review, 51*(3), 1149–1210.

Beer, D. (2017). The social power of algorithms. *Information Communication and Society, 20*(1), 1–13. DOI: 10.1080/1369118X.2016.1216147

Benkler, Y. (2016). Degrees of freedom, dimensions of power. *Daedalus, 145*(1), 18–32. DOI: 10.1162/DAED_a_00362

Bennett, C. J., & Raab, C. D. (2017). *The governance of privacy: Policy instruments in global perspective*. Routledge. DOI: 10.4324/9781315199269

Bennett, W. L. (2017). The personalization of politics. *The Annals of the American Academy of Political and Social Science, 644*(1), 20–39. DOI: 10.1177/0002716212451428

Binns, R., Veale, M., Van Kleek, M., & Shadbolt, N. (2018). "It's reducing a human being to a percentage": Perceptions of justice in algorithmic decisions. In *Proceedings of the 2018 CHI Conference on Human Factors in Computing Systems* (pp. 1–14). DOI: 10.1145/3173574.3173951

Bösch, M., & Divon, T. (2024). The sound of disinformation: TikTok, computational propaganda, and the invasion of Ukraine. New Media & Society, 26(9), 5081–5106. (Original work published 2024)DOI: 10.1177/14614448241251804

Bradshaw, S., & Howard, P. N. (2017). *Troops, trolls and troublemakers: A global inventory of organized social media manipulation*. Computational Propaganda Research Project.

Bradshaw, S., & Howard, P. N. (2019). *The global disinformation order: 2019 global inventory of organised social media manipulation*. Oxford Internet Institute.

Brady, W. J., Wills, J. A., Jost, J. T., Tucker, J. A., & Van Bavel, J. J. (2021). Emotion shapes the diffusion of moralized content in social networks. *Proceedings of the National Academy of Sciences of the United States of America, 118*(1).

Bucher, T. (2018). *If...Then: Algorithmic power and politics*. Oxford University Press. DOI: 10.1093/oso/9780190493028.001.0001

Burrell, J. (2016). How the machine 'thinks': Understanding opacity in machine learning algorithms. *Big Data & Society, 3*(1), 2053951715622512. DOI: 10.1177/2053951715622512

Caplan, R., Donovan, J., Hanson, L., & Matthews, J. (2018). *Algorithmic accountability: A primer*. Data & Society Research Institute.

Castells, M. (2015). *Networks of outrage and hope: Social movements in the Internet age*. Polity Press.

Chadwick, A. (2017). *The hybrid media system: Politics and power*. Oxford University Press. DOI: 10.1093/oso/9780190696726.001.0001

Chemerys, H. (2023). Deepfakes and synthetically reproduced media content as a form of disinformation in the context of the Russian aggression against Ukraine. In Протидія дезінформації в умовах російської агресії проти України: виклики і перспективи: тези доп. учасників міжн. наук.-практ. конф. (Харків, 12-13 груд. 2023р.) (p. 400). Харків: НДІ ППСН. DOI: 10.32782/PPSS.2023.1.8

Cinelli, M., Morales, G. D. F., Galeazzi, A., Quattrociocchi, W., & Starnini, M. (2021). The echo chamber effect on social media. *Proceedings of the National Academy of Sciences of the United States of America, 118*(9), e2023301118. DOI: 10.1073/pnas.2023301118

Cohen, J. E. (2019). *Between truth and power: The legal constructions of informational capitalism*. Oxford University Press. DOI: 10.1093/oso/9780190246693.001.0001

Couldry, N., & Hepp, A. (2017). *The mediated construction of reality*. Polity Press.

Couldry, N., & Mejias, U. A. (2019). *The costs of connection: How data is colonizing human life and appropriating it for capitalism*. Stanford University Press.

Eubanks, V. (2018). *Automating inequality: How high-tech tools profile, police, and punish the poor*. St. Martin's Press.

Floridi, L. (2020). The fight for digital sovereignty: What it is, and why it matters, especially for the EU. *Philosophy & Technology*, *33*(3), 369–378. DOI: 10.1007/s13347-020-00423-6

Foucault, M. (1975). *Discipline and punish: The birth of the prison*. Vintage Books.

Foucault, M. (2008). *The birth of biopolitics*. Palgrave Macmillan.

Freelon, D., Marwick, A., & Kreiss, D. (2022). False equivalencies: Online activism from left to right. *Science*, *369*(6508), 1197–1201. DOI: 10.1126/science.abb2428

Fuchs, C. (2017). Social media: A critical introduction. *Sage (Atlanta, Ga.)*.

Fuchs, C. (2020). *Communication and capitalism: A critical theory*. University of Westminster Press. Dawsey, J., Dou, E., & Siddiqui, F. (2024). How Elon Musk came to endorse Donald Trump. The Washington Post, NA-NA.

Gensburger, S., & Clavert, F. (2024). Is Artificial Intelligence the Future of Collective Memory? *Memory Studies Review*, *1*(2), 195–208. DOI: 10.1163/29498902-202400019

Gerbaudo, P. (2024). TikTok and the algorithmic transformation of social media publics: From social networks to social interest clusters. *New Media & Society*, *0*(0), 14614448241304106. Advance online publication. DOI: 10.1177/14614448241304106

Gillespie, T. (2014). The relevance of algorithms. In Gillespie, T., Boczkowski, P., & Foot, K. (Eds.), *Media technologies: Essays on communication, materiality, and society* (pp. 167–194). MIT Press. DOI: 10.7551/mitpress/9042.003.0013

Gillespie, T. (2018). *Custodians of the Internet: Platforms, content moderation, and the hidden decisions that shape social media*. Yale University Press.

Greene, T., Martens, D., & Shmueli, G. (2022). Barriers to academic data science research in the new realm of algorithmic behaviour modification by digital platforms. *Nature Machine Intelligence*, *4*(4), 323–330. DOI: 10.1038/s42256-022-00475-7

Habermas, J. (1989). *The structural transformation of the public sphere*. MIT Press.

Helberger, N., Pierson, J., & Poell, T. (2020). Governing online platforms: From contested to cooperative responsibility. *The Information Society*, *36*(1), 1–14. DOI: 10.1080/01972243.2017.1391913

Helbing, D., Frey, B. S., Gigerenzer, G., Hafen, E., Hagner, M., Hofstetter, Y., & Zicari, R. V. (2021). Will democracy survive big data and artificial intelligence? *Scientific American*.

Hinds, J., Williams, E. J., & Joinson, A. N. (2020). "It wouldn't happen to me": Privacy concerns and perspectives following the Cambridge Analytica scandal. *International Journal of Human-Computer Studies*, *143*, 102498. DOI: 10.1016/j.ijhcs.2020.102498

Howard, P. N. (2020). *Lie machines: How to save democracy from troll armies, deceitful robots, junk news operations, and political operatives*. Yale University Press.

Huq, A. Z. (2024). (Forthcoming). The Geopolitics of Digital Regulation. U of Chicago, Public Law. *Working Paper*.

Kitchens, B., Johnson, S. L., & Gray, P. (2020). Understanding echo chambers and filter bubbles: The impact of social media on diversification and partisan shifts in news consumption. *Management Information Systems Quarterly*, *44*(4), 1619–1649. DOI: 10.25300/MISQ/2020/16371

Kitchin, R. (2014). The data revolution: Big data, open data, data infrastructures and their consequences. *Sage (Atlanta, Ga.)*. Advance online publication. DOI: 10.4135/9781473909472

Lyon, D. (2010). Liquid surveillance. *Polity*.

Mittelstadt, B. D., Allo, P., Taddeo, M., Wachter, S., & Floridi, L. (2016). The ethics of algorithms: Mapping the debate. *Big Data & Society*, *3*(2), 2053951716679679. DOI: 10.1177/2053951716679679

Moreno Rubio, Á. (2022). Zelensky's discourse during the Russian invasion of Ukraine: How the war of narratives influences conflicts.

Morozov, E. (2018). *The net delusion: The dark side of Internet freedom*. PublicAffairs.

Munger, K. (2021). All the news that's fit to click: The economics of clickbait. *Journal of Media Economics*.

Napoli, P. M. (2019). *Social media and the public interest: Media regulation in the disinformation age*. Columbia University Press. DOI: 10.7312/napo18454

Nye, J. S. (2004). *Soft power: The means to success in world politics*. PublicAffairs.

Pariser, E. (2011). *The filter bubble: What the Internet is hiding from you*. Penguin Press.

Pasquale, F. (2015). *The black box society: The secret algorithms that control money and information*. Harvard University Press. DOI: 10.4159/harvard.9780674736061

Pomerantsev, P. (2019). *This is not propaganda: Adventures in the war against reality*. Faber & Faber.

Reuters. (2024, December 6). Musk spent over quarter billion dollars to help elect Trump. Reuters. https://www.reuters.com/world/us/musk-spent-over-quarter-billion-dollars-help-elect-trump-2024-12-06/

Ribeiro, M. H., Ottoni, R., West, R., Almeida, V. A., & Meira, W., Jr. (2020). Auditing radicalization pathways on YouTube. In *Proceedings of the 2020 FAT* Conference.

Rid, T. (2020). *Active measures: The secret history of disinformation and political warfare*. Farrar, Straus and Giroux.

Rowley, J. (2007). The wisdom hierarchy: Representations of the DIKW hierarchy. *Journal of Information Science*, *33*(2), 163–180. DOI: 10.1177/0165551506070706

Seattle University. (n.d.). The European Union's Digital Services Act: A new era for the internet. Seattle University – Albers School of Business and Economics. https://www.seattleu.edu/business/news-events/pov/ethics-matter/posts/the-european-unions-digital-services-act-a-new-era-for-the-internet.php

Sunstein, C. R. (2018). *Republic: Divided democracy in the age of social media*. Princeton University Press.

Tambini, D. (2017). *Fake news: Public policy responses. Media Policy Brief 20*. London School of Economics.

The Guardian. (2024). Elon Musk's Super Pac spent $200m to help elect Donald Trump https://www.theguardian.com

Tucker, J. A., Theocharis, Y., Roberts, M. E., & Barberá, P. (2017). From liberation to turmoil: Social media and democracy. *Journal of Democracy*, *28*(4), 46–59. DOI: 10.1353/jod.2017.0064

Tufekci, Z. (2015). *Algorithmic harms beyond Facebook and Google: Emergent challenges of computational agency*. Colorado Technology Law Journal.

Tufekci, Z. (2017). *Twitter and tear gas: The power and fragility of networked protest*. Yale University Press.

Tufekci, Z. (2018). YouTube, the great radicalizer. *The New York Times*.

Van Dijck, J. (2013). *The culture of connectivity: A critical history of social media*. Oxford University Press. DOI: 10.1093/acprof:oso/9780199970773.001.0001

Van Dijck, J. (2014). Datafication, dataism and dataveillance: Big data between scientific paradigm and ideology. *Surveillance & Society*, *12*(2), 197–208. DOI: 10.24908/ss.v12i2.4776

Van Dijck, J., & Poell, T. (2013). Understanding social media logic. *Media and Communication*, *1*(1), 2–14. DOI: 10.17645/mac.v1i1.70

Van Dijck, J., Poell, T., & de Waal, M. (2018). *The platform society: Public values in a connective world*. Oxford University Press. DOI: 10.1093/oso/9780190889760.001.0001

Walsh, T. (2024). TikTok as a site of social protest in Iran's Gen-Z uprising. *Discourse & Society*, *35*(5), 625–650. DOI: 10.1177/09579265241234351

Zeng, J., Stevens, T., & Chen, Y. (2017). China's solution to global cyber governance: Unpacking the domestic discourse of "internet sovereignty". *Politics & Policy*, *45*(3), 432–464. DOI: 10.1111/polp.12202

Zuboff, S. (2019). *The age of surveillance capitalism: The fight for a human future at the new frontier of power*. PublicAffairs.

Chapter 6
The Impact of Facial Recognition Technology on Migrant Communities at EU Borders:
Surveillance, Privacy, and Discrimination

Gianina Anemona Radu
https://orcid.org/0009-0001-0624-1038
Police Academy, Bucharest, Romania

ABSTRACT

This chapter critically examines the increasing use of Facial Recognition Technology (FRT) in EU border management and its implications for migrant communities, asylum seekers, and displaced persons. While FRT is often promoted as a tool for enhancing security and streamlining identity verification, its deployment raises significant concerns related to privacy violations, algorithmic bias, and systemic discrimination. This study explores these challenges through legal, ethical, and human rights lenses, offering an interdisciplinary analysis of biometric surveillance practices at borders. The chapter underscores the urgent need for robust regulatory frameworks, oversight mechanisms, and alternative, rights-based approaches to border security.

DOI: 10.4018/979-8-3373-7406-2.ch006

1. INTRODUCTION

The increasing digitization of border management has introduced new technologies aimed at enhancing efficiency and security. Among these, FRT has gained prominence as an identity verification tool used to streamline border crossings and detect unauthorized migration. However, while proponents highlight its ability to curb fraudulent travel and strengthen security, its implementation raises fundamental questions about privacy, discrimination, and the disproportionate targeting of marginalized communities (Bigo et al., 2021).

The deployment of facial recognition technology (FRT) at EU external borders has dramatically expanded surveillance of migrant communities, raising profound concerns about privacy, discrimination, and fundamental rights. Recent analyses warn that FRT systems "raise fundamental rights issues, particularly privacy, non-discrimination, and human dignity". In the EU legal order, the Charter of Fundamental Rights explicitly enshrines a right to respect for private life (Art. 7) and a right to the protection of personal data (Art. 8), mirroring the protections of the European Convention on Human Rights (Art. 8 ECHR) .The European Court of Human Rights has underscored that the very act of collecting biometric identifiers (e.g. DNA, fingerprints, facial images) interferes with private life, often without infringing the core of that right only if tightly controlled. For example, in *S. and Marper v. UK* the Court struck down indefinite retention of DNA and fingerprints of innocent persons, emphasizing that *any* biometric capture "is in principle an interference with the private life" and must be justified by strict safeguards In the EU context, the Court of Justice has similarly recognized data retention and processing as a "serious interference" with privacy, requiring clear legal basis and proportionate limits (e.g. *Tele2/Watson* C-203/15)

However, FRT at borders often skirts these protections. EU proposals and practices increasingly treat migrants themselves as security risks to be detected by "automated border control" systems. One commentator notes that policy shifts towards the right have explicitly justified new border technologies – including biometrics and AI – as necessary to "detect and avert the potential threat and danger migrants and refugees pose" to Europe's stability. Over €3 billion has been invested in EU border tech since 2007 and tools like automated surveillance drones and "virtual fences" now surround migration routes. In this "digitalization of border security," basic aspects of human movement are turned into data points, and migrants are often "viewed as a security threat" to be managed by technology. The trend is to treat people *not* as individuals entitled to rights, but as profiles to be matched or flagged by algorithmic systems

2. LITERATURE REVIEW AND THEORETICAL FOUNDATIONS

This section provides an overview of the theoretical and scholarly landscape surrounding facial recognition technology (FRT), biometric surveillance, and their intersection with migration governance. It contextualizes the current deployment of FRT at EU borders within broader debates on surveillance, algorithmic governance, and state power.

2.1 *Surveillance Theory and the Digital Border*

Surveillance theory provides a vital lens through which the use of FRT at borders can be understood. Michel Foucault's concept of the panopticon serves as a foundational framework for understanding how surveillance produces disciplined subjects. In the context of border management, FRT represents a form of automated panopticons, in which the mere possibility of being watched conditions behavior. Agamben's notion of the "state of exception" is also relevant, where borders become spaces of legal ambiguity, enabling the suspension of normative legal protections for migrants.

Lyon (2001) and Zuboff (2019) argue that surveillance has evolved into a form of "surveillance capitalism" wherein personal data becomes a commodity. The biometric border, thus, is not merely a security measure but a site of data extraction and categorization, contributing to what Amoore (2020) calls "algorithmic governance." Within this framework, individuals are reduced to data points used to forecast and manage risk.

2.2 *Algorithmic Governance and Migration*

Scholars such as Eubanks (2018) and Dencik et al. (2019) highlight how algorithmic decision-making systems can entrench structural inequalities, particularly for marginalized groups. In the context of migration, AI-based systems like FRT amplify the exclusionary logic of borders by pre-emptively categorizing and controlling migrant populations. This produces what Molnar (2019) refers to as the "datafied refugee," a figure managed through predictive analytics and biometric surveillance.

The growing literature on "digital borders" (Broeders and Dijstelbloem 2015) underscores how technological infrastructures reconfigure the spatial and temporal dynamics of border control. Surveillance is no longer limited to checkpoints; it extends into the digital and predictive realms, creating a constant monitoring apparatus.

2.3 *Intersectionality and Discrimination in Biometric Systems*

Facial recognition systems have been widely criticized for encoding racial, gender, and age-based biases. Research by Buolamwini and Gebru (2018) reveals stark disparities in error rates across demographic groups, with dark-skinned women being disproportionately misidentified. These biases are not accidental but reflect the sociotechnical systems within which the algorithms are trained and deployed (Thomi, 2021).

An intersectional perspective is critical in assessing the impact of FRT. Scholars argue that biometric systems often ignore the complex identities of migrants, treating them as a homogenous risk category. Feminist and critical race theorists emphasize the need to examine how surveillance technologies reproduce existing hierarchies based on gender, race, and legal status.

2.4 *Historical Context of EU Border Technologies*

Historically, the EU's border governance has evolved from paper-based visa systems to digital databases like SIS, VIS, and Eurodac. The integration of biometrics began in the early 2000s but has accelerated rapidly post-9/11, coinciding with the securitization of migration (Balzacq et al., 2016). Current developments, such as interoperability of EU databases and the use of predictive analytics, represent the latest phase in a long trajectory of technocratic border control.

The literature suggests that these systems not only regulate movement but also reinforce narratives of risk, danger, and illegitimacy associated with non-EU migrants. The border thus becomes a site of both symbolic and material exclusion, where FRT functions as a key enabler of digital bordering.

3. LEGAL AND INSTITUTIONAL FRAMEWORK

3.1 Introduction to AI in Border Control

The European Union (EU) is increasingly relying on artificial intelligence (AI)-driven tools for border and migration management. While these systems offer efficiency and predictive capability, they also raise significant legal and ethical concerns. Biometric data—particularly facial recognition technology (FRT)—plays a central role in this new infrastructure. Given the sensitive nature of biometric information, its use is subject to strict legal scrutiny under EU law. This section outlines the key legal instruments governing biometric data processing and the safeguards designed to uphold fundamental rights such as privacy, data protection, and human dignity.

3.2 Key Surveillance Tools and Systems

Under the **General Data Protection Regulation (GDPR)**, biometric data is classified as a special category of personal data (Art. 4(14), Art. 9 GDPR), triggering heightened protections. Processing of such data is generally prohibited unless it falls under a limited set of exceptions—such as explicit consent or substantial public interest—and must strictly comply with core data protection principles: purpose limitation, data minimization, accuracy, integrity, and confidentiality.

The **Law Enforcement Directive (LED)** further narrows the scope for biometric processing by police or border authorities. Article 10 LED stipulates that biometric data may be processed only when "strictly necessary" for defined and serious criminal purposes, and must be grounded in clear, precise legal provisions. The **CJEU judgment in Ministry of the Interior v. Biuro Projektów (C-205/21, 2023)** confirmed that indiscriminate or preventive biometric collection by police is unlawful unless it meets high thresholds of necessity and proportionality.

FRT systems used at borders, therefore, cannot function as standalone automated filters. They must operate under a regime that allows for human oversight and meaningful safeguards. For instance, when a facial recognition system flags an individual as a potential "irregular migrant," the final determination must involve a human officer to ensure fairness and compliance with Article 22 GDPR, which prohibits fully automated decision-making except under specific, limited conditions.

3.3 Interoperability and Predictive Systems

Legal frameworks also govern how biometric data can be shared and combined across different databases. The EU's move toward **interoperability**—mandated through Regulations (EU) 2019/817 and 2019/818—creates an integrated data environment linking systems such as SIS, VIS, Eurodac, EES, ETIAS, and ECRIS-TCN. While this facilitates real-time cross-checking and border enforcement, it also raises the risk of "function creep," where data collected for one purpose is reused for unrelated surveillance or enforcement.

From a legal standpoint, such data sharing must remain within the **principle of purpose limitation** under Article 5 GDPR and Article 4(1)(b) LED. Additionally, the systems must embed **privacy by design and by default** (Article 25 GDPR), ensuring technical and organizational measures are built in from the outset to minimize rights intrusions. Moreover, the GDPR's transparency and accountability requirements mean that individuals must be informed about how their data is being processed—even in complex, multi-system environments.

Predictive analytics and algorithmic risk profiling present additional legal challenges. While not always explicitly covered by biometric rules, they often rely on sensitive data that can reinforce biases and create discriminatory outcomes. If used for automated border decisions, these tools must also comply with Article 22 GDPR and ensure the availability of human intervention and recourse.

3.4 The Digital Border and Securitization

The deployment of AI in border contexts must also be evaluated through the lens of broader fundamental rights protections provided by the **Charter of Fundamental Rights of the European Union (CFR)** and the **European Convention on Human Rights (ECHR)**. Article 1 CFR guarantees **human dignity**, while Article 7 (respect for private life) and Article 8 (protection of personal data) further strengthen privacy protections.

The **CJEU has repeatedly emphasized** that the processing of biometric data constitutes a serious interference with the right to private life and data protection. In **Digital Rights Ireland (C-594/12)** and **Schwarz (C-291/12)**, the Court ruled that such processing must be clearly justified and narrowly tailored to a legitimate aim.

Recent **EDPB Guidelines (2023)** take this further, warning that facial recognition systems risk **reducing individuals to "machine-readable" entities**, violating the very essence of human dignity: "Human dignity requires that individuals are not treated as mere objects. FRT calculates existential and highly personal characteristics into a machine-readable form... thereby objectifying the face."

The Guidelines also caution against the real-world impacts of **false positives and algorithmic bias**, which may lead to unjustified detentions, erroneous security classifications, or denial of asylum rights. These are not hypothetical concerns: real cases have already demonstrated how mismatches and opaque systems disproportionately affect racialized and marginalized groups.

Considering these issues, any FRT deployment at the EU's borders must not only meet legal thresholds under the GDPR and LED but must also align with the **spirit of dignity, justice, and non-discrimination** enshrined in EU fundamental rights law.

4. SURVEILLANCE AND THE DEPLOYMENT OF FACIAL RECOGNITION AT EU BORDERS

4.1 Algorithmic Bias, Discrimination, and Equality

The integration of facial recognition technology (FRT) and other AI-based systems into EU border control practices has intensified concerns regarding discrimination and unequal treatment. While AI promises objectivity and efficiency, its application in migration contexts often reinforces structural inequalities. Algorithmic bias—stemming from skewed training data, technical limitations, or socio-political assumptions—can result in **disproportionate harms to racialized, ethnic, or religious minority groups**.

FRT, in particular, has been shown to exhibit **lower accuracy rates for non-white individuals**, women, and children. These discrepancies are not merely technical flaws—they translate into real-world consequences such as unjustified detentions, suspicion, or denial of entry or asylum. Border control decisions based on faulty or biased outputs not only undermine procedural fairness but also exacerbate the precarity of already vulnerable individuals.

This gives rise to a **two-tier model of rights protection**: one in which EU citizens enjoy a presumption of legitimacy, while migrants are subjected to increased surveillance, risk scoring, and algorithmic suspicion. Such a framework risks violating Article 21 of the **EU Charter of Fundamental Rights**, which prohibits discrimination on any ground including race, ethnicity, or nationality. By embedding racial profiling into technical systems, these practices threaten to hollow out the very foundations of equality before the law.

4.2 Privacy, Consent, and Fundamental Rights

FRT's deployment across EU borders raises profound questions about **privacy, consent, and autonomy**. Migrants are often subjected to biometric data collection—such as face scans or fingerprints—without meaningful explanation or the opportunity to opt out. The logic of "security necessity" is frequently used to override traditional data protection guarantees.

However, under both the **GDPR** and **Law Enforcement Directive (LED)**, biometric processing must meet strict criteria of necessity, proportionality, and purpose limitation. Consent cannot be presumed or coerced—especially in contexts of vulnerability, such as asylum or detention. Moreover, fully automated decision-making (Article 22 GDPR) must include safeguards such as human intervention and the right to challenge outcomes.

In addition to data protection concerns, there are broader **rights-based implications**. The **Charter of Fundamental Rights** and the **European Convention on Human Rights (ECHR)** enshrine the right to private life, dignity, and effective remedy. Facial recognition systems—particularly when used for real-time monitoring or profiling—constitute significant interferences with these rights. The **European Data Protection Board (EDPB)** has warned that reducing human faces to machine-readable patterns risks objectifying individuals and undermining their dignity.

The concept of **"digital borders"**—where surveillance extends beyond checkpoints into predictive, biometric, and remote monitoring—raises further legal and ethical challenges. These technologies enable states to **track migrants from ori-**

gin to destination, blurring the lines between migration governance and policing. What begins as a border control tool easily morphs into a generalized surveillance infrastructure with little accountability or transparency.

4.3 Lived Experiences and Ethnographic Insights

Legal frameworks often abstract the human cost of AI-driven border control. Yet ethnographic studies and field interviews conducted by organizations like **Privacy International**, **Médecins Sans Frontières**, and **Refugee Rights Europe** offer powerful counter-narratives. These testimonies reveal the psychological, emotional, and procedural burdens that surveillance systems place on displaced individuals.

Migrants report being **fingerprinted or facially scanned without explanation**, and many are warned that refusal would delay or jeopardies their asylum claims. Others discover they have been flagged as "security risks" due to algorithmic misidentification—often with no understanding of how the classification occurred or how to challenge it. This lack of transparency creates a Kafkaesque environment where individuals are monitored, categorized, and penalized without due process.

The **emotional toll** is equally profound. Migrants describe FRT checkpoints as moments of fear and humiliation, not safety. Some liken the experience to being treated as a **criminal suspect**, not a person seeking protection. These narratives speak to broader themes of **disempowerment, alienation, and dehumanization** in digital border regimes.

Ethnographic insights help reframe the conversation around AI and migration, shifting focus from technological efficiency to **human dignity**. They underscore the reality that **data-driven governance does not occur in a vacuum**, but within asymmetrical power structures marked by coercion, exclusion, and lack of redress. Without participatory mechanisms or oversight, migrants remain **subjects of data, not bearers of rights**.

5. DISCRIMINATION AND HUMAN RIGHTS IMPLICATIONS

The ethical implications of FRT at borders cannot be overstated. As one human rights commentator put it, EU border policy now treats people "not as people, but as a security problem"[4]. Facial scans turn faces into machine-readable identifiers, stripping away context and dignity. The EDPB emphasizes that individuals must not be treated as "mere objects" of surveillance. Yet, without strict controls, FRT does exactly that: it automates recognition and tracking without human engagement.

Various oversight bodies have raised alarm. The EDPS (European Data Protection Supervisor) has repeatedly urged caution or bans on remote FRT uses. The EDPB/

EDPS have even called for an *outright ban* on public facial recognition systems because of human dignity concerns. National data protection authorities have struck down programs (as in Italy) or demanded impact assessments before deployment (as with the Greek police project). The EU's new AI Act will ban "remote biometric identification" for law enforcement in public spaces as high-risk (with limited exceptions), acknowledging these severe rights implications.

5.1. *Algorithmic Bias, Discrimination, and Equality*

Facial recognition technology has well-documented accuracy issues that pose specific dangers for migrants. Many studies find that commercial FRT algorithms are far less accurate on darker-skinned and female faces than on lighter-skinned male faces. Pioneering research (e.g. Buolamwini & Gebru 2018) showed error rates for dark-skinned women up to 34.7% versus <1% for fair-skinned men. In practice, a migrant from Africa or Asia is more likely to be misidentified by an FRT system than a European tourist. This bias can lead to **false positives** (incorrect "matches" with someone in a criminal database) or **false negatives** (failure to recognize a legitimate identity). As the EDPB has warned, false positives by FRT "may lead to severe implications… a person being subject to further policing" or even criminal prosecution. Conversely, a false negative might result in a person evading detection – which could also have human rights effects if authorities then use overly broad methods (like detention or pushback) to compensate.

Ethnic or racial profiling is a real risk. Because many border databases contain records of migrants who have claimed asylum or crossed irregularly, targeted FRT use could disproportionately mark certain nationalities as "high risk." The *Risking Lives* report notes specific profiles targeted (e.g. Arabic, Pashto, Dari names) for surveillance. Algorithmic decision-making tends to reflect the biases of its training data: if European police feeds primarily contain EU citizen faces, the system may wrongly flag non-European faces as anomalies.

The EU Charter prohibits discrimination (Art. 21 CFR) and guarantees equality before the law (Art. 20). Courts would likely view racially biased FRT as an infringement of these rights. Humanitarian migrants, already marginalized by language and legal status, have little opportunity to contest an algorithmic "hit" on the spot. There is also a gender dimension: female migrants may find facial systems failing to recognize them equally, potentially subjecting them to extra checks or delays. One master's thesis note that algorithmic gender bias (such as recruitment tools excluding women) signals how even facial match systems can disproportionately disadvantage female refugees.

In sum, FRT at borders embodies *algorithmic discrimination* risks. From a sociotechnical perspective, the tech is not "neutral." Its design choices – which populations were included in datasets, whose data it was tuned on – inevitably reflect social biases. Left unchecked, these systems could systematically violate principles of equal treatment. The GDPR's fairness principle demands that algorithms be trained on representative data and evaluated for disparate impact. GDPR Art. 9 also bans processing of "special categories" of data (e.g. ethnic origin) unless a narrow exception applies – meaning that if an FRT system implicitly infers race from facial features, it could be illegal processing of sensitive data.

In practice, algorithmic bias means migrants are doubly vulnerable: first as migrants with limited rights, and second as members of over-policed racial or ethnic groups. Even if the raw surveillance is justified by security claims, discriminatory technology can aggravate historical inequities. Rights bodies like the EDPS now insist that any biometric system be tested and calibrated to the highest performance standards. The EDPB guidelines explicitly demand that FRT at least match or exceed the accuracy of a well-trained human border guard. If an algorithm cannot reliably identify all demographic groups equally, it should not be used. So far, EU deployments fall short of this standard.

5.2. *Privacy, Consent, and Fundamental Rights*

Beyond bias, FRT raises acute privacy and autonomy issues. Migrants at EU borders often have little real choice. For example, in the Eurodac fingerprint system (for asylum seekers), fingerprints of asylum applicants are legally mandatory. The EU regulation explicitly forbids storing any biometric data other than fingerprints for asylum procedures. However, research shows some applicants fear that fingerprinting tags them for future police checks or restrictions. The FRA warns that when asylum seekers are compelled to biometrically register in "hotspots," this can feel coercive: are migrants truly giving informed consent, or simply facing detention if they refuse?

Even taking the fingerprint or face image creates a privacy intrusion. In *P.G. and J.H. v. UK* (2022), the ECHR held that police drone surveillance over a park violated Art. 8 due to lack of clear legal basis. The lesson carries over: migrants, too, have the same right to know when the state is capturing their biometric data. EU law requires any restriction of privacy rights to be "provided by law, necessary and proportionate". Yet many FRT deployments lack a specific legal basis spelled out in national law. For instance, the Italian Ombudsman faulted the SARI project for the absence of any "normative basis" specifying when and how FRT could be used. Such practices risk breaching Article 52(1) CFR, which insists that any limitation of rights must "respect the essence" of those rights and be clearly and precisely defined.

Another issue is data security. Biometric databases are highly sensitive targets. A breach of border agency FRT data – say from a Frontex or national police server – would expose migrants' identities and vulnerabilities. The GDPR requires "integrity and confidentiality" and even "privacy by design" (using state-of-art encryption) for such data. However, EU practice has seen multiple data leaks (e.g. unsecured spreadsheets of asylum applicants). Any large-scale FRT deployment amplifies this risk. The stakes are high: migrants often flee persecution precisely because they lack political or financial power to protect themselves against surveillance.

5.3 *Private Sector Influence in Border Technology*

Private corporations play a central role in the development and deployment of biometric systems at EU borders. Companies such as IDEMIA, Gemalto, Thales, and Palantir provide technical infrastructure for FRT, data storage, and analytics. These firms often win large EU procurement contracts, yet their operations lack meaningful transparency.

For example, Frontex's Project Euclid involved partnerships with AI vendors to match live facial images with law enforcement watchlists. The procurement process, largely closed to public scrutiny, included minimal human rights vetting. Similarly, Italy's SARI system was purchased using EU Internal Security Funds, with little clarity about the technical accuracy or safeguards built into the software.

These public-private partnerships blur accountability. Corporate lobbying also influences EU tech policy, promoting security-driven narratives while downplaying risks. As scholars argue, the biometric border is not only shaped by state power but also by market incentives that prioritize efficiency and control over dignity and rights.

6. KEY CASE STUDIES: FRONTEX, EURODAC, AND NATIONAL BORDER PROGRAMS

6.1. Case Law on Biometric Surveillance

EU and European courts have begun grappling with biometric surveillance. In the EU courts, *Willems v. Belgium* (C-446/12) and *Schwarz v. Stadt Bochum* (C-291/12) upheld mandatory fingerprinting for passports, reasoning it was necessary to prevent identity fraud and illegal migration. Similarly, audio-visual systems like eGates with facial scans have been deemed lawful if covered by a clear legal framework. But the CJEU also maintains that biometric data capture must be carefully proportioned: for example, in *Willems*, taking two fingerprints was allowed, but doing *more* (e.g. scanning an iris) would exceed what is needed for border control.

At the Council of Europe level, the European Court of Human Rights has issued several landmark rulings on biometrics. In *S. and Marper v. UK* (2008), the Court held that indefinite retention of DNA and fingerprints violated Article 8 ECHR, especially for innocent persons. It stressed that even the **collection** of biometric data – separate from retention – is an interference requiring justification. In *Gaughran v. UK* (2020), the Grand Chamber struck down blanket retention of DNA from convicted persons, reaffirming that retention policies must be strictly tailored. Very recently, in *Glukhin v. Russia* (2023), the Court found that photographing and scanning a protester's face without legal basis infringed Article 8, again highlighting the sensitivity of face data. These cases collectively underscore that facial images are part of private life and cannot be handled permissively.

6.2. EU Border Surveillance in Practice: Case Studies

Frontex and Pan-EU Programs. The European Border and Coast Guard Agency (Frontex) is central to EU surveillance policy. In 2022, Frontex released a *Technology Foresight on Biometrics* envisioning "paperless travel" with multimodal biometric checkpoints Frontex ambitions include using face recognition in drones, cars, and patrols. Reports note that "at least eleven EU Member States have biometric databases with facial recognition" for law enforcement and border checks, and Frontex can tap into these via data-sharing networks. Frontex's initiatives like "Project Euclid" have explored matching live camera feeds against large "watchlists" (Europol and Interpol databases). Investigations by NGOs show Frontex pursued a Pan-European Data Retrieval Architecture (PeDRA) to funnel migrants' data into crime databases. For example, Queen Mary University security expert Niovi Vavoula revealed in 2022 that Frontex and the Commission had quietly tried to expand data collection under PeDRA – an effort to "feed" migrants' biometric and biographical data into Europol's criminal information systems. This was roundly criticized as blurring the line between migrants and criminal suspects, risking "discriminatory criminalization" of refugees (Vavoula, N. (2022).

Italy (SARI). Italy's experiments with FRT have been particularly controversial. In 2017 Italy acquired a mobile Facial Recognition System (called SARI) intended to check identities in public. In 2021 the Interior Ministry issued a tender to upgrade SARI for monitoring migrants arriving on coasts. Investigations showed EU Internal Security funds (€246,000) were to pay for a facial recognition license for SARI. The Italian Data Protection Authority (Garante) issued a stern opinion in March 2021: it warned that SARI would constitute "indiscriminate mass surveillance" of migrants and others Both the EDPB and EDPS explicitly stated that FRT in public spaces should be broadly banned, citing threats to privacy and free expression. Human-rights NGOs highlighted the potential for ethnic profiling in using SARI on migrants. In April 2021, the Italian Ombudsman declared SARI *unlawful.* The Ombudsman noted that SARI lacked any legal basis for automated biometric processing and would pull "everybody in the monitored space" into a universal surveillance net. The system was funded partly by the EU's Internal Security Fund – ironically the same fund sponsoring mobile FRT kits for the Greek police. By late 2022 Italy banned facial recognition in public by law (with an exception "to fight crime"), a measure widely seen as a belated response to criticisms of SARI.

Greece. Greece has also moved towards biometric policing. Data Justice research (2023) reports that Greek police discussed using portable FRT and fingerprint scanners to check "illegalized" migrants during street stops. Under this plan, a migrant's face or fingerprint would be matched against the EU's six interoperable migration databases (Eurodac, VIS, SIS, ETIAS, EES, ECRIS-TCN). If rolled out, this would effectively create a mega-database conflating migration and crime, undermining the asylum process. The Greek Data Protection Authority is investigating the legality of these plans, and it remains unclear if the devices are used. Meanwhile, in a grim twist, some Greek reception centers now require refugees to scan a biometric card to receive food or services – a form of ID-control attached to humanitarian aid that human rights advocates say violates dignity. (In *A.I. and Others v. Greece* (ECHR 2020) the court has already condemned Greek officials for abusing asylum seekers' data to deter further migration, though that case focused on generalized pushbacks more than biometric tech.)

Other Contexts. Migrant communities also face surveillance indirectly. For example, the Entry/Exit System (EES) now in operation at Schengen borders will capture both fingerprints and a facial image of every third-country national crossing the EU's external borders. All these data feed into shared EU databases. In practice, that means a migrant carrying biometric data from a previous EU journey (say, in Italy) can be automatically re-identified months later at another border if their facial biometrics are in an Interpol or EU watchlist. This function creep has worried privacy experts. The FRA has warned that requiring biometric identification at multiple "hotspots" or registrations can be coercive. And in the EU's newly proposed Screening Regulation, authorities are empowered to process refugees' fingerprints and facial images without consent, potentially for social control. Each of these measures has implications under EU privacy law that have been insufficiently tested in court.

7. LEGAL CHALLENGES AND CIVIL SOCIETY RESISTANCE

Despite growing deployment of facial recognition technology (FRT) at EU borders, legal resistance has mounted from various civil society groups and legal actors. Strategic litigation has sought to challenge the proportionality, legality, and transparency of these technologies.

7.1. Strategic Litigation

Cases before domestic courts and European institutions have addressed the legality of biometric data processing. Notably, the European Court of Human Rights (ECtHR) has ruled in *S. and Marper v. United Kingdom* (2008) that indefinite retention of biometric data (including photographs) violates Article 8 of the European Convention on Human Rights (ECHR).

More recently, the use of facial recognition in public spaces was challenged in *R. (Bridges) v. Chief Constable of South Wales Police* [2020] EWCA Civ 1058. Although not an EU case, the ruling set a powerful precedent in recognizing the necessity of oversight, non-discrimination, and human rights impact assessments.

7.2. NGO Advocacy

Organizations such as Privacy International, EDRi, and Statewatch have consistently advocated for a moratorium on FRT at borders. Their efforts emphasize the opacity of data-sharing agreements and lack of clear legal bases under the GDPR and Law Enforcement Directive (Directive (EU) 2016/680).

They also criticize Frontex's expanding role in biometric surveillance, arguing that it has outpaced appropriate accountability mechanisms, particularly concerning third-country data transfers and interoperability systems like the European Travel Information and Authorization System (ETIAS).

8. THE EU AI ACT AND THE FUTURE REGULATION OF FACIAL RECOGNITION

The forthcoming EU Artificial Intelligence Act (AI Act), currently in final negotiations (as of 2025), represents the most comprehensive regulatory framework for artificial intelligence in the EU. It categorizes biometric remote identification systems as high-risk or prohibited depending on their context of deployment.

8.1 High-Risk and Prohibited Uses

Article 5 of the proposed AI Act prohibits certain uses of AI deemed unacceptable, including real-time remote biometric identification in publicly accessible spaces for law enforcement purposes—except in narrowly defined cases involving serious crimes or imminent threats. While this prohibition is a significant step, it includes carve-outs for border control, allowing FRT to remain operational in certain high-risk migration contexts.

FRT systems used for border management are categorized as "high-risk AI" under Annex III of the Act. This classification triggers a series of obligations for developers and deployers, including the requirement to conduct fundamental rights impact assessments, implement robust human oversight, and maintain transparency in system design and deployment. Moreover, these systems must be subjected to conformity assessments to ensure compliance with EU standards for safety, reliability, and fundamental rights protection.

However, critics argue that the high-risk framework may not go far enough. The exemptions allowed for border authorities potentially create a regulatory loophole that undermines the Act's broader rights-based objectives. Without strict enforcement and narrow interpretation of exceptions, FRT could continue to be used in ways that disproportionately affect vulnerable populations.

8.2. Implications for Border Technology

If effectively implemented, the AI Act could significantly reshape the governance of FRT at EU borders. By mandating transparency and accountability, the Act would require agencies such as Frontex, national police forces, and private contractors to document how biometric systems are deployed, audited, and reviewed. This could lead to greater harmonization of practices and reduce the fragmented legal landscape currently governing FRT use across member states.

Furthermore, the AI Act empowers national supervisory authorities and the European Data Protection Board (EDPB) to monitor compliance and enforce sanctions where necessary. These enforcement mechanisms could serve as a check on overreach, particularly if used to prevent the deployment of discriminatory or insufficiently tested biometric systems.

Nonetheless, significant implementation challenges remain. Member states may interpret obligations differently, and border contexts may be seen as exceptional zones where rights protections are diluted. For the AI Act to deliver meaningful safeguards, it must be complemented by robust guidance, judicial oversight, and a commitment to fundamental rights as the guiding principle of border technology.

In sum, the AI Act marks a crucial development in regulating the use of FRT in Europe. Its success, however, will depend on how consistently and rigorously it is enforced, especially in politically sensitive areas such as migration control.

9. RETHINKING BIOMETRIC BORDER GOVERNANCE: RIGHTS-BASED ALTERNATIVES AND REGULATORY PATHWAYS

The rapidly expanding integration of Facial Recognition Technology (FRT) and biometric surveillance into EU border management frameworks raises acute concerns not only regarding privacy and data protection, but also with respect to fundamental rights, democratic legitimacy, and structural discrimination. In response, this section articulates a set of policy alternatives that shift the normative foundation of EU migration governance from surveillance-driven risk management to rights-based, legally accountable models of technological deployment. The recommendations provided below are structured thematically, encompassing technological design strategies, legal and institutional reform, democratic oversight, and long-term ethical foresight. Each is grounded in existing legal norms (e.g., the Charter of Fundamental Rights of the EU, GDPR), technological feasibility, and emerging scholarship on surveillance governance.

9.1 Designing for Rights: Alternatives to Biometric Automation

Rather than presuming biometric surveillance as a default mode of border control, EU institutions should prioritize human-centered, proportionate, and transparent verification systems. One such approach involves the recalibration of identity checks to reintroduce human-led or hybrid verification mechanisms, where automation is assistive rather than determinative. Empirical evidence suggests that automated facial recognition systems systematically underperform on marginalized demographic groups; therefore, mandatory escalation protocols for ambiguous or contested matches—triggering secondary human review—should be standard.

Further, the development of tiered identity assurance frameworks—where the level of verification corresponds to contextual risk—offers a legally defensible alternative to blanket biometric collection. Routine or low-risk interactions (e.g., short-stay visa entries) do not meet the threshold of necessity and proportionality for invasive data capture, particularly where less intrusive alternatives suffice.

Digital identity wallets based on decentralized architectures, such as W3C Verifiable Credentials, present an emerging rights-preserving model. These allow individuals to selectively disclose specific attributes (e.g., age or vaccination status) without exposing sensitive biometric identifiers. However, any deployment of such tools must be accompanied by robust safeguards including revocation capabilities, key recovery protocols, and privacy-preserving off-chain storage.

Where biometric data collection is deemed unavoidable, data minimization must be embedded by design. This includes exclusive reliance on hashed or template-reduced representations, clear prohibitions on raw image retention, and retention schedules tightly bound to legal purpose limitations under Article 5 of the GDPR. Moreover, transparency in the algorithmic performance of these systems is essential. Procurement processes must prioritize auditable systems—whether through open-source publication or code escrow agreements—and publish accuracy metrics disaggregated by relevant demographic and situational variables (e.g., skin tone, age, protective facial wear).

9.2 Legal and Institutional Realignment

A durable rights-based framework requires recalibration of the legal foundations governing biometric technologies in the EU, beginning with an amendment of the Schengen Borders Code. The revised Code must enshrine explicit prohibitions on real-time or indiscriminate biometric surveillance in border contexts, conditioning deployment on demonstrated necessity, legal specificity, and evidence-based proportionality.

To prevent the normalization of function creep—where data collected for one purpose is silently repurposed for others—future legislation must include binding purpose limitation clauses. Biometric data initially gathered for identity verification must not be reused for law enforcement, intelligence profiling, or migration deterrence without renewed, democratically validated legal authorization.

Additionally, all biometric system deployments must be preceded by ex ante Human Rights Impact Assessments (HRIAs) that assess legality, discrimination risk, redress mechanisms, and cross-border data transfer implications. These assessments must be independently reviewed and periodically updated in cases of system scaling, vendor change, or the addition of new datasets.

Legal accountability can also be enhanced by integrating compliance conditionality into procurement contracts, linking access to EU funding with performance benchmarks such as demographic accuracy audits, publication of technical summaries, and contractually mandated termination clauses for human rights violations.

9.3 Strengthening Oversight and Democratic Controls

Ensuring effective legal oversight over biometric surveillance requires expanding the mandates and operational capacity of EU-level supervisory authorities. The European Data Protection Supervisor (EDPS) and the European Data Protection Board (EDPB) must be legally empowered to investigate biometric deployments in cross-border contexts, issue binding remedial measures, and coordinate enforcement where systems span multiple jurisdictions.

Oversight structures should be democratized through the creation of independent multistakeholder monitoring bodies at both the EU and regional "hotspot" levels.

These should include not only data protection experts and legal practitioners but also civil society representatives, migrant-led organizations, and technical auditors. Such bodies must be granted access to systems for independent auditing and publish annual transparency reports detailing system performance, rights violations, and remedial actions.

Institutional transparency can be further advanced by requiring formal notification and parliamentary review of all high-risk biometric systems. Member States and EU agencies (notably Frontex) should be mandated to notify both the European Parliament and relevant national parliaments prior to deployment, with provisions for judicial fast-tracking to the CJEU in the event of systemic rights infringements.

Finally, accessible complaint and redress mechanisms are essential for meaningful accountability. These must be multilingual, low-threshold, and embedded into migration infrastructure—offering mobile interfaces, partnerships with legal aid NGOs, and in-person services at reception centers. Migrants should have the right to contest biometric misclassifications, request data correction or deletion, and suspend automated risk assessments pending review.

9.4 Embedding Ethical Foresight and Preventive Risk Governance

As biometric technologies become increasingly predictive, affective, and opaque, a long-term governance strategy must adopt anticipatory ethics and scenario-based risk analysis. Technologies such as emotion recognition, intent inference, and predictive "risk of irregularity" scoring—which lack scientific reliability and carry high rights risk—must be preemptively regulated or banned, in line with the precautionary principle enshrined in EU risk governance doctrine.

Structured red teaming and misuse cascade analysis must be institutionalized to identify how interoperable biometric datasets could be redirected during future crises for mass deportations, politically motivated targeting, or discriminatory mobility controls. These foresight practices enable institutions to map and mitigate emergent risks before deployment occurs.

Additionally, Technology Ethics Councils should be embedded within institutional decision-making processes. Comprising ethicists, migration law specialists, technologists, and directly affected community members, these bodies must be authorized to issue binding ethical opinions as a condition for system approval.

All high-intrusion biometric pilots must also be subject to sunset and review clauses, whereby experimental systems automatically expire unless affirmatively renewed through independent evaluation. These reviews should assess legal compliance, accuracy, proportionality, and broader human rights impacts, thus preventing the entrenchment of exceptional surveillance infrastructures under conditions of regulatory inertia.

10. CONCLUSION

Facial Recognition Technology (FRT) is rapidly becoming embedded in the architecture of European border governance, often framed as a necessary tool for enhancing security, combating irregular migration, and modernising border procedures. However, this study has shown that the widespread deployment of FRT at EU borders is far from neutral or benign. It raises serious ethical, legal, and social questions that strike at the core of the European Union's constitutional commitments to human rights, non-discrimination, accountability, and the rule of law.

Through an analysis of applicable legal frameworks—including the General Data Protection Regulation (GDPR), the Law Enforcement Directive (LED), the Charter of Fundamental Rights of the European Union, and the jurisprudence of the Court of Justice of the EU—this report has demonstrated that the deployment of biometric surveillance technologies frequently exceeds the bounds of necessity and proportionality. Case law such as *Biuro Projektów* confirms that indiscriminate or disproportionate biometric data collection is incompatible with EU data protection principles and fundamental rights protections. Additionally, guidance from the European Data Protection Board (EDPB), the European Data Protection Supervisor (EDPS), and academic literature converges on a clear normative baseline: biometric surveillance must be subject to strict legal limits, robust oversight, and demonstrable rights-based justification.

Moreover, the empirical realities of FRT implementation—biased algorithms, flawed vendor procurement, lack of redress for false positives, and opaque inter-agency data flows—have led to the normalisation of systemic discrimination at Europe's borders. Migrants, asylum seekers, and racialised individuals are disproportionately subjected to surveillance, with limited avenues for challenge or accountability. These technologies do not merely process identities—they construct risk profiles, influence access to territory, and shape who is seen as deserving of protection or suspicion.

The policy alternatives outlined in this report—ranging from privacy-respecting identity tools and transparent algorithmic procurement to mandatory Human Rights Impact Assessments and participatory oversight structures—demonstrate that more humane, effective, and rights-compliant governance models are possible. Importantly, these are not anti-security proposals; they are efforts to ensure that security measures operate within the legal and ethical boundaries that underpin democratic legitimacy in the European Union.

Ultimately, the governance of Europe's borders is a litmus test for its democratic credibility. The use of FRT at borders must not become a Trojan horse for broader normalisation of surveillance, profiling, and the erosion of legal safeguards. Instead, it must trigger renewed vigilance: to foreground human dignity, to ensure that innovation does not outrun accountability, and to reaffirm that every individual—regardless of migration status—is a bearer of inalienable rights.

The road forward must prioritise not only smarter technologies, but more just institutions. This will require legislative reform, institutional courage, and persistent engagement from civil society, regulators, courts, and affected communities. At stake is nothing less than the integrity of the EU's commitment to a border policy that is lawful, proportionate, and fundamentally humane.

REFERENCES

Amoore, L. (2020). *Cloud Ethics: Algorithms and the Attributes of Ourselves and Others*. Duke University Press.

Balzacq, T., Léonard, S., & Ruzicka, J. (2016). "Securitization" Revisited: Theory and Cases. *International Relations*, 30(4), 494–531. SAGE Publications. DOI: 10.1177/0047117815596590

Bigo, D., Guild, E., & Kuskonmaz, E. M. (2021). Obedience in times of COVID-19 pandemics: A renewed governmentality of unease? *Global Discourse*, *11*(3), 471–489. DOI: 10.1332/204378921X16158113910675

Biuro Projektów Regionalnych, S. A. v. (2022). Vyriausioji tarnybinės etikos komisija, Case C-184/20, ECLI:EU:C:2022:601 (Court of Justice of the European Union, 2022). https://eur-lex.europa.eu/legal-content/EN/TXT/?uri=CELEX%3A62020CJ0184

Buolamwini, J., & Gebru, T. (2018). Gender Shades: Intersectional accuracy disparities in commercial gender classification. *Proceedings of the 1st Conference on Fairness, Accountability and Transparency (FAT*)*, 81, 77–91. PMLR. https://proceedings.mlr.press/v81/buolamwini18a.html

Charter of Fundamental Rights of the European Union. 2012/C 326/02. (2012). *Official Journal of the European Union*, C 326, 391–407. https://eur-lex.europa.eu/legal-content/EN/TXT/?uri=CELEX:12012P/TXT

Directive (EU) 2014/24 of the European Parliament and of the Council of 26 February 2014 on public procurement and repealing Directive 2004/18/EC. (2014). *Official Journal of the European Union*, L 94, 65–242. https://eur-lex.europa.eu/legal-content/EN/TXT/?uri=CELEX%3A32014L0024

Directive (EU) 2016/680 of the European Parliament and of the Council of 27 April 2016 on the protection of natural persons regarding the processing of personal data by competent authorities for law enforcement purposes. (2016). *Official Journal of the European Union*, L 119, 89–131. https://eur-lex.europa.eu/legal-content/EN/TXT/?uri=CELEX%3A32016L0680

Eubanks, V. (2018). *Automating Inequality: How High-Tech Tools Profile, Police, and Punish the Poor*. St. Martin's Press.

European Commission. (2021). *Proposal for a regulation laying down harmonised rules on artificial intelligence (Artificial Intelligence Act)* (COM/2021/206 final). https://eur-lex.europa.eu/legal-content/EN/TXT/?uri=CELEX%3A52021PC0206

European Commission. (n.d.). *Better Regulation Toolbox – Tool #30: Fundamental rights and human rights impacts*. https://commission.europa.eu/law/law-making-process/planning-and-proposing-law/better-regulation/better-regulation-toolbox_en

European Data Protection Board. (2019). *Guidelines 3/2019 on processing of personal data through video devices*. https://edpb.europa.eu/our-work-tools/our-documents/guidelines/guidelines-32019-processing-personal-data-through-video_en

European Data Protection Board. (2020). *Guidelines 4/2019 on Article 25 Data Protection by Design and by Default*. https://edpb.europa.eu/our-work-tools/our-documents/guidelines/guidelines-42019-article-25-data-protection-design-and_en

European Parliament. (2021, October 6). *Resolution on artificial intelligence in criminal law and its use by the police and judicial authorities in criminal matters* (2020/2016(INI)). https://www.europarl.europa.eu/doceo/document/TA-9-2021-0405_EN.html

General Data Protection Regulation (GDPR). 2016). Regulation (EU) 2016/679 of the European Parliament and of the Council of 27 April 2016. (*Official Journal of the European Union*, L 119, 1–88. https://eur-lex.europa.eu/legal-content/EN/TXT/?uri=CELEX:32016R0679

Lyon, D. (2001). *Surveillance Society: Monitoring Everyday Life*. Open University Press, 2001.

Regulation (EU) 2016/399 of the European Parliament and of the Council of 9 March 2016 on a Union Code on the rules governing the movement of persons across borders (Schengen Borders Code). (2016). *Official Journal of the European Union*, L 77, 1–52. https://eur-lex.europa.eu/legal-content/EN/TXT/?uri=CELEX:32016R0399

Regulation - EU - 2018/1725 - EN - EUR-Lex

Regulation (EU) 2018/1725 of the European Parliament and of the Council of 23 October 2018 on the protection of natural persons by the Union institutions regarding processing of personal data. (2018). *Official Journal of the European Union*, L 295, 39–98.

Thomi, L. B. (2021). *The impact of biometric systems at EU outside borders on the human rights of irregular migrating women* (Master's thesis). Gender, Conflict and Humanitarian Study.

Vavoula, N. (2022). *Frontex and the EU Commission quietly expand biometric data collection on migrants under PeDRA, risking discriminatory criminalization*. Queen Mary University of London. Web.: https://left.eu/frontex-europol-collusion-in-targeting-migrants

Zuboff, S. (2019). *The Age of Surveillance Capitalism: The Fight for a Human Future at the New Frontier of Power*. Profile Books / PublicAffairs.

Chapter 7
Protection of Critical Digital Infrastructure:
Cyber Attacks and Threats to Energy, Water, and Financial Systems

Yusuf Dinçel
https://orcid.org/0000-0002-2615-6025
Turkish National Police Academy, Turkey

ABSTRACT

This chapter provides a comprehensive examination of the cybersecurity threats facing critical digital infrastructure systems in an era of rapid digital transformation. Focusing on three essential sectors—energy, water, and financial systems—the analysis reveals how cyber attackers exploit vulnerabilities in these infrastructures, posing significant risks to economic stability, public safety, and national security. The increasing interconnectivity of critical systems, while improving efficiency and accessibility, has also expanded the attack surface for malicious actors, ranging from state-sponsored hackers to criminal organizations.

INTRODUCTION

Digital transformation today emerges as a process that comprehensively reshapes the fundamental dynamics of societies and economies. This transformation does not merely refer to the development of technological infrastructures; it also extensively addresses the social, economic, and political impacts brought about by these infrastructures. The influence of digitalization has profoundly changed not

DOI: 10.4018/979-8-3373-7406-2.ch007

only individuals' daily lives but also states' perceptions of security in the modern world. With the increasing integration of digital technologies into daily life, systems reliant on internet infrastructure have become indispensable for societies. While this transformation offers significant opportunities for the functioning of many sectors -from communication to energy, from finance to water infrastructure- it has also amplified cybersecurity vulnerabilities and threats. As can be seen, the digitalization of critical infrastructures today presents new opportunities, but it also encompasses serious risks faced by both the public and private sectors. The digitalization of these systems may render these sectors prime targets for cyber attacks and may hinder the development of adequate defense mechanisms against the potentially devastating consequences of such attacks.

This chapter aims to conduct an in-depth analysis of the cyber threats faced by critical digital infrastructures and to develop ideas regarding potential countermeasures. Within this framework, cyber attacks aimed at contaminating water infrastructure systems, ransomware attacks targeting energy facilities, and identity fraud faced by financial institutions will be examined in detail. The central research question of this chapter is as follows: What cyber threats do critical digital infrastructures face, and how can effective defense mechanisms be developed against these threats? In line with this question, the chapter's hypothesis is that the cybersecurity of critical infrastructures must be reinforced not only through technical measures but also through international cooperation, political strategies, and public-private partnerships. The originality of this chapter lies in its comparative analysis of cyber threats within the specific contexts of the water, energy, and financial sectors. Different sectors are evaluated together, and their shared and distinct aspects in the face of cyber attacks are identified. Furthermore, the negative impacts of state-sponsored cyber attacks on critical infrastructures are discussed individually through concrete examples.

In this chapter, a qualitative research method has been employed. Specifically, the case study technique was adopted, and cyber attack incidents targeting the water, energy, and financial sectors were examined through examples from different countries. For instance, the Stuxnet attack (targeting Iran's nuclear energy infrastructure), the case involving a wastewater treatment plant in Pennsylvania (targeting the U.S. water infrastructure), and the Bangladesh Central Bank heist (targeting financial institutions) were analyzed within this framework.

This chapter aims to provide policymakers, security experts, and academics with a comprehensive assessment regarding the protection of critical infrastructures in an increasingly digitalized world. Additionally, it will address recommendations on how public-private sector cooperation can be strengthened to prevent potential future cyber threats. In conclusion, in this era of rapid digitalization, the security of critical infrastructures is no longer solely the responsibility of technology experts; it has become a security issue that directly affects national security, societal welfare, and economic sustainability. This chapter seeks to demonstrate this reality through examples from different sectors and to highlight the necessity of adopting a holistic approach to the defense of digital infrastructures.

DIGITALIZATION AND NEW SECURITY THREATS

Looking at the etymology of the word "digital," it is known to derive from the Latin word *digitus*, referring to early methods of counting (Möller, 2020). In general terms, the concept of digitalization refers to the integration of digital technologies into our daily lives (Barcik et al., 2023). Digitalization is rapidly transforming societies, and keeping up with the technological developments it brings is becoming increasingly difficult (Salminen & Hossain, 2018). Digitalization manifests itself in all areas of society, and dependence on digital systems is growing in key fields such as communication, commerce, and governance (Petersons, 2024). The opportunities that digitalization offers in our daily lives are undeniable. For example, with the increasing number of autonomous vehicles, people are able to travel more safely in traffic. Another example is how integrated machines can complete complex tasks in a short time, simplifying previously difficult operations. In addition, thanks to digital advancements in the healthcare sector, the analysis of big data has led to results that create significant comfort in human health. Alongside all these positive developments, it must be understood that data security is a fundamental element for the success of digitalization. In an environment where such opportunities are offered, if security is not ensured, people will not be able to benefit from these services. For this reason, not only governments but also sectors such as science and business must develop a clear roadmap to ensure that society can access services at the desired level (Kremer, 2017). As new technologies continue to emerge each day in the digital age, making life easier, digital threats also continue to grow. According to the *Global Risks Report* of the World Economic Forum in 2017, the likelihood of cyber attacks occurring worldwide is increasing with each passing day (Dalal, 2018).

The internet, as a crucial component of digitalization, has significantly expanded its influence worldwide over the past two decades and has led to major advancements in the field of communication. Thanks to its innovative nature and low cost, the internet is widely accessible across the globe. Moreover, it has established a global economic network through which transactions worth billions of dollars are conducted. Under current conditions, countries are conducting many of their economic, commercial, cultural, and social activities in cyberspace (Li & Liu, 2021). Before defining cyberspace, it is important to consider the term "cyber." The word "cyber" first appeared in Norbert Wiener's 1948 work "*Cybernetics; or Control and Communication in the Animal and the Machine*". This work focused on the interaction between humans and machines within the framework of cybernetics. Within this context, the importance of the human element in cyber systems was emphasized; it was stated that systems or technologies have no meaningful existence without humans. Cyberspace is described as a "new frontier" for humanity. In cyberspace, geographical borders have lost their significance, and transnational data flows occur at high speeds. It is known that technologies and digitalization are not distributed equally among countries across the globe. This leads to imbalances in the power dynamics between states in cyberspace. As a result, states are engaged in a struggle for power to establish sovereignty in the cyber domain (Mikhaylova & Mikhaylov, 2024; Alexei & Alexei, 2022). Hans Morgenthau, a prominent international relations theorist, defined national security in 1948 as the protection of a state's borders and institutions. Today, national security threats still include invasion or terrorist attacks. However, considering the role of the internet in daily life and the digitalization of critical infrastructures, it becomes evident that threats to national security are now emerging in new forms (Geers, 2009).

As digital technologies are increasingly utilized by both the public and private sectors, it has become essential to develop a general security perspective that addresses how these smart and interconnected complex systems operate, and how they can be protected against potential attacks. Within this framework, the field of cybersecurity -closely linked with information technology- focuses on countering cyber attacks carried out by adversarial actors. The concept of cybersecurity encompasses various subfields such as data security, cryptography, network and system security, and software and hardware protection. To ensure data security in cyberspace, various defense mechanisms must be established. Due to the interconnected nature of technological infrastructures, the threat of cyber attacks frequently comes to the forefront (Möller, 2020). The significance of cybersecurity is not only apparent during global political crises but also emerges as a crucial field beyond traditional security notions due to the increasing digitalization in business and society (Cavelty & Egloff, 2019). The security of digital information possessed by governments or individual users becomes a central issue (Azmi et al., 2018). At this point, it is evident that there is a close relationship between the concepts of digitalization and cybersecurity. In both the public and private sectors, the importance of building robust defense systems against cyber attacks and ensuring data security continues to grow day by day. The wide range of activities carried out in cyberspace, coupled with the high volume of security threats, highlights the complexity of this process.

The primary goal of cybersecurity is to protect large-scale data and systems from cyber attacks. Particularly, cyber attacks targeting the political and military assets of states represent one of the most dangerous threats a nation can face (Seemma et al., 2018). As a result, state leaders are taking strict measures to shield their citizens and economies from the impacts of such attacks, giving rise to what is termed the "Cyber

Westphalian Age" (Demchak & Dombrowski, 2011). In the Cyber Westphalian Age, states cannot define their borders as clearly as in the classical Westphalian order, making it difficult for them to assert sovereignty. Moreover, states are unable to fully control activities taking place in cyberspace (Mueller, 2020). In this ambiguous environment, in addition to cyber attacks, problems may also arise in physical devices and wireless communication systems (Sha et al., 2009).

Since cybersecurity involves many interconnected factors, it is impossible to propose simple and definitive solutions in the event of an attack (Cavelty & Wenger, 2022). When examining the nature of cyber conflicts, it appears that some commentators have reached a consensus around the idea of "waging war without fighting." States are developing various strategies to gain an advantage over their rivals in cyberspace and to achieve success without bloodshed (Carr, 2012). However, according to Thomas Rid, not only is cyber war not currently taking place, but it will also not emerge in the future. All past and present cyber attacks, in his view, are actually a combination of sabotage, subversion, and espionage activities. In Clausewitz's classical definition of war, emphasis is placed on the presence of violence, the instrumental nature of war, and its use for political purposes. Rid argues that no cyber conflict has ever met all three of these criteria simultaneously (Rid, 2012). On the other hand, John Stone considers cyber conflicts as part of the broader act of war. Given today's technological capabilities, the mere press of a button could result in the deaths of hundreds or even thousands of people (Stone, 2013). While there is ongoing debate in the literature over whether cyber conflicts should be considered acts of war, former United States (U.S.) Director of National Intelligence Mike McConnell has asserted that states are already engaged in warfare in cyberspace (Hayden, 2011). As can be seen, cybersecurity cannot be viewed merely as a technical issue; it also has significant strategic and political dimensions. Furthermore, based on Clausewitz's definition of war, various interpretations and discussions about cyber conflicts have emerged in the literature. However, it must be remembered that states are increasingly taking precautions in cyberspace, and the competition among them continues to intensify. In this context, any approach to cybersecurity should not only focus on preventing attacks but also carefully examine their nature, scope, and consequences.

In cyber attacks, the primary objective is to catch the target off guard and unprotected. When examining the variety of violations caused by cyber attacks, it becomes clear how crucial it is for states to take early precautions against such threats. Generally speaking, a cyber attack can be described as unauthorized access. In this context, attackers gain access to computer systems and carry out attacks on targeted areas to inflict damage. Hackers who infiltrate systems can steal data or gain access to target individuals' emails and publicly disclose them. Cyber espionage involves the theft of data that should remain confidential. It is conducted in a manner similar to traditional, physically executed espionage activities. Accordingly, there are two main types of cyber espionage: industrial espionage, which is carried out for material gain, and espionage aimed at uncovering highly classified information and documents belonging to states. In cyber operations, it is not always intended for the attacks carried out by rival states to have an immediate impact. Just as traditional armies prepare physically for war, many cyber operations focus on actions whose effects do not manifest right away. For example, in cyber operations, it is common for programs such as logic bombs or Trojan horses to be embedded in computers and remain dormant for a period of time before activation (Rosenzweig, 2013). With globalization, digitalization, and technological advancement, cybercrime has significantly increased. At this point, it is essential to invest heavily in cyber-security defense systems at both national and international levels. If the necessary precautions are not taken, the consequences of cyber attacks can be severe - in 2020 alone, cyber attacks are estimated to cause a global financial loss of $945 billion (Cremer et al., 2022).

Today, cyber attacks have become a method of resistance used by groups seeking to challenge political ideologies (Herzog, 2011). Additionally, states use cyber attacks to establish political dominance over one another. Throughout the 1990s and 2000s, Russia closely followed actions in the Baltic states, particularly those related to political figures significant to Soviet history. After several World War II monuments were damaged in Estonia in 2005, Russia accused Estonia of distorting historical facts and glorifying Nazism. On 26 April 2007, the Estonian government became the target of protests by certain Russia-linked groups during the relocation of a World War II monument related to Soviet history from Tallinn. Following the events, members of the Russian parliament (the Duma) called for the severing of diplomatic relations with Estonia. Furthermore, Russia imposed export restrictions on Estonia. As a result, trade volume between the two countries decreased, and disruptions occurred in railway transportation. On 27 April 2007, Russia launched intensive cyber attacks targeting Estonian government institutions, news agencies, political parties, and banks. The cyber attacks lasted for three weeks and initially involved mostly Denial of Service (DoS) and Distributed Denial of Service (DDoS) attacks aimed at websites and email systems. Later, the network infrastructure of Estonian telecommunications companies was targeted, resulting in a cyber attack on Estonia's critical infrastructure. These attacks significantly disrupted Estonia's banking and communication systems (Pernik, 2018). Russia denied any involvement in the cyber attacks (Libicki, 2009). In this context, it is evident that cyber attacks are not only technical in nature but also an extension of social and political disputes. Cyber attacks should not only be considered from a defensive point of view, but also from a national and international security perspective.

A similar process also occurred in Georgia outside of Estonia. Due to a dispute between Russia and Georgia over the regions of South Ossetia and Abkhazia, an armed conflict broke out in 2008. Following the entry of Georgian forces into South Ossetia on 7 August 2008, Russian troops intervened in the area, and Georgian soldiers were forced to withdraw. While Russian forces were operating on the ground, hackers directed by Russia launched DDoS attacks on Georgian government websites and Georgian news outlets. As a result, efforts were made to block Georgian authorities from receiving and disseminating information. Cyber attacks targeted the official websites of Georgian institutions, and images were published portraying Georgian leader Mikheil Saakashvili as Adolf Hitler. During this time, no emails could be sent out of Georgia. Although Georgia initially attempted to block the DDoS attacks, it was largely unsuccessful. In addition to the collapse of Georgia's banking system, major disruptions also occurred in telephone lines. As in the case of Estonia, the Russian government denied any involvement in the attacks. However, Georgia and some Western countries claimed that Russian intelligence was behind the operations (Clarke & Knake, 2010). Georgia was ultimately able to neutralize the cyber attacks thanks to technological support provided by the U.S. Geographically, Georgia is under pressure from Russia, but in terms of "cyber geography," it is under the protection of the US (Libicki, 2009). What happened in Georgia is significant in showing how cyber attacks can be coordinated simultaneously with traditional military conflict. In the international system, it can be observed that powerful states are attempting to exert dominance over one another through cyber operations.

Lastly, the cyber espionage operation conducted by China, which was uncovered in 2009 through the malicious software known as Gh0stNet, can be examined. Gh0stNet is a type of software that can be remotely controlled and can infiltrate computers via a Trojan horse program. Through this capability, a single keystroke can activate the target computer's microphone and camera, allowing full access to all information stored on the device. Using this software, China was able to infiltrate computers in the embassies of India, Malaysia, and Indonesia, as well as in some NATO systems. It is evident that cyber espionage is just as important as physical espionage. In order to avoid falling victim to such cyber attacks, states must conduct risk assessments. In this context, it is crucial to eliminate elements that create vulnerabilities (Rosenzweig, 2013).

DEFINITION AND IMPORTANCE OF CRITICAL INFRASTRUCTURE

When evaluated from a historical perspective, attacking the critical infrastructure facilities of a target country is an old warfare tactic. Throughout history, armies have aimed to destroy each other's long-term warfighting capacity in order to gain superiority during conflicts. In his book *The Art of War*, Sun Tzu noted that fire could be used effectively in five different ways in enemy territory: burning military zones, setting fire to storage facilities, targeting supply trains critical to logistics, destroying arsenals with fire, and killing enemy troops using fire (Geers, 2009). In today's context, the term "critical infrastructure" refers to systems essential for the security, economy, health, and social welfare of a society -systems whose disruption or destruction would have significant consequences (Luiijf & Klaver, 2019). Furthermore, the concept encompasses sectors such as energy, water, financial services, transportation, healthcare, and telecommunications, which are evaluated in terms of national security, economic stability, and public safety. With the increase in digitalization, the interconnection and integration of these sectors have come to the fore, leading to a rise in cyber attacks from both states and hacker groups targeting these areas. Ensuring smooth and secure operations in these sectors is crucial for national security. However, the widespread use of digital technologies and the internet within critical infrastructure sectors introduces new vulnerabilities (Bellamkonda, 2020). The reason for using the internet in these sectors is to enable remote management of infrastructure through advanced software, thereby reducing operational costs. Yet, as mentioned above, this also brings new threats (Geers, 2009). The security of critical infrastructure is closely tied to the sophistication of network technologies. The process of managing critical infrastructure through network technologies began to gain importance in the 1990s. During the same period, national and international efforts to develop defense techniques against cyber threats became more widespread (Darıcılı & Çelik, 2021). On 22 May 1998, U.S. President Bill Clinton signed Directive No. 63, which emphasized the potential security vulnerabilities of critical infrastructure. It also underlined the need to approach national critical infrastructure from a security perspective. In this framework, U.S. decision-makers advocated for taking preventive measures related to critical infrastructure (Hemme, 2015). Thus, states must make maximum efforts not only to protect their critical infrastructure from cyber attacks but also from threats posed by natural disasters and terrorist attacks. A disruption in energy, water, transportation, or communication networks would negatively affect the functioning of many other sectors. According to the Global Risks Report published in 2021, weather conditions, climate change, natural disasters, pandemics, and cyber attacks are listed among the most significant risk factors today (Roshanaei, 2021).

After the 11 September 2001 attack on the U.S., numerous documents on the protection of critical infrastructure were published by international organizations, governments, and research institutions (Aradau, 2010). Some institutions argue that the concept of critical infrastructure extends beyond the sectors mentioned earlier. Within the European Union (EU), the European Programme for Critical Infrastructure

Protection (EPCIP) emphasizes that protecting critical infrastructure is an important responsibility for all member states and EU citizens. EPCIP classifies energy, information and communication technologies, water, food and agriculture, health, financial systems, civil administration, public order, transportation, the chemical industry, nuclear energy, and space as sectors of critical infrastructure. According to the U.S. *National Infrastructure Protection Plan* published by the Department of Homeland Security, in addition to the aforementioned areas, national monuments, the defense industry, and commercial facilities are also considered part of critical infrastructure (Alcaraz & Zeadally, 2015). Germany's *National Strategy for Critical Infrastructure Protection* states that a disruption in critical infrastructure could lead to dramatic consequences for a nation in terms of public safety, society, and the economy. Looking at the United Kingdom (UK)'s definition of critical infrastructure, nuclear and chemical facilities -which may not be essential for the continuity of basic services but pose potential dangers to the public -are also evaluated within the scope of critical infrastructure (Gallais & Filiol, 2017). It is evident that there is no standard definition of critical infrastructure. Comparing the definitions in the EU and the U.S., it is apparent that areas such as cultural assets and national defense are also included within the scope of critical infrastructure. In this context, the security of critical infrastructure should be approached in a multidimensional way, and flexible security measures should be developed according to the nature of the threats.

Today, among the most complex threats to the security of critical infrastructures, *Advanced Persistent Threats* (APTs) rank at the top. These attacks are particularly difficult to detect because they combine various cyber and physical threats into sophisticated attack strategies. APT attacks are typically executed against specific, high-value targets. In such attacks, traditional security measures or antivirus software may prove insufficient. The goal of a cyber attack via APT is often to gain long-term control of a system, infiltrate it stealthily, and use it as a platform for further attacks. In some cases, APT-based cyber attacks on critical infrastructures aim to shut down systems entirely or cause permanent damage. For instance, compromising computers at a nuclear facility to harm a nuclear reactor could result in a catastrophic disaster. Another key aspect of APT attacks is their ability to remain undetected within a system for extended periods. It is widely known that many APT operations are carried out by state-sponsored groups with virtually no budget constraints (Rass et al., 2020). APTs are particularly effective in cyber attacks targeting critical infrastructure. These attacks are recognized as threats to national security, and states must engage in vigorous efforts to minimize the potential damage they may cause.

Some critical infrastructures are under the control of the private sector. For example, Internet Service Providers (ISPs) can lease communication lines to both governments and commercial enterprises. This highlights the necessity for cooperation between states and private sector entities to ensure the security of critical infrastructures. In public-private partnerships, the clarity of each party's objectives increases the likelihood of success. Furthermore, governments must take the lead in securing critical infrastructures that are under private sector control. The private sector must fully understand what is expected of it in its cyber cooperation with the state. If companies perceive that governments are not making the necessary investments in cybersecurity measures, this could undermine the nation's overall cybersecurity posture. States, especially during military operations, are often subject to a significant number of cyber attacks from hackers. In this context, it is highly likely that DoS attacks will occur during military operations. Such attacks can result in data alterations or even the physical destruction of hardware. For instance, during the Kosovo war in 1999, hackers attempted to infiltrate computers used by soldiers in an effort to disrupt NATO operations, and some missions were hindered before the intrusion was detected. These developments underscore the need for governments to determine the extent to which the internet poses a threat to national security. For this reason, states must ensure the security of numerous critical infrastructure components, particularly electrical grids (Geers, 2009; Tiirmaa-Klaar, 2016). Governments pursuing a sustainable digitalization approach are striving to make digitalized critical infrastructures more resilient to cyber attacks. To this end, states primarily work to prevent data loss in the face of cyber attacks by backing up information within critical infrastructure systems (Goswami et al., 2023). In theory, critical infrastructure systems should not be directly connected to the internet; however, in practice, these systems are increasingly becoming digitalized (Tiirmaa-Klaar, 2016). Cooperation between the state and the private sector on critical infrastructure is not only important for technical reasons but also for strategic purposes, and thus must be jointly planned and implemented. The fact that the management of critical infrastructures is not solely in the hands of the public sector underlines that responsibility for protective measures must also be shared with the private sector.

Attacks targeting critical infrastructure have emerged as a significant risk factor in an increasingly globalized world. When examining the perpetrators of such attacks, one can cite state-sponsored espionage groups, terrorist organizations, or malicious hackers. British intelligence reports that these groups have carried out cyber attacks against government institutions in the UK, attempting to steal sensitive information by disabling computer systems. While many cyber attackers are financially motivated, those driven by political or ideological motives often focus their efforts on critical infrastructures. In the initial phase of a cyber attack, it is often very difficult to determine whether it was carried out by state-sponsored actors or by individual malicious hackers. Moreover, understanding the motivation behind the attack requires in-depth investigation. Some cyber attacks on computer networks may be carried out as a form of protest. However, attacks conducted directly against critical infrastructure by hackers pose a serious threat to national security

(Rudner, 2013). It is evident that the actors and motivations behind cyber attacks are highly diverse. The difficulty of identifying the perpetrators behind such attacks necessitates more detailed analysis of intelligence and cyber operations within the field of cybersecurity.

In order to combat cyber attacks, states generally engage their ministries of interior and judicial systems. However, depending on each country's internal dynamics, different institutions may be tasked with this responsibility. While some countries have established national cyber agencies, European nations tend to involve IT agencies, intelligence organizations, and interior ministries in the fight against cyber crime. As dependence on digital infrastructure systems increases, the issue of preventing cyber attacks will continue to be a topic of discussion among decision-makers. Moreover, when examining investments in cybersecurity across countries, even among developed nations, a growing imbalance is evident. At the same time, the number of hackers with various motivations is steadily increasing. While the number of internet users was 2.5 billion in 2015, it has doubled to reach 5 billion by 2025. This surge in users has led to a rise in the number of actors seeking to infiltrate and damage critical infrastructure systems. Neglecting cybersecurity in both developed and developing countries poses serious threats in terms of both national security and economic stability (Tiirmaa-Klaar, 2016). France has attempted to build a centralized system in its fight against cyber attacks, whereas the UK conducts its efforts by involving multiple actors. In the UK, private sector actors responsible for the security of critical infrastructures have more authority compared to those in France (Weiss & Biermann, 2021). Cybersecurity has become vital for states today. In response to cyber threats, countries do not adopt standard or one-size-fits-all solutions. Each country establishes institutional structures based on its specific context. France has adopted a centralized approach, promoting a more controlled security strategy, while the UK has pursued a flexible and inclusive response method by cooperating with a broader range of actors. Cybersecurity should be addressed not only from a technological perspective but also in a multidimensional manner that includes governance, investment priorities, and international strategy.

In addition to the concept of protecting critical infrastructure, the term critical infrastructure preparedness is also used in the literature. This concept aims to prevent risks, threats, and vulnerabilities targeting critical infrastructures through cyber attacks or physical interventions, thereby emphasizing the necessity of proactive measures. Training programs should be organized concerning the measures to be taken by both the public and private sectors. Furthermore, awareness among personnel working in critical infrastructure sectors should be increased so they can report any unusual activity to the authorities (Radvanovsky, 2006). Most defense measures focus on a proactive security approach. However, the measures taken do not always yield positive results. Therefore, it is necessary to consider proactive and reactive measures together. To deter individuals who attack critical infrastructures, additional precautions -such as identity card scanning along with computer passwords -can be implemented. Yet even this measure may not be enough to deter hackers (Hermann & Pridöhl, 2020). Taking measures to prevent cyber attacks is of great importance. However, attackers continuously develop new methods, so assuming that every precaution will be effective is not a realistic approach. In addition to digital precautions, physical measures are not always deterrent either. For this reason, instead of seeking absolute solutions in cybersecurity, a flexible and continuously evolving approach should be adopted.

There are several reasons why critical infrastructure facilities are targeted by cyber attacks. First, countries possess a large number of critical infrastructures that are widely dispersed across national territories. This makes it difficult to protect all critical infrastructure facilities and renders them vulnerable targets. In most cases, critical infrastructure facilities operate in an integrated manner, and as a result, disruption in one sector can affect others. For example, a cyber attack on a country's power grid can negatively impact transportation and communication infrastructures as well. Moreover, cyber attacks on critical infrastructures can have severe psychological effects on the public. For this reason, attackers often carry out such sensational actions to increase their visibility. In critical infrastructures controlled by either the public or private sector, inadequate security investments due to cost concerns can lead to intelligence weaknesses in detecting potential attacks. While increasing digitalization in critical infrastructures reduces human error, it also introduces new security vulnerabilities. The use of foreign-origin technologies in critical infrastructure systems points to another potential security issue (Haber & Zarsky, 2018). Cyber attacks not only cause financial damage but also create fear and insecurity among the public, which can lead to more serious consequences. Therefore, in addition to ensuring the security of critical infrastructures, raising public awareness of cyber threats is also essential. Although the use of advanced technology in critical infrastructure systems produces beneficial outcomes, it does not mean these technologies are entirely secure. In particular, technology transfers from foreign countries may lead to issues that could pose threats to national security.

CYBER THREATS TO ENERGY INFRASTRUCTURE

Energy infrastructure is a key component of critical infrastructures and provides services to many other sectors. In modern society, the uninterrupted functioning of sectors depends on the resilience and security of energy infrastructure. Today, cyber attacks are carried out in more dangerous and complex ways. It is well known that both developed and developing countries heavily use network-connected technologies in the energy sector. While states face small-scale cyber attacks on a daily basis, large-scale attacks typically span longer periods (Venkatachary et al., 2017). When examining the electricity infrastructure in the U.S., it is estimated that there are more than 7.000 power plants, 55.000 transformers, and 160.000 miles of transmission lines. A large-scale cyber attack on this massive critical infrastructure system in the U.S. could have dangerous consequences. According to the World Economic Forum's 2020 Global Risks Report, cyber attacks on critical infrastructures -including energy systems- are considered high-risk threats. The International Energy Agency reports that cyber attacks targeting energy infrastructures are increasing day by day, and that the individuals carrying out these attacks are becoming more skilled in identifying security vulnerabilities (Smith, 2021). Power plants, which are among the critical infrastructure components, are usually constructed in a multilayered manner; however, they still possess security vulnerabilities against cyber attacks. With the digitalization of electric grids, these systems have become vulnerable to cyber threats, which negatively affect human life, the environment, and businesses (Plėta et al., 2020).

One of the earliest known attacks on critical infrastructure occurred in 1982, when the CIA allegedly created a malicious software and indirectly sold it to the Soviet Union. This ultimately led to the explosion of a pipeline in Siberia. In more recent times, one of the most striking cyber attacks on critical infrastructure was the 2010 Stuxnet attack, a malicious software operation that targeted Iran's nuclear development facility in Natanz (Onyeji et al., 2014). The goal of the Stuxnet malware was not to disable the entire centrifuge array, but to target a specific number and type of centrifuges. The software disrupted uranium enrichment and caused equipment failure due to unexpected vibrations. However, for a long time, it was not recognized that the facility was under cyber attack (Singer, 2015). After Stuxnet was discovered, it was determined that the software had actually been deployed as early as 2007. The infiltration plan into Natanz was initiated via a mole working for Dutch intelligence. This mole was later presented as a technician working for a front company jointly established by the U.S. and Israel. In the spring of 2007, under the pretext of work, the mole successfully gained access to the Natanz nuclear facility. He introduced the Stuxnet virus into the facility through a USB device, uploading it into the internal computer systems. As a result of Stuxnet, Iran's nuclear program slowed down, and the incident exposed vulnerabilities in Iran's national security. Clearly, Stuxnet was a cyber operation conducted through U.S.-Israeli collaboration, which also involved the use of HUMINT (human intelligence) tactics. Stuxnet is considered one of the first targeted attacks against critical infrastructure (Çahmutoğlu, 2021; Stevens, 2018). Former CIA Director Michael Hayden stated that the Stuxnet operation clearly demonstrated how a country's critical infrastructure could be targeted. Following the Stuxnet attack, other spyware programs such as Duqu (discovered in Iran in September 2011) and Flame (discovered in May 2012) were identified in Iran's computer networks. These spyware programs are known to have inflicted serious damage on Iran's critical infrastructure. This indicates that Iran failed to develop adequate defense mechanisms against cyber attacks (Bahgat, 2020). Moreover, the Flame spyware infiltrated the computer networks of many countries in the Middle East and went undetected for a long time. When Stuxnet infiltrated a targeted system, it was programmed to damage nuclear enrichment equipment and then self-destruct. Additionally, Iranian technicians working at the nuclear facility were misled by inaccurate data caused by the malware when monitoring the plant's safety systems. According to some commentators, the Stuxnet and Flame spyware were developed to be used simultaneously in order to disrupt Iran's nuclear program. Similarly, such malware-based cyber attacks have been described by some researchers as weapons of mass destruction (Wilson, 2013). The Stuxnet operation is significant because it demonstrated that cyber operations are not limited to intelligence gathering; they can also cause physical harm to critical infrastructure. Alongside the use of cyber tactics and strategies, the operation also highlights the importance of HUMINT. If states fail to address vulnerabilities in cybersecurity, they may face serious consequences.

Stuxnet represents a turning point in the targeting of critical infrastructure. It was a significant cyber attack that embodied the elements of deniability and ambiguity. In this context, it is easier for states in cyberspace to deny responsibility for accusations and to absolve themselves of blame. While identifying the attacker in traditional armed conflicts is relatively easy, this becomes significantly more difficult in cyber conflicts (Farwell & Rohozinski, 2011). After the Stuxnet attack, Iran was able to resume its nuclear program activities within just over a year (Lindsay, 2013). In modern nuclear power plants, computers that handle large volumes of data play a major role. These computers are used to operate the reactor itself or to control the functions of auxiliary systems. If any change is made to the software or hardware in nuclear plants, it can result in an accident within the reactor. In the event of such an accident, emergency response systems are activated; however, these do not always lead to positive outcomes (Shea et al., 2013).

The increase in cyber attacks targeting critical infrastructure demonstrates that state-sponsored cybercriminal groups are carrying out serious attacks on both the public and private sectors, causing significant financial losses. Russia, with its high technical capabilities in cyberspace, actively uses cyber attack methods against rival states to achieve military and political objectives. It is known that Russia launched cyber attacks on Ukraine during the armed conflict that began between the two countries in 2014. During this period, Russia had the opportunity to test its cyber power through the use of cyber weapons. In 2015 and 2016, Russia conducted cyber attacks on Ukraine's electrical infrastructure, causing extensive damage to the country's power plants. In 2017, Russia used malicious software called NotPetya, causing billions of dollars in damages both across Ukraine and on a global scale (Aljohani, 2022). Looking at its global impact, the NotPetya attack caused Danish shipping company Maersk to suffer losses of approximately $300 million (Dutta & Navy, 2022). The NotPetya incident is one of the most striking examples in the history of cyber warfare. Although it initially targeted Ukraine, it quickly turned into a global crisis by affecting multinational companies. Through the NotPetya attack, Russia aimed to disrupt Ukraine's economy and erode the Ukrainian public's trust in the state. The attack was also a display of Russia's cyber power and determination on both regional and global levels. Furthermore, Russia sought to strengthen its position in Eastern Europe, highlighting the fact that cyber warfare can be as important as traditional warfare. As a result of the NotPetya attack, Ukraine's electricity infrastructure, traffic systems, and government institutions suffered major damage. Poland and the Baltic states were also economically affected due to their strong trade relations with Ukraine. It is estimated that the NotPetya attack caused approximately $10 billion in damages globally. Due to the risks posed by cyber attacks, insurance companies had to reevaluate their policies, which have since become more expensive. The NotPetya incident exposed the inadequacy of the digital infrastructure of the region's economies. Most government institutions lacked a proactive approach and were found to be weak in terms of cybersecurity (Hassam, 2025). It was determined that the Russian military intelligence agency GRU was behind the NotPetya attack. U.S. intelligence officials identified the group responsible for the cyber attacks on Ukraine since 2014 as Fancy Bear/APT28, which is known to operate on behalf of the GRU (Bronk et al., 2023). It is evident that Ukraine was not the sole target of the NotPetya attack. The cyber attack caused global economic damage and revealed the critical importance of digital infrastructure security. In addition to causing financial harm, such attacks also damage diplomatic relations between states. Therefore, cybersecurity must be evaluated on a global scale, and it is becoming increasingly clear that the boundaries between states are becoming blurred in cyberspace.

In Russia's cyber attacks against Ukraine, the objective has been to collapse the entire electrical grid system and disable natural gas pipelines, thereby preventing the population from meeting their heating needs. According to many cyber analysts, during the Russia-Ukraine war that began on 24 February 2022, cyber attacks were used more sparingly compared to traditional military operations. For instance, according to Nadiya Kostyuk and Erik Gartzke, the goals of Russia's recent cyber attacks were to collect intelligence, mobilize Ukrainian public opinion against the Ukrainian government, and gain leverage in diplomatic negotiations. Unit 74455, operating under the Russian GRU, carried out a cyber attack on electrical substations in Ukraine during the early months of the ongoing conflict. In this operation, the

Russians attempted to infiltrate Ukraine's central electrical system using a malicious software called *Industroyer2*. Ukrainian officials reported that these attacks were thwarted by Ukrainian cyber experts, but approximately two million Ukrainians were at risk of being left without electricity. Ukrainian authorities also noted that the tactics used by the Russians in this cyber attack resembled those employed in 2015 and 2016. To defend against the cyber attacks Ukraine faced, countries such as the U.S., NATO member states, and EU countries provided cybersecurity support. In particular, the U.S. and UK cybersecurity agencies took steps to strengthen Ukraine's cyber defense capabilities. In this context, the U.S. Department of Energy worked to enhance cybersecurity mechanisms in Ukraine's energy sector, while the U.S. Treasury Department provided similar support in the area of financial operations. Additionally, since 2021, many U.S.-based private companies, especially Microsoft, have supported Ukraine against Russian cyber attacks. Microsoft alone reportedly spent $239 million in this effort. Since 2020, the U.S. has also sent cyber experts to Ukraine and provided software support to help secure the country's critical infrastructure. In the UK, the Government Communications Headquarters (GCHQ), which combats cyber attacks, provided intelligence and consultancy support to Ukraine (Lin, 2022; Willett, 2022). On 15 January 2022, Microsoft detected a ransomware named *WhisperGate* that targeted various Ukrainian government institutions. As can be seen, Ukraine faces serious difficulties in protecting not only its energy sector but also other critical infrastructure from cyber attacks. As regional tensions escalate into conflict, state-sponsored cyber attacks come to the forefront, and combating them requires significant financial investment. In this regard, outdated security systems that protect energy infrastructure must be modernized (Borychenko et al., 2024). Thanks to the support it has received from foreign states, Ukraine has adopted a cyber-strategic perspective to minimize damage, focusing on data backups and strengthening firewalls (Aviv & Ferri, 2023). Russia's targeting of Ukraine's electrical and energy infrastructure cannot be evaluated solely as a military strategy. Rather, it reveals Russia's intention to expand its sphere of influence. In response to these attacks, Ukraine has been compelled to rely on the support of both the private sector and foreign governments.

When looking at recent cyber attacks targeting the energy sector, it is observed that in February 2021, two Brazilian state-run electricity distribution companies, Eletrobras and Copel, experienced ransomware attacks that temporarily disabled their systems. Additionally, there was a significant data exfiltration from Copel's system. Similarly, on 5 May 2021, a Norwegian energy company, Volue ASA, announced that it had fallen victim to a cyber attack due to ransomware found in its systems. To prevent further data theft by hackers, the company temporarily shut down its systems (Georgiadou et al., 2023). In May 2021, a major fuel pipeline owned by Colonial Pipeline, located on the southeastern coast of the U.S., was targeted by a cyber attack, leading to a temporary fuel shortage in the region. Hackers used ransomware to halt the flow through the pipeline and demanded a ransom for the restoration of the system. Increasing numbers of cyber attacks are being carried out against the energy sector every day. According to IBM's February 2021 report, in 2020, the energy sector was the third most affected industry by cyber attacks, following manufacturing and banking. Researchers focusing on energy security argue that critical elements of the U.S. energy network, such as pipelines and power plants, remain insufficiently protected against cyber threats (Plumer, 2021). After the Colonial Pipeline attack, the company was forced to pay a ransom of $4.4 million to regain control of its systems from the hackers (Smith, 2021). In the U.S., cyber attacks targeting critical infrastructure increased by approximately 70% in 2024 compared to 2023. Despite growth and digitalization in energy networks, the lack of necessary investment is making critical infrastructure systems in the U.S. increasingly vulnerable (Dareen & Srivastava, 2024). The above-mentioned cyber incidents demonstrate that attacks on critical infrastructure pose not only economic damages but also a significant threat to national security. To prevent future cyber attacks that may have global implications, critical infrastructures must be redesigned with a modern cybersecurity approach.

In Iran's regional political struggle, Israel and Saudi Arabia stand as its primary rivals. In this context, there have been occasional cyber attacks between the parties, particularly targeting the energy sector. A hacker group named *Gonjeshke Darande*, operating on behalf of Israel, launched a cyber attack on Iran's gas stations in December 2023. Iranian Oil Minister Javad Owji stated that gas stations across the country were out of service and experiencing disruptions. As a result of this cyber attack, approximately 70% of gas stations in Iran were rendered inoperative (Ribeiro, 2023). Another example is the cyber attack on Saudi Arabia's oil company Aramco in August 2012 using a piece of malware called *Shamoon*. This attack led to the complete deletion of data on 30.000 computers at Aramco facilities. The most notorious feature of the Shamoon malware was that the deleted data was unrecoverable. It is widely believed that Iran was behind the Shamoon cyber attack. It took Aramco approximately two weeks to fully restore its systems (Alelyani & Kumar, 2018). These examples show that the global energy sector remains highly vulnerable to cyber attacks. The ongoing cyber conflict between Iran, Israel, and Saudi Arabia demonstrates that states are now engaging in digital confrontations. As a result of such cyber attacks, electronic systems have suffered severe damage, and restoring them to full functionality has often taken weeks.

CYBER ATTACKS ON WATER INFRASTRUCTURE SYSTEMS

Drinking water and wastewater services constitute key components of critical infrastructure. Water infrastructure systems are threatened by factors such as floods, droughts, earthquakes, pollution, or cyber attacks (Sinha et al., 2023). For example, after the 1995 earthquake in Kobe, Japan, the city's water infrastructure system suffered extensive damage. Water infrastructure provides water for agricultural activities, industrial operations, businesses, and households. In the 1997 report prepared in the U.S. on the protection of critical infrastructure, water systems were identified as part of critical infrastructure, and it was noted that there were significant security vulnerabilities in this area. Water infrastructure systems are highly vulnerable to physical, terrorist, and cyber attacks (Panguluri et al., 2011; Clark et al., 2011). There are different ways in which damage can be inflicted on water infrastructure. First, attacks may target water distribution systems by disrupting telecommunications or electronic control systems. Second, water contamination through chemical attacks may be intended, posing serious threats to public health. Finally, cyber attacks on the computers that control water infrastructure systems can lead to data theft or service disruptions (Bahadur & Samuels, 2011). Considering natural disasters and new threats emerging from technological advances, comprehensive strategic plans must be developed to enhance the security of water infrastructure systems.

It was previously noted that the regional rivalry between Israel and Iran also manifests itself in the cyber domain. The power struggle between the two countries continues through cyber attacks targeting water infrastructure facilities. In April 2021, water pumps in Israel were targeted in a cyber attack. Israeli officials stated that the attack was carried out by Iran. The main goal of the attackers was to infiltrate the computers at the water facilities and increase the chlorine levels in the water. Following the attack, the Israel National Cyber Directorate announced that all passwords for computers at the water facilities had to be changed (Goud, 2021). After the cyber attacks, the directorate responsible for Israel's water infrastructure signed an agreement with the cybersecurity company SIGA OT Solutions to ensure the security of the facilities. The company stated that it would eliminate cyber threats targeting devices used in critical infrastructure and provide protection against hackers who infiltrate computer systems and demand ransom (Gross, 2021). It is evident that water infrastructure systems are vulnerable to state-sponsored cyber attacks. Due to the increase in cyber attacks, cooperation between the private and public sectors must be strengthened.

Water infrastructure in the U.S. is vulnerable to cyber attacks due to aging facilities. As cyber attacks on U.S. water systems -especially by actors such as Iran and Russia- continue, security vulnerabilities are increasingly exposed. Furthermore, the growing digitalization of water infrastructure systems significantly raises the likelihood of cyber intrusions. In the winter of 2024, a hacker group directed by the Russian military infiltrated the system of a water treatment plant in Texas, causing a systemic malfunction. Cyber experts believe that this incident was carried out by Russia's military intelligence agency, the GRU. Similarly, Russia has recently launched cyber attacks against a dam system in France and water infrastructure in Poland. The primary aim behind these attacks appears to be sending a political message to countries with which Russia has strained relations. Consequently, it is likely that similar attacks will increase in NATO member states in the near future. In addition to Russia, Iran is also making efforts to carry out cyber attacks against the U.S. In 2023, a group named *Cyber Av3ngers,* affiliated with Iran's Islamic Revolutionary Guard Corps (IRGC) and operating under its Cyber Electronic Command, disabled systems controlling pumps and valves at a wastewater facility in Pennsylvania. Following this attack, the U.S. Department of the Treasury announced sanctions against six senior Iranian officials working within the IRGC. Given Iran's advancing cyber capabilities, both the U.S. and Israel have recently shown an increasing tendency to take precautions against potential cyber attacks on their critical infrastructure. Cyber attacks on U.S. water facilities have negatively impacted the daily lives of American citizens. Former U.S. National Security Advisor Jake Sullivan stated that investments in defense should be increased to prevent such attacks on water systems. Cyber attacks targeting water infrastructure include activities that could seriously affect public health, such as altering or contaminating water quality. Moreover, cyber attacks that cause prolonged water outages in homes, businesses, or hospitals can create fear and panic among the public. The growing trend of remotely managing water infrastructure systems for the sake of cost reduction and operational efficiency has increased their vulnerability, as these systems are connected to the internet (Cyfirma Decoding Threats, 2024). The security of water infrastructure systems should not be viewed merely as a technical issue. The serious impacts of cyber attacks on national security and public health must not be overlooked. Updates and improvements must be made to ensure cybersecurity at water infrastructure facilities.

On 22 September 2024, a cyber attack occurred at the Arkansas City Water Treatment in Arkansas, U.S. However, the attack was detected in time, and there were no restrictions on water supply. After the incident, it was observed that cybersecurity experts and local authorities cooperated closely. There was a prevailing belief among officials that this incident could be a precursor to a larger cyber attack in the future. It was found that the attackers typically targeted water facilities that were connected to the internet and used outdated systems. Experts believe that operators of small and medium-sized water infrastructure systems are particularly vulnerable to such attacks due to the lack of cybersecurity experts at their facilities. They also predict that the number of such attacks will increase in the future. The damage caused by cyber attacks on critical infrastructure has been quite costly. According to IBM's

2024 Data Breach Report, a cyber attack on critical infrastructure resulted in an average loss of approximately $5.56 million, marking an 18% increase in costs compared to 2023 (Reed, 2025). The cyber attack incident in Arkansas highlights the importance of investing in cybersecurity. The use of outdated systems and the lack of specialized personnel in water infrastructure facilities make these facilities more vulnerable to cyber attacks.

CYBERSECURITY OF FINANCIAL SYSTEMS

With the increase in digitization, cyber attacks on financial institutions continue. Both the number of cyber attacks on financial systems and their intensity and complexity levels are increasing. These attacks threaten not only personal data theft or targeting personal assets in banks, but also the entire economic structure. According to a study, the increase in ransomware attacks in the banking sector in 2021 was 1,318% annually. Looking at the data for 2022, cyber attacks on financial institutions increased by 38% compared to the previous year. Jonah Force Hill, who previously served as the director within the U.S. Secret Service Cyber Investigations Advisory Board, emphasized that many global sectors are exposed to cyber attacks, but the financial sector is regularly and frequently targeted. Attackers use various methods such as ransomware, DDoS attacks, and email fraud to conduct cyber attacks (Gulyás & Kiss, 2023; Jimmy, 2024). In the banking sector, a large portion of financial transactions is carried out by networked computers, and communication between bank employees and customers usually occurs over the internet. With the increasing impact of online banking, banks have more opportunities to focus on high-value transactions. However, these developments also present a very favorable situation for hackers. Furthermore, the ease of conducting financial transactions online is also highly attractive to attackers (Marchetti et al., 2012; Ho & Mallick, 2010). Although significant changes have occurred in the global banking sector in the digital field, it should not be forgotten that technology also brings along cyber threats. Banks serve their customers with the help of digital systems, but during this process, they rely on third-party systems that are beyond their control. This situation gives hackers the opportunity to hack digital banking systems and steal money from bank accounts. In this context, banks need to take measures against unauthorized access or cyber threats to ensure the security of their customers (Al-Alawi & Al-Bassam, 2020). Like other critical infrastructures, the financial sector has followed the trend of digitization and, as a result, has become increasingly exposed to cyber threats. While banks follow the digitization processes, they must also develop new security measures against threats. Additionally, financial institutions must establish a cybersecurity strategy not only for the security measures in their own systems but also for all the digital systems they are connected to.

In addition to being exposed to cyber attacks on web applications, institutions in the banking sector also face attacks such as botnets or trojans, targeting employees or customers to gain access to authentication mechanisms. With the increase in cyber threats to the financial sector, both the public and private sectors are taking new measures every day to protect assets. In 2016, the Reserve Bank of India published a statement highlighting the difference between information security and cybersecurity. According to this statement, all banks in India were required to develop a comprehensive cybersecurity strategy. Similarly, international organizations such as the International Monetary Fund (IMF) and the World Economic Forum (WEF) have issued a series of directives to ensure that banks worldwide remain vigilant against cyber threats. In this context, banking institutions have chosen to redesign their computer infrastructure systems to be resilient to cyber attacks. Additionally, to test the validity of new technologies and teach employees how to respond to attacks, active defense methods are being employed by simulating cyber attacks. Just like in traditional warfare, during cyber warfare, both public and private sector entities resort to tactics and strategies that will bring them success (Creado & Ramteke, 2020). Looking at these developments, it is clear that actors in the financial sector prioritize cybersecurity. With the implementation of active defense methods, they are not only combating existing threats but also taking measures to prepare for potential attacks. From this, it can be concluded that in the coming years, banks will invest more in cybersecurity infrastructure and engage in more international cooperation on this matter.

The primary goal of cyber attackers targeting financial institutions is fraud or bank robbery. In 2016, the Bangladesh Central Bank fell into the trap of cybercriminals and lost approximately 81 million dollars. The impact of such a cyber attack can indirectly affect all institutions involved in the transaction process. Therefore, it is essential for banking institutions to allocate sufficient budgets for cybersecurity so that they can design their infrastructure to be more resilient to cyber attacks. In this regard, the banking sector typically resorts to methods such as procuring reliable software and hardware systems, establishing data encryption systems, and creating risk detection systems (Uddin et al., 2020). Additionally, by adopting multi-factor authentication in banking systems, multiple security barriers are created to prevent hackers from executing data breaches. This way, access to systems is not solely through passwords, making unauthorized access more difficult. If passwords are created strongly, even if data is stolen, attackers will not be able to access the contents of that data. Cyber attackers generally target financial institutions using outdated software. Therefore, keeping security system software up to date is crucial (SentinelOne, 2024). Banks around the world are constantly facing the threat of cyber attacks. According to data from December 2024, banks in Singapore encountered an average of 1.830 cyber attacks per week in the last six months. According to the IMF, the financial sector has been subjected to over 20.000 cyber attacks in the last 20 years, resulting in a global loss of approximately 12 billion dollars. Data losses caused by cyber attacks also tarnish the reputation of banks. Furthermore, during cyber attacks, a halt in credit flow can occur, negatively impacting the global financial system (Staff Reporter, 2024). For banks to protect critical data and prevent disruptions in operations, investing in cybersecurity infrastructure has become a necessity, not a choice.

CONCLUSION

This chapter thoroughly examines the threats faced by critical digital infrastructure facilities as digitalization increases, with a focus on energy, water, and financial infrastructure systems. The dynamics of cyber attacks and their impacts are analyzed, considering the vulnerabilities that come with the opportunities provided by digitalization. The findings in this chapter highlight that, while digitalization offers opportunities, the security gaps it creates pose significant threats to critical infrastructure facilities. The widespread use of the internet and digital technologies in critical infrastructure facilities has facilitated remote management of systems but has also opened the door for new cyber attacks by cybercriminals.

Looking at cyber attacks on energy critical infrastructures, it is evident that the Stuxnet attack not only involved data theft but also reached levels capable of causing direct physical damage. Similarly, in cyber attacks on water infrastructure facilities, risks that directly threaten public health, such as water contamination or disruption of water distribution services, arise. As seen in the examples of Israel and the U.S., cyber attacks on water infrastructures appear to have political objectives. In the financial sector, identity fraud, data breaches, and cyber attacks targeting banking transactions are causing significant economic damage. The Bangladesh Central Bank case starkly revealed that a low level of defense resilience in financial institutions' digital infrastructures could lead to negative consequences.

Another key finding of this chapter is that state-backed actors play an important role in cyber attacks and attempt to exert political and economic pressure on rival states by targeting critical infrastructures. Russia's attacks on Estonia and Georgia, China's Gh0stNet operation, Iran's cyber attack attempts on U.S. water facilities, and the mutual cyber attacks between Israel and Iran clearly demonstrate this. It is understood that states view cyberspace as a real battlefield and have increasingly incorporated it into their military strategies. However, due to the nature of cyberspace, it is difficult to definitively identify the perpetrators of attacks and assign direct responsibility. As a result, states adopt denial strategies after attacks, allowing them to avoid international legal responsibility.

In conclusion, the most fundamental finding of this chapter is that, in addition to enhancing the technical capacity of the public sector for cybersecurity, there is a need to strengthen international cooperation, coordinate with the private sector, conduct public awareness campaigns, and develop fast and effective intervention strategies in times of crisis. In this context, the security of critical digital infrastructures will become more prominent in international relations and national security policies in the future. In an environment where cyber threats are continuously evolving, developing a flexible, innovative, and multi-layered security approach is no longer a choice but a necessity.

REFERENCES

Al-Alawi, A. I., & Al-Bassam, S. A. (2020). The Significance of Cybersecurity System in Helping Managing Risk in Banking and Financial Sector. *Journal of Xidian University*, *14*(7), 1523–1536. DOI: 10.37896/jxu14.7/174

Alcaraz, C., & Zeadally, S. (2015). Critical infrastructure protection: Requirements and challenges for the 21st century. *International Journal of Critical Infrastructure Protection*, *8*, 53–66. DOI: 10.1016/j.ijcip.2014.12.002

Alelyani, S., & Kumar, H. (2018). Overview of Cyberattack on Saudi Organizations. *Journal of Information Security & Cybercrimes Research*, *1*(1), 32–39. DOI: 10.26735/16587790.2018.004

Alexei, A., & Alexei, A. (2022). The Difference Between Cyber Security vs Information Security. *Journal of Engineering Science*, *29*(4), 72–83. DOI: 10.52326/jes.utm.2022.29(4).08

Aljohani, T. M. (2022). Cyberattacks on Energy Infrastructures: Modern War Weapons. doi: /arXiv.2208.14225DOI: 10.48550

Aradau, C. (2010). Security That Matters: Critical Infrastructure and Objects of Protection. *Security Dialogue*, *41*(5), 491–514. DOI: 10.1177/0967010610382687

Aviv, I., & Ferri, U. (2023). Russian-Ukraine armed conflict: Lessons learned on the digital ecosystem. *International Journal of Critical Infrastructure Protection*, *43*, 1–15. DOI: 10.1016/j.ijcip.2023.100637

Azmi, R., Tibben, W., & Win, K. T. (2018). Review of cybersecurity frameworks: Context and shared concepts. *Journal of Cyber Policy*, *3*(2), 1–26. DOI: 10.1080/23738871.2018.1520271

Bahadur, R., & Samuels, W. B. (2011). Drinking Water Critical Infrastructure and Its Protection. In Clark, R. M., Hakim, S., & Ostfeld, A. (Eds.), *Handbook of Water and Wastewater Systems Protection* (pp. 65–85). Springer International Publishing. DOI: 10.1007/978-1-4614-0189-6_4

Bahgat, G. (2020). Iran and Its Neighbors Face Risks and Opportunities in Cyber Security. *Orbis*, *64*(1), 78–97. DOI: 10.1016/j.orbis.2019.12.006

Barcik, P., Coufalikova, A., Frantis, P., & Vavra, J. (2023). The Future Possibilities and Security Challenges of City Digitalization. *Smart Cities*, *6*(1), 137–155. DOI: 10.3390/smartcities6010008

Bellamkonda, S. (2020). Cybersecurity in Critical Infrastructure: Protecting the Foundations of Modern Society. [IJCNIS]. *International Journal of Communication Networks and Information Security, 12*(2), 273–280.

Borychenko, O., Cherniavskyi, A., Muliarevych, O., Yurii Shelekh, Y. & Sabat, M. (2024). Cybersecurity in the energy industry of Ukraine: protection measures and challenges in the context of energy security. *Revista Gestão & Tecnologia (Journal of Management & Technology), 24*(4), p. 67-90. DOI: 10.20397/2177-6652/2024.v24i4.2876

Bronk, C., Collins, G., & Wallach, D. S. (2023). The Ukrainian Information and Cyber War. *The Cyber Defense Review, 8*(3), 33-50. https://www.jstor.org/stable/48755360

Çahmutoğlu, E. (2021). *Iran's Cyber Power.* IRAM Publications. https://iramcenter.org/en/irans-cyber-power_en-441

Carr, J. (2012). *Inside Cyber Warfare: Mapping the Cyber Underworld.* O'Reilly Media, Inc.

Cavelty, M. D., & Egloff, F. J. (2019). The Politics of Cybersecurity: Balancing Different Roles of the State. *St. Antony's International Review, 15*(1), 37–57. https://papers.ssrn.com/sol3/papers.cfm?abstract_id=3403971

Cavelty, M. D., & Wenger, A. (2022). Introduction: Cyber security between socio-technological uncertainty and political fragmentation. In Cavelty, M. D., & Wenger, A. (Eds.), *Cyber Security Politics: Socio-Technological Transformations and Political Fragmentation* (pp. 1–13). Routledge. DOI: 10.4324/9781003110224-1

Clark, R. M., Hakim, S., & Ostfeld, A. (2011). Securing Water and Wastewater Systems: An Overview. In Clark, R. M., Hakim, S., & Ostfeld, A. (Eds.), *Handbook of Water and Wastewater Systems Protection* (pp. 1–25). Springer International Publishing. DOI: 10.1007/978-1-4614-0189-6_1

Clarke, R. A., & Knake, R. K. (2010). *Cyber War: The Next Threat to National Security and What to Do About It.* HarperCollins Publishers.

Creado, Y., & Ramteke, V. (2020). Active cyber defence strategies and techniques for banks and financial institutions. *Journal of Financial Crime, 27*(3), 771–780. DOI: 10.1108/JFC-01-2020-0008

Cremer, F., Sheehan, B., Fortmann, M., Kia, A. N., Martin, M., Murphy, F., & Materne, S. (2022). Cyber risk and cybersecurity: A systematic review of data availability. *The Geneva Papers on Risk and Insurance. Issues and Practice, 47*(3), 698–736. DOI: 10.1057/s41288-022-00266-6

Cyfirma Decoding Threats. (2024, August 16). U.S. Water Structure's Vulnerability to Cyber Attacks. https://www.cyfirma.com/research/u-s-water-structures-vulnerability-to-cyber-attacks/

Dalal, A. (2018). Cybersecurity And Artificial Intelligence: How AI Is Being Used in Cybersecurity To Improve Detection And Response To Cyber Threats. [TURCOMAT]. *Turkish Journal of Computer and Mathematics Education*, *9*(3), 1416–1423. DOI: 10.61841/turcomat.v9i3.14670

Dareen, S., & Srivastava, V. (2024, September 11). Cyberattacks on US utilities surged 70% this year, says Check Point. *Reuters*. https://www.reuters.com/technology/cybersecurity/cyberattacks-us-utilities-surged-70-this-year-says-check-point-2024-09-11/

Darıcılı, A. B., & Çelik, S. (2021). National Security 2.0: T he Cyber Security of Critical Infrastructure. *PERCEPTIONS: Journal of International Affairs*, *26*(2), 259–276.

Demchak, C. C., & Dombrowski, P. (2011). Rise of a Cybered Westphalian Age. *Strategic Studies Quarterly, 5*(1), 32-61. https://www.jstor.org/stable/26270509

Dutta, S., & Navy, I. (2022). Cyber Operations Associated with the Ukraine-Russia Conflict: An Open-Source Assessment. *Maritime perspectives*, 346-361. https://maritimeindia.org/cyber-operations-associated-with-the-ukraine-russia-conflict-an-open-source-assessment/

Farwell, J. P., & Rohozinski, R. (2011). Stuxnet and the Future of Cyber War. *Survival. Survival*, *53*(1), 23–40. DOI: 10.1080/00396338.2011.555586

Gallais, C., & Filiol, E. (2017). Critical Infrastructure: Where Do We Stand Today? A Comprehensive and Comparative Study of the Definitions of a Critical Infrastructure. *Journal of Information Warfare*, *16*(1), 64–87. https://www.jstor.org/stable/26502877

Geers, K. (2009). The Cyber Threat to National CriticalInfrastructures: Beyond Theory. *Information Security Journal: A Global Perspective, 18*(1), 1-7. DOI: 10.1080/19393550802676097

Georgiadou, A., Michalitsi, A., & Askounis, P. D. (2023). A security awareness and competency evaluation in the energy sector. *Computers & Security*, *129*, 103199. Advance online publication. DOI: 10.1016/j.cose.2023.103199

Goswami, S. S., Sarkar, S., Gupta, K. K., & Mondal, S. (2023). The role of cyber security in advancing sustainable digitalization: Opportunities and challenges. *Journal of Decision Analytics and Intelligent Computing*, *3*(1), 270–285. DOI: 10.31181/jdaic10018122023g

Goud, N. (2021). Cyber Attack on Israel water system. *Cybersecurity Insiders.* https://www.cybersecurity-insiders.com/cyber-attack-on-israel-water-system/

Gross, J. A. (2021, July 21). After alleged Iranian cyberattack, Israel's Water Authority beefs up defenses. *The Times of Israel.* https://www.timesofisrael.com/after-alleged-iranian-cyberattack-israels-water-authority-beefs-up-defenses/

Gulyás, O., & Kiss, G. (2023). Impact of cyber-attacks on the financial institutions. *Procedia Computer Science, 219*, 84–90. DOI: 10.1016/j.procs.2023.01.267

Haber, E., & Zarsky, T. (2018). Cybersecurity for Infrastructure: A Critical Analysis. *Florida State University Law Review. Florida State University. College of Law, 44*(2), 515–577. https://ir.law.fsu.edu/lr/vol44/iss2/3

Hassam, S. (2025). The notpetya cyber-attack: Russia-Ukraine conflict and its impact on the regional economies. *Advance Social Science Archive Journal, 3*(1), 373-385. https://assajournal.com/index.php/36/article/view/152

Hayden, M. V. (2011). The Future of Things "Cyber". *Strategic Studies Quarterly, 5*(1), 3-7. https://www.jstor.org/stable/26270507

Hemme, K. (2015). Critical Infrastructure Protection: Maintenance is National Security. *Journal of Strategic Security, 8*(5), 25–39. DOI: 10.5038/1944-0472.8.3S.1471

Hermann, D., & Pridöhl, H. (2020). Basic Concepts and Models of Cybersecurity. In Christen, M., Gordijn, B., & Loi, M. (Eds.), *The Ethics of Cybersecurity* (pp. 11–44). Springer International Publishing. DOI: 10.1007/978-3-030-29053-5_2

Herzog, S. (2011). Revisiting the Estonian Cyber Attacks: Digital Threats and Multinational Responses. *Journal of Strategic Security, 4*(2), 49–60. DOI: 10.5038/1944-0472.4.2.3

Ho, S. J., & Mallick, S. K. (2010). The impact of information technology on the banking industry. *The Journal of the Operational Research Society, 61*(2), 211–221. DOI: 10.1057/jors.2008.128

Jimmy, F. (2024). Assessing the Effects of Cyber Attacks on Financial Markets. *Journal of Artificial Intelligence General Science, 6*(1), 288–305. DOI: 10.60087/jaigs.v6i1.254

Kremer, T. (2017). Trust Is the Basis of Digitization. In Abolhassan, F. (Ed.), *Cyber Security. Simply. Make it Happen: Leveraging Digitization Through IT Security* (pp. v–viii). Springer International Publishing.

Li, Y., & Liu, Q. (2021). A comprehensive review study of cyber-attacks and cyber security; Emerging trends and recent developments. *Energy Reports*, *7*, 8176–8186. DOI: 10.1016/j.egyr.2021.08.126

Libicki, M. C. (2009). *Cyberdeterrence and Cyberwar*. RAND Corporation.

Lin, H. (2022). Russian Cyber Operations in the Invasion of Ukraine. *The Cyber Defense Review, 7*(4), 31-46. https://www.jstor.org/stable/48703290

Lindsay, J. R. (2013). Stuxnet and the Limits of Cyber Warfare. *Security Studies, 22*(3), 365–404. DOI: 10.1080/09636412.2013.816122

Luiijf, E., & Klaver, M. (2019). Resilience Approach to Critical Information Infrastructures. In Gritzalis, D., Theocharidou, M., & Stergiopoulos, G. (Eds.), *Critical Infrastructure Security and Resilience: Theories, Methods, Tools and Technologies* (pp. 3–16). Springer International Publishing. DOI: 10.1007/978-3-030-00024-0_1

Marchetti, M., Colajanni, M., Messori, M., Aniello, L., & Vigfusson, Y. (2012). Cyber Attacks on Financial Critical Infrastructures. In Baldoni, R., & Chockler, G. (Eds.), *Collaborative Financial Infrastructure Protection: Tools, Abstractions, and Middleware* (pp. 53–82). Springer International Publishing. DOI: 10.1007/978-3-642-20420-3_3

Mikhaylova, A. A., & Mikhaylov, A. S. (2024). Cyberspace: A systematic review of 30 years of social and economic research. *Journal of Infrastructure. Policy and Development.*, *8*(8), 1–22. DOI: 10.24294/jipd.v8i8.6178

Möller, D. P. F. (2020). *Cybersecurity in Digital Transformation: Scope and Applications*. Springer International Publishing. DOI: 10.1007/978-3-030-60570-4

Mueller, M. L. (2020). Against Sovereignty in Cyberspace. *International Studies Review*, *22*(4), 779–801. DOI: 10.1093/isr/viz044

Onyeji, I., Bazilian, M., & Bronk, C. (2014). Cyber Security and Critical Energy Infrastructure. *The Electricity Journal*, *27*(2), 52–60. DOI: 10.1016/j.tej.2014.01.011

Panguluri, S., Philips, W., & Cusimano, J. (2011). Protecting water and wastewater infrastructure from cyber attacks. *Frontiers of Earth Science*, *5*(4), 406–413. DOI: 10.1007/s11707-011-0199-5

Pernik, P. (2018, October). The Early Days of Cyberattacks: The Cases of Estonia, Georgia and Ukraine. In N. Popescu & S. Secrieru (Eds.), *Hacks, Leaks and Disruptions: Russian Cyber Strategies* (pp. 53-64). Chaillot Paper No. 148, European Union Institute for Security Studies.

Petersons, E. (2024, February 12). Cybersecurity challenges in the era of digitalization. DOI: 10.2139/ssrn.4723047

Plėta, T., Tvaronavičienė, M., Casa, S. D., & Agafonov, K. (2020). Cyber-attacks to critical energy infrastructure and management issues: Overview of selected cases. *Insights into Regional Development*, *2*(3), 703–715. DOI: 10.9770/IRD.2020.2.3(7)

Plumer, B. (2021, May 13). Pipeline Hack Points to Growing Cybersecurity Risk for Energy System. *The New York Times*. https://www.nytimes.com/2021/05/13/climate/pipeline-ransomware-hack-energy-grid.html

Radvanovsky, R. (2006). *Critical Infrastructure: Homeland Security and Emergency Preparedness*. CRC/Taylor & Francis. DOI: 10.1201/9781420007428

Rass, S., Schauer, S., König, S., & Zhu, Q. (2020). *Cyber-Security in Critical Infrastructures: A Game-Theoretic Approach*. Springer International Publishing. DOI: 10.1007/978-3-030-46908-5

Reed, J. (2025, January 10). Is the water safe? The state of critical infrastructure cybersecurity. *IBM*. https://www.ibm.com/think/insights/is-the-water-safe-state-of-critical-infrastructure-cybersecurity

Reporter, S. (2024, December 5). SG banks see over 1,800 cyberattacks weekly in past six months. *Asian Banking & Finance*. https://asianbankingandfinance.net/banking-technology/news/sg-banks-see-over-1800-cyberattacks-weekly-in-past-six-months

Ribeiro, A. (2023, December 18). Iranian petrol stations hit by cyber attack allegedly linked to Israeli hacker group. *Industrial Cyber*. https://industrialcyber.co/critical-infrastructure/iranian-petrol-stations-hit-by-cyber-attack-allegedly-linked-to-israeli-hacker-group/

Rid, T. (2012, February). Cyber War Will Not Take Place. *The Journal of Strategic Studies*, *35*(1), 5–32. DOI: 10.1080/01402390.2011.608939

Rosenzweig, P. (2013). *Cyber Warfare: How Conflicts in Cyberspace Are Challenging America and Changing the World*. Bloomsbury Publishing USA. DOI: 10.5040/9798400636493

Roshanaei, M. (2021). Resilience at the Core: Critical Infrastructure Protection Challenges, Priorities and Cybersecurity Assessment Strategies. *Journal of Computer and Communications*, *9*(8), 80–102. DOI: 10.4236/jcc.2021.98006

Rudner, M. (2013). Cyber-Threats to Critical National Infrastructure: An Intelligence Challenge. *International Journal of Intelligence and CounterIntelligence*, *26*(3), 453–481. DOI: 10.1080/08850607.2013.780552

Salminen, M., & Hossain, K. (2018). Digitalisation and human security dimensions in cybersecurity: An appraisal for the European High North. *The Polar Record, 54*(2), 108–118. DOI: 10.1017/S0032247418000268

Seemma, P. S., Nandhini, S., & Sowmiya, M. (2018, November). Overview of Cyber Security. *International Journal of Advanced Research in Computer and Communication Engineering*, *7*(11), 125–128. DOI: 10.17148/IJARCCE.2018.71127

SentinelOne. (2024, September 23). Cyber Security in Finance: Key Threats and Strategies. https://www.sentinelone.com/cybersecurity-101/cybersecurity/cyber-security-in-finance/

Sha, L., Gopalakrishnan, S., Liu, X., & Wang, Q. (2009). Cyber-Physical Systems: A New Frontier. In Tsai, J. J. P., & Yu, P. S. (Eds.), *Machine Learning in Cyber Trust: Security, Privacy, and Reliability* (pp. 1–13). Springer International Publishing. DOI: 10.1007/978-0-387-88735-7_1

Shea, T., Gaycken, S., & Martellini, M. (2013). Cyber Security for Nuclear Power Plants. In Martellini, M. (Ed.), *Cyber Security: Deterrence and IT Protection for Critical Infrastructures* (pp. 25–35). Springer International Publishing. DOI: 10.1007/978-3-319-02279-6_3

Singer, P. W. (2015). Stuxnet and Its Hidden Lessons on the Ethics of Cyberweapons. *Case Western Reserve Journal of International Law*, *47*(1), 79–86. https://scholarlycommons.law.case.edu/jil/vol47/iss1/10

Sinha, S. K., Davis, C., Gardoni, P., Babbar-Sebens, M., Stuhr, M., Huston, D., Cauffman, S., Williams, W. D., Alanis, L. G., Anand, H., & Vishwakarma, A. (2023). Water sector infrastructure systems resilience: A social–ecological–technical system-of-systems and whole-life approach. *Cambridge Prisms*, *1*, 1–24. DOI: 10.1017/wat.2023.3

Smith, D. C. (2021). Cybersecurity in the energy sector: Are we really prepared? *Journal of Energy & Natural Resources Law*, *39*(3), 265–270. DOI: 10.1080/02646811.2021.1943935

Stevens, T. (2018). Cyberweapons: Power and the governance of the invisible. *International Politics*, *55*(3-4), 482–502. DOI: 10.1057/s41311-017-0088-y

Stone, J. (2013). Cyber War Will Take Place! *The Journal of Strategic Studies, 36*(1), 101–108. DOI: 10.1080/01402390.2012.730485

Tiirmaa-Klaar, H. (2016). Building national cyber resilience and protecting critical information infrastructure. *Journal of Cyber Policy*, *1*(1), 94–106. DOI: 10.1080/23738871.2016.1165716

Uddin, H., Ali, H., & Hassan, M. K. (2020). Cybersecurity hazards and fnancial system vulnerability: A synthesis of literatüre. *Risk Management, 22*(4), 239–309. DOI: 10.1057/s41283-020-00063-2

Venkatachary, S. K., Prasad, J., & Samikannu, R. (2017). Economic Impacts of Cyber Security in Energy Sector: A Review. *International Journal of Energy Economics and Policy*, *7*(5), 250–262. http://hdl.handle.net/11159/1315

Weiss, M., & Biermann, F. (2021). Cyberspace and the protection of critical national infrastructure. *Journal of Economic Policy Reform*, *26*(3), 250–267. DOI: 10.1080/17487870.2021.1905530

Willet, M. (2022). The Cyber Dimension of the Russia–Ukraine War. *Survival. Survival*, *64*(5), 7–26. DOI: 10.1080/00396338.2022.2126193

Wilson, C. (2013). Cybersecurity and Cyber Weapons: Is Nonproliferation Possible? In Matellini, M. (Ed.), *Cyber Security: Deterrence and IT Protection for Critical Infrastructures* (pp. 11–24). Springer International Publishing. DOI: 10.1007/978-3-319-02279-6_2

KEY TERMS AND DEFINITIONS

Cyber Attack: This term refers to all the conflicts that occur in cyberspace as digitalization increases worldwide. Cyber attacks can be carried out for personal gain or with state support.

Cyber Espionage: Just like physical espionage, cyber espionage refers to activities carried out in cyberspace to acquire confidential information. In cyber espionage, it is very difficult to identify the perpetrators.

Cyberspace: This refers to the area where all activities occur in a digital environment, in which physical borders lose significance due to technological developments.

Critical Infrastructure: This refers to the systems essential for the continuity of access to basic services such as electricity, transportation, and telecommunications, as well as the security of these sectors in a society.

Firewall: In cyberspace, especially in critical infrastructure facilities, a security system developed to ensure security and prevent unauthorized access is called a firewall.

Shamoon: This is the name of the malware used by Iran during the 2012 cyber attack on Saudi Arabia's Aramco facilities. It is known that 30.000 computers in the facility were disabled, and significant data loss occurred as a result of this attack.

Stuxnet: This refers to a malicious software targeting computers used in Iran's nuclear development program, which was discovered in 2010. After the attack, Iran spent a long time trying to fix the damage caused by the attack.

Chapter 8
Extremism in the Age of the Internet:
The Rise of Algorithmic Radicalization

Yağız Atay
https://orcid.org/0009-0007-4420-9737
National Defense University, Turkey

ABSTRACT

Despite the growing attention algorithmic radicalization has received in recent years, academic research on the subject remains relatively scarce. This study aims to contribute to this emerging field by examining algorithmic radicalization through the lenses of social and cognitive psychology. In an era where social media increasingly permeates everyday life, understanding how people are influenced by algorithmic content is essential. Furthermore, the study conceptualizes algorithmic radicalization not only as a sociotechnical phenomenon but also as an emerging security threat, with significant implications for national security, public safety, and the prevention of violent extremism. It explores potential technology policy interventions that could be implemented to mitigate the risks posed by algorithmically driven pathways to radicalization.

INTRODUCTION

Although radicalization is a phenomenon frequently discussed in the field of social sciences, there is no clear consensus on its definition. (Kılıç, 2024) While the dictionary definition refers to it as "the adoption of radical views by an individual or group," what is considered radical can vary greatly from person to person and from

DOI: 10.4018/979-8-3373-7406-2.ch008

context to context. The use of the word "radical" in a social and political context can be traced back to early 19th-century Great Britain. In its earliest usage, it meant "an advocate of fundamental change" or "a reformist." (Encyclopædia Britannica, n.d.) Despite its vague definition, radicalization can be broadly described as "the process of adopting views that are distant from the center, or in other words, marginal." Even though there is no definitive agreement on what constitutes radical, the acceptance of violence as a legitimate means in the name of political ideologies is generally considered a major indicator of radicalization. Radicalism, which in almost every definition shares the common element of "the adoption of certain radical views by individuals or groups," will be addressed in this article as a cognitive process, and this phenomenon will be examined through the principles of psychology.

THE HISTORICAL ROOTS OF RADICALIZATION

The introduction of the word "radical" into political literature in the 19th century is no coincidence. The French Revolution of 1789 led to the collapse of the absolute monarchy in France and forced the Catholic Church into sweeping reforms. In the years following the revolution, during the period known as "The Reign of Terror," tens of thousands of people were executed by the Jacobins. The nationalist movements and revolutionary ideologies that began to spread from France to Europe—and eventually the world—also contributed to the dissemination of similar radical ideas. Around the same period, the First and Second Industrial Revolutions in Great Britain began to spread across Continental Europe in the following decades, leading to the rise of socialist and Marxist ideologies, particularly among the urban working classes. In the years following World War I, the destructive consequences of the war created fertile ground for the spread of radical views; Germany, Italy, and Spain came under the rule of radical right-wing governments, while Tsarist Russia fell under radical left-wing control with the Bolshevik Revolution. After World War II and throughout the Cold War era, both far-right ideologies and fundamentalist religious views gained traction in various regions such as China, South America, and the Middle East. British historian Eric Hobsbawm referred to the period between the beginning of World War I and the end of the Cold War—namely, the years from 1914 to 1991—as "The Age of Extremes," a time when ideologies like fascism and socialism spread widely among the masses. (Hobsbawm, 1994, pp. 109–141)

When examining the mechanisms that historically contributed to the radicalization of masses, one observes the prominent role played by print media and direct social interaction. *L'Ami du peuple*, a newspaper published by Jean-Paul Marat during the French Revolution, gained considerable influence among the Jacobins and actively promoted revolutionary and violent ideologies. The publication frequently targeted individuals by name, advocating that the execution of counter-revolutionaries—through decapitation—was essential for the preservation of the revolution. Ironically, Marat himself was assassinated. (Darnton & Roche, 1989)

Similarly, *Iskra*—a publication founded by Vladimir Lenin and later serving as the official newspaper of the Russian Social Democratic Labour Party—was clandestinely distributed throughout Russia, contributing to the dissemination of communist ideologies.[1] *Die Rote Fahne*, a newspaper published by Rosa Luxemburg and Karl Liebknecht, was instrumental in the spread of communist ideas among the German working class. It is important to note that such publications were not exclusive to far-left or anarchist ideologies. Following World War I, *Il Popolo d'Italia*, founded by Benito Mussolini, played a significant role in the dissemination of pro-war, irredentist, and militarist ideologies to a wide audience in Italy. In the United States, far-right, racist, and antisemitic ideologies were propagated through various media, including magazines such as *Attack!*, *National Vanguard*, and *American Renaissance*, as well as fictional propaganda texts like *The Turner Diaries*. These materials served as ideological resources for white supremacist terrorist organizations such as *The Order*, and for lone actors like Timothy McVeigh—responsible for the 1995 Oklahoma City bombing that resulted in 167 deaths—who are known to have been influenced by such publications. (Hoffman & Ware, 2024)

When radical ideologies succeed in seizing control of central political authority, the scope and efficacy of their propaganda mechanisms are significantly amplified. *Pravda*, a communist publication founded in 1912, became the official newspaper of the Central Committee of the Communist Party of the Soviet Union following the October Revolution, eventually reaching millions of readers. Similarly, *Der Angriff*, established in 1927 by Joseph Goebbels, gained prominence alongside the National Socialist German Workers' Party (NSDAP) and functioned as a key instrument in disseminating official ideology and maintaining public morale during wartime. *El Alcázar*, a newspaper that came under the control of the Nationalist faction following their victory in the Spanish Civil War in 1936, operated in Francoist Spain as a mouthpiece for far-right Falangist ideology. (Voltmer, 2006)

In addition to print media, radio broadcasts were also employed as powerful tools of propaganda by totalitarian regimes. In Nazi Germany, Joseph Goebbels, as Minister of Propaganda, implemented policies to develop and distribute low-cost radios known as *Volksempfänger* in order to make the regime's messaging more accessible to the general population. Likewise, the Union of Soviet Socialist Republics (USSR) utilized radio broadcasting extensively to propagate its official ideology across vast territories.

In addition to the media, direct social interaction has historically served as a significant vehicle for radicalization. Associations, ideological clubs, student unions, labor organizations, and even cafés and bars frequented by individuals aligned with specific ideologies could function as environments conducive to the adoption of radical ideas. *A particularly relevant example can be seen in the Beer Hall Putsch.* The Beer Hall Putsch was a failed coup attempt by Adolf Hitler and the early Nazi Party in Munich, Germany, on November 8–9, 1923. Hitler and his followers tried to overthrow the Weimar Republic and seize power by force. It's called the *Beer Hall Putsch* because the coup began in a beer hall—specifically the Bürgerbräukeller, a large beer hall in Munich. At the time, beer halls in Bavaria were popular venues for political meetings and speeches. (Gordon, 1972)

While the underlying dynamics of radicalization have largely remained consistent, the channels through which it manifests have evolved in contemporary contexts. One phenomenon frequently discussed in this regard is algorithmic radicalization. To fully grasp the implications of algorithmic radicalization, it is essential to consider the historical developments in information technologies that have shaped the current media and communication landscape.

INFORMATION AGE AND THE RISE OF ALGORITHMIC RADICALIZATION

The patent for the telephone was granted to Alexander Graham Bell in 1876. By 1945, it is estimated that only 45% of households in the United States had access to a telephone. It would not be unreasonable to assume that this figure was significantly lower in other parts of the world. During the same period, the first personal computers began to be developed in the United States. Models such as the ENIAC, created in these early years, were designed exclusively for professional use. In the 1970s, devices like the Commodore PET 2001-8, Apple II, and TRS-80 Model I began to enter homes in the 1980s for purposes such as coding, gaming, and basic computation. In subsequent decades—the 1990s and 2000s—the internet also became increasingly common in private households. While in 2005 only 16% of the global population had access to the internet, this figure rose to 67% by 2023. (Statista, 2024) In developed countries, internet penetration is estimated to be as high as 93%. (Statista, 2023)

Another major technological development in the realm of information and communication technologies occurred in the 2010s with the widespread adoption of smartphones. A study conducted by the Pew Research Center revealed that while only 35% of the U.S. population owned a smartphone in 2011, this figure had increased to 91% by 2024. (Pew Research Center, 2024) When considered alongside the famous remark attributed to Alexander Graham Bell—“One day there will be a telephone in every major city in the United States”—these radical advancements in information technology appear all the more astonishing.

The internet revolution of the 2000s, followed by the widespread adoption of smartphones in the 2010s, has led to a dramatic increase in the role of social media platforms in our daily lives. As a result of these technological advancements, it is currently estimated that over five billion people around the world have access to the internet. However, the notable increase during this period is not limited to the number of individuals with internet access. Equally significant is the substantial rise in the amount of time people spend in front of screens. A public survey conducted in 2024 reported that the average daily screen time for an adult in the United States was 7 hours and 3 minutes. The global average, by comparison, stood at 6 hours and 40 minutes per day. Among members of Generation Z, this figure is even higher, with average daily screen time reaching up to 9 hours. (Dean, 2023)

The global phenomenon of intensive social media use cannot be attributed solely to the increased accessibility of the internet. As advertising constitutes the primary source of revenue for these platforms, they are designed to maximize the time users spend on screen. To achieve this, social media platforms employ algorithms that are specifically engineered to promote prolonged engagement. While there is no universally applicable model governing how such algorithms operate, it can generally be stated that they are complex systems intended to deliver content based on users' interests and behavioral patterns. These algorithms aim to personalize the user experience, ranking and presenting content according to various engagement metrics such as interactions, likes, shares, comments, and screen time.

In fact, the idea of content personalization in digital environments has a much longer history than many people assume. The concept was first introduced in 1995 by Nicholas Negroponte, the founder of the MIT Media Lab. Inspired by the notion that individuals seek out different types of news in newspapers, Negroponte coined the term *"Daily Me"*. This concept was grounded in the principle that digital platforms could tailor content to align with the personal preferences and interests of individual users. (Sunstein, 2009, pp. 1–18)

At their core, social media algorithms are designed to maximize the time users spend on the platform. To achieve this, these algorithms often exploit a cognitive bias inherent to the human mind: the tendency to prefer interacting with those who share similar beliefs and perspectives. This notion is often summarized by the well-known phrase, "Our modern skulls house a stone age mind," which highlights the evolutionary mismatch between contemporary environments and the cognitive architecture shaped by ancestral conditions. (Stankus, 2011) Although openness and tolerance are celebrated values in today's world, tribalism remains deeply ingrained in human psychology—a legacy of the hundreds of thousands of years our species spent living in small, tightly-knit groups. Social media platforms are not exempt from this evolutionary predisposition. Most users prefer to encounter others who support the same sports teams, share the same hobbies, or hold similar social and political views. Consequently, social media algorithms learn and adapt to this preference, curating user experiences accordingly.

In the years when social media networks were rapidly expanding across the globe, many believed that this development would contribute positively to democratization. Social media platforms such as Twitter and Facebook helped opposition groups organize and amplify their voices in authoritarian regimes where mainstream media was heavily censored, such as Tunisia, Syria, and Egypt. (Carty, 2014) In a similar vein, social media played a vital role in enabling civil society to express itself during various events such as the 2019–2020 Hong Kong Protests and the 2013 Brazilian Protests. (Anonymous Author, 2019) (The Guardian, 2013) It is also widely believed that social media fosters pluralism by giving voice to groups that lack the financial means to gain exposure in mainstream media. The anonymity provided by these platforms and the relative difficulty of enforcing censorship were, until recently, characteristics that were predominantly discussed in a positive light.

Nonetheless, there have also been critiques and concerns—expressed even in earlier periods—regarding the notion that social media use may not always yield democratic outcomes. Media theorist Steven Johnson, in his 2001 book *Emergence: The Connected Lives of Ants, Brains, Cities, and Software*, criticized the "Daily Me" project. He expressed concern that allowing individuals to permanently determine the types of content they are exposed to could, in the long term, lead to fragmented realities and societal polarization. Johnson also has argued that such forms of hyper-personalization would lead not to a "mind-expanding" but rather a "mind-narrowing" experience, while simultaneously paving the way for groupthink within communities. (Johnson, 2001) In this context, it would not be an exaggeration to suggest that Johnson's insight was ahead of its time.

Cass Sunstein, a prominent figure in the field of behavioral sciences, was another early critic of personalized content on digital platforms. In his 2009 book *Republic 2.0*, Sunstein argued that the ability to filter "what people read, see, and hear," as he put it, could evolve into a dystopian scenario. While he acknowledged that personalized content may not be especially dangerous when used to follow topics such as sports or music, he warned that in the realm of social and political issues, exposure to differing perspectives is essential. Sunstein conceded that mainstream media is not entirely objective, but he emphasized its role in creating shared narratives, serving as a form of "social glue" essential for societal cohesion. He further asserted that diversity is a vital component of democracy, and prolonged exposure to homogeneous content could have detrimental consequences for democratic systems. (Sunstein, 2009, pp. 97–118)

COGNITIVE DRIVERS OF ALGORITHMIC RADICALISM

The phenomenon of algorithmic radicalization enters the picture at this point. According to many experts, the inherent design of social media algorithms can, over time, lead individuals to adopt increasingly radical viewpoints. At the heart of this dynamic lies a process known as the *positive feedback loop*. A positive feedback loop refers to a system in which the output reinforces the input, thereby generating even greater output. In other words, a change within the system produces an effect that amplifies that very change, increasing its intensity or rate. In such a loop, a small initial shift can grow over time, eventually producing radical outcomes. The concept of the positive feedback loop has been adopted across multiple disciplines, from biology to political science.

Instability itself can be seen as a textbook example of a positive feedback loop. If a disturbance within a system is not dampened while still below a certain threshold, it can intensify over time, leading to greater systemic instability. In this context, social media algorithms can be understood as an instance of the positive feedback loop. These algorithms are designed to show users more of the content with which they frequently interact. If a user engages repeatedly with a specific type of content, the algorithm responds by suggesting similar content more frequently. As this content receives further interaction, the algorithm continues to promote it, gradually shaping the user's feed into an increasingly one-dimensional stream. This cycle may narrow the user's range of interests over time. While users may be satisfied with the content recommended to them—and thus spend more time on the platform—the cognitive and social consequences of this dynamic are highly complex.

The fact that algorithms are designed to continually expose users to people and content that align with their own views eventually leads to the phenomenon known as the *echo chamber*. In this environment, individuals become insulated within networks that reinforce their existing beliefs. A closely related concept is the *filter bubble*. The filter bubble refers to a personalized digital environment in which internet users are exposed only to content that aligns with their own views and interests. Coined by tech entrepreneur and author Eli Pariser, the term describes the effect of algorithms on platforms such as social media and search engines, which filter the flow of information in an attempt to deliver more "relevant" content to users. (Kitchens, Johnson, & Gray, 2020).

Filter bubbles and *echo chambers* are two concepts that describe the same underlying algorithmic mechanisms in different terms. Both phenomena are grounded in the way social media algorithms analyze users' past engagement metrics to deliver personalized content. Put simply, these algorithms identify the types of content users prefer to engage with and construct individualized experiences based on these preferences.

Echo chambers refer to situations in which individuals interact primarily with like-minded people on specific topics. This homogeneity in social interactions and information exposure reduces tolerance toward differing perspectives, potentially contributing to the radicalization of users over time. Research conducted on various social media platforms has shown that virtually all platforms create echo chambers to differing degrees of homogeneity. (Cinelli, Morales, Galeazzi, Quattrociocchi, & Starnini, 2021) Although seemingly benign at first glance, such phenomena have significant implications for human cognitive processes.

Political scientist Ian Bremmer interprets the rise of anti-globalism through the lens of *cultural anxiety*. He argues that globalization is not merely an economic phenomenon but also a cultural one, and that certain outcomes of globalization—such as mass migration—tend to trigger cultural anxiety, particularly among groups that perceive themselves as the "losers" of globalization. Bremmer notes that even prior to the advent of social media, individuals tended to socialize with those who shared similar views and consumed ideologically aligned media. Nevertheless, he emphasizes the concept of the filter bubble, asserting that social media has played a pivotal role in exacerbating polarization and fostering radicalization, particularly among these already disaffected groups. (Bremmer, 2018, pp. 20–24)

The psychological dimensions of this issue are not limited to individuals' tendencies to associate with others who share similar views. Although people were long conceptualized as rational actors, numerous studies in the field of experimental psychology have shown that human beings are not as rational as once assumed. In this context, the concept of *cognitive bias* is highly relevant to understanding algorithmic radicalization.

Cognitive biases are defined in psychology as systematic deviations in judgment, in which decisions are made with partiality toward or against a person, idea, or proposition. Although philosophers have debated the rationality and objectivity of human thought for centuries, the term *cognitive bias* was first introduced by Israeli cognitive psychologists Amos Tversky and Daniel Kahneman in 1972. (Gilovich, Griffin, & Kahneman, 2002)

In their pioneering work on decision-making, Tversky and Kahneman observed that participants consistently deviated from rational models in systematic ways, and they sought to categorize these deviations. They defined cognitive biases as patterns of systematic deviation from rationality embedded within human cognition. Following their foundational work, many scholars in the field of experimental psychology have designed various experiments to investigate this tendency, identifying a range of cognitive biases that can be classified under different categories. These same biases have been observed across individuals of varying cultures, races, genders, and social classes, suggesting that cognitive biases represent a universal tendency inherent to human decision-making processes.

Similarly, individuals tend to focus on content that confirms their existing beliefs and attitudes. Although this tendency has been discussed by philosophers for centuries, it was in the twentieth century that cognitive psychologists—most notably Peter Wason—empirically demonstrated and theorized it as *confirmation bias*. This cognitive bias refers to the human inclination to interpret, accept, or reject new information in ways that align with one's pre-existing beliefs. Often, confirmation bias leads individuals to dismiss evidence that contradicts their current opinions or ideologies. This bias significantly distorts decision-making processes and remains a subject of extensive research.

One of the most prominent demonstrations of confirmation bias is Peter Wason's *Wason Rule Discovery Task*. In this experiment, participants are shown cards displaying a letter on one side and a number on the other. Given a rule such as "If there is a vowel on one side, then there must be an even number on the other," participants are asked which cards need to be flipped to test the rule. Most participants tend to choose cards that could confirm the rule rather than disprove it, demonstrating a preference for confirmatory evidence even in experimental settings. This illustrates how individuals are generally inclined to seek out and focus on information and people that validate their views. (Wagner-Egger, 2007)

Another relevant cognitive bias that influences human decision-making and perception is *availability bias*. This refers to the tendency to base judgments on the ease with which information can be recalled or accessed. It functions as an unconscious mental shortcut and is closely tied to the structure of human memory. (Manis, Shedler, Jonides, & Nelson, 1993) People are more likely to recall unusual or emotionally charged events, which explains why such events are disproportionately represented in the media. For instance, deaths caused by murder, plane crashes, or terrorist attacks are reported far more frequently than those caused by car accidents, diabetes, or domestic accidents. This discrepancy can lead to distorted perceptions, with individuals overestimating the frequency of dramatic causes of death. In this sense, availability bias is directly relevant to the content produced and circulated through both mainstream and social media.

A third significant bias is the *in-group–out-group bias*. This bias involves a tendency to evaluate one's own group (the in-group) more positively than outside groups (the out-group), often attributing favorable characteristics to one's own group while stereotyping others negatively. As a result, people perceive both their in-groups and out-groups as more homogeneous than they actually are. Many social psychologists explain phenomena such as racism or sexism through this lens, particularly within the framework of social identity theory.

Social psychologist Jonathan Haidt argues that human beings have evolved to form groups and describes people as inherently *groupish*. He claims that individuals are so committed to their group identities that they may remain loyal even when doing so contradicts their own interests. Haidt presents this tendency as a key part of the evolutionary origins of human morality, noting that groups characterized by cooperation and solidarity are more likely to succeed than others. Thus, from an evolutionary perspective, group loyalty is interpreted as an adaptive trait that strengthens social bonds and enhances intergroup competition. Events such as the September 11 attacks or times of war tend to intensify these groupish tendencies. In this context, Haidt suggests that human beings are, at their core, predisposed to *polarization*. (Haidt, 2012)

When these cognitive tendencies are combined with the *positive feedback loops* generated by algorithmic content curation, the effects can be particularly destructive. As people are already inclined to defend their pre-existing beliefs and favor their in-groups, social media algorithms amplify these tendencies by surrounding users with content that reinforces their perspectives. This dynamic further entrenches individuals in *echo chambers* and exacerbates polarization.

Moreover, the psychological dynamics of online social interaction are not limited to cognitive biases alone. The *online disinhibition effect* describes individuals' tendencies to behave more rudely or aggressively in digital interactions compared to face-to-face contexts. Several psychological factors contribute to this effect, one of the most significant being the anonymity provided by social media platforms. When users can conceal their real identities, their sense of social responsibility diminishes, and normative behavioral constraints weaken. This anonymity allows users to create alternative personas and act more recklessly online, as they no longer perceive their online behavior as directly linked to their real lives. (Suler, 2004)

Another contributing factor is the nature of online communication itself. Unlike face-to-face interactions, digital communication often lacks non-verbal cues such as eye contact, body language, and tone of voice—elements that have shaped human communication for thousands of years. The absence of these cues can reduce empathy, enabling individuals to say things online that they would hesitate to express in person. Additionally, the asynchronous nature of online communication removes the immediate social consequences of one's statements, increasing the likelihood of aggressive or impulsive responses.

The *deindividuation effect* is another relevant factor. It describes how individuals in group settings may feel a diminished sense of personal responsibility, which can lead to more aggressive or antisocial behavior. (Diener, 1977) While not unique to social media—having been observed in phenomena such as riots, vandalism, or war crimes—deindividuation is readily observable in online echo chambers. These environments foster a sense of group identity while simultaneously diffusing personal accountability, thereby reinforcing disinhibited and extreme behavior.

Taken together, these psychological mechanisms suggest that individuals are more prone to irresponsible and aggressive conduct in online settings than in face-to-face interactions. In this regard, the online disinhibition effect can also be considered a cognitive driver of radicalization via digital platforms. (Suler, 2004)

Some studies in cognitive psychology and neuroscience support this explanation. Over thousands of years, the human mind has adapted not only to language but also to perceive social cues such as tone of voice and facial expressions. While these cues are present in face-to-face communication, online interaction largely takes place in written form. As a result, users' mirror neurons are activated far less than they would be during in-person interactions, leading to reduced empathy toward others. This diminished empathetic engagement may explain why individuals are more likely to violate social norms and behave aggressively or rudely on social media. (Doheny & Lighthall, 2023)

Another way echo chambers on social media may contribute to radicalization is through the concept of social reward. Humans are inherently social beings, and experiences of approval, recognition, and acceptance from others are psychologically rewarding. In other words, social validation activates strong reward signals in the brain. (Meshi et al., 2015) This desire for acceptance can, at times, cause individuals to abandon their own beliefs to conform to group expectations.

Asch's Conformity Experiment serves as a compelling illustration of this phenomenon. In a study conducted in 1951 by Solomon Asch, participants were shown lines of varying lengths and asked to identify which one matched a reference line. Unbeknownst to the true participant, other members of the group were confederates who intentionally gave incorrect answers. Despite knowing the correct answer, the real participants often conformed to the group's incorrect response. This experiment demonstrated how the fear of social rejection and the desire for social approval can override individual judgment. (Asch, 1951)

This need for social validation is not exclusive to face-to-face interaction; it is equally present on social media. Users receive feedback in the form of likes, comments, and shares, which activate the brain's reward system in ways similar to in-person praise. (Meshi, Tamir, & Heekeren, 2015) Consequently, users are incentivized to produce and share content that yields more social rewards. In this sense, echo chambers are fertile grounds for the reinforcement of social reward dynamics. Once a user is drawn into an echo chamber by algorithmic curation, they begin tailoring their content to gain acceptance and approval within that group—potentially accelerating their own radicalization and that of others.

Social media's impact on cognitive psychology can also be observed in declining attention spans. Numerous studies suggest that the fast-paced and ever-changing nature of content on social media platforms leads to increased boredom and decreased attention spans. The rapid influx of bite-sized content has conditioned users to seek constant stimulation, reducing their capacity for sustained focus. Some researchers argue that social media directly impacts the brain's reward mechanisms, thereby shortening attention spans. One recent study found that the ideal length for a TikTok video is considered to be between 21 and 31 seconds—an illustration of this attention deficit. (Center for Humane Technology, n.d.)

Some scholars argue that shortened attention spans may also relate to radicalization. This viewpoint holds that the brevity of content on social media tends to promote shallow and one-sided perspectives. The character limit on platforms like Twitter or the prevalence of under-one-minute videos on TikTok, Shorts, or Reels exemplifies this trend. A shorter attention span may also encourage impulsive and reactive decision-making. (Vaidhyanathan, 2018)

LOSS OF COMMON GROUND, POLARIZATION, AND MANIPULATION

One of the primary threats that echo chambers pose to democratic societies is the spread of disinformation. (Diaz Ruiz & Nilsson, 2022) Disinformation refers to intentionally false or misleading content created to deceive audiences, often for political or financial gain. A study on Twitter found that "fake news" is 70% more likely to be retweeted than accurate news. As a result, false stories reach 1,500 people six times faster than true stories. This phenomenon is especially dangerous during global crises such as pandemics, natural disasters, and wars.

The concept of "post-truth"—a term that gained significant traction in intellectual circles in recent years—can also be understood in this context. Named the Oxford Dictionaries' 2016 "Word of the Year," post-truth is defined as circumstances in which "objective facts are less influential in shaping public opinion than appeals to emotion and personal belief." (BBC News, 2016) The rise of post-truth is largely associated with the widespread use of social media. As more individuals obtain information from filter bubbles rather than mainstream media, shared realities have fragmented into competing versions of truth. Social media platforms reinforce users' tendencies to seek content that validates their existing beliefs and emotions rather than objective sources. (Viner, 2016) The post-truth era has been characterized by the increasing inability of individuals to distinguish between what is factually true and false, the growing influence of beliefs and emotions in shaping perceptions of reality, and the erosion of a shared public sphere for deliberation. This condition has been referred to by some scholars as an *epistemic crisis*. (Cosentino, 2020) In this light, Cass Sunstein's prediction that the erosion of shared narratives would lead to increased polarization has proven accurate, particularly in the rise of populist leaders across the democratic West.

One of the most significant consequences of echo chambers and filter bubbles is polarization. Political polarization refers to a shift of individuals within a society toward more extreme ideological positions, often fostering hostility among groups. Because of its potential for social fragmentation, polarization is a closely monitored societal indicator. A Pew Research Center study found that between 1994 and 2014, the proportion of Democrats and Republicans in the U.S. identifying with ideologically extreme views nearly doubled. (Doherty, 2014) A separate 2022 Pew Research study, widely reported in the media, showed an increase in Americans using negative descriptors to characterize members of the opposing political party—an explicit sign of rising polarization. (The Economist, 2022) Some social psychologists now refer to this dynamic as "tribalism." (Kelly, 2021) A 2021 Brookings Institution article titled "How tech platforms fuel U.S. political polarization" described this issue as a national security threat. (Brookings Institution, 2021)

Another serious threat posed by social media algorithms to democratic institutions is the increased susceptibility of the public to manipulation. Both domestic and foreign actors may exploit these vulnerabilities to interfere with electoral processes. One of the most well-known examples of such abuse is the Cambridge Analytica scandal. At the heart of the controversy was the unauthorized collection of personal data from millions of Facebook users by a private company, Cambridge Analytica, which used the data to influence electoral outcomes. Unlike conventional algorithms, Cambridge Analytica employed a personality test app called "thisisyourdigitallife" to harvest personal and psychological data. (Hern & Cadwalladr, 2018)

Using a profiling system developed by researcher Aleksandr Kogan, individuals were categorized based on the Big Five personality traits: openness, conscientiousness, extraversion, agreeableness, and emotional stability. These traits were used to tailor political messaging to each user's psychological profile and political preferences. This allowed for "tailored" propaganda to be delivered to users based on highly specific characteristics. While similar methods may have been in use earlier, the scandal gained global attention after the 2016 U.S. Presidential Election.

In 2018, former Cambridge Analytica employee Christopher Wylie came forward with revelations that exposed the inner workings of the company. The scandal sparked worldwide outrage, with allegations that Cambridge Analytica had intervened not only in the 2016 U.S. elections but also in events such as Brexit and numerous other referenda and elections worldwide. Facebook founder Mark Zuckerberg was called to testify before the U.S. Congress, and the #DeleteFacebook campaign went viral, resulting in a loss of trust and a decline in the company's stock value. The U.S. Federal Trade Commission (FTC) fined Facebook $5 billion for mishandling personal data and imposed new privacy restrictions. (Federal Trade Commission, 2019) Cambridge Analytica subsequently ceased operations.[2] The Cambridge Analytica scandal remains one of the most striking examples of how personalized content and social media algorithms can be weaponized for large-scale political manipulation.

Another widely discussed example of the influence of social media algorithms is the 2024 Romanian presidential election. One of the candidates, Călin Georgescu, diverged from traditional political communication strategies by heavily utilizing TikTok in his campaign. His approach focused on targeting young voters with viral content, including videos of Georgescu practicing judo, wearing traditional attire, and participating in religious rituals. These videos reached wide audiences through TikTok's algorithmic recommendation systems. Georgescu, who started his election campaign as an unknown candidate, quickly gained popularity, thanks in part to his social media hype.

Following Georgescu's victory, some sources questioned the authenticity of his TikTok rise, suggesting it was coordinated rather than organic. Documents revealed that the campaign was allegedly orchestrated through platforms like Telegram and Discord, with specific instructions on how to circumvent TikTok's security mechanisms. There were also serious allegations regarding campaign financing, with claims that tens of thousands of TikTok accounts were used to disseminate Georgescu's videos and manipulate the algorithm. (The Loop – ECPR, 2024)

These developments spurred further controversy, including allegations that Russia supported Georgescu's campaign due to his anti-NATO stance. Subsequently, on December 6, 2024, Romania's Constitutional Court annulled the first round of the election, citing manipulation and voter misinformation. Georgescu's TikTok campaign has since been cited as a striking case of how digital platforms can influence political processes and how algorithmic systems may be exploited. The event sparked international discussions on digital media literacy, platform transparency, and electoral security. (Ross, Paun, & Popoviciu, 2024)

The polarizing potential of social media is not confined to domestic societal dynamics—it can also become a matter of international concern. One of the most frequently discussed examples in this context is the Russian Federation. The Internet Research Agency (IRA), an organization reportedly established in the early 2010s with close ties to the Putin administration, has been widely accused of weaponizing social media platforms to serve geopolitical objectives. (Prier, 2017). Various investigations suggest that this group has actively manipulated online discourse, particularly in the United States and Ukraine, by amplifying narratives favorable to Russian interests while discrediting opposing political figures and policies. These activities exemplify how algorithmically driven platforms can be exploited not only to influence public opinion but also to destabilize democratic processes and international relations. Allegations have gone so far as to assert that Russia directly interfered in the 2016 U.S. presidential election. According to these claims, Russia sought to polarize American public opinion and influence voter behavior through fake accounts on social media platforms. The Trump campaign's various foreign contacts were subject to investigation; however, it could not be definitively proven whether these interactions constituted criminal conduct. The Mueller Report, published in 2019, confirmed that Russia did interfere in the election, though it found no conclusive evidence of a direct conspiracy with the Trump campaign. (Mueller, 2019) Similar disinformation efforts were observed during the 2020 election as well, although their impact was comparatively limited. IRA instrumentalizes social movements as part of its broader strategy to destabilize and undermine international rivals. One of the most prominent examples of this tactic is the Black Lives Matter (BLM) movement. During the 2016 U.S. presidential election, it was revealed that fake social media accounts affiliated with the IRA disseminated dual narratives by appearing to support the BLM movement while simultaneously promoting counter-propaganda against it. Among these accounts were pages such as "Blacktivist," which amassed thousands of followers and were reportedly involved in organizing physical protests. The underlying objective is interpreted as an effort to exacerbate social tensions, incite racial discord, and erode public trust in American institutions. Consequently, it is argued that the IRA did not genuinely support BLM but rather exploited the movement as a tool for influence operations. (Bradshaw, DiResta, & Miller, 2022) Russia's use of social media to exploit both political and racial fault lines in order to destabilize other countries has become increasingly evident.

FROM CONSPIRACY THEORIES TO POLITICAL VIOLENCE

Much like fake news, conspiracy theories also spread rapidly online. A conspiracy theory is a belief that an event or situation is secretly manipulated by a malevolent group, despite more plausible explanations being available. Though conspiracy theories predate the internet—some sources trace the term to the mid-1800s—there is little doubt that the internet and especially social media have significantly accelerated their dissemination. This trend became particularly evident during the COVID-19 pandemic, when conspiracy theories regarding vaccine skepticism and claims that the virus was a biological weapon spread rapidly.

Although conspiracy theories generally rely on similar psychological dynamics, scholars have attempted to categorize them. Jesse Walker, for example, outlines five main types: "Enemy Outside" theories suggest that conspirators are external to the community; "Enemy Within" theories posit that hidden enemies exist within the population; "Enemy Above" attributes manipulation to powerful elites; "Enemy Below" blames social unrest on subversive lower-class groups; and "Benevolent Conspiracies" involve secretive forces working for the good of humanity. (Walker, 2013)

Michael Barkun, meanwhile, categorizes conspiracy theories into three types: event-specific conspiracies, such as those surrounding 9/11; systemic conspiracies that claim a single evil entity is trying to control entire institutions or regions; and superconspiracies, which combine multiple independent conspiracies under a single overarching narrative involving omnipotent forces. (Barkun, 2003)

Some studies argue that conspiracy theories were prevalent before the internet and that while the web has not necessarily increased their general popularity, it has intensified radicalization within echo chambers. Even so, many conspiracy theories have originated and flourished directly on the internet and social media. One of the most prominent is *QAnon*, a conspiracy movement that emerged in 2017 in the United States and later spread globally. At its core, QAnon posits the existence of a "deep state" in the U.S., run by a cabal of satanic, pedophilic elites. The movement takes its name from an anonymous internet user, "Q", who shared cryptic messages on forums such as 4chan.

QAnon gained further traction over time, notably when a police officer photographed with then–Vice President Mike Pence was seen wearing a QAnon patch in 2018. (The New York Times, 2018) The movement culminated in its involvement in the January 6, 2021 Capitol Hill insurrection. Believing the election was stolen and Trump was fighting the deep state, QAnon followers saw the event as "The Great Awakening" in which evil would be overthrown. Adorned with Q symbols, they stormed the U.S. Capitol in an attempt to disrupt the democratic process—an incident that underscored QAnon's evolution from digital mythology into a real-world, radicalizing force. (Liyanage, 2021)

Another conspiracy theory born and spread rapidly through social media was *Pizzagate*. Emerging before the 2016 U.S. presidential election, Pizzagate falsely claimed that high-ranking members of the Democratic Party operated a child trafficking ring out of a Washington D.C. pizzeria. The theory gained traction after misinterpretations of leaked emails shared by WikiLeaks, and it spread quickly on Reddit, 4chan, and other platforms. (Bleakley, 2021) The baseless nature of the claims did not prevent real-world consequences; in late 2016, a heavily armed individual entered the pizzeria, believing the conspiracy. The attacker was arrested by the police and the attack was terminated without anyone being seriously injured. (Siddiqui, & Svrluga, 2016) The incident serves as a stark reminder of the tangible dangers posed by internet-borne conspiracy theories.

Another prominent conspiracy theory that has gained significant traction on social media is the "Great Replacement" theory. Although its roots can be traced back further, it was first articulated in a systematic manner by French writer Renaud Camus in 2011. The theory posits that Western societies, particularly white Europeans, are being demographically "replaced" by immigrants—especially Muslims and people of African descent—through a deliberate plan orchestrated by elites, globalists, or so-called "deep state" actors. While the theory originated from Camus's book of the same name, it has since spread rapidly among racist and anti-immigrant groups on social media. (Murthy, 2023)

Although conspiracy theories are commonly associated with the far-right, research indicates that individuals on the far-left may also be prone to such beliefs. (van Prooijen, Krouwel, & Pollet, 2015)

When these types of conspiracy theories circulate within echo chambers, they can easily escalate into acts of social or individual violence under the right conditions. A major example of collective violence influenced by social media is the January 6, 2021 Capitol Hill insurrection in the United States, widely regarded as one of the most severe threats to American democracy in recent history. That day, while Congress convened to certify the results of the 2020 presidential election, thousands of mostly armed Trump supporters stormed the Capitol building, interrupting the proceedings and exposing severe security lapses. It is well documented that the attackers organized through social media. (The New York Times, 2021)

Many participants livestreamed the assault, took selfies, and shared content across platforms like Instagram, TikTok, and Twitter. This turned a violent collective action into a form of social media performance. Beyond just organizing online, it is clear that the radicalization processes leading up to the attack were significantly influenced by social media. Protesters used numerous symbols that had already become memes in far-right internet culture. (The Washington Post, 2021) (CNN, 2021)

Another example of how echo chambers can lead to collective violence is the 2017 “Unite the Right” rally. Organized primarily by white supremacist and alt-right groups, the rally relied heavily on social media coordination. The flags and banners on display during the rally reflected numerous elements of far-right internet culture. (Southern Poverty Law Center, 2017) Several prominent far-right influencers were known to have played a role in planning the rally, with Facebook and Discord serving as key platforms during the organizational phase. (Hendrix, 2022)

In addition to collective violence, social media's role in individual acts of political violence—particularly lone-wolf attacks—is increasingly evident. Lone actors, unlike members of organized terrorist groups, carry out attacks independently. While conventional terrorists often radicalize through face-to-face socialization, lone actors typically experience radicalization via online platforms.

One of the most striking lone-wolf attacks was perpetrated by Anders Breivik in 2011 in Oslo and Utøya, Norway. On that day, Breivik first detonated a car bomb near a government building in Oslo, then traveled to Utøya Island disguised as a police officer and carried out a mass shooting at a youth camp organized by the Norwegian Labour Party. It is believed that the initial bombing was intended to distract law enforcement from the subsequent attack. The dual attacks resulted in 77 deaths and over 300 injuries. It is known that Breivik had increasingly isolated himself from social life in the years prior and had become deeply immersed in online forums promoting Islamophobia, anti-immigration, and far-right ideologies. Given that mainstream social media platforms were less popular at the time, Breivik spent much of his time on niche extremist forums, where his views were significantly shaped.

Breivik did not only absorb content from social media; he also used digital platforms to disseminate his own radical ideas. Just hours before the attacks, he uploaded an ideological video collage to YouTube, expressing his worldview, listing his perceived enemies, and glorifying historical figures he considered heroic. He also released a 1,500-page manifesto titled *2083: A European Declaration of Independence*, in which he laid out his ideology, motivations, and detailed preparations for the attack. The manifesto appears to have been designed not only to justify his own actions but also to serve as a how-to guide for future attacks. It reflects Breivik's psychological instability and self-image as a misunderstood savior. Although the manifesto has been banned in several countries due to its incitement to violence and detailed instructions on attack planning, it continues to circulate in far-right online communities. Breivik is believed to have inspired other attackers since then, making his case a disturbing example of how online radicalization can culminate in extreme real-world violence. (Macklin & Bjørgo, 2021)

Another illustrative example is the Christchurch mosque shootings, carried out by Australian-born attacker Brenton Tarrant in 2019. During Friday prayers, Tarrant executed mass shootings at two mosques in succession and was intercepted by police before reaching a third location. These consecutive attacks resulted in the deaths of 51 individuals and injuries to 89 others. The attack prompted international condemnation of Islamophobia and led the United Nations to designate March 15—the date of the shootings—as the International Day to Combat Islamophobia.

Tarrant's attack bore clear marks of internet culture and social media influence. Like Anders Breivik, Tarrant produced a so-called manifesto before the attack—a 74-page document titled *The Great Replacement*, which he emailed to about 30 recipients, including New Zealand's Prime Minister's Office and leading media organizations. Links to the document were also shared on platforms like Twitter and 4chan. The manifesto was heavily influenced by Breivik's ideology and writings, as well as far-right internet subcultures. In one example, Tarrant described himself as a "kebab removalist," referencing a meme derived from an anti-Muslim propaganda video from the Yugoslav Wars. The meme has been widely adopted among far-right and alt-right communities.

In addition to using social media to spread his ideology, Tarrant livestreamed the attack via a body camera on Facebook. The attack was broadcast for 17 uninterrupted minutes and became the first terrorist act in history to be livestreamed in such a manner. Facebook faced heavy criticism for its delayed response in removing the video. Although it has since been taken down from mainstream platforms, the footage continues to circulate in extremist online communities. (Kupper et al., 2022)

This leads to the phenomenon known as the "copycat effect." Simply defined, this is when an individual is inspired to replicate a terrorist attack after being exposed to it—emulating the methods, ideology, or visibility of the original attacker. In the age of social media, where such events are widely disseminated, copycat incidents have become more frequent. The widespread circulation of the Breivik and Tarrant attacks in far-right circles has demonstrated how such acts can serve as blueprints for future violence. Some media outlets have reported that Tarrant has been elevated to "saint" status among extremists, and his writings may inspire future attackers. (The Independent, 2019)

A powerful example of the copycat phenomenon is the 2019 El Paso Walmart shooting. On August 3, 2019, 21-year-old Patrick Crusius entered a Walmart in El Paso, Texas, and opened fire with an automatic weapon, killing 23 people and injuring more than 20. Most of the victims were of Mexican descent. Authorities classified the event not only as a hate crime but also as an act of domestic terrorism. Prior to the attack, Crusius published a manifesto online, referencing the Great Replacement theory and claiming that Latin American immigrants were "invading" the U.S. His manifesto drew direct inspiration from Tarrant's 2019 writings. (Newsweek, 2022)

Another recent example of copycat violence is the 2022 Buffalo supermarket shooting. On May 14, 2022, 18-year-old Payton Gendron targeted a predominantly Black neighborhood's Tops Friendly Market in Buffalo, New York. Gendron fatally shot 10 people and injured three others. Like Tarrant, Gendron inscribed white supremacist slogans and references to previous shooters on his weapons, including direct nods to Breivik and Tarrant's manifestos. (Anti-Defamation League, 2022) Gendron also livestreamed the attack using a body camera, but opted for Twitch instead of Facebook. (The New York Times, 2022) He published a manifesto prior to the attack, which showed significant influence from far-right internet culture and was peppered with memes. Some reports indicate that large portions of his manifesto were directly plagiarized from Tarrant's. (WIVB News 4, 2022)

Numerous other incidents similarly underscore the contagious nature of terrorism. In this context, every attack should be regarded not only as an outcome but also as a potential catalyst for future acts of violence. Echo chambers on social media further intensify this contagion factor. While the copycat phenomenon appears more visible among far-right perpetrators, far-right terrorism is not the only movement that has leveraged social media.

Although radicalism is not a new phenomenon, academic interest in the subject has significantly increased alongside the rise of terrorism, particularly after the September 11 attacks. (Kılıç & Selçuk, 2023) In this regard, while radicalism is not limited to terrorism, studies on terrorism play a significant role in enhancing our understanding of radicalism. Groups such as ISIS, with jihadist-fundamentalist motivations, have also used social media for propaganda and recruitment. In its early years, ISIS exploited mainstream platforms like YouTube and Twitter to disseminate its ideology and radicalize audiences. By 2015, an estimated 125,000 ISIS-affiliated Twitter accounts were reported. (WIRED, 2016) In 2016, Twitter announced that it had removed a total of 325,000 ISIS-related accounts. (Twitter, 2016) Many of these suspended users created new profiles to remain active. ISIS sympathizers also organized hashtag campaigns to increase reach. Additionally, ISIS utilized TikTok to spread fear and propaganda by posting execution videos. (Wells, 2019)

Beyond recruiting for direct participation in the group, ISIS sought to inspire lone-wolf attacks among Muslims living in Western countries. Over recent years, individuals with no direct contact or logistical support from ISIS, but who were radicalized online through its propaganda, have committed lone-wolf terror attacks. (Mandelson, 2016) Such attacks are particularly difficult for intelligence services to detect in advance, given the absence of communication with the central organization or cells. Recognizing the danger, EUROPOL emphasized that social media could be weaponized for the spread of terrorism and established the EU Internet Referral Unit in 2015 to counter this threat. (Council of the European Union, n.d.)

Despite the influential role of social media in radicalization, other contributing factors exist, with mental health being among the most prominent. A 2021 study on the relationship between radicalization and mental health found a significant link between lone-wolf attackers and mental disorders. (Weenink, 2022) Another 2020 study suggested that conditions such as depression and PTSD may increase an individual's susceptibility to radical ideologies. However, the study also emphasized that radicalization is a complex phenomenon and cannot be explained solely by psychiatric diagnoses. (Corner & Gill, 2020)

COMBATING ALGORITHMIC RADICALIZATION

The societal threat posed by algorithmic radicalization is evident. Given the role polarization plays in enabling populist leaders, this phenomenon arguably poses a risk to international security. Thus, governments must develop effective techno-policies to combat the echo chambers and filter bubbles created by algorithmic radicalization.

One of the most immediate policy tools that comes to mind is censorship. Censorship refers to the partial or complete suppression of information, ideas, or content by an authority. Although generally controversial, there is broad consensus around censoring content that incites violence or targets individuals or groups. In mainstream media, censorship typically occurs before publication, whereas on social media it takes place after content is posted. In recent years, social media platforms have adopted proactive stances on this issue. Many posts that incite violence, promote terrorist organizations, or spread dangerous conspiracy theories are removed, and offending accounts are often suspended. These actions are guided by human moderation and artificial intelligence (AI). AI systems analyze text, images, videos, and audio to detect illegal, violent, hateful, or spam content. (Johannes Kepler University Linz, n.d.) However, censorship alone is insufficient. Many radical views have migrated from mainstream, tightly regulated platforms to less regulated spaces—a phenomenon some liken to "migration." (Ganesh & Amarasingam, 2023)

Telegram serves as a prime example. Unlike Facebook, Instagram, or Twitter, Telegram is less strictly moderated. This weak oversight allows radical groups to disseminate propaganda and incite violence with relative impunity. Telegram also offers features such as public channel creation and anonymous group participation, which amplify its potential as a haven for extremism. Today, radical groups of varying ideological motivations actively use the platform. (Mak & Lindeman, 2023) (PBS NewsHour, 2022)

Among the most effective strategies is increasing citizens' media literacy. At its core, media literacy is the ability to understand, analyze, and evaluate media content. Unlike traditional media outlets, social media platforms rarely engage in editorial oversight. Consequently, determining their accountability for misinformation remains contentious. This makes social media fertile ground for the spread of misinformation. Media literacy can be taught. Individuals can be trained to assess the credibility of news sources, verify claims, and question narratives. Such skills are essential in combating algorithmic radicalization. (Boston University, 2023) The European Commission has described media literacy as "crucial" for fighting disinformation. (European Commission, n.d.)

Another important intervention is fact-checking. Platforms have implemented tools to verify content accuracy and counter misinformation in echo chambers. This not only informs users but also enhances their critical thinking, thus mitigating the effects of algorithmic radicalization. However, who conducts the fact-checking is a vital consideration. Meta, for instance, delegates this responsibility to independent organizations through its Third-Party Fact-Checking program. Users can report suspicious content, which is then reviewed by independent fact-checkers. (Meta, n.d.) The International Fact Checking Network (IFCN), founded in 2015, includes more than 170 organizations and provides objective standards for reliable fact-checking. (RAND Corporation, n.d.) Twitter, now X, by contrast, developed the Community Notes system, which relies on user contributions. Volunteer users can annotate misleading or decontextualized posts, and these annotations become visible only if endorsed by users with differing perspectives. While Meta's approach relies on institutional expertise, Twitter's emphasizes collective user input.

Transparency in algorithmic design is another critical measure. Many platforms operate with black-box algorithms—systems whose internal logic is opaque. Critics argue this lack of transparency obscures crucial decisions, while companies cite user privacy, security, and competitive concerns. (Hussain, Hussain, & Hossain, 2021) These justifications often clash with public interest. The EU's Digital Services Act aims to address these concerns by increasing democratic oversight and minimizing risks such as manipulation and disinformation. (European Commission, n.d.-a)

Beyond regulation, platforms have initiated voluntary transparency measures. For instance, YouTube introduced the "Why this video?" feature to explain recommendation logic. Meta offers users tools to manage content visibility and publishes transparency reports. TikTok provides explanations for recommendations and allows users to reject certain content. While commendable, these steps are limited; core algorithms remain inaccessible to independent scrutiny. Moreover, algorithm transparency is not only a corporate issue but sometimes a geopolitical one. TikTok, owned by a China-based company, has raised concerns over data handling and international security. (Reuters, 2024) Therefore, algorithmic transparency should not be left solely to corporate discretion—it requires oversight from states and international bodies.

Lastly, algorithms should be redesigned to expose users to a diversity of perspectives. Social media platforms could use interest-based recommendations to introduce varying viewpoints, encouraging users to escape their echo chambers. For instance, a politically engaged user could be shown content from multiple ideological perspectives. Such interventions serve as nudges rather than coercive measures and may reduce cognitive radicalization. (Shahrezaye et al., 2024)

CONCLUSION

This study has approached the phenomenon of algorithmic radicalization from a multidimensional perspective, beginning with its historical and social roots and extending to its current manifestations shaped through digital media. Historically, radicalization has referred to the process by which individuals or groups, motivated by ideological, political, or religious beliefs, are drawn toward marginal positions. In earlier times, this process was largely shaped through print media, propaganda tools, and face-to-face social networks. However, in the current digital age, radicalization occurs in more invisible, rapid, and widespread ways—primarily through new media technologies and, in particular, social media algorithms.

The widespread adoption of the internet and smart devices has fundamentally transformed how individuals access information. Social media platforms, via algorithms tailored to user behavior, now influence not just what users access, but how they think. These algorithmic recommendation systems are designed to prioritize content that maximizes engagement and attention. As a result, users are often funneled into echo chambers and filter bubbles dominated by homogeneous perspectives. This limits exposure to diverse viewpoints and intensifies societal polarization.

This process is not merely technological in nature—it is deeply rooted in the cognitive and evolutionary tendencies of the human mind. Human beings, as social creatures, have evolved over hundreds of thousands of years with an inherent inclination toward group identity. Despite modern values that emphasize tolerance and open-mindedness, the human tendency to form groups remains strong. Cognitive biases such as confirmation bias, in-group bias, and availability bias create fertile ground for online radicalization. Users gravitate toward content that reinforces their worldview and become less tolerant of opposing views, which fuels societal polarization and political tension.

Furthermore, digital features like anonymity, asynchronous communication, and the absence of face-to-face interaction exacerbate aggression and irresponsibility in online behavior. In other words, the positive feedback loops created by social media algorithms reinforce the groupish tendencies already present in the human psyche.

One of the most dangerous outcomes of algorithmic radicalization is the translation of digital ideologies into real-world violence. Lone-actor attacks—violent acts carried out by individuals radicalized through online exposure—highlight this threat. Examples such as Anders Breivik, Brenton Tarrant, and Patrick Crusius demonstrate how individuals have used social media and forums both for ideological radicalization and for the dissemination of propaganda related to their actions. These acts of violence can lead not only to individual harm but also to widespread societal unrest and threats to democratic institutions. Without proper interventions, social media platforms may become incubators not only for radical lone actors but also for organized terrorist groups and hate organizations. Even when radicalization does not result in violence, it contributes to polarization and erodes the shared foundations necessary for democratic cohesion.

The alignment of users with extremist groups on social media is not solely a function of individual psychology—it is also shaped by the algorithmic policies of platform operators. Social media companies analyze user behavior in great detail to maximize engagement, which in turn leads to greater ad exposure and more data collection. Consequently, there is often a conflict between corporate interests and the public good, necessitating oversight and transparency in algorithmic systems.

Thus, tackling algorithmic radicalization requires not only individual awareness and media literacy but also legal and institutional interventions. Regulations like the European Union's Digital Services Act impose transparency and accountability requirements on platforms regarding how their algorithms function. Moreover, platform-based interventions such as fact-checking and community notes are vital tools in combating disinformation and manipulative content. Meta's collaboration with third-party fact-checkers and Twitter's user-driven Community Notes represent two different models—both useful but limited in terms of speed, scope, and effectiveness.

In conclusion, algorithmic radicalization is not solely a byproduct of digital technology—it exists at the intersection of human psychology and political structures. Therefore, the solution must be multilayered: media literacy at the individual level, algorithmic transparency and ethical design at the corporate level, and regulatory policies at the governmental level. Without such comprehensive strategies, social media platforms will continue to evolve from spaces of information exchange into dangerous arenas where radical ideologies flourish and violence is normalized.

Social media must now be recognized as a critical domain for hybrid warfare. States and non-state actors alike exploit the inherently polarizing nature of social media platforms to advance their own strategic interests. This dynamic further amplifies the threat of algorithmic radicalization. In this regard, it is essential that intelligence agencies maintain familiarity with this domain, as doing so is crucial for effectively countering both internal and external threats.

Radicalization, much like many other social phenomena, possesses a contagious nature that enables its diffusion within societies. This transmissibility must never be underestimated or overlooked. Indeed, addressing radicalization before it spreads is considerably more feasible than attempting to contain it after it has taken root. The human mind's inherent tendency toward group formation—combined with the reinforcing dynamics of echo chambers on social media—further intensifies this risk. In this context, algorithmic radicalization emerges as a critical threat that must be addressed not only by individual states but also through coordinated action by international institutions. The development and implementation of effective techno-political strategies is, therefore, not a matter of choice, but a necessity for safeguarding the resilience and cohesion of democratic societies.

REFERENCES

Anti-Defamation League. (2022, May 16). Buffalo shooter's weapons covered in white supremacist messaging. https://www.adl.org/resources/article/buffalo-shooters-weapons-covered-white-supremacist-messaging

Asch, S. E. (1951). Effects of group pressure upon the modification and distortion of judgments. In Guetzkow, H. (Ed.), *Groups, leadership and men* (pp. 177–190). Carnegie Press.

Barkun, M. (2003). A culture of conspiracy: Apocalyptic visions in contemporary [University of California Press.]. *America*, •••, 3–8.

BBC News. (2016, November 15). Post-truth declared word of the year by Oxford Dictionaries. https://www.bbc.com/news/uk-37995600

Bleakley, P. (2021). Panic, pizza and mainstreaming the alt-right: A social media analysis of Pizzagate and the rise of the QAnon conspiracy. *Current Sociology*, *71*(3), 509–525. DOI: 10.1177/00113921211034896

Boston University. (2023, May 15). Media literacy skills important to counter disinformation, survey says. https://www.bu.edu/com/articles/media-literacy-skills-important-to-counter-disinformation-survey-says/

Bradshaw, S., DiResta, R., & Miller, C. (2022). Playing both sides: Russian state-backed media coverage of the #BlackLivesMatter movement. The International Journal of Press/Politics, 28(4), 791–817. (Original work published 2023)DOI: 10.1177/19401612221082052

Bremmer, I. (2018). *Us vs. them: The failure of globalism*. Portfolio/Penguin.

Brookings Institution. (2021, November 15). How tech platforms fuel U.S. political polarization—and what government can do about it. https://www.brookings.edu/articles/how-tech-platforms-fuel-u-s-political-polarization-and-what-government-can-do-about-it/

Carty, V. (2014). Arab Spring in Tunisia and Egypt: The impact of new media on contemporary social movements and challenges for social movement theory. *International Journal of Contemporary Sociology*, *51*(1), 51–80.

Center for Humane Technology. (n.d.). Attention & mental health. https://www.humanetech.com/attention-mental-health

Cinelli, M., Morales, G. D. F., Galeazzi, A., Quattrociocchi, W., & Starnini, M. (2021). The echo chamber effect on social media. *Proceedings of the National Academy of Sciences of the United States of America, 118*(9), e2023301118. DOI: 10.1073/pnas.2023301118

CNN. (2021, January 9). Extremist flags and symbols seen at the US Capitol insurrection: Their meanings and origins. https://edition.cnn.com/2021/01/09/us/capitol-hill-insurrection-extremist-flags-soh/index.html

Corner, E., & Gill, P. (2020). Is mental illness a factor in lone-actor terrorism? *The British Journal of Psychiatry, 217*(2), 709–711. DOI: 10.1192/bjp.2019.14

Cosentino, G. (2020). The post-truth world order. In *Social media and the post-truth world order: The global dynamics of disinformation* (pp. 10–41). Springer. DOI: 10.1007/978-3-030-43005-4_1

Council of the European Union. (n.d.). EU response to terrorism. https://www.consilium.europa.eu/en/eu-response-to-terrorism/

Darnton, R., & Roche, D. (Eds.). (1989). *Revolution in print: The press in France, 1775–1800* (p. 162). University of California Press.

Dean, B. (2023, May 4). Screen time statistics: Average usage data 2023. Exploding Topics. https://explodingtopics.com/blog/screen-time-stats?utm_source=chatgpt.com

Diaz Ruiz, C., & Nilsson, T. (2022). Disinformation and echo chambers: How disinformation circulates on social media through identity-driven controversies. *Journal of Public Policy & Marketing*, •••, 1–18. DOI: 10.1177/07439156221103852

Diener, E. (1977). Deindividuation: Causes and consequences. *Social Behavior and Personality, 5*(1), 143–155. DOI: 10.2224/sbp.1977.5.1.143

Doheny, M. M., & Lighthall, N. R. (2023). Social cognitive neuroscience in the digital age. *Frontiers in Human Neuroscience, 17*, 1168788. Advance online publication. DOI: 10.3389/fnhum.2023.1168788

Doherty, C. (2014, June 17). Which party is more to blame for political polarization? It depends on the measure. Pew Research Center. https://www.pewresearch.org/short-reads/2014/06/17/which-party-is-more-to-blame-for-political-polarization-it-depends-on-the-measure/

Encyclopædia Britannica. (n.d.). Radical | Political Theory, Social Change & Activism. https://www.britannica.com/topic/radical-ideologist

European Commission. (n.d.). Media literacy. https://digital-strategy.ec.europa.eu/en/policies/media-literacy

European Commission. (n.d.-a). Digital Services Act. https://commission.europa.eu/strategy-and-policy/priorities-2019-2024/europe-fit-digital-age/digital-services-act_en

Federal Trade Commission. (2019, July 24). FTC imposes $5 billion penalty and sweeping new privacy restrictions on Facebook. https://www.ftc.gov/news-events/news/press-releases/2019/07/ftc-imposes-5-billion-penalty-sweeping-new-privacy-restrictions-facebook

Ganesh, B., & Amarasingam, A. (2023, June 23). How do terrorists utilise and exploit small, covert online spaces? Global Network on Extremism & Technology (GNET). https://gnet-research.org/2023/06/23/how-do-terrorists-utilise-and-exploit-small-covert-online-spaces

Gilovich, T., Griffin, D., & Kahneman, D. (2002). Heuristics and biases: The psychology of intuitive judgment. *Academy of Management Review*, *29*(4), 695–698.

Gordon, H. J.Jr. (1972). *Hitler and the Beer Hall Putsch*. Princeton University Press.

Haidt, J. (2012). *The righteous mind: Why good people are divided by politics and religion*. Pantheon Books.

Hendrix, J. (2022, March 17). Evidence in trial of 2017 Unite the Right rally organizers reveals role of Facebook, Discord. Tech Policy Press. https://www.techpolicy.press/evidence-in-trial-of-2017-unite-the-right-rally-organizer-reveals-role-of-facebook-discord

Hobsbawm, E. (1994). *The age of extremes: The short twentieth century, 1914–1991*. Pantheon Books.

Hoffman, B., & Ware, J. (2024, April 26). Ropes, accelerationism, and the enduring legacy of the Turner Diaries. International Centre for Counter-Terrorism. https://icct.nl/publication/ropes-accelerationism-and-enduring-legacy-turner-diaries

Hussain, F., Hussain, R., & Hossain, E. (2021). Explainable artificial intelligence (XAI): An engineering perspective. arXiv preprint arXiv:2101.03613. https://arxiv.org/abs/2101.03613

Johannes Kepler University Linz. (n.d.). An update on our efforts to combat violent extremism. https://epub.jku.at/download/pdf/11380643.pdf

Johnson, S. (2001). *Emergence: The connected lives of ants, brains, cities, and software*. Scribner.

Kelly, M. (2021, December 9). Political polarization and its echo chambers: Surprising new, cross-disciplinary perspectives from Princeton. Princeton University. https://www.princeton.edu/news/2021/12/09/political-polarization-and-its-echo-chambers-surprising-new-cross-disciplinary

Kılıç, K. (2024). Radikalleşme ve şiddet içeren aşırıcılığı uzaklarda önlemek: Afrika Boynuzu'nda şiddet içeren aşırıcılığa karşı direncin güçlendirilmesi. *Türkiye Siyaset Bilimi Dergisi*, *7*(2), 97–109.

Kılıç, K., & Selçuk, Z. (2023). Radikalleşme ile mücadelede istihbarat örgütlerinin rolü: Danimarka Güvenlik ve İstihbarat Servisi (Politiets Efterretningstjeneste–PET) örneği. *Güvenlik Stratejileri Dergisi*, *19*(45), 421–453. DOI: 10.17752/guvenlik-strtj.1288297

Kitchens, B., Johnson, S. L., & Gray, P. (2020). Understanding echo chambers and filter bubbles: The impact of social media on diversification and partisan shifts in news consumption. *Management Information Systems Quarterly*, *44*(4), 1619–1649. DOI: 10.25300/MISQ/2020/16371

Kupper, J., Christensen, T. K., Wing, D., Hurt, M., Schumacher, M., & Meloy, R. (2022). The contagion and copycat effect in transnational far-right terrorism: An analysis of language evidence. *Perspectives on Terrorism*, *16*(4), 4–26. https://www.jstor.org/stable/27158149

Liyanage, C. (2021, June 14). QAnon and the Great Awakening: How the Deep Web rewrites ideologies and beliefs. GNET. https://gnet-research.org/2021/06/14/qanon-and-the-great-awakening-how-the-deep-web-rewrites-ideologies-and-beliefs/

Macklin, G., & Bjørgo, T. (2021). Breivik's long shadow? The impact of the July 22, 2011 attacks on the modus operandi of extreme-right lone actor terrorists. *Perspectives on Terrorism*, *15*(3), 14–36. https://www.jstor.org/stable/27030880

Mak, T., & Lindeman, T. (2023, March 30). The rise and fall of Terrorgram: Inside a global online hate network. ProPublica. https://www.propublica.org/article/rise-and-fall-terrorgram-inside-global-online-hate-network-frontline-telegram

Manis, M., Shedler, J., Jonides, J., & Nelson, T. E. (1993). Availability heuristic in judgments of set size and frequency of occurrence. *Journal of Personality and Social Psychology*, *65*(6), 448–457. DOI: 10.1037/0022-3514.65.3.448

Meshi, D., Morawetz, C., & Heekeren, H. R. (2015). Nucleus accumbens response to gains in reputation for the self relative to gains for others predicts social media use. *Social Cognitive and Affective Neuroscience*, *10*(2), 173–180. DOI: 10.1016/j.scan.2014.08.018

Meshi, D., Tamir, D. I., & Heekeren, H. R. (2015). The emerging neuroscience of social media. *Trends in Cognitive Sciences, 19*(12), 771–782. DOI: 10.1016/j.tics.2015.09.004

Meta. (n.d.). How fact-checking works. Meta Transparency Center. https://transparency.meta.com/tr-tr/features/how-fact-checking-works/

Mueller, R. S., III. (2019, March). Report on the investigation into Russian interference in the 2016 presidential election: Volume I of II. U.S. Department of Justice. https://www.justice.gov/storage/report.pdf

Murthy, D. (2023, April 17). "They're coming to take over our country": Researching global circuits of racist misinformation. MediaWell, Social Science Research Council. https://mediawell.ssrc.org/articles/theyre-coming-to-take-over-our-country-researching-global-circuits-of-racist-misinformation/

Newsweek. (2022, May 16). The Great Replacement theory has inspired several terror attacks in recent years. https://www.newsweek.com/great-replacement-theory-inspired-terror-attacks-recent-years-1706953

PBS NewsHour. (2022, May 4). How the Telegram app became a hub for hate crime and radical extremists. PBS. https://www.pbs.org/newshour/show/how-the-telegram-app-became-a-hub-for-hate-crime-and-radical-extremists

Pew Research Center. (2024, November 13). Mobile fact sheet. https://www.pewresearch.org/internet/fact-sheet/mobile/

Prier, J. (2017). Commanding the trend: Social media as information warfare. Strategic Studies Quarterly, 11(4), 50–85. https://www.jstor.org/stable/26271634

RAND Corporation. (n.d.). International Fact-Checking Network (IFCN) codes and principles. https://www.rand.org/research/projects/truth-decay/fighting-disinformation/search/items/international-fact-checking-network-ifcn-codes-and.html

Reuters. (2024, December 6). Why does the US want to ban TikTok? The allegations against it. https://www.reuters.com/technology/why-does-us-want-ban-tiktok-allegations-against-it-2024-12-06/

Ross, T., Paun, C., & Popoviciu, A. (2024, December 6). Romanian court cancels presidential election amid Russian influence fears. Politico. https://www.politico.eu/article/romania-court-cancels-presidential-election-runoff-tiktok-russian-influence-calin-georgescu/

Shahrezaye, M., Stier, S., & Neubaum, G. (2024). Designing algorithms to increase exposure to counter-attitudinal content. In de León, A., Esser, A., & Friemel, N. (Eds.), *The Routledge companion to media disinformation and populism* (pp. 265–278). Springer., DOI: 10.1007/978-3-031-78554-2_16

Southern Poverty Law Center. (2017, August 12). Flags and other symbols used by far-right groups in Charlottesville. https://www.splcenter.org/resources/hatewatch/flags-and-other-symbols-used-far-right-groups-charlottesville/

Stankus, T. (2011). Our modern skulls house a stone age brain: An overview and annotated bibliography of evolutionary psychology, Part I. *Behavioral & Social Sciences Librarian, 30*(3), 131–150. DOI: 10.1080/01639269.2011.591276

Statista. (2023). Internet penetration rate worldwide in 2023, by country income level. https://www.statista.com/statistics/1361735/internet-penetration-rate-by-country-income-level/

Statista. (2024). Number of internet users worldwide from 2010 to 2024. https://www.statista.com/statistics/617136/digital-population-worldwide/

Suler, J. (2004). The online disinhibition effect. *Cyberpsychology & Behavior, 7*(3), 321–326. DOI: 10.1089/1094931041291295

Suler, J. (2004). The online disinhibition effect. *Cyberpsychology & Behavior, 7*(3), 321–326. DOI: 10.1089/1094931041291295

Sunstein, C. R. (2009). *Republic.com 2.0.* Princeton University Press.

The Economist. (2022, August 17). How Democrats and Republicans see each other. https://www.economist.com/graphic-detail/2022/08/17/how-democrats-and-republicans-see-each-other

The Guardian. (2013, July 4). Brazilian protesters use Twitter, Microsoft data shows. https://www.theguardian.com/news/datablog/2013/jul/04/brazilian-protesters-twitter-microsoft

The Independent. (2019, August 24). Revered as a saint by online extremists: How Christchurch shooter inspired copycat terrorists around the world. https://www.independent.co.uk/news/world/australasia/brenton-tarrant-christchurch-shooter-attack-el-paso-norway-poway-a9076926.html

The Loop – ECPR. (2024, April 8). How Călin Georgescu's TikTok tactics rewired Romanian politics. https://theloop.ecpr.eu/how-calin-georgescus-tiktok-tactics-rewired-romanian-politics/

The New York Times. (2018, December 4). SWAT leader demoted after wearing QAnon patch while meeting Vice President Pence. https://www.nytimes.com/2018/12/04/us/swat-leader-qanon-patch.html

The New York Times. (2021, January 6). Protesters storm Capitol Hill building. https://www.nytimes.com/2021/01/06/us/politics/protesters-storm-capitol-hill-building.html

The New York Times. (2022, May 16). Buffalo shooting: What we know about the attack. https://www.nytimes.com/2022/05/16/nyregion/buffalo-shooting-attack.html

The Washington Post. (2021, January 15). Far-right symbols seen at the U.S. Capitol riot: What they mean and where they come from. https://www.washingtonpost.com/nation/interactive/2021/far-right-symbols-capitol-riot/

Twitter. (2016, August 18). An update on our efforts to combat violent extremism. https://blog.x.com/en_us/a/2016/an-update-on-our-efforts-to-combat-violent-extremism

Vaidhyanathan, S. (2018). *Antisocial media: How Facebook disconnects us and undermines democracy*. Oxford University Press.

Van Prooijen, J.-W., Krouwel, A. P. M., & Pollet, T. V. (2015). Political extremism predicts belief in conspiracy theories. *Social Psychological & Personality Science*, *6*(5), 570–578. DOI: 10.1177/1948550614567356

Viner, K. (2016, July 12). How technology disrupted the truth. The Guardian. https://www.theguardian.com/media/2016/jul/12/how-technology-disrupted-the-truth

Voltmer, K. (2006). *Mass media and political communication in new democracies*. Psychology Press.

Wagner-Egger, P. (2007). Conditional reasoning and the Wason selection task: Biconditional interpretation instead of reasoning bias. *Thinking & Reasoning*, *13*(4), 484–505. DOI: 10.1080/13546780701415979

Walker, J. (2013). *The United States of paranoia: A conspiracy theory*. Harper.

Weenink, A. W. (2022). Mental health and terrorism: A review of the literature. *Journal of Psychiatric Research*, *146*, 141–149. DOI: 10.1016/j.jpsychires.2021.12.057

Wells, G. (2019, October 23). Islamic State's TikTok posts include beheading videos. The Wall Street Journal. https://www.wsj.com/articles/islamic-states-tiktok-posts-include-beheading-videos-11571855833

WIRED. (2016, March 8). Why ISIS is winning the social media war—and how to beat it. https://www.wired.com/2016/03/isis-winning-social-media-war-heres-beat/

WIVB News 4. (2022, May 16). Racist screed linked to Buffalo mass shooter plagiarized manifesto portions from Christchurch mosque shooter, Great Replacement theory. https://www.wivb.com/news/buffalo-supermarket-mass-shooting-tops/racist-screed-linked-to-buffalo-mass-shooter-plagiarized-manifesto-portions-from-christchurch-mosque-shooter-great-replacement-theory/

ENDNOTES

1 *"Iskra" means "spark" in Russian. The newspaper adopted the motto "From a spark a flame will flare up," a metaphor that aptly reflects the conceptualization of radicalization as a cognitive process.*

2 Cambridge Analytica's former CEO, Alexander Nix, reportedly continued his business activities through a consultancy firm called Emerdata.

Chapter 9
Bangladesh Quota Reform Movement 2024:
The Impact of Internet Shutdown on the ICT Sector

Psychee Zaman
https://orcid.org/0009-0007-0494-5836
University of Frontier Technology, Bangladesh

Md. Sanaullah
https://orcid.org/0009-0008-2006-3785
University of Frontier Technology, Bangladesh

Md. Ashrafuzzaman
https://orcid.org/0000-0003-2100-9998
University of Frontier Technology, Bangladesh

ABSTRACT

Access to the internet is increasingly recognized as a fundamental human right, essential for promoting freedom of expression and communication. The internet's infrastructure plays a critical role in facilitating modern business, online education, and overall economic stability. Unfortunately, this right is often restricted in many countries to prevent riots and political unrest. A notable example of the adverse effects of internet restrictions occurred during a two-week blackout in Bangladesh in 2024, which took place amidst student-led protests advocating for quota reform. This internet outage severely disrupted essential services and resulted in an estimated loss of $341 million. The shutdown negatively impacted on the ICT sector, making it more difficult for them to work with clients and meet project deadlines.

DOI: 10.4018/979-8-3373-7406-2.ch009

main objectives: firstly, to address historical inequalities and, secondly, to ensure representation for specific population groups, such as women and ethnic minorities.

Introduced in 1972, the civil service quota system reserves 55% of positions for various quotas, leaving 45% to be filled based on merit (Rahman, 2009). This distribution has evolved over time, especially following the liberation war of Bangladesh. In 1976, the first formal recruitment rules for the civil service were established, replacing an interim policy that had been in place since September 1972 (Ali, 2004). At that time, the allocation was as follows: 40% for merit, 20% for the district quota, 10% for women, and 30% for freedom fighters (See Table 1).

Table 1. Reservation under Quota for Class-I and Class-II Officers

Quota Category	1972	1976	1985–2011	2012–2018
Merit	20	40	45	44
District	40	20	10	10
Freedom Fighters	30	30	30	30
Women	10	10	10	10
Tribal	–	–	05	05
Disabled	–	–	–	01
Total	100	100	100	100

Source. (Uddin & Chowdhury, 2016 cited in Hasan et al., 2022)

In 1996, the quota privileges for freedom fighters were expanded to include their children (Yasmin, 2010). Subsequently, in 2009, these privileges were further extended to their grandchildren (Yasmin, 2010). This extension led to significant frustration and confusion among job seekers.

The quota system has undergone numerous reforms, leading to adjustments in the percentages allocated for various groups. However, the 30% reserved quota for the descendants of freedom fighters has remained unchanged. Several administrative reform commissions have recommended the gradual abolition of this quota (Hasan et al., 2022). Despite these recommendations, every government has been reluctant to implement the suggested changes.

2.1 Protest and Revocation of Quotas in Government Jobs

The disparity in employment opportunities has raised concerns among job seekers and university students in Bangladesh. However, it has also benefited certain political parties, allowing them to secure jobs for their supporters (Reuters, 2024). As students opposed this arrangement in public employment, numerous debates and discussions emerged. Unfortunately, the government has failed to provide a reasonable solution, leaving job seekers to navigate a biased job market on their own. There had been several protests against the quota system, which many considered unjust, discriminatory, and biased toward the followers of a particular political party. However, no movement achieved significant success until 2018.

In 2009, a small-scale protest took place on the Dhaka University campus after the government issued an order stating that reserved posts would remain vacant if no candidates were found. However, this movement ended without any significant outcomes. In 2013, a larger protest arose in response to the imposition of quotas in the Bangladesh Civil Service Preliminary Examination results (The Asia Post, 2013). Unfortunately, this movement also did not achieve much success since the authorities promptly addressed the concerns raised.

In 2018, another major protest took place in Dhaka, calling for the reform of the quota system. This movement was led by the Sadharon Chatro Odhikar Songrokshon Parishad (General Students Rights Preservation Council), and that year, the government revoked all quotas in Bangladesh's public services (The Economist, 2018, April 21). At that time, Bangladeshi government jobs were allocated with a 56% quota: 5% reserved for small ethnic groups, 10% for women, 10% for district quotas, and 30% for the children and grandchildren of freedom fighters. Additionally, if no suitable disabled candidates met the criteria for this 55% quota, a provision allowed for 1% of the seats to be occupied by people with disabilities.

Students from several universities in Bangladesh demanded a rational reform of the system to ensure adequate representation for every group while maintaining meritocracy. At the time of their movement, a national election was approaching, which put significant pressure on the government. Responding to this mass movement, the government decided to revoke the entire quota system (The Economist,2018, April 21). While the government's response elicited mixed reactions—since the demand was for reform rather than complete abolition, the movement was generally considered a success.

In 2024, the issue resurfaced following a Supreme Court verdict that annulled the notification of revocation of the quota system for entry into public services. This decision surprised job seekers and students across Bangladesh, leading to widespread protests. These protests significantly altered the political and administrative landscape, ultimately ending the fifteen-and-a-half-year rule of the Awami League, which had been criticized for establishing autocratic governance in the country. The student movement of 2024 is now regarded as a landmark event in Bangladesh's political history.

2.2 Quota Protest and Violent Attacks on Protesters

After the reinstatement of quotas in government jobs on June 5, 2024, by an order from the Supreme Court (Reuters, 2024), general students without any quota faced potential discrimination. This decision agitated students at several universities and colleges, prompting them to protest on the streets. They formed a group called "Students Against Discrimination". Initially, the protest was peaceful, with students from Dhaka University and other institutions demonstrating in the center of Dhaka.

The protest programs were very attractive and innovative, as no political party used such terms as those before. Students from various regions, with diverse ideologies and social backgrounds, participated in this movement. But the government was adamant about not taking any action. They did not initially plan to appeal in the Supreme Court, nor did they demand suspension of the verdict. Their reluctance was due to an excellent chance of appointing their own political followers to government jobs if the quota system prevailed. Students demanded an executive decision on the quota, arguing that the executive, not the judiciary, should make policy decisions. But the government failed to realise the seriousness of the matter.

Following weeks of protests, then-Prime Minister Sheikh Hasina, who was the president of the Awami League, responded to a journalist who referred to the protesters as "the grandchildren of Razakars." The Awami League asserts its claim to the political leadership of Bangladesh's liberation war. Over the past fifteen years, one of their main political agendas has been to eradicate the "Razakars," a paramilitary group that collaborated with the Pakistani army during the liberation war. Supporters and think tanks associated with the Awami League have created a narrative suggesting that anyone who does not align with their agenda could potentially be labeled a "Razakar."

Sheikh Hasina's comments ignited further outrage among the protesting students. In response, the protesters began chanting satirical slogans: "Tumi ke, ami ke, razakar, razakar" (Who are you, who am I, Razakar, Razakar). Following this, the secretary of the Awami League party and a powerful government minister directed the student wing of the Awami League, known as the Bangladesh Student League, to take action against the protesting students who chanted the "rajakar" slogans (Prothomalo, July 15, 2024).

The student wing of the ruling party attacked protesting students on the Dhaka University campus following an order from the Bangladesh Awami League secretary and government minister. Images of these assaults incited protests across Bangladesh. In a violent response, police and other law enforcement agencies, including the Border Guards, opened fire on the protesting students, resulting in the deaths of six students on July 17th. This deadly incident ignited further unrest among private universities and colleges in Dhaka and other regions of the country. By the evening of July 18th, violence escalated, leading to the deaths of dozens of students. The Armed Forces were deployed heavily to protect the government as the protesting students demanded justice and accountability for the killings. More than 875 students and civilians lost their lives during the protests (The Daily Star, 2024, Sep 13).

Although the original death toll is quite high, many bodies were buried anonymously (New Age, 12 April 2025). According to a report by the UN Office of the High Commissioner for Human Rights (OHCHR), around 1,400 people were killed (United Nations Human Rights, 2025) by August 5th, when longtime dictator Sheikh Hasina fled the country.

3. THE INTERNET SHUTDOWN

As the protest intensified, the government ordered a nationwide shutdown of all internet sites. Previously, the authorities had blocked Facebook, YouTube, TikTok, and other social media platforms in Bangladesh. Such actions were not uncommon or unexpected in the country. There have been several instances of internet shutdowns aimed at suppressing protests. These frequent shutdowns have led to significant criticism regarding human rights, transparency, the rule of law, and the protection of citizens' basic rights. The internet is regarded as a tool for free speech worldwide, but in Bangladesh, the authorities sometimes attempt to manipulate it through the Digital Security Act (2018) and other similar legislation.

Many countries, such as India, Egypt, Myanmar, and Pakistan, impose restrictions on internet use to suppress protests (Joshi, 2020). Internet shutdowns are viewed as violations of human rights. These shutdowns disrupt various aspects of daily life, including employment, education, healthcare, and financial transactions (Hasan, 2024). They hinder journalism, impede free speech, and limit activism, making it difficult to document human rights abuse. Additionally, internet shutdowns obstruct the flow of essential information and emergency assistance during crises, which can endanger lives (Access Now, 2024).

Internet shutdowns create significant economic damage because research shows that nations experiencing interruptions experience a 15.6 percentage point drop in GDP per capita (Tagat et al., 2024). Similarly, the Internet shutdown in India caused digital economies to suffer from more than 50% reduced activity (Gunsilius & David, 2023). Data from Access Now shows that these shutdowns have become more frequent, and this escalation leads to increased economic effects that damage GDP levels, employment statistics, and foreign direct investment values (Oxford Analytica, 2024).

Shutdowns have significant effects on a country's entire economy. The digital infrastructure connects all aspects of trade and commerce, and any disruption to this infrastructure can hinder various business operations. The consequences of these shutdowns can be better understood through network theory and economic shock theory.

Network theory serves as a flexible framework that links micro-level relationships with macro-level organizational structures to create interdisciplinary insights (Daniels, 2022; Gamper, 2022). It examines the dynamics of intermediation, pricing, and trust among interconnected systems in internet-based trade and commerce. This theory emphasizes how networks influence market power and competition, particularly through the coordination among traders and intermediaries, which can result in different levels of efficiency in pricing equilibria (Choi et al., 2017). Economic shock theory explores significant changes in the economy that disrupt stability and affect the growth patterns of economic systems. This theory outlines various types of shocks, including those triggered by external events, which can lead to either negative or positive economic changes (Pilipenko, 2019; Pesotskiy, 2023).

3.1 Internet Shutdown: Global and Local Precedents

Many nations recognize that limiting free speech can help them manage their countries more smoothly. Reports indicate that there have been numerous internet shutdowns worldwide, with India experiencing the highest number. Out of at least 283 reported incidents globally, 116 occurred in India alone (Access Now, 2024). Table 2 displays the top 20 countries that have faced internet shutdowns.

Table 2. Top 20 countries in the world that have faced the internet shutdown

Country	Affected Network	No. of Shutdown	Ordered by	Government Justification	Actual Events
India	Broadband, Mobile	116	State Government	Fake news, hate speech, and incendiary content promote violence.	Communal violence, protests, information control, exam cheating and religious holidays or anniversaries, etc.
Myanmar	Broadband, Mobile	37	Military Junta	Fake news, dissidents, and any kind of planning of actions harmful to the country through digital conduits.	The military council cut off the internet in an area during active conflict; the net was shut down in an active conflict zone due to deliberate infrastructure attacks or targeted disruptions, mobilisation, etc.
Iran	Broadband, Mobile	34	State Government	Flow of information, limit mobilization efforts, and prevent the dissemination of protest footage to international audiences.	Government officials visits, protests, Masha Amini's death in police custody etc.
Palestine	Broadband, Mobile	16	Non-government (Military of the State of Israel)	Sabotage and third-party action.	Destruction of telecommunication infrastructure, a combination of targeted bombings of network installations, disabling of 2 out of 3 primary mobile communication lines for all of the Gaza Strip, and targeted airstrikes on ISP offices and infrastructure.
Ukraine	Broadband, Mobile	8	Non-government	Sabotage and third-party action.	Cyberattack on the Kyivstar ISP, missile strikes, etc.
Pakistan	Broadband, Mobile	7	Executive Government	Fake news, hate speech, and incendiary content violence.	Fighting between the Pakistani army and Baloch separatist troops, protests, etc.
Iraq	Broadband, Mobile	6	Government	School examinations.	Exam cheating.

continued on following page

Table 2. Continued

Country	Affected Network	No. of Shutdown	Ordered by	Government Justification	Actual Events
Azerbaijan	Broadband, Mobile	5	Government	Unknown.	Ongoing blockade in Lachin corridor, Azerbaijani military offensive into the Nagorno-Karabakh region, etc.
Ethiopia	Broadband, Mobile	4	State Government	Protect lives and national property.	Protests, conflict between federal military forces and Amhara Fano fighters.
Senegal	Broadband, Mobile	4	Government	Public safety: quell unrest and public order.	Protests
Bangladesh	Broadband, Mobile	3	Executive Government	Technical problems and infrastructural failure.	Protests, rally of the opposition party, military operations, etc.
Russia	Broadband, Mobile	3	Executive Government	The Internet was shut down to test the sovereign "Runet".	Disconnecting from the international internet served as a test of the sovereign internet.
Jordan	Broadband, Mobile	3	Executive Government	Unknown.	Information control.
Libya	Mobile	3	Unknown	Technical problems and infrastructure failure.	Protests.
China	Broadband, Mobile	2	CAC (Cyberspace Administration of China)	Unknown.	The Cyberspace Administration of China shut down over 4,200 websites and removed 55 apps for violations, such as unauthorised news services and spreading harmful content.
Guinea	Broadband, Mobile	2	Executive Government	Technical problems and infrastructure failure.	Protests: the shutdown was taken to suppress the voices of critical journalists amid political unrest.
Tanzania	Broadband, Mobile	2	Executive Government	Unknown.	Information control.

continued on following page

Table 2. Continued

Country	Affected Network	No. of Shutdown	Ordered by	Government Justification	Actual Events
Turkmenistan	Mobile	2	Executive Government	Unknown.	The shutdown coincided with the opening of a new "smart" city (Arkadag) named in honour of ex-president Gurbanguly Berdymukhammedov, referred to as Arkadag ("the Protector").
Sudan	Broadband, Mobile	2	Executive Government	Unknown.	Amid the conflict between SAF and RSF, MTN shut down internet services at the request of the government telecom regulator.
Syria	Broadband, Mobile	2	Executive Government	School examinations.	Examination cheating.

Source: Access Now. (2024, November 12). *#KeepItOn: fighting internet shutdowns around the world – Access Now*. https://www.accessnow.org/campaign/keepiton/#global-tracker

3.2 Case-specific Discussions on Internet Shutdowns

Case I: Jammu and Kashmir Issue in India

Following the revocation of the region's special status in 2019, the longest internet blackout in any democracy lasted over seven months (Shah & Junaid-ul-Shafi, 2024). Authorities in India, often justifying these shutdowns as measures to maintain public safety and curb unrest, have adversely affected local entrepreneurs, leading to the closure of small businesses reliant on online operations in India (Qadir & Dar, 2021; Collyer & Wright, 2021). The government of India imposed a total communication blackout in Jammu and Kashmir to quell the protest there, which was provoked by the government policy. Internet shutdown is very common in Jammu and Kashmir. Between 2012 and 2017, the total duration of internet shutdown was 16315 hours (Qadir & Dar, 2021). Precisely, the government of Jammu and Kashmir snapped internet services whenever any anti-military and anti-government operation happened, and for these small businesses, health centres, entrepreneurs, software firms, and cybersecurity platforms were hampered (S. Qadir et al., 2021). These blackouts caused all educational institutions, including universities, engineering colleges, medical schools, and secondary schools, to close without providing formal notice. Completely ceased employment at Jammu and Kashmir's nine state universities and two central universities. Jammu and Kashmir's internet ban is a clear illustration of how political unrest may seriously impede advancements in science, education, and professional growth. The UN acknowledged that the shutdown violated human rights and added to the political and social unrest in the area (Firdosi, 2020). The government has justified those measures as necessary to guarantee national security and public order, despite continuous criticisms coming from human rights organisations because such actions encroach on freedom of expression and economic activities (Momen et al., 2020).

Case II: Manipur Conflict in India

The internet shutdown in Manipur, India, which lasted for 80 consecutive days in 2023, stands as one of the longest state-imposed digital blackouts in the country's history. This drastic measure emerged from escalating tensions between the Meitei community, the majority ethnic group in the Imphal Valley, and the Kuki-Zomi tribes, a Scheduled Tribe (ST) minority predominantly residing in the hill districts. The conflict was The Meitei community's demand for inclusion in the ST category—a constitutional designation that grants marginalised groups access to reserved quotas in education, employment, and political representation—triggered the situation. The Kuki-Zomi tribes, already classified as STs, vehemently opposed this move, arguing that it would dilute their existing privileges and exacerbate competition for limited resources (Chakraborty, 2023). Authorities argued that social media platforms were being used to circulate inflammatory content, coordinate attacks, and instigate communal hatred. The shutdown initially targeted mobile internet services but later expanded to broadband in conflict-prone districts. For 80 days, residents were forced to rely on offline modes of communication, severely hampering crisis response, humanitarian aid, and journalistic reporting (Shirin, 2023). In addition, this shutdown impacts democracy, civil rights, and economic stability. Along with worsening social tensions and disinformation, the disruption had a significant impact on emergency services, companies, education, and healthcare (Maurya, 2024). The broader global trend of digital authoritarianism is exemplified by the Manipur incident, a troubling misuse of power with severe consequences for democracy, human rights, and economic stability, and it has called for stronger legal protections, judicial oversight, and alternative measures for conflict resolution that do not involve blanket digital blackouts (Maurya, 2024).

Case III: Internet Blackout in Pakistan

Between 2012 and 2017, there were 41 internet shutdowns in Pakistan (Wagner, 2018). The reasons behind internet shutdowns in Pakistan are multifaceted, primarily revolving around national security concerns, religious gatherings, elections, protests and the suppression of civil unrest. The government uses these shutdowns as a preventive measure to stop protests and minimise violent extremist activities that use networks to plan attacks (Wagner, 2018; Purdon et al., 2014). The sudden failure of the nation's online connectivity had a profound impact on numerous economic sectors and disrupted the lives of innumerable individuals who depend on the Internet for their livelihoods. Social media content creators found it challenging to keep up relationships with their followers, and people who worked remotely or from home noticed that they were unable to finish their duties. The sudden disappearance of online health services, which are necessary for remote consultations and medical assistance, has caused many people to worry about their safety. Confusion and suffering among the populace were exacerbated by malfunctions in even basic equipment like ATMs and biometric systems (Hussain et al., 2024). Digital growth suffered a setback which negatively affected freelancers and startups and technology companies because they lost potential opportunities. Internet and mobile shutdowns were imposed as a tool by the governments of Pakistan to control political mobilisation; this reduces the dissemination of information during protests or rallies, and it keeps power in their hands (Wagner, 2018).

Case IV: Internet Shutdown in Myanmar

The February 1, 2021, military coup in Myanmar provoked civil unrest, and medical professionals, together with other public workers, started the Civil Disobedience Movement against military rule (Sharma et al., 2021). The military government responded with strong internet censorship policies that blocked social media platforms, restricted cellular data and enforced nightly internet blackouts to stop dissident information and maintain control (Padmanabhan et al., 2021; Bischof et al., 2023). These actions pose an additional and increasing risk to various facets of human rights, freedom of speech, and public health worldwide. Myanmar's authorities have entirely shut down the internet during periods of political unrest, civil disobedience, or alleged threats to national security, depriving millions of people of access. Internet shutdowns harm the wellbeing of the populace by restricting freedom of expression and violating human rights. Disconnected people lack access to essential services, which affect many aspects of life, including work, education, health care, and financial stability, especially for freelancers and those in the ICT sector (Hussain et al., 2024). The government employed these measures to stop the spread of protest content and maintain control over power because such actions align with authoritarian patterns where internet blackouts accompany political protest events (Bischof et al., 2023). The justification from the government and authorities for the blackouts was that it would constrain insurgents' ability to spread fake news, dissent and plan any sort of action through digital conduits (Khine, 2023).

3.3 Previous Instances of Internet Shutdowns in Bangladesh

Bangladesh has experienced various internet shutdowns and slow speeds for multiple reasons. Since 2009, internet users in the country have faced different forms of shutdown almost every year (see Table 3). These restrictions have included complete network blackouts, the blocking of communication apps and social media sites, and deliberate slowdowns of mobile internet speeds. An estimated cost of a one-day internet shutdown in Bangladesh was more than $78 million (Prepare Prevent Resist, 2023).

Table 3. Incidence of Internet Shutdown (Government Ordered) in Bangladesh

Starting Date	Ending Date	Duration	Affected Network	Excuse (Government Justification)	Actual Events
25th February, 2009	1st March, 2009	5 Days	Broadband and Mobile Internet	Maintain public order during a period of unrest following violent clashes in Dhaka.	The armed conflict in the Bangladesh Rifles revolt continues.
6th May, 2013	8th May, 2013	3 Days	Broadband	There is escalating violence and unrest.	Hefajat-e Islam demonstration in Motijheel.
4th January, 2015	5th January, 2015	1 Day	Broadband	The national elections, citing security concerns.	Elections and political events.
1 July, 2016	4th July, 2016	3 Days	Broadband and Mobile Internet	Spread fake news and rumors, creating a dark environment.	Militant attack on Holey Artisan Bakery, Gulshan, Dhaka.
4th August, 2018	7th August, 2018	3 Days	Broadband and Mobile Internet	Prevent the spread of rumors and misinformation and curb the protests via social media.	Massive student protests demanding road safety followed the death of two college girls by road accident.
29th November, 2018	4th December, 2018	5 Days	Broadband and Mobile Internet	Public safety, controlling unrest, and ensuring national security.	National election and political unrest.
26th February, 2021	1st March, 2021	3 Days	Broadband and Mobile Internet	There are tensions between the government and civil society over freedom of expression and access to information.	Demonstrations against the Digital Security Act.
26th March, 2021	27th March, 2021	1 Day	Broadband and Mobile Internet	The spread of inflammatory content...	Protests erupted when Indian Prime Minister Narendra Modi visited Bangladesh.

continued on following page

Table 3. Continued

Starting Date	Ending Date	Duration	Affected Network	Excuse (Government Justification)	Actual Events
5th January, 2024	8th January, 2024	3 Days	Broadband and Mobile Internet	Control sensitive political organisations and suppress dissent and communication.	National election.
18th July, 2024	28th July, 2024	10 Days	Broadband and Mobile Internet	To control the spread of misinformation, public safety, and protect against violence and clashes.	Quota reform movement by the students against discrimination.

Source: Access Now. (2024, November 12). *#KeepItOn: fighting internet shutdowns around the world – Access Now*. https://www.accessnow.org/campaign/keepiton/#global-tracker

4. THE ICT INDUSTRY IN BANGLADESH

The information communication technology (ICT) sector has emerged as very important for the economic growth and development of Bangladesh. It has developed this industry into one of its fastest-growing sectors that adds substantial economic value to the national economy. The IT sector in Bangladesh has demonstrated substantial growth since recent times, generating $1.5 billion in revenue and employing 300,000 IT professionals; it is projected to increase to 440,000 by 2025 (Hossain, 2022). This would reach $5 billion by 2025 and $20 billion by 2031, indicating rapid growth and future scope of the industry (Tanner, 2024). More important is the fact that the new generation is highly keen on learning about software and technology, and the IT industry has provided a career opportunity for this generation. Indeed, at least 100,000 jobs in that industry have been created by another team of software and customer service providers and most importantly, they can hire freelancers who have been working (Ahmed, 2018).

A major impact of information and communication technology (ICT) has been on trade in Bangladesh. It was seen that improved infrastructures of ICT affected increased trade flows, hence showing how that form of technology can boost trade. The impact of ICTs on trade patterns indicates improved connectivity and digitalised services, making access to markets easier for Bangladeshi businesses. IT companies' competencies include business process optimisation and operational efficiency, and other industries can benefit from that. The economy has been driven by access to bigger markets that SMEs have obtained through e-commerce and mobile financial services. So far, more than 4500 IT companies are working, and 750,000 are ICT employers in Bangladesh (Mahmud, 2024). As for now, however, Bangladesh is situated as an insourcing back office in this market. It is still a low-cost labour region compared to some regional players like India or Malaysia. Already, large international corporations are investing more and more in the Bangladesh market, becoming attracted by highly qualified labour forces and favourable economic conditions. Although information technology in this country is at a growth stage, it faces certain problems related to shortages of highly skilled professionals and the poor condition of infrastructure. Their solution could provide better assurance for growth and competitiveness. The IT industry in Bangladesh plays a very vital role. Therefore, it has great potential to become one of the significant players in the international context of IT if continuous investment in education and infrastructure is well supported by government policies.

4.1 Impact of Internet Shutdown on the ICT Sector

The government's shutdown of access to the internet in response to increasing student protests severely hampered the information technology sector in many ways. On July 17, authorities reportedly suspended mobile internet services, supposedly to calm public anxieties over the quota reform movement. The situation worsened when, on July 18, broadband internet services were throttled, negatively impacting society and numerous enterprises. This shutdown just about rendered impossible essential activities such as paying energy bills, conducting online banking and shopping, global communication, digital trade, and customs clearance. The government-forced internet outage greatly hurt telecommunications companies, software developers, producers, e-commerce entrepreneurs, business process outsourcing firms, and freelancers alike. Partial restoration of broadband internet was done on July 23 (Al Jazeera, 2024, July 28).

A national ban has been effective since the start of the shutdown on all social media outlets, including Facebook, Instagram, TikTok, WhatsApp, and YouTube. Mobile internet services were restored on July 28, but access to social media platforms was only restored on July 31. On August 2, an interruption in mobile internet services was again witnessed when Facebook and Messenger were inaccessible for some seven hours in the morning. These actions had far-reaching consequences for export-oriented IT companies whose brand images suffered adversely, therefore. Many internet-based organisations in Bangladesh have also lost significant amounts of income in the given period (The Daily Star, 2024, August 10).

According to a report of The Internet Society Pulse (2025), Bangladesh's economy faced $21,965,222 USD losses due to the five-day, twelve-hour internet shutdown. The total two-week shutdown in July-August of 2024 cost around $341 million USD (Internet Society, 2024).

According to the ICT and telecom ministry, the financial losses from the shutdown amounted to BDT 18,000 crore (The Daily Star, 2024, August 10). Industry experts pointed to the most damaging issue being the blow that had been dealt to the global reputation of Bangladesh's ICT sector because of the five-day internet blackout. According to the Bangladesh Association of Software and Information Services, its members incurred a loss amounting to Tk 500 crore during this period (The Daily Star, 2024, August 10). e-CAB estimated that the loss in the e-commerce sector was about Tk 1,700 crore during the 13 days of July when the internet services were unavailable. About 5% of e-commerce transactions were put on hold due to the outage and a nationwide curfew and public safety.

Freelancers of Bangladesh, dependent on Fiverr, Guru, and People Per Hour, were among the worst sufferers. Many freelancers faced huge stress and fear since they could not communicate with their clients or deliver projects with their deadlines. According to BFDS (Bangladesh Freelancer Development Society), 161 freelancers went to Nepal, and 33 others moved to India, continuing their work without disturbance during the blackout (Adib, 2024). Many of the freelancers and businesses did not survive this disruption, which plagued the sector for the good. The e-commerce sectors, entrepreneurs and some influencers have faced many problems, and they are noted in figure 1 below:

Figure 1. Breakdown of Issues Impacting Business Operations for Internet Shutdown

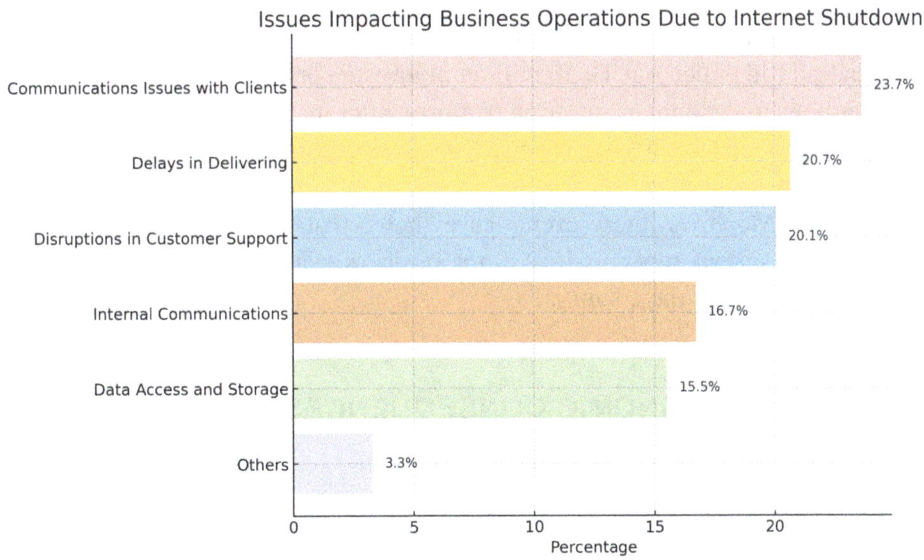

(Suroy, 2024).

This figure describes how the internet shutdown impacted more than 400 outsourcing businesses. The problems with communication due to the internet shutdown were that 23.7% of the respective firms communicated with clients, 20.7% delayed project deliveries, 20.1% disrupted customer support, 16.7% reported internal communications, 15.5% faced challenges in data access and storage and 3.3% had other issues. Further, 54.2% of these companies had to decrease their staffing by more than 70%, showing the operational severity due to the internet outage (Suroy, 2024).

The shutdown of the internet also hugely affected the education sector. Just after the violent clashes occurred on July 16, the government announced the closure of schools that very night. The government initially implemented the shutdown in city corporation areas but later expanded it to the entire country. The quota reform protests disrupted educational institutions, especially among students at primary, secondary, and higher secondary levels. This delayed regular class tests, half-yearly exams, and SSC and HSC preparations, which left the students struggling to keep up with their academic schedules. The long closure made many students lose their interest in studying at home and hindered their focus and motivation even more (Rahman, 2024).

The learning disruptions also caused a big worry for the teachers, whose challenge to address the burgeoning educational gaps was getting bigger with each passing day. During the shutdown, several online educational platforms, like Shikho, 10 Minute School, Eshikhon, Amar Pathshala, and Fahad's Tutorial, among others, had to suspend their services. Furthermore, several teachers were harassed, and some were arrested for showing solidarity with students during protests. The Startup Bangladesh Ltd pulled out Tk 50 million in investment with 10 Minute School, in a major blow to the online education platform, after its founder came out in public support for the quota reform movement on Facebook (bdnews24, 2024, July 16). This singular event unveiled how the autocracy affects the business decision of Bangladesh. Moreover, these events have shown that the internet shutdown has brought very serious repercussions to the business, education, and livelihoods of many citizens across the country.

5. BROADER ECONOMIC CONSEQUENCES OF THE INTERNET SHUTDOWN

The 2024 Bangladesh internet shutdown caused severe economic damage which devastated e-commerce industries and every digital service as well as banking and FinTech operations. The shutdown destroyed the foundation of digital economic growth throughout the country, leading to massive financial losses. The e-commerce industry suffered a Tk 1,700 crore deficit during the 13-day Internet outage period.

The economic losses from the shutdown amounted to Tk 600 crore for e-commerce, Tk 300 crore for e-tourism and Tk 100 crore for e-logistics (The Business Standard, 2024, July 31).

There was no feasibility to process the customer orders, communicate with the clients, or do financial transactions due to a lack of reliable access to the internet. Alone, F-commerce depended on online sales and suffered losses of around Tk 120 crore every day. Besides this, strikes resulted in losses of about US $3 million a day to the industry that served international clients because it could not sustain the operations. Due to these strikes, industry accounted for losses of approximately $3 million per day (The Business Standard 2024, July 31). The digital economy faced sustained damage and reputation losses, which caused investors to lose confidence.

Through its years of development, the Bangladesh economy has encountered multiple interruptions. The internet shutdowns in 2024 exposed numerous vulnerabilities in the economic infrastructure, serving as a harsh wake-up call. Experts have drawn parallels between the economic consequences of the COVID-19 pandemic, which significantly impacted the garment industry, the backbone of the nation's export economy. The situation resulted in the massive factory closure, loss of jobs, and people spending less on consumer goods, further plunging the most vulnerable into poverty. Commodity prices also increased, and the budgets of governments stretched to their breaking point; strong mechanisms were needed in protecting economies from disasters like the pandemic (Bodrud-Doza et al., 2020).

Similarly, in 2007, when the world faced a financial crisis, Bangladesh also suffered with exports, remittances, and foreign aid. However, a solid banking regulatory framework dampened its worst effects and helped them avoid catastrophic collapses like many other countries. This has given importance to diversification and flexibility if growth is to be sustained in an increasingly volatile global economy (Reza & Khan, 2011). The shutdown of the internet also caused disturbance in digital banking and FinTech practices. Nationwide, the internet shutdown hindered online banking services. These failures in processing transactions created organisational blockages and raised costs for both organisations as well as consumers. Even after partial restoration, banks struggled to conduct foreign transactions since the speed of the internet was way too slow, affecting their operational capacity immensely.

This resulted in an immediate decline in the number of users and transaction volumes for FinTech firms dependent on digital payments. Several firms operating on cash-on-delivery models were under the imminent threat of a liquidity crisis, as those were the only valid mode of transaction. These circumstances raised doubts about the situation and the long-term sustainability of digital payment solutions in Bangladesh. This hence slowed down the pace of adaptation to digital financial technologies in Bangladesh (Roy, 2024).

The internet shutdown has badly affected the image of Bangladesh on the world platform and simultaneously shaken the confidence of businesses. According to FICCI, which has considered only the direct effects of a shutdown, the economic impact stands estimated at $10 billion daily and BGMEA estimated losses of Tk 6,400 crore, thus heightening the economic strain even more (The Business Standard, 2024, August 3).

These disruptions therefore bring in a lot of uncertainty that has put off potential investors, and net FDI inflow has sharply fallen to $3.8 billion during the July-May period of FY24, due to various perceptions like political instability and lack of reliability in infrastructure (Chakma, 2024). Moreover, such shutdowns virtually paralyse the international communications of local businesses and damage the country's reputation as a reliable partner. The shutdown of the internet made Bangladesh's economic setup susceptible to fatal flaws – especially dependence on digital infrastructure. It will be a task now for the government and businesses in unison to reassure the world about operational stability and reliable channels of communication. To overcome the long-term consequences of this crisis, foreign investors need both a favourable investment environment and restored international trust.

6. SOCIO POLITICAL REPERCUSSIONS OF THE SHUTDOWN

The quota protest in Bangladesh in 2024, driven principally by students who had much passion for government job quota reforms, exposed widespread social problems, including the erosion of democratic practices coupled with the growth of authoritarian practices. These protests led to violent clashes, which killed over 100 people within a day, which became the turning point, as these actions significantly affected the legitimacy and responsiveness of the government in the public eye.

The national response to the protests by the government was to turn off the internet throughout the nation. To many, this represented an attempt to strangle the voice of dissent, substantially reduce the flow of information, and muzzle the movement. Being in blackout conditions from both local and global news cultivated this sense of helplessness and lack of confidence in government institutions. The critics had then argued that the move reflected a broader authoritarian trend in which control of information was turning into a tool for maintaining power.

This internet shutdown devastated education in Bangladesh, which increasingly relies on digital platforms for learning. Students of the country could not access important online resources, participate in virtual classes, or seek academic support. The disruption paralysed major online learning platforms, exacerbating the struggles the students were facing. The uncertainty caused by the protests and subsequent restrictions created a very stressful and chaotic environment that may have long-term effects, such as anxiety and reduced motivation to pursue education.

The blackout also impeded political activities and restricted freedom of expression. It divided the opposition movements, making it almost impossible for political parties to marshal any support or communicate appropriately. Things turned ugly when then Prime Minister Sheikh Hasina termed the agitating students "Razakars", a term deeply rooted in historical and political memory. The remark further incensed public sentiment and fuelled the protests, turning into a general call for the government to act and reform.

The media's role in the protest was multilayered, developing in three sharp stages. The few media outlets that reported on the events more objectively at the very beginning, when the protests were orientated towards changes in the job quota system in public services, were swiftly labelled "Islamists" or "terrorists". Social media became a key channel for the recording of police violence cases and dissemination of information in real time, although the government tried to suppress such reports. The shutdown of the internet hampered the dissemination of the news of brutal crackdown over the protesting students. Violence was more serious in the second phase of the movement when the Chhatra League, the student wing of the ruling Awami League, collaborated with the police to assault protesters. The local media could not or did not perform their duty of publishing truth. Several government agencies had put tremendous pressure on them to not publish anything that was unfavourable for the government. International media such as DW, Al Jazeera, and Reuters also played an important role in exposing government actions, including allegations of the military using UN logos during operations. These events invited international pressure on the Bangladeshi military, including from the UN itself.

The government also resorted to the Digital Security Act to muzzle opposition voices by criminalising legitimate expressions of opinion. So far, more than 1,700 DSA cases have been filed against journalists, activists, and ordinary citizens critical of the government (Amnesty International, 2024). These moves further weakened freedom of speech and increased discontent among the people.

When the internet restored, the protests in this last stage started to demand the resignation of the then Prime Minister, Sheikh Hasina. In this stage of the protests, media coverage was increased, and some of them did their work terrifically. For example, Jamuna TV broadcast news without bias but presented a general view of the incidents. Other media were politically biased, either supporting the government or secretly withholding critical information. The movement faced challenges, including injuries and fatalities among journalists and media representatives during the protests.

The internet shutdown catalysed further public resentment and showed critical defects in governance and transparency. Such a step by the government alienated its people through isolation and suppression of democratic discourse. These incidents are indicative that there is an emergent need to institute more safeguards protecting freedom of expression and transparency in nature to uphold the democratic principles of Bangladesh.

7. POLICY RECOMMENDATIONS

In 2024, the government's response to the quota reform movement, particularly the decision to impose a nationwide internet blackout, heightened tensions and significantly impacted both freedom of expression and the IT and digital sectors. These actions were extremely unpopular, violating fundamental democratic values and undermining the potential of information technology (IT), software, and the rapidly growing ICT sector in Bangladesh. These industries have shown great promise, supported by government initiatives, skilled talent, and progressive digitalization. However, the internet shutdowns have severely hindered their growth and raised concerns about the sustainability of Bangladesh's digital infrastructure. Given the critical role of IT and digital infrastructure in the country's economic development, several policy recommendations have been proposed to address these disruptions and mitigate future impacts.

i. The government should establish a legal framework that prohibits internet shutdowns. Such shutdowns hinder freedom of speech and create barriers to ensuring human rights and access to essential information. There should be no justification for shutting down the internet unless there is a state of emergency that poses a direct threat to the country's digital infrastructure.
ii. Instead of implementing a nationwide blackout, the government should consider alternative methods to address security concerns. This could involve targeted measures, such as restricting access in specific regions experiencing unrest.
iii. In cases of national security threats, blackouts should not be imposed arbitrarily. Instead, they should require judicial approval, with decisions made by a Supreme Court judge or a standing committee of judges. This process should involve careful consideration of the potential economic, social, and democratic impacts of such actions.
iv. If an internet shutdown is unavoidable, its duration should not be extended unnecessarily. Continuous blackouts should not last more than three hours, and relevant authorities should provide advance notice to the affected areas. Implementing this policy would alleviate significant stress for both businesses and individuals while addressing security threats.

v. Laws should be enacted to penalize unauthorized or arbitrary internet shutdowns. This legal safeguard would discourage misuse of power and reinforce the notion that digital access is a fundamental right.
vi. The government should also expand initiatives to create and support remote IT-based job opportunities, particularly for freelancers. Effective management and infrastructure development are essential to ensure these jobs remain resilient during crises.
vii. Additionally, ad hoc advisory councils should be established, consisting of government ICT stakeholders, industry professionals, lawyers, and representatives from NGOs. These councils can offer advice and oversight on digital policies, such as internet management during crises.
viii. Develop effective communication protocols to ensure timely information dissemination during crises. This includes clearly explaining the reasons for implementing internet restrictions and providing recommendations for avoiding similar disruptions in the future.
ix. Political turmoil often raises cybersecurity issues. By investing in strong cybersecurity infrastructure, the government can reduce digital risks without resorting to internet shutdowns, thus maintaining trust in the nation's digital ecosystem.
x. Bangladesh should explore global best practices for managing digital infrastructure during political crises. Collaborating with international organizations and adhering to global standards can enhance the country's reputation as a responsible player in the digital economy.
xi. Promote digital literacy and awareness among citizens to reduce the exploitation of internet platforms during times of chaos. Informed individuals are less likely to spread disinformation or engage in actions that escalate tensions.

By implementing these strategies, Bangladesh can establish itself as a reliable and competitive player in the IT sector. Strategic initiatives will not only foster IT growth but also drive economic development. A balanced and transparent approach to digital governance will enhance investor confidence, protect democratic values, and sustain the digital economy.

8. CONCLUSION

In the 21st century, the internet has become an essential platform for exercising freedom of expression, allowing individuals to share ideas and opinions on a global scale. However, governments and dominant political factions often impose restrictions on internet access to suppress dissent and maintain their authority. By censoring content, blocking websites, or throttling connectivity, these groups stifle opposition and control public discourse. Such measures undermine democratic principles and limit citizens' ability to engage in open dialogue. While the internet empowers voices that challenge the status quo, the regulation of this platform by those in power indicates a troubling effort to manipulate information and maintain political control in the digital age. The 2024 Bangladesh quota reformation movement turned violent when the government attempted to quell the protests forcefully, using lethal weapons. Due to the leaders of the movement using social media, the authorities attempted to limit the dissemination of information through the internet. Incidents of obstruction and disturbing footage spread rapidly to billions of users, both locally and globally. For example, the police shooting that resulted in the death of Abu Saeed during a protest in Rangpur was broadcast live on numerous national television channels and social media platforms. In an effort to restrict access to this disturbing footage, the government ordered internet shutdowns (Ahmed, 2024). These widespread shutdowns across the nation severely impacted the country's IT industry, highlighting its vulnerability to digital dependency. This study demonstrates that the sectors most affected included the IT industry, software companies, freelancing, e-commerce, and social media platforms. But the worst affected were the students who relied on various online educational platforms for their studies. In the case of the IT industry in Bangladesh, the shutdown has led to immediate losses that could hinder long-term growth, international partnerships, and the country's reputation as an emerging destination for IT outsourcing. Furthermore, these effects have extended to the broader ecosystem, impacting IT training institutions, innovation centers, and supply chains. A cascading economic effect has been observed in the reduced contribution of the IT sector to the GDP, which has damaged Bangladesh's reputation as an increasingly important destination for IT outsourcing. Businesses in this sector have experienced disrupted workflows, missed deadlines, and a significant loss of client trust, particularly among freelancers and small businesses working under international contracts. The findings of this research highlight an urgent need for a strategic policy framework that balances national security requirements with the critical importance of digital connectivity. Additionally, proactive crisis management strategies will be necessary for resilient infrastructure investment. Future efforts should involve coordination among policymakers, industry stakeholders, and global partners to support Bangladesh's IT industry.

REFERENCES

Access Now. (2024, November 12). #KeepItOn: fighting internet shutdowns around the world - Access Now. https://www.accessnow.org/campaign/keepiton/#global-tracker

Adib, A. A. H. (2024). Internet exodus: Bangladeshi freelancers flee to Nepal, India for connectivity. *jagonews24.com*. https://www.jagonews24.com/en/tech/news/75838

Ahmed, R. (2024, July 28). The government shut down the internet. Prothomalo. https://www.prothomalo.com/bangladesh/0l53ciu95t

Ahmed, S. (2018). Opportunities and Challenges of software development business in Bangladesh. In Brac University. https://dspace.bracu.ac.bd/xmlui/handle/10361/10129

Al Jazeera. (2024, July 28). Bangladesh restores mobile internet after 11-day blackout to quell protests. *Al Jazeera*. https://www.aljazeera.com/news/2024/7/28/bangladesh-restores-mobile-internet-after-11-day-blackout-to-quell-protests

Alam, J., Emrun Garjon, A., & Pathi, K. (2024, July 19). *Bangladesh quota protests: Internet and mobile services cut off | AP News*. AP News. https://apnews.com/article/bangladesh-student-protests-violence-internet-shutdown-622c6c464c47860afee293e80550c051

Alam, M. A., Roy, P. C., & Bíró, J. (2025). Breaking the Chains of Fear: Civil Society's role in defying autocracy and shaping Bangladesh's 2024 July Revolution. *Civil Szemle*, *22*(2), 71–96. DOI: 10.62560/csz.2025.02.4

Ali, A. M. M. S. (2004). *Bangladesh civil service : a political-administrative perspective*. CiNii Research. The University Press Limited. https://cir.nii.ac.jp/crid/1130282269418922880

Amnesty International. (2024, July 19). *Stop Bangladesh's crackdown on freedom of expression online - Amnesty International*. https://www.amnesty.org/en/petition/stop-crackdown-on-freedom-of-expression-online-in-bangladesh/

bdnews24.com. (2024, July 16). Startup Bangladesh cancels TK 50m investment for 10 minute school. *Bdnews24*. https://bdnews24.com/bangladesh/8cde64566eb9

Bhatia, K. V., Elhussein, M., Kreimer, B., & Snapp, T. (2023). Internet shutdown and Regime-Imposed disinformation campaigns. *Communicatio*, *49*(2), 53–71. DOI: 10.1080/02500167.2023.2230391

Bischof, Z. S., Pitcher, K., Carisimo, E., Meng, A., Nunes, R. B., Padmanabhan, R., Roberts, M. E., Snoeren, A. C., & Dainotti, A. (2023). Destination unreachable: characterizing internet outages and shutdowns. *In ACM SIGCOMM '23: Proceedings of the ACM SIGCOMM 2023 Conference* (pp. 608–621). DOI: 10.1145/3603269.3604883

Bodrud-Doza, M., Shammi, M., Bahlman, L., Islam, A. R. M. T., & Rahman, M. M. (2020). Psychosocial and Socio-Economic crisis in Bangladesh due to COVID-19 Pandemic: A Perception-Based Assessment. *Frontiers in Public Health*, *8*, 341. Advance online publication. DOI: 10.3389/fpubh.2020.00341 PMID: 32676492

Chakma, J. (2024, July 28). Internet outage, curfew leave foreign investors in a bind. *The Daily Star*. https://www.thedailystar.net/business/economy/news/internet-outage-curfew-leave-foreign-investors-bind-3663536

Chakraborty, S. (2023, July 3). India dispatch: ethnic violence continues to plague India's Manipur State as internet shutdown continues. *Gujarat National Law U., IN*. https://www.jurist.org/news/2023/07/india-dispatch-ethnic-violence-continues-to-plague-indias-manipur-state-as-internet-shutdown-continues/

Choi, S., Galeotti, A., & Goyal, S. (2017). Trading in Networks: Theory and Experiments. *Journal of the European Economic Association*, *15*(4), 784–817. DOI: 10.1093/jeea/jvw016

Collyer, M., & Wright, J. (2021). A Bayesian Analysis of Collective Action and Internet Shutdowns in India. In *13th ACM Web Science Conference 2021* (pp. 309–318). DOI: 10.1145/3447535.3462480

Daniels, M. (2022). Aspects of Network Theory - (L.) Foxhall (ed.) Interrogating Networks. Investigating Networks of Knowledge in Antiquity. Pp. x + 134, figs, ills, maps. Oxford and Philadelphia: Oxbow Books, 2021. Paper, £16.95. ISBN: 978-1-78925-627-7. *The Classical Review, 73*(1), 169–172. DOI: 10.1017/S0009840X22001676

Firdosi, M. (2020). STEM on hold: The impacts of the internet shutdown in Jammu and Kashmir. *Science for the People*, *23*(1). https://www.researchgate.net/publication/342339149_STEM_on_Hold_The_Impacts_of_the_Internet_Shutdown_in_Jammu_and_Kashmir

Gamper, M. (2022). Social Network Theories: An Overview. In *Springer eBooks* (pp. 35–48). DOI: 10.1007/978-3-030-97722-1_3

Gunsilius, F., & David, V. D. (2023). Free discontinuity design: with an application to the economic effects of internet shutdowns. *arXiv (Cornell University)*. https://doi.org//arxiv.2309.14630DOI: 10.48550

Hasan, A. R., Jahan, M., & Islam, Md. R. (2022). Recruitment and Selection of Civil Servants in Bangladesh: An Expository Study. Bangladesh Journal of Public Administration (BJPA), 30(2), 115–128. https://www.researchgate.net/publication/375755842_Recruitment_and_Selection_of_Civil_Servants_in_Bangladesh_An_Expository_Study

Hasan, M. (2024, July 23). *Internet blackout wallops life and living.* The Daily Star. https://www.thedailystar.net/business/news/internet-blackout-wallops-life-and-living-3660021

Hasnat, S. (2024, July 11). Students protest job quotas in Bangladesh's streets. *The New York Times.* https://www.nytimes.com/2024/07/11/world/asia/bangladesh-student-protests-job-quotas.html

Hossain, M. (2022). IT and IT Enabled Service (ITES) sector in Bangladesh: Current status and future potentials. In *Digital Transformation and Economic Development in Bangladesh* (pp. 83–104). DOI: 10.1007/978-981-19-2753-9_5

Hussain, R., Kabir, R., Kar, S. K., & Arafat, S. Y. (2024). Internet Shutdown with Violations of Human Rights and Freedom of Speech. *Asian Journal of Public Health and Nursing.*, *1*(3), 47–50. Advance online publication. DOI: 10.62377/x3zp6t02

Internet Society. (2024, July 18). *Shutdown - Bangladesh - Internet Society Pulse.* Internet Society Pulse. https://pulse.internetsociety.org/shutdowns/mobile-internet-shut-down-in-bangladesh-amidst-protests

Joshi, N. (2020). Internet shutdowns during protests: A practice in digital authoritarianism. Diplomová práce, vedoucí Schlotti, Jivanta. Praha: Univerzita Karlova, Fakulta sociálních věd, Katedra bezpečnostních studií. https://dspace.cuni.cz/bitstream/handle/20.500.11956/150279/120400013.pdf?sequence=1

Khine, N. K. (2023, December 30). *Digital rights in the post-coup Myanmar: Enabling factors for digital authoritarianism.* https://so03.tci-thaijo.org/index.php/HRPS/article/view/266778

Mahmud, F. (2024, July 30). Bangladesh's internet blackout immobilizes its booming tech industry. Rest of World. https://restofworld.org/2024/bangladesh-curfew-internet-shutdown/

Maurya, R. (2024). Darkening Digital Democracy: A case study of Manipur Internet shutdown. *Global Media Journal-Indian Edition, 16(2).* https://www.researchgate.net/profile/Riya-Maurya-2/publication/387207553_Darkening_Digital_Democracy_A_Case_Study_of_Manipur_Internet_Shutdown/links/676403f672316e5855fe15e8/Darkening-Digital-Democracy-A-Case-Study-of-Manipur-Internet-Shutdown.pdf

Momen, M. N., S, H., & Das, D. (2020). Mediated democracy and internet shutdown in India. *Journal of Information Communication and Ethics in Society*, *19*(2), 222–235. DOI: 10.1108/JICES-07-2020-0075

Morshed, M. B., Dye, M., Ahmed, S. I., & Kumar, N. (2017). When the Internet Goes Down in Bangladesh. In *Proceedings of the 2017 ACM Conference on Computer Supported Cooperative Work and Social Computing* (pp. 1591–1604). DOI: 10.1145/2998181.2998237

New Age. (2025, April 12). 1,581 killed in mass uprising: students. New Age. https://www.newagebd.net/post/country/246450/1581-killed-in-mass-uprising-students

Oxford Analytica. (2024). *Socio-economic cost of internet shutdowns is rising*. Emerald Expert Briefings., DOI: 10.1108/OXAN-DB287653

Padmanabhan, R., Filastò, A., Xynou, M., Raman, R. S., Middleton, K., Zhang, M., Madory, D., Roberts, M., & Dainotti, A. (2021). A multi-perspective view of internet censorship in Myanmar. In *ACM SIGCOMM 2021 Workshop on Free and Open Communications on the Internet* (pp. 27–36). DOI: 10.1145/3473604.3474562

Pesotskiy, A. A. (2023). The Economic Shock from the Introduction of the Sanctions Regime in the Regional Context. *Collection of Scientific Papers*, 118–128. DOI: 10.52897/978-5-7310-6226-8-2023-51-118-128

Pilipenko, Z. A. (2019). Shock theory. In *Practice, progress, and proficiency in sustainability* (pp. 150–174). DOI: 10.4018/978-1-7998-1033-9.ch008

Prepare Prevent Resist. (2023, December 14). *Home - Prepare Prevent resist*. Prepare Prevent Resist -. https://preparepreventresist.org/wp-content/uploads/2022/12/Bangladesh-Summary-Report.pdf

Prothomalo. (2024, July 15). *Chhatra League ready to respond to audacity on campus: Obaidul Quader*. Prothomalo. https://en.prothomalo.com/bangladesh/bi054q9uaz

Purdon, L., Ashraf, A., & Wagner, B. (2014). Security v Access: The impact of mobile network shutdowns, Case Study Telenor Pakistan. *Internet Policy Observatory*. https://core.ac.uk/download/pdf/76396194.pdf

Qadir, S., & Dar, A. A. (2021). How internet shutdowns affects the entrepreneurs in Jammu and Kashmir. *International Journal of Asian Business and Information Management*, *12*(3), 109–116. DOI: 10.4018/IJABIM.20210701.oa7

Rahman, A. L. M. A. (2009). Quota Intervention in Civil Service: A Critical Review And Recommendations. *NDC E-JOURNAL, 8(1)*, 1-17. https://ndcjournal.ndc.gov.bd/ndcj/index.php/ndcj/article/view/64

Rahman, K. N. (2024, July 29). Quota movement: How will education system recover? *Bdnews24*. https://bdnews24.com/education/abed7e6b5262

Reuters. (2024, July 18). Why are Bangladesh students protesting government job quotas? *Voice of America*. https://www.voanews.com/a/why-are-bangladesh-students-protesting-government-job-quotas-/7703253.html

Reza, Md. S., & Khan, M. M. H. (2011). Impact of global financial crisis on the economy of Bangladesh. *Bangladesh Journal of Political Economy, 27(1 & 2)*, 61–83. https://bea-bd.org/assets/articlesPhoto/VolNo_20230301155239.pdf

Roy, G. (2024). Quota reform movement, internet shutdown and economic shock: Bangladesh. *SSRN*, Preprint. https://papers.ssrn.com/sol3/papers.cfm?abstract_id=4911644

Shah, M. G., & Junaid-Ul-Shafi, N. (2024). COVID-19, Internet and Education: Loss of a generation. *Peace Review*, *36*(3), 443–454. DOI: 10.1080/10402659.2024.2352411

Sharma, V., Oo, P. P., Hollaender, J., & Scott, J. (2021). COVID-19 and a coup: Blockage of internet and social media access further exacerbate gender-based violence risks for women in Myanmar. *BMJ Global Health*, *6*(6), e006564. DOI: 10.1136/bmjgh-2021-006564 PMID: 34193476

Shirin, B. (2023, December 3). Internet ban lifted in violence-hit Manipur, restrictions in border areas till Dec 18. *India Today*. https://www.indiatoday.in/india/story/manipur-violence-internet-services-restored-border-areas-exception-meiteis-kukis-2471548-2023-12-04

Suroy, H. S. (2024, August 5). Bangladesh BPO sector faces $34Mn loss after internet shutdown. *Outsource Accelerator*. https://news.outsourceaccelerator.com/bangladesh-bpo-sector-faces-loss/

Tagat, A., Phokeer, A., & Kreitem, H. M. (2024). Net Loss: An econometric method to measure the impact of Internet shutdowns. *ACM Journal on Computing and Sustainable Societies*, *2*(2), 1–22. DOI: 10.1145/3659466

Tanner, J. (2024, July 22). *Bangladesh internet goes dark amid protest violence*. Developing Telecoms. https://developingtelecoms.com/telecom-business/telecom-regulation/17035-bangladesh-internet-goes-dark-amid-protest-violence.html

The Business Standard. (2024, August 3). Bangladesh faces $10b setback, image crisis: Biz leaders. The Business Standard. https://www.tbsnews.net/economy/bangladesh-faces-10b-setback-image-crisis-biz-leaders-905336

The Business Standard. (2024, July 31). Internet, FB shutdown: Digital commerce loses Tk1,700cr in 13 days. *The Business Standard*. https://www.tbsnews.net/economy/e-cab-leaders-seek-govt-assistance-reviving-e-commerce-sector-amid-ongoing-crisis-907356

The Daily Star. (2024, August 1). E-commerce sector lost TK 1,700 crore for internet shutdown, violence: e-CAB. The Daily Star. https://www.thedailystar.net/business/news/e-commerce-sector-lost-tk-1700-crore-internet-shutdown-violence-e-cab-3667231

The Daily Star. (2024, August 10). Ledger of losses. The Daily Star. https://www.thedailystar.net/business/news/ledger-losses-3673416

The Daily Star. (2024, August 5). Mobile internet, social media blocked again. *The Daily Star*. https://www.thedailystar.net/news/bangladesh/news/mobile-internet-social-media-blocked-again-3669681

The Daily Star. (2024, September 13). At least 875 killed in July mass uprising. The Daily Star. https://www.thedailystar.net/news/bangladesh/crime-justice/news/least-875-killed-july-mass-uprising-3702451

The Economist. (2018, April 21). Protests in Bangladesh put an end to a corrupt quota system. The Economist. https://www.economist.com/asia/2018/04/21/protests-in-bangladesh-put-an-end-to-a-corrupt-quota-system

Uddin, M. M., & Chowdhury, M. J. A. (2016). Quota reservations in civil service: Arguments for a class based preference system. *Chittagong University Journal of Law*, *21*, 1–22.

United Nations. Human Rights. (2025). Fact-Finding: Report Human Rights Violations and Abuses related to the Protests of July and August 2024 in Bangladesh. In *UN Office of the High Commissioner for Human Rights (OHCHR)*. https://www.ohchr.org/sites/default/files/documents/countries/bangladesh/ohchr-fftb-hr-violations-bd.pdf

Wagner, B. (2018, September 18). *Authoritarian Practices in the Digital Age| Understanding Internet Shutdowns: A Case Study from Pakistan*. Wagner | International Journal of Communication. https://ijoc.org/index.php/ijoc/article/view/8545/2465

World Trade Organization. (2022). Digital connectivity, e-commerce and sustainable trade. In *Aid for Trade Global Review 2022* (pp. 86–127). Aid for Trade Global Review., DOI: 10.30875/9789287072085c006

Yasmin, N. (2010). Quota system in Bangladesh Civil Service: an appraisal [MA thesis], BRAC University. https://dspace.bracu.ac.bd/xmlui/bitstream/handle/10361/2085/Quota%20System%20in%20Bangladesh%20Civil%20Service%20An.pdf?isAllowed=y&sequence=1

Compilation of References

Access Now. (2024, November 12). #KeepItOn: fighting internet shutdowns around the world - Access Now. https://www.accessnow.org/campaign/keepiton/#global-tracker

Adib, A. A. H. (2024). Internet exodus: Bangladeshi freelancers flee to Nepal, India for connectivity. *jagonews24.com*. https://www.jagonews24.com/en/tech/news/75838

Afzal, M., & Panagiotopoulos, P. (2024). Data in Policing: An Integrative Review. *International Journal of Public Administration*, *48*(7), 411–430. DOI: 10.1080/01900692.2024.2360586

Agrawal, A. (1995). Dismantling the divide between indigenous and scientific knowledge. *Development and Change*.

Ahmed, R. (2024, July 28). The government shut down the internet. Prothomalo. https://www.prothomalo.com/bangladesh/0l53ciu95t

Ahmed, S. (2018). Opportunities and Challenges of software development business in Bangladesh. In Brac University. https://dspace.bracu.ac.bd/xmlui/handle/10361/10129

Aho, B., & Duffield, R. (2020). Beyond surveillance capitalism: Privacy, regulation and big data in Europe and China. *Economy and Society*, *49*(2), 187–212. DOI: 10.1080/03085147.2019.1690275

Al Jazeera. (2024, July 28). Bangladesh restores mobile internet after 11-day blackout to quell protests. *Al Jazeera*. https://www.aljazeera.com/news/2024/7/28/bangladesh-restores-mobile-internet-after-11-day-blackout-to-quell-protests

Al-Alawi, A. I., & Al-Bassam, S. A. (2020). The Significance of Cybersecurity System in Helping Managing Risk in Banking and Financial Sector. *Journal of Xidian University*, *14*(7), 1523–1536. DOI: 10.37896/jxu14.7/174

Alam, J., Emrun Garjon, A., & Pathi, K. (2024, July 19). *Bangladesh quota protests: Internet and mobile services cut off | AP News*. AP News. https://apnews.com/article/bangladesh-student-protests-violence-internet-shutdown-622c6c464c47860afee293e80550c051

Alam, M. A., Roy, P. C., & Bíró, J. (2025). Breaking the Chains of Fear: Civil Society's role in defying autocracy and shaping Bangladesh's 2024 July Revolution. *Civil Szemle*, *22*(2), 71–96. DOI: 10.62560/csz.2025.02.4

Alcaraz, C., & Zeadally, S. (2015). Critical infrastructure protection: Requirements and challenges for the 21st century. *International Journal of Critical Infrastructure Protection*, *8*, 53–66. DOI: 10.1016/j.ijcip.2014.12.002

Alelyani, S., & Kumar, H. (2018). Overview of Cyberattack on Saudi Organizations. *Journal of Information Security & Cybercrimes Research*, *1*(1), 32–39. DOI: 10.26735/16587790.2018.004

Alexei, A., & Alexei, A. (2022). The Difference Between Cyber Security vs Information Security. *Journal of Engineering Science*, *29*(4), 72–83. DOI: 10.52326/jes.utm.2022.29(4).08

Ali, A. M. M. S. (2004). *Bangladesh civil service : a political-administrative perspective*. CiNii Research. The University Press Limited. https://cir.nii.ac.jp/crid/1130282269418922880

Almasoud, A. S., & Idowu, J. A. (2025). Algorithmic fairness in predictive policing. *AI and Ethics*, *5*(3), 2323–2337. DOI: 10.1007/s43681-024-00541-3

Alyukov, M., Kunilovskaya, M., & Semenov, A. (2023). Wartime Media Monitor (WarMM-2022): A Study of Information Manipulation on Russian Social Media during the Russia-Ukraine War. Proceedings of the 7th Joint SIGHUM Workshop on Computational Linguistics for Cultural Heritage, Social Sciences, Humanities and Literature. DOI: 10.18653/v1/2023.latechclfl-1.17

Amnesty International. (2024, July 19). *Stop Bangladesh's crackdown on freedom of expression online - Amnesty International*. https://www.amnesty.org/en/petition/stop-crackdown-on-freedom-of-expression-online-in-bangladesh/

Amoore, L. (2020). *Cloud Ethics: Algorithms and the Attributes of Ourselves and Others*. Duke University Press.

Andrejevic, M. (2013). *Infoglut: How too much information is changing the way we think and know*. Routledge. DOI: 10.4324/9780203075319

Andrejevic, M. (2014). Surveillance and alienation in the online economy. *Surveillance & Society, 12*(3), 381–393.

Andrejevic, M. (2019). *Automated media*. Routledge. DOI: 10.4324/9780429242595

Anti-Defamation League. (2022, May 16). Buffalo shooter's weapons covered in white supremacist messaging. https://www.adl.org/resources/article/buffalo-shooters-weapons-covered-white-supremacist-messaging

Appel, E. J. (2011). *Internet searches for vetting, investigations, and open-source intelligence*. CRC Press.

APPRAISE. (2021). fAcilitating Public & Private secuRity operAtors to mitigate terrorIsm Scenarios against soft targEts – APPRAISE: the future for preventing and providing security for soft targets. https://appraise-h2020.eu

Aradau, C. (2010). Security That Matters: Critical Infrastructure and Objects of Protection. *Security Dialogue, 41*(5), 491–514. DOI: 10.1177/0967010610382687

Arafat, R., & Khamis, S. (2025). Unveiling the online dynamics influencing the success and virality of TikTok social movements: A case study on pro and anti hijab feminist activism. *Media, War & Conflict, 18*(2), 251–272. Advance online publication. DOI: 10.1177/17506352241308152

Asch, S. E. (1951). Effects of group pressure upon the modification and distortion of judgments. In Guetzkow, H. (Ed.), *Groups, leadership and men* (pp. 177–190). Carnegie Press.

Astuti, Y. D., Attaymini, R., & Dewi, M. S. R. (2022). Digital media and war: Social media as a propaganda tool for the Russia-Ukraine conflict in the post-truth era.

Atlantic Council. (2024). *Russian Telegram in 2024: A growing ecosystem for propaganda and information operations*. Atlantic Council's Digital Forensic Research Lab.

Aviv, I., & Ferri, U. (2023). Russian-Ukraine armed conflict: Lessons learned on the digital ecosystem. *International Journal of Critical Infrastructure Protection, 43*, 1–15. DOI: 10.1016/j.ijcip.2023.100637

Azmi, R., Tibben, W., & Win, K. T. (2018). Review of cybersecurity frameworks: Context and shared concepts. *Journal of Cyber Policy, 3*(2), 1–26. DOI: 10.1080/23738871.2018.1520271

Bagaric, M., Svilar, J., Bull, M., Hunter, D., & Stobbs, N. (2022). The solution to the pervasive bias and discrimination in the criminal justice system: Transparent and fair Artificial Intelligence. *The American Criminal Law Review, 59*(1), 95–148. https://ssrn.com/abstract=3795911

Bahadur, R., & Samuels, W. B. (2011). Drinking Water Critical Infrastructure and Its Protection. In Clark, R. M., Hakim, S., & Ostfeld, A. (Eds.), *Handbook of Water and Wastewater Systems Protection* (pp. 65–85). Springer International Publishing. DOI: 10.1007/978-1-4614-0189-6_4

Bahgat, G. (2020). Iran and Its Neighbors Face Risks and Opportunities in Cyber Security. *Orbis*, *64*(1), 78–97. DOI: 10.1016/j.orbis.2019.12.006

Bail, C. A., Guay, B., Maloney, E., Combs, A., Hillygus, D. S., Merhout, F., Freelon, D., & Volfovsky, A. (2020). Assessing the Russian Internet Research Agency's impact on the political attitudes and behaviors of American Twitter users in late 2017. *Proceedings of the National Academy of Sciences of the United States of America*, *117*(1), 243–250. DOI: 10.1073/pnas.1906420116 PMID: 31767743

Baker, R. L. (2023). *Deep dive: Exploring the real-world value of open source intelligence*. Wiley.

Balkin, J. M. (2018). Free speech in the algorithmic society: Big data, private governance, and new school speech regulation. *U.C. Davis Law Review*, *51*(3), 1149–1210.

Balzacq, T., Léonard, S., & Ruzicka, J. (2016). "Securitization" Revisited: Theory and Cases. *International Relations*, 30(4), 494–531. SAGE Publications. DOI: 10.1177/0047117815596590

Barcik, P., Coufalikova, A., Frantis, P., & Vavra, J. (2023). The Future Possibilities and Security Challenges of City Digitalization. *Smart Cities*, *6*(1), 137–155. DOI: 10.3390/smartcities6010008

Barkun, M. (2003). A culture of conspiracy: Apocalyptic visions in contemporary [University of California Press.]. *America*, •••, 3–8.

BBC News. (2016, November 15). Post-truth declared word of the year by Oxford Dictionaries. https://www.bbc.com/news/uk-37995600

bdnews24.com. (2024, July 16). Startup Bangladesh cancels TK 50m investment for 10 minute school. *Bdnews24*. https://bdnews24.com/bangladesh/8cde64566eb9

Bean, H. (2011). *No more secrets: Open source information and the reshaping of U.S. intelligence*. Praeger Security International. DOI: 10.5040/9798400691799

Beer, D. (2017). The social power of algorithms. *Information Communication and Society*, *20*(1), 1–13. DOI: 10.1080/1369118X.2016.1216147

Bellamkonda, S. (2020). Cybersecurity in Critical Infrastructure: Protecting the Foundations of Modern Society. [IJCNIS]. *International Journal of Communication Networks and Information Security*, *12*(2), 273–280.

Benkler, Y. (2016). Degrees of freedom, dimensions of power. *Daedalus*, *145*(1), 18–32. DOI: 10.1162/DAED_a_00362

Bennett, C. J., & Raab, C. D. (2017). *The governance of privacy: Policy instruments in global perspective*. Routledge. DOI: 10.4324/9781315199269

Bennett, W. L. (2017). The personalization of politics. *The Annals of the American Academy of Political and Social Science*, *644*(1), 20–39. DOI: 10.1177/0002716212451428

Berk, R. A. (2021). Artificial intelligence, predictive policing, and risk assessment for law enforcement. *Annual Review of Criminology*, *4*(1), 209–237. DOI: 10.1146/annurev-criminol-051520-012342

Bhatia, K. V., Elhussein, M., Kreimer, B., & Snapp, T. (2023). Internet shutdown and Regime-Imposed disinformation campaigns. *Communicatio*, *49*(2), 53–71. DOI: 10.1080/02500167.2023.2230391

Bielska, A., Stępień, M., Terefenko, M., & Węgrzyn, P. (2020). *Open source intelligence tools and resources handbook*. I-Intelligence.

Bigo, D., Guild, E., & Kuskonmaz, E. M. (2021). Obedience in times of COVID-19 pandemics: A renewed governmentality of unease? *Global Discourse*, *11*(3), 471–489. DOI: 10.1332/204378921X16158113910675

Binns, R., Veale, M., Van Kleek, M., & Shadbolt, N. (2018). "It's reducing a human being to a percentage": Perceptions of justice in algorithmic decisions. In *Proceedings of the 2018 CHI Conference on Human Factors in Computing Systems* (pp. 1–14). DOI: 10.1145/3173574.3173951

Bischof, Z. S., Pitcher, K., Carisimo, E., Meng, A., Nunes, R. B., Padmanabhan, R., Roberts, M. E., Snoeren, A. C., & Dainotti, A. (2023). Destination unreachable: characterizing internet outages and shutdowns. *In ACM SIGCOMM '23: Proceedings of the ACM SIGCOMM 2023 Conference* (pp. 608–621). DOI: 10.1145/3603269.3604883

Biuro Projektów Regionalnych, S. A. v. (2022). Vyriausioji tarnybinės etikos komisija, Case C-184/20, ECLI:EU:C:2022:601 (Court of Justice of the European Union, 2022). https://eur-lex.europa.eu/legal-content/EN/TXT/?uri=CELEX%3A62020CJ0184

Bleakley, P. (2021). Panic, pizza and mainstreaming the alt-right: A social media analysis of Pizzagate and the rise of the QAnon conspiracy. *Current Sociology*, *71*(3), 509–525. DOI: 10.1177/00113921211034896

Bodrud-Doza, M., Shammi, M., Bahlman, L., Islam, A. R. M. T., & Rahman, M. M. (2020). Psychosocial and Socio-Economic crisis in Bangladesh due to COVID-19 Pandemic: A Perception-Based Assessment. *Frontiers in Public Health, 8,* 341. Advance online publication. DOI: 10.3389/fpubh.2020.00341 PMID: 32676492

Bonta, J., & Andrews, D. A. (2023). *The Psychology of Criminal Conduct.*

Bordes Perez, A. (2024). What is really open source intelligence? A conceptual analysis of the different notions of OSINT. *Romanian Intelligence Studies Review, 1*(31), 51–74.

Borychenko, O., Cherniavskyi, A., Muliarevych, O., Yurii Shelekh, Y. & Sabat, M. (2024). Cybersecurity in the energy industry of Ukraine: protection measures and challenges in the context of energy security. *Revista Gestão & Tecnologia (Journal of Management & Technology), 24*(4), p. 67-90. DOI: 10.20397/2177-6652/2024.v24i4.2876

Bösch, M., & Divon, T. (2024). The sound of disinformation: TikTok, computational propaganda, and the invasion of Ukraine. New Media & Society, 26(9), 5081–5106. (Original work published 2024)DOI: 10.1177/14614448241251804

Boston University. (2023, May 15). Media literacy skills important to counter disinformation, survey says. https://www.bu.edu/com/articles/media-literacy-skills-important-to-counter-disinformation-survey-says/

Bowers, K. J., Johnson, S. D., & Pease, K. (2004). Prospective hot-spotting: The future of crime mapping? *British Journal of Criminology.*

Bradford, A. (2020). *The Brussels Effect: How the European Union Rules the World.* Oxford University Press. DOI: 10.1093/oso/9780190088583.001.0001

Bradshaw, S., DiResta, R., & Miller, C. (2022). Playing both sides: Russian state-backed media coverage of the #BlackLivesMatter movement. The International Journal of Press/Politics, 28(4), 791–817. (Original work published 2023)DOI: 10.1177/19401612221082052

Bradshaw, S., & Howard, P. N. (2017). *Troops, trolls and troublemakers: A global inventory of organized social media manipulation.* Computational Propaganda Research Project.

Bradshaw, S., & Howard, P. N. (2019). *The global disinformation order: 2019 global inventory of organised social media manipulation.* Oxford Internet Institute.

Brady, W. J., Wills, J. A., Jost, J. T., Tucker, J. A., & Van Bavel, J. J. (2021). Emotion shapes the diffusion of moralized content in social networks. *Proceedings of the National Academy of Sciences of the United States of America, 118*(1).

Brayne, S. (2017). Big data surveillance: The case of policing. *American Sociological Review*, *82*(5), 977–1008. DOI: 10.1177/0003122417725865 PMID: 38322733

Brayne, S. (2020). *Predict and surveil: Data, policing, and the future of criminal justice*. Oxford University Press. DOI: 10.1093/oso/9780190684099.001.0001

Bremmer, I. (2018). *Us vs. them: The failure of globalism*. Portfolio/Penguin.

Bronk, C., Collins, G., & Wallach, D. S. (2023). The Ukrainian Information and Cyber War. *The Cyber Defense Review, 8*(3), 33-50. https://www.jstor.org/stable/48755360

Brooker, C., Bridges, W., & Armstrong, J. (2011 -). Black mirror [TV series]. Zeppotron Productions; House of Tomorrow Productions; Broke & Bones Productions.

Brookings Institution. (2021, November 15). How tech platforms fuel U.S. political polarization—and what government can do about it. https://www.brookings.edu/articles/how-tech-platforms-fuel-u-s-political-polarization-and-what-government-can-do-about-it/

Browne, T. O., Abedin, M., & Chowdhury, M. J. M. (2024). A systematic review on research utilising artificial intelligence for open source intelligence (OSINT) applications. *International Journal of Information Security*, *23*(4), 2911–2938. DOI: 10.1007/s10207-024-00868-2

Bucher, T. (2018). *If...Then: Algorithmic power and politics*. Oxford University Press. DOI: 10.1093/oso/9780190493028.001.0001

Buolamwini, J., & Gebru, T. (2018). Gender Shades: Intersectional accuracy disparities in commercial gender classification. *Proceedings of the 1st Conference on Fairness, Accountability and Transparency (FAT*)*, 81, 77–91. PMLR. https://proceedings.mlr.press/v81/buolamwini18a.html

Buolamwini, J., & Gebru, T. (2018). Gender Shades: Intersectional Accuracy Disparities in Commercial Gender Classification. *Proceedings of the 1st Conference on Fairness, Accountability and Transparency*, 77–91.

Burrell, J. (2016). How the machine 'thinks': Understanding opacity in machine learning algorithms. *Big Data & Society*, *3*(1), 2053951715622512. DOI: 10.1177/2053951715622512

Çahmutoğlu, E. (2021). *Iran's Cyber Power.* IRAM Publications. https://iramcenter.org/en/irans-cyber-power_en-441

California Consumer Privacy Act (CCPA), Cal. Civ. Code § 1798.100 et seq. (2018).

California Privacy Rights Act (CPRA), California Proposition 24 (2020).

Cameron, J. (1991). Terminator 2: Judgment day [Movie]. Carolco Pictures, Pacific Western Productions, Lightstorm Entertainment, Le Studio Canal+; TriStar Pictures.

Caplan, R., Donovan, J., Hanson, L., & Matthews, J. (2018). *Algorithmic accountability: A primer.* Data & Society Research Institute.

Carr, J. (2012). *Inside Cyber Warfare: Mapping the Cyber Underworld.* O'Reilly Media, Inc.

Carty, V. (2014). Arab Spring in Tunisia and Egypt: The impact of new media on contemporary social movements and challenges for social movement theory. *International Journal of Contemporary Sociology, 51*(1), 51–80.

Castells, M. (2015). *Networks of outrage and hope: Social movements in the Internet age.* Polity Press.

Castets-Renard, C. (2021). Human Rights and Algorithmic Impact Assessment for Predictive Policing Constitutional Challenges in the Algorithmic Society, Cambridge University Press, Forthcoming, Available at SSRN: https://ssrn.com/abstract=3890283

Catlett, C., Portugali, J., & Venkatakrishnan, V. (2023). Privacy and trust in artificially intelligent cities. In Portugali, J. (Ed.), *The Crisis of Democracy in the Age of Cities* (pp. 167–183). Edward Elgar Publishing. DOI: 10.4337/9781803923055.00018

Cavelty, M. D., & Egloff, F. J. (2019). The Politics of Cybersecurity: Balancing Different Roles of the State. *St. Antony's International Review, 15*(1), 37–57. https://papers.ssrn.com/sol3/papers.cfm?abstract_id=3403971

Cavelty, M. D., & Wenger, A. (2022). Introduction: Cyber security between socio-technological uncertainty and political fragmentation. In Cavelty, M. D., & Wenger, A. (Eds.), *Cyber Security Politics: Socio-Technological Transformations and Political Fragmentation* (pp. 1–13). Routledge. DOI: 10.4324/9781003110224-1

Center for Humane Technology. (n.d.). Attention & mental health. https://www.humanetech.com/attention-mental-health

Chadwick, A. (2017). *The hybrid media system: Politics and power.* Oxford University Press. DOI: 10.1093/oso/9780190696726.001.0001

Chainey, S., & Ratcliffe, J. (2013). *GIS and crime mapping* (2nd ed.). Wiley.

Chakma, J. (2024, July 28). Internet outage, curfew leave foreign investors in a bind. *The Daily Star*. https://www.thedailystar.net/business/economy/news/internet-outage-curfew-leave-foreign-investors-bind-3663536

Chakraborty, S. (2023, July 3). India dispatch: ethnic violence continues to plague India's Manipur State as internet shutdown continues. *Gujarat National Law U., IN*. https://www.jurist.org/news/2023/07/india-dispatch-ethnic-violence-continues-to-plague-indias-manipur-state-as-internet-shutdown-continues/

Charter of Fundamental Rights of the European Union, 2000/C 364/01. (2000). *Official Journal of the European Communities*, C 364, 1–22.

Charter of Fundamental Rights of the European Union. 2012/C 326/02. (2012). *Official Journal of the European Union*, C 326, 391–407. https://eur-lex.europa.eu/legal-content/EN/TXT/?uri=CELEX:12012P/TXT

Chemerys, H. (2023). Deepfakes and synthetically reproduced media content as a form of disinformation in the context of the Russian aggression against Ukraine. In Протидія дезінформації в умовах російської агресії проти України: виклики і перспективи: тези доп. учасників міжн. наук.-практ. конф. (Харків, 12-13 груд. 2023р.) (p. 400). Харків: НДІ ППСН. DOI: 10.32782/PPSS.2023.1.8

Choi, S., Galeotti, A., & Goyal, S. (2017). Trading in Networks: Theory and Experiments. *Journal of the European Economic Association*, *15*(4), 784–817. DOI: 10.1093/jeea/jvw016

Cinelli, M., Morales, G. D. F., Galeazzi, A., Quattrociocchi, W., & Starnini, M. (2021). The echo chamber effect on social media. *Proceedings of the National Academy of Sciences of the United States of America*, *118*(9), e2023301118. DOI: 10.1073/pnas.2023301118

Clarke, R. A., & Knake, R. K. (2010). *Cyber War: The Next Threat to National Security and What to Do About It*. HarperCollins Publishers.

CNN. (2021, January 9). Extremist flags and symbols seen at the US Capitol insurrection: Their meanings and origins. https://edition.cnn.com/2021/01/09/us/capitol-hill-insurrection-extremist-flags-soh/index.html

Cohen, J. E. (2019). *Between truth and power: The legal constructions of informational capitalism*. Oxford University Press. DOI: 10.1093/oso/9780190246693.001.0001

Collyer, M., & Wright, J. (2021). A Bayesian Analysis of Collective Action and Internet Shutdowns in India. In *13th ACM Web Science Conference 2021* (pp. 309–318). DOI: 10.1145/3447535.3462480

Colorado Privacy Act (CPA), Colo. Rev. Stat. § 6-1-1301 et seq. (2021).

Commission Nationale de l'Informatique et des Libertés (CNIL). (n.d.). *1970–2021: la protection des données essaime le monde*. LINC. Retrieved June 29, 2025, from https://linc.cnil.fr/1970-2021-la-protection-des-donnees-essaime-le-monde

Convention 108+, Council of Europe Modernised Convention for the Protection of Individuals with regard to Processing of Personal Data. (2018). Council of Europe.

Corner, E., & Gill, P. (2020). Is mental illness a factor in lone-actor terrorism? *The British Journal of Psychiatry*, *217*(2), 709–711. DOI: 10.1192/bjp.2019.14

Cosentino, G. (2020). The post-truth world order. In *Social media and the post-truth world order: The global dynamics of disinformation* (pp. 10–41). Springer. DOI: 10.1007/978-3-030-43005-4_1

Cossette-Lefebvre, H., & Maclure, J. (2023). AI's fairness problem: Understanding wrongful discrimination in the context of automated decision-making. *AI and Ethics*, *3*(4), 1255–1269. DOI: 10.1007/s43681-022-00233-w

Couldry, N., & Hepp, A. (2017). *The mediated construction of reality*. Polity Press.

Couldry, N., & Mejias, U. A. (2019). *The costs of connection: How data is colonizing human life and appropriating it for capitalism*. Stanford University Press.

Council of Europe. (1981). *Convention for the Protection of Individuals with regard to Automatic Processing of Personal Data* (ETS No. 108). Strasbourg: Council of Europe.

Council of the European Union. (n.d.). EU response to terrorism. https://www.consilium.europa.eu/en/eu-response-to-terrorism/

Creado, Y., & Ramteke, V. (2020). Active cyber defence strategies and techniques for banks and financial institutions. *Journal of Financial Crime*, *27*(3), 771–780. DOI: 10.1108/JFC-01-2020-0008

Cremer, F., Sheehan, B., Fortmann, M., Kia, A. N., Martin, M., Murphy, F., & Materne, S. (2022). Cyber risk and cybersecurity: A systematic review of data availability. *The Geneva Papers on Risk and Insurance. Issues and Practice*, *47*(3), 698–736. DOI: 10.1057/s41288-022-00266-6

Cybersecurity Law of the People's Republic of China. (2017).

Cyfirma Decoding Threats. (2024, August 16). U.S. Water Structure's Vulnerability to Cyber Attacks. https://www.cyfirma.com/research/u-s-water-structures-vulnerability-to-cyber-attacks/

Dalal, A. (2018). Cybersecurity And Artificial Intelligence: How AI Is Being Used in Cybersecurity To Improve Detection And Response To Cyber Threats. [TURCOMAT]. *Turkish Journal of Computer and Mathematics Education*, *9*(3), 1416–1423. DOI: 10.61841/turcomat.v9i3.14670

Dale, D. S. (2023). *Open source intelligence for cybersecurity events via Twitter data* (Master's thesis, California State University, San Bernardino). ProQuest Dissertations Publishing.

Daniels, M. (2022). Aspects of Network Theory - (L.) Foxhall (ed.) Interrogating Networks. Investigating Networks of Knowledge in Antiquity. Pp. x + 134, figs, ills, maps. Oxford and Philadelphia: Oxbow Books, 2021. Paper, £16.95. ISBN: 978-1-78925-627-7. *The Classical Review, 73*(1), 169–172. DOI: 10.1017/S0009840X22001676

Dareen, S., & Srivastava, V. (2024, September 11). Cyberattacks on US utilities surged 70% this year, says Check Point. *Reuters.* https://www.reuters.com/technology/cybersecurity/cyberattacks-us-utilities-surged-70-this-year-says-check-point-2024-09-11/

Darıcılı, A. B., & Çelik, S. (2021). National Security 2.0: T he Cyber Security of Critical Infrastructure. *PERCEPTIONS: Journal of International Affairs, 26*(2), 259–276.

Darnton, R., & Roche, D. (Eds.). (1989). *Revolution in print: The press in France, 1775–1800* (p. 162). University of California Press.

Data Security Law of the People's Republic of China. (2021).

Dean, B. (2023, May 4). Screen time statistics: Average usage data 2023. Exploding Topics. https://explodingtopics.com/blog/screen-time-stats?utm_source=chatgpt.com

Demchak, C. C., & Dombrowski, P. (2011). Rise of a Cybered Westphalian Age. *Strategic Studies Quarterly, 5*(1), 32-61. https://www.jstor.org/stable/26270509

Department of the Army. (2012). *Open-source intelligence (ATP 2-22.9).* Headquarters, Department of the Army. https://irp.fas.org/doddir/army/atp2-22-9.pdf

Diaz Ruiz, C., & Nilsson, T. (2022). Disinformation and echo chambers: How disinformation circulates on social media through identity-driven controversies. *Journal of Public Policy & Marketing*, •••, 1–18. DOI: 10.1177/07439156221103852

Diener, E. (1977). Deindividuation: Causes and consequences. *Social Behavior and Personality*, *5*(1), 143–155. DOI: 10.2224/sbp.1977.5.1.143

Dinušová, D. (2024). *Dôveryhodnosť Policajného zboru v perspektívach filozofie a etiky (The Credibility of Police Force in Philosophical and Ethical Perspectives)*. Academy of the Police Force in Bratislava.

Directive (EU) 2014/24 of the European Parliament and of the Council of 26 February 2014 on public procurement and repealing Directive 2004/18/EC. (2014). *Official Journal of the European Union*, L 94, 65–242. https://eur-lex.europa.eu/legal-content/EN/TXT/?uri=CELEX%3A32014L0024

Directive (EU) 2016/680 of the European Parliament and of the Council of 27 April 2016 on the protection of natural persons regarding the processing of personal data by competent authorities for law enforcement purposes. (2016). *Official Journal of the European Union*, L 119, 89–131. https://eur-lex.europa.eu/legal-content/EN/TXT/?uri=CELEX%3A32016L0680

Directive 95/46/EC of the European Parliament and of the Council of 24 October 1995 on the protection of individuals with regard to the processing of personal data and on the free movement of such data. (1995). *Official Journal of the European Communities*, L 281, 31–50.

Doheny, M. M., & Lighthall, N. R. (2023). Social cognitive neuroscience in the digital age. *Frontiers in Human Neuroscience*, *17*, 1168788. Advance online publication. DOI: 10.3389/fnhum.2023.1168788

Doherty, C. (2014, June 17). Which party is more to blame for political polarization? It depends on the measure. Pew Research Center. https://www.pewresearch.org/short-reads/2014/06/17/which-party-is-more-to-blame-for-political-polarization-it-depends-on-the-measure/

Donahoe, E., & Metzger, M. M. (2019). Artificial intelligence and human rights. *Journal of Democracy*, *30*(2), 115–126. DOI: 10.1353/jod.2019.0029

Doshi-Velez, F., & Kim, F. (2017). Towards a rigorousscience of interpretable machine learning. arXiv preprint arXiv:1702.08608.

Dudek, A., Dąbek, A., Zborowska, I., & Lichosik, J. (2023). Integrating artificial intelligence in forensic science. *E-methodology*, *10*(10), 15–28. DOI: 10.15503/emet2023.15.28

Dutta, S., & Navy, I. (2022). Cyber Operations Associated with the Ukraine-Russia Conflict: An Open-Source Assessment. *Maritime perspectives*, 346-361. https://maritimeindia.org/cyber-operations-associated-with-the-ukraine-russia-conflict-an-open-source-assessment/

Elluri, L., Mandalapu, V., Vyas, P., & Roy, N. (2025). Recent advancements in machine learning for cybercrime prediction. *Journal of Computer Information Systems*, *65*(2), 249–263. DOI: 10.1080/08874417.2023.2270457

Encyclopædia Britannica. (n.d.). Radical | Political Theory, Social Change & Activism. https://www.britannica.com/topic/radical-ideologist

Eubanks, V. (2018). *Automating inequality: How high-tech tools profile, police, and punish the poor*. St. Martin's Press.

Eubanks, V. (2018). *Automating Inequality: How High-Tech Tools Profile, Police, and Punish the Poor*. St. Martin's Press.

European Commission. (2010). *Communication from the Commission to the European Parliament, the Council, the Economic and Social Committee and the Committee of the Regions: A comprehensive approach on personal data protection in the European Union* (COM(2010) 609 final). Brussels: European Commission: https://eur-lex.europa.eu/legal-content/EN/TXT/?uri=CELEX%3A52010DC0609

European Commission. (2019). Regulation (EU) 2016/679 of the European Parliament and of the Council of 27 April 2016 on the protection of natural persons with regard to the processing of personal data and on the free movement of such data, and repealing Directive 95/46/EC (General Data Protection Regulation). Official Journal of the European Union, L 119, 4.5.2016, p. 1–88.

European Commission. (2021). *Proposal for a regulation laying down harmonised rules on artificial intelligence (Artificial Intelligence Act)* (COM/2021/206 final). https://eur-lex.europa.eu/legal-content/EN/TXT/?uri=CELEX%3A52021PC0206

European Commission. (2021a). Proposal for a Regulation of the European Parliament and of the Council Laying Down Harmonised Rules on Artificial Intelligence (Artificial Intelligence Act) and Amending Certain Union Legislative Acts. COM(2021) 206 final.

European Commission. (2021b). Communication from the Commission to the European Parliament, the Council, the European Economic and Social Committee and the Committee of the Regions on the European strategy for data. COM(2020) 66 final.

European Commission. (n.d.). *Better Regulation Toolbox – Tool #30: Fundamental rights and human rights impacts.* https://commission.europa.eu/law/law-making-process/planning-and-proposing-law/better-regulation/better-regulation-toolbox_en

European Commission. (n.d.). Media literacy. https://digital-strategy.ec.europa.eu/en/policies/media-literacy

European Commission. (n.d.-a). Digital Services Act. https://commission.europa.eu/strategy-and-policy/priorities-2019-2024/europe-fit-digital-age/digital-services-act_en

European Data Protection Board. (2019). *Guidelines 3/2019 on processing of personal data through video devices.* https://edpb.europa.eu/our-work-tools/our-documents/guidelines/guidelines-32019-processing-personal-data-through-video_en

European Data Protection Board. (2020). *Guidelines 4/2019 on Article 25 Data Protection by Design and by Default.* https://edpb.europa.eu/our-work-tools/our-documents/guidelines/guidelines-42019-article-25-data-protection-design-and_en

European Parliament. (2021, October 6). *Resolution on artificial intelligence in criminal law and its use by the police and judicial authorities in criminal matters* (2020/2016(INI)). https://www.europarl.europa.eu/doceo/document/TA-9-2021-0405_EN.html

European Parliament. (2023). EU AI Act: first regulation on artificial intelligence. https://www.europarl.europa.eu/topics/en/article/20230601STO93804/eu-ai-act-first-regulation-on-artificial-intelligenceEuropean

European Union Agency for Fundamental Rights. (2018). *Fundamental rights implications of the future development of AI systems in policing*. Publications Office of the European Union.

European Union. (2022). *Regulation (EU) 2022/1925 of the European Parliament and of the Council of 14 September 2022 on contestable and fair markets in the digital sector (Digital Markets Act) and amending Directives (EU) 2019/1937 and (EU) 2020/1828.* Official Journal of the European Union, L 265, 1–66. https://eur-lex.europa.eu/legal-content/EN/TXT/?uri=CELEX%3A32022R1925

European Union. (2022). *Regulation (EU) 2022/2065 of the European Parliament and of the Council of 19 October 2022 on a Single Market for Digital Services (Digital Services Act) and amending Directive 2000/31/EC.* Official Journal of the European Union, L 277, 1–102. https://eur-lex.europa.eu/legal-content/EN/TXT/?uri=CELEX%3A32022R2065

European Union. (2022). *Regulation (EU) 2022/868 of the European Parliament and of the Council of 30 May 2022 on European data governance (Data Governance Act) and amending Regulation (EU) 2018/1724*. Official Journal of the European Union, L 152, 1–44. https://eur-lex.europa.eu/legal-content/EN/TXT/?uri=CELEX%3A32022R0868

European Union. (2024). *Regulation (EU) 2023/2854 of the European Parliament and of the Council of 13 December 2023 on harmonised rules on fair access to and use of data (Data Act)*. Official Journal of the European Union, L 2023/2854, 1–64. https://eur-lex.europa.eu/legal-content/EN/TXT/?uri=CELEX%3A32023R2854

Farwell, J. P., & Rohozinski, R. (2011). Stuxnet and the Future of Cyber War. *Survival. Survival, 53*(1), 23–40. DOI: 10.1080/00396338.2011.555586

Federal Trade Commission. (2019, July 24). FTC imposes $5 billion penalty and sweeping new privacy restrictions on Facebook. https://www.ftc.gov/news-events/news/press-releases/2019/07/ftc-imposes-5-billion-penalty-sweeping-new-privacy-restrictions-facebook

Ferguson, A G (2017) The rise of big data policing: Surveillance, race, and the future of law enforcement NYU Press

Firdosi, M. (2020). STEM on hold: The impacts of the internet shutdown in Jammu and Kashmir. *Science for the People, 23*(1). https://www.researchgate.net/publication/342339149_STEM_on_Hold_The_Impacts_of_the_Internet_Shutdown_in_Jammu_and_Kashmir

Floridi, L. (2020). The fight for digital sovereignty: What it is, and why it matters, especially for the EU. *Philosophy & Technology, 33*(3), 369–378. DOI: 10.1007/s13347-020-00423-6

Foucault, M. (1975). *Discipline and punish: The birth of the prison*. Vintage Books.

Foucault, M. (2008). *The birth of biopolitics*. Palgrave Macmillan.

Freelon, D., Marwick, A., & Kreiss, D. (2022). False equivalencies: Online activism from left to right. *Science, 369*(6508), 1197–1201. DOI: 10.1126/science.abb2428

Fuchs, C. (2020). *Communication and capitalism: A critical theory*. University of Westminster Press. Dawsey, J., Dou, E., & Siddiqui, F. (2024). How Elon Musk came to endorse Donald Trump. The Washington Post, NA-NA.

Fuchs, C. (2017). Social media: A critical introduction. *Sage (Atlanta, Ga.)*.

Gallais, C., & Filiol, E. (2017). Critical Infrastructure: Where Do We Stand Today? A Comprehensive and Comparative Study of the Definitions of a Critical Infrastructure. *Journal of Information Warfare, 16*(1), 64–87. https://www.jstor.org/stable/26502877

Gamper, M. (2022). Social Network Theories: An Overview. In *Springer eBooks* (pp. 35–48). DOI: 10.1007/978-3-030-97722-1_3

Ganesh, B., & Amarasingam, A. (2023, June 23). How do terrorists utilise and exploit small, covert online spaces? Global Network on Extremism & Technology (GNET). https://gnet-research.org/2023/06/23/how-do-terrorists-utilise-and-exploit-small-covert-online-spaces

Geers, K. (2009). The Cyber Threat to National CriticalInfrastructures: Beyond Theory. *Information Security Journal: A Global Perspective, 18*(1), 1-7. DOI: 10.1080/19393550802676097

General Data Protection Regulation (GDPR), Regulation (EU) 2016/679 of the European Parliament and of the Council of 27 April 2016 on the protection of natural persons with regard to the processing of personal data and on the free movement of such data, and repealing Directive 95/46/EC. (2016). *Official Journal of the European Union*, L 119, 1–88.

General Data Protection Regulation (GDPR). 2016). Regulation (EU) 2016/679 of the European Parliament and of the Council of 27 April 2016. (*Official Journal of the European Union*, L 119, 1–88. https://eur-lex.europa.eu/legal-content/EN/TXT/?uri=CELEX:32016R0679

Gensburger, S., & Clavert, F. (2024). Is Artificial Intelligence the Future of Collective Memory? *Memory Studies Review, 1*(2), 195–208. DOI: 10.1163/29498902-202400019

Georgiadou, A., Michalitsi, A., & Askounis, P. D. (2023). A security awareness and competency evaluation in the energy sector. *Computers & Security, 129*, 103199. Advance online publication. DOI: 10.1016/j.cose.2023.103199

Geradts, Z., & Franke, K. (Eds.). (2023). *Artificial Intelligence (AI) in Forensic Sciences*. Wiley.

Gerbaudo, P. (2024). TikTok and the algorithmic transformation of social media publics: From social networks to social interest clusters. *New Media & Society, 0*(0), 14614448241304106. Advance online publication. DOI: 10.1177/14614448241304106

Gerbrandy, A., & Zweers, K. (2019). Artificial intelligence and law enforcement: Impacts on legal certainty and fundamental rights. Research Paper, Vrije Universiteit Amsterdam.

Gille, M., Tropmann-Frick, M., & Schomacker, T. (2024). Balancing public interest, fundamental rights, and innovation: The EU's governance model for non-high-risk AI systems. *Internet Policy Review, 13*(3). Advance online publication. DOI: 10.14763/2024.3.1797

Gillespie, T. (2014). The relevance of algorithms. In Gillespie, T., Boczkowski, P., & Foot, K. (Eds.), *Media technologies: Essays on communication, materiality, and society* (pp. 167–194). MIT Press. DOI: 10.7551/mitpress/9042.003.0013

Gillespie, T. (2018). *Custodians of the Internet: Platforms, content moderation, and the hidden decisions that shape social media.* Yale University Press.

Gill, P., & Phythian, M. (2018). *Intelligence in an insecure world* (3rd ed.). Polity Press.

Gilovich, T., Griffin, D., & Kahneman, D. (2002). Heuristics and biases: The psychology of intuitive judgment. *Academy of Management Review, 29*(4), 695–698.

Gioti, A. (2023). Advancements in open source intelligence techniques and the role of artificial intelligence in cyber threat intelligence (Master's thesis). University of the Aegean.

Goldstein, H. (1990). *Problem-oriented policing*. McGraw Hill.

Gordon, H. J.Jr. (1972). *Hitler and the Beer Hall Putsch.* Princeton University Press.

Goswami, S. S., Sarkar, S., Gupta, K. K., & Mondal, S. (2023). The role of cyber security in advancing sustainable digitalization: Opportunities and challenges. *Journal of Decision Analytics and Intelligent Computing, 3*(1), 270–285. DOI: 10.31181/jdaic10018122023g

Goud, N. (2021). Cyber Attack on Israel water system. *Cybersecurity Insiders.* https://www.cybersecurity-insiders.com/cyber-attack-on-israel-water-system/

Greene, T., Martens, D., & Shmueli, G. (2022). Barriers to academic data science research in the new realm of algorithmic behaviour modification by digital platforms. *Nature Machine Intelligence, 4*(4), 323–330. DOI: 10.1038/s42256-022-00475-7

Gross, J. A. (2021, July 21). After alleged Iranian cyberattack, Israel's Water Authority beefs up defenses. *The Times of Israel.* https://www.timesofisrael.com/after-alleged-iranian-cyberattack-israels-water-authority-beefs-up-defenses/

Gulyás, O., & Kiss, G. (2023). Impact of cyber-attacks on the financial institutions. *Procedia Computer Science, 219*, 84–90. DOI: 10.1016/j.procs.2023.01.267

Haber, E., & Zarsky, T. (2018). Cybersecurity for Infrastructure: A Critical Analysis. *Florida State University Law Review. Florida State University. College of Law, 44*(2), 515–577. https://ir.law.fsu.edu/lr/vol44/iss2/3

Habermas, J. (1989). *The structural transformation of the public sphere*. MIT Press.

Haidt, J. (2012). *The righteous mind: Why good people are divided by politics and religion*. Pantheon Books.

Harding, S (1998) Is science multicultural? Postcolonialisms, feminisms, and epistemologies Indiana University Press

Hasan, A. R., Jahan, M., & Islam, Md. R. (2022). Recruitment and Selection of Civil Servants in Bangladesh: An Expository Study. Bangladesh Journal of Public Administration (BJPA), 30(2), 115–128. https://www.researchgate.net/publication/375755842_Recruitment_and_Selection_of_Civil_Servants_in_Bangladesh_An_Expository_Study

Hasan, M. (2024, July 23). *Internet blackout wallops life and living*. The Daily Star. https://www.thedailystar.net/business/news/internet-blackout-wallops-life-and-living-3660021

Hasnat, S. (2024, July 11). Students protest job quotas in Bangladesh's streets. *The New York Times*. https://www.nytimes.com/2024/07/11/world/asia/bangladesh-student-protests-job-quotas.html

Hassam, S. (2025). The notpetya cyber-attack: Russia-Ukraine conflict and its impact on the regional economies. *Advance Social Science Archive Journal, 3*(1), 373-385. https://assajournal.com/index.php/36/article/view/152

Hassan, N. A., & Hijazi, R. (2018). *Open source intelligence methods and tools: A practical guide to online intelligence*. Apress. DOI: 10.1007/978-1-4842-3213-2

Hayden, M. V. (2011). The Future of Things "Cyber". *Strategic Studies Quarterly, 5*(1), 3-7. https://www.jstor.org/stable/26270507

Helberger, N., Pierson, J., & Poell, T. (2020). Governing online platforms: From contested to cooperative responsibility. *The Information Society, 36*(1), 1–14. DOI: 10.1080/01972243.2017.1391913

Helbing, D., Brockmann, D., Chadefaux, T., Donnay, K., Blanke, U., Woolley-Meza, O., Moussaid, M., Johansson, A., Krause, J., Schutte, S., & Perc, M. (2015). Saving human lives: What complexity science and information systems can contribute. *Journal of Statistical Physics, 158*(3), 735–781. DOI: 10.1007/s10955-014-1024-9 PMID: 26074625

Helbing, D., Frey, B. S., Gigerenzer, G., Hafen, E., Hagner, M., Hofstetter, Y., & Zicari, R. V. (2021). Will democracy survive big data and artificial intelligence? *Scientific American.*

Hemme, K. (2015). Critical Infrastructure Protection: Maintenance is National Security. *Journal of Strategic Security, 8*(5), 25–39. DOI: 10.5038/1944-0472.8.3S.1471

Hendrix, J. (2022, March 17). Evidence in trial of 2017 Unite the Right rally organizers reveals role of Facebook, Discord. Tech Policy Press. https://www.techpolicy.press/evidence-in-trial-of-2017-unite-the-right-rally-organizer-reveals-role-of-facebook-discord

Hermann, D., & Pridöhl, H. (2020). Basic Concepts and Models of Cybersecurity. In Christen, M., Gordijn, B., & Loi, M. (Eds.), *The Ethics of Cybersecurity* (pp. 11–44). Springer International Publishing. DOI: 10.1007/978-3-030-29053-5_2

Herzog, S. (2011). Revisiting the Estonian Cyber Attacks: Digital Threats and Multinational Responses. *Journal of Strategic Security, 4*(2), 49–60. DOI: 10.5038/1944-0472.4.2.3

Hinds, J., Williams, E. J., & Joinson, A. N. (2020). "It wouldn't happen to me": Privacy concerns and perspectives following the Cambridge Analytica scandal. *International Journal of Human-Computer Studies, 143*, 102498. DOI: 10.1016/j.ijhcs.2020.102498

Hobbs, C., Moran, M., & Salisbury, D. (Eds.). (2014). *Open source intelligence in the twenty-first century: New approaches and opportunities*. Palgrave Macmillan. DOI: 10.1057/9781137353320

Hobsbawm, E. (1994). *The age of extremes: The short twentieth century, 1914–1991*. Pantheon Books.

Hoch, N. (2020). Russian Internet Research Agency disinformation activities on Tumblr: Identity, privacy, and ambivalence. *Media, War & Conflict, 13*(3), 309–326.

Hoffman, B., & Ware, J. (2024, April 26). Ropes, accelerationism, and the enduring legacy of the Turner Diaries. International Centre for Counter-Terrorism. https://icct.nl/publication/ropes-accelerationism-and-enduring-legacy-turner-diaries

Hoffman, M. (2019). *Open source (OSINT) intelligence gathering and analysis (SANS SEC487 Coursebook).* SANS Institute.

Holden-Rhodes, J. F. (1997). *Sharing the secrets: Open source intelligence and the war on drugs.* Praeger.

Ho, S. J., & Mallick, S. K. (2010). The impact of information technology on the banking industry. *The Journal of the Operational Research Society, 61*(2), 211–221. DOI: 10.1057/jors.2008.128

Hossain, M. (2022). IT and IT Enabled Service (ITES) sector in Bangladesh: Current status and future potentials. In *Digital Transformation and Economic Development in Bangladesh* (pp. 83–104). DOI: 10.1007/978-981-19-2753-9_5

Howard, P. N. (2020). *Lie machines: How to save democracy from troll armies, deceitful robots, junk news operations, and political operatives.* Yale University Press.

Huang, D. F. (2021). *Nowhere to hide: Open source intelligence gathering.* DFH Press.

Huq, A. Z. (2024). (Forthcoming). The Geopolitics of Digital Regulation. U of Chicago, Public Law. *Working Paper.*

Hussain, F., Hussain, R., & Hossain, E. (2021). Explainable artificial intelligence (XAI): An engineering perspective. arXiv preprint arXiv:2101.03613. https://arxiv.org/abs/2101.03613

Hussain, R., Kabir, R., Kar, S. K., & Arafat, S. Y. (2024). Internet Shutdown with Violations of Human Rights and Freedom of Speech. *Asian Journal of Public Health and Nursing., 1*(3), 47–50. Advance online publication. DOI: 10.62377/x3zp6t02

International Labour Organisation. (2022) Global Estimates of Modern Slavery: Forced Labour and Forced Marriage https://www.ilo.org/publications/major-publications/global-estimates-modern-slavery-forced-labour-and-forced-marriage

Internet Society. (2024, July 18). *Shutdown - Bangladesh - Internet Society Pulse.* Internet Society Pulse. https://pulse.internetsociety.org/shutdowns/mobile-internet-shut-down-in-bangladesh-amidst-protests

Jaitner, M., & Mattsson, P. A. (2015). "Russian information warfare of 2014". In M. Maybaum, A.-M. Osula, and L. Lindström (Eds.), *7th International Conference on Cyber Conflict: Architectures in Cyberspace,* pp. 39–51. NATO CCD COE Publications.

Jasanoff, S. (2004). The idiom of co-production. In *States of knowledge* (pp. 1–12). Routledge. DOI: 10.4324/9780203413845-6

Jimmy, F. (2024). Assessing the Effects of Cyber Attacks on Financial Markets. *Journal of Artificial Intelligence General Science*, *6*(1), 288–305. DOI: 10.60087/jaigs.v6i1.254

Johannes Kepler University Linz. (n.d.). An update on our efforts to combat violent extremism. https://epub.jku.at/download/pdf/11380643.pdf

Johnson, S. (2001). *Emergence: The connected lives of ants, brains, cities, and software*. Scribner.

Jones, R., Schur, M., & Brooker, C. (Writer) & Wright, J. (Director) (2016, 21 de Outubro). Nosedive (Series 3, Episode 1) [TV series episode]. In C. Brooker, B. Reisz, & A. Jones (Executive Ptoducers), Black Mirror. Zeppotron Productions; House of Tomorrow Productions; Broke & Bones Productions.

Joshi, N. (2020). Internet shutdowns during protests: A practice in digital authoritarianism. Diplomová práce, vedoucí Schlotti, Jivanta. Praha: Univerzita Karlova, Fakulta sociálních věd, Katedra bezpečnostních studií. https://dspace.cuni.cz/bitstream/handle/20.500.11956/150279/120400013.pdf?sequence=1

Kavoliūnaitė-Ragauskienė, E. (2024). Right to Privacy and Data Protection Concerns Raised by the Development and Usage of Face Recognition Technologies in the European Union. *Journal of Human Rights Practice*, *16*(2), 658–674. DOI: 10.1093/jhuman/huad065

Kelly, M. (2021, December 9). Political polarization and its echo chambers: Surprising new, cross-disciplinary perspectives from Princeton. Princeton University. https://www.princeton.edu/news/2021/12/09/political-polarization-and-its-echo-chambers-surprising-new-cross-disciplinary

Kent, S. (1949). *Strategic Intelligence for American World Policy*. Princeton University Press.

Khine, N. K. (2023, December 30). *Digital rights in the post-coup Myanmar: Enabling factors for digital authoritarianism*. https://so03.tci-thaijo.org/index.php/HRPS/article/view/266778

Kılıç, K. (2024). Radikalleşme ve şiddet içeren aşırıcılığı uzaklarda önlemek: Afrika Boynuzu'nda şiddet içeren aşırıcılığa karşı direncin güçlendirilmesi. *Türkiye Siyaset Bilimi Dergisi*, *7*(2), 97–109.

Kılıç, K., & Selçuk, Z. (2023). Radikalleşme ile mücadelede istihbarat örgütlerinin rolü: Danimarka Güvenlik ve İstihbarat Servisi (Politiets Efterretningstjeneste–PET) örneği. *Güvenlik Stratejileri Dergisi*, *19*(45), 421–453. DOI: 10.17752/guvenlikstrtj.1288297

Kitchens, B., Johnson, S. L., & Gray, P. (2020). Understanding echo chambers and filter bubbles: The impact of social media on diversification and partisan shifts in news consumption. *Management Information Systems Quarterly*, *44*(4), 1619–1649. DOI: 10.25300/MISQ/2020/16371

Kitchin, R. (2014). The data revolution: Big data, open data, data infrastructures and their consequences. *Sage (Atlanta, Ga.)*. Advance online publication. DOI: 10.4135/9781473909472

Kohan, J., Hess, S., & Hermann (Executive Producers) (2013-2019). Orange is the new black [TV series]. Lionsgate Television; Titled.

Kremer, T. (2017). Trust Is the Basis of Digitization. In Abolhassan, F. (Ed.), *Cyber Security. Simply. Make it Happen: Leveraging Digitization Through IT Security* (pp. v–viii). Springer International Publishing.

Kupper, J., Christensen, T. K., Wing, D., Hurt, M., Schumacher, M., & Meloy, R. (2022). The contagion and copycat effect in transnational far-right terrorism: An analysis of language evidence. *Perspectives on Terrorism*, *16*(4), 4–26. https://www.jstor.org/stable/27158149

Leslie, D. (2020). Understanding bias in facial recognition technologies. arXiv preprint arXiv:2010.07023. https://doi.org//arXiv.2010.07023DOI: 10.48550

Libicki, M. C. (2009). *Cyberdeterrence and Cyberwar*. RAND Corporation.

Limantė, A. (2024). Bias in facial recognition technologies used by law enforcement: Understanding the causes and searching for a way out. *Nordic Journal of Human Rights*, *42*(2), 115–134. DOI: 10.1080/18918131.2023.2277581

Lin, H. (2022). Russian Cyber Operations in the Invasion of Ukraine. *The Cyber Defense Review, 7*(4), 31-46. https://www.jstor.org/stable/48703290

Lindsay, J. R. (2013). Stuxnet and the Limits of Cyber Warfare. *Security Studies, 22*(3), 365–404. DOI: 10.1080/09636412.2013.816122

Li, Y., & Liu, Q. (2021). A comprehensive review study of cyber-attacks and cyber security; Emerging trends and recent developments. *Energy Reports*, *7*, 8176–8186. DOI: 10.1016/j.egyr.2021.08.126

Liyanage, C. (2021, June 14). QAnon and the Great Awakening: How the Deep Web rewrites ideologies and beliefs. GNET. https://gnet-research.org/2021/06/14/qanon-and-the-great-awakening-how-the-deep-web-rewrites-ideologies-and-beliefs/

Lowenthal, M. M. (2008). *Intelligence: From secrets to policy* (4th ed.). CQ Press.

Luiijf, E., & Klaver, M. (2019). Resilience Approach to Critical Information Infrastructures. In Gritzalis, D., Theocharidou, M., & Stergiopoulos, G. (Eds.), *Critical Infrastructure Security and Resilience: Theories, Methods, Tools and Technologies* (pp. 3–16). Springer International Publishing. DOI: 10.1007/978-3-030-00024-0_1

Lum, K., & Isaac, W. (2016). To predict and serve? *Significance*, *13*(5), 14–19. DOI: 10.1111/j.1740-9713.2016.00960.x

Lynch, J. (2020). Face off: Law enforcement use of face recognition technology. Available at *SSRN* 3909038. DOI: 10.2139/ssrn.3909038

Lyon, D. (2001). *Surveillance Society: Monitoring Everyday Life*. Open University Press, 2001.

Lyon, D. (2010). Liquid surveillance. *Polity*.

Macklin, G., & Bjørgo, T. (2021). Breivik's long shadow? The impact of the July 22, 2011 attacks on the modus operandi of extreme-right lone actor terrorists. *Perspectives on Terrorism*, *15*(3), 14–36. https://www.jstor.org/stable/27030880

Mahmud, F. (2024, July 30). Bangladesh's internet blackout immobilizes its booming tech industry. Rest of World. https://restofworld.org/2024/bangladesh-curfew-internet-shutdown/

Mak, T., & Lindeman, T. (2023, March 30). The rise and fall of Terrorgram: Inside a global online hate network. ProPublica. https://www.propublica.org/article/rise-and-fall-terrorgram-inside-global-online-hate-network-frontline-telegram

Malek, M. A. (2022). Criminal courts' artificial intelligence: The way it reinforces bias and discrimination. *AI and Ethics*, *2*(1), 233–245. DOI: 10.1007/s43681-022-00137-9

Manis, M., Shedler, J., Jonides, J., & Nelson, T. E. (1993). Availability heuristic in judgments of set size and frequency of occurrence. *Journal of Personality and Social Psychology*, *65*(6), 448–457. DOI: 10.1037/0022-3514.65.3.448

Marchetti, M., Colajanni, M., Messori, M., Aniello, L., & Vigfusson, Y. (2012). Cyber Attacks on Financial Critical Infrastructures. In Baldoni, R., & Chockler, G. (Eds.), *Collaborative Financial Infrastructure Protection: Tools, Abstractions, and Middleware* (pp. 53–82). Springer International Publishing. DOI: 10.1007/978-3-642-20420-3_3

Markovets, O., Buchyn, M., Kovalchuk, A., & Basyuk, T. (2023). Russian information-psychological special operations in Ukraine and peculiarities of system design for their countermeasures. *Proceedings of the 2nd International Workshop on Social Communication and Information Activity in Digital Humanities (SCIA 2023)*, 3564, pp. 87–104.

Maurya, R. (2024). Darkening Digital Democracy: A case study of Manipur Internet shutdown. *Global Media Journal-Indian Edition, 16(2)*. https://www.researchgate.net/profile/Riya-Maurya-2/publication/387207553_Darkening_Digital_Democracy_A_Case_Study_of_Manipur_Internet_Shutdown/links/676403f672316e5855fe15e8/Darkening-Digital-Democracy-A-Case-Study-of-Manipur-Internet-Shutdown.pdf

Mazur, J. (2023). Artificial Intelligence vs Data Protection: How the GDPR Can Help to Develop a Precautionary Regulatory Approach to AI? In Kornilakis, A., Nouskalis, G., Pergantis, V., & Tzimas, T. (Eds.), *Artificial Intelligence and Normative Challenges. Law, Governance and Technology Series* (Vol. 59, pp. 215–233). Springer., DOI: 10.1007/978-3-031-41081-9_12

Meresi, M. (2025). *Pattern recognition models, neural networks and machine learning for risk assessment: Building JA.I.Net.1 engine & scalable applications, predictive criminology, Amazon.com*. KDP.

Meshi, D., Morawetz, C., & Heekeren, H. R. (2015). Nucleus accumbens response to gains in reputation for the self relative to gains for others predicts social media use. *Social Cognitive and Affective Neuroscience*, *10*(2), 173–180. DOI: 10.1016/j.scan.2014.08.018

Meshi, D., Tamir, D. I., & Heekeren, H. R. (2015). The emerging neuroscience of social media. *Trends in Cognitive Sciences*, *19*(12), 771–782. DOI: 10.1016/j.tics.2015.09.004

Meta. (n.d.). How fact-checking works. Meta Transparency Center. https://transparency.meta.com/tr-tr/features/how-fact-checking-works/

Migliorini, S. (2023). Biometric harm. Law. *Technology & Humans*, *5*(2), 238–251. DOI: 10.5204/lthj.2830

Mikhaylova, A. A., & Mikhaylov, A. S. (2024). Cyberspace: A systematic review of 30 years of social and economic research. *Journal of Infrastructure. Policy and Development.*, *8*(8), 1–22. DOI: 10.24294/jipd.v8i8.6178

Mittelstadt, B. D., Allo, P., Taddeo, M., Wachter, S., & Floridi, L. (2016). The ethics of algorithms: Mapping the debate. *Big Data & Society*, *3*(2), 2053951716679679. DOI: 10.1177/2053951716679679

Möller, D. P. F. (2020). *Cybersecurity in Digital Transformation: Scope and Applications.* Springer International Publishing. DOI: 10.1007/978-3-030-60570-4

Momen, M. N., S, H., & Das, D. (2020). Mediated democracy and internet shutdown in India. *Journal of Information Communication and Ethics in Society*, *19*(2), 222–235. DOI: 10.1108/JICES-07-2020-0075

Moreno Rubio, Á. (2022). Zelensky's discourse during the Russian invasion of Ukraine: How the war of narratives influences conflicts.

Morgado, S. M. A. (2013). Crime and socio-economic context: A framework approach. In Z. V. Sovreski, M. Mokryš, Š. Badura, A., Lieskovský (Eds.), Proceedings in Advanced Research in Scientific Areas (ARSA 2013), (pp. 139 – 142.). Slovakia: EDIS - Publishing Institution of the University of Zilina.

Morgado, S. M. A. (2023). Inteligência artificial e metamorfose dos paradigmas: Economia na era da transformação. Congresso Nacional da Ordem dos Economistas – Portugal e os Desafios do Presente: O papel dos Economistas e Gestores.https://www.ordemeconomistas.pt/xportalv3/file/XEOCM_Documento/74260936/file/S%C3%B3nia%20Aniceto%20Morgado.pdf

Morgado, S. M. A., Carvalho, M., & Felgueiras, S. (2024b). Diagnosis model for detection of e-threats against soft-targets. In A. Rocha, H. Adeli, G., Dzemyda, F., Moreira, and V. Colla (eds). Information Systems and Technologies. WorldCIST 2023. Lecture Notes in Networks and Systems, vol 800 (pp. 249–262). Springer, Cham. DOI: 10.1007/978-3-031-45645-9_24

Morgado, S. M. A., Nabais, T., & Felgueiras, S. (2024a). Unveiling the project fAcilitating Public & Private secuRity operAtors to mitigate terrorIsm Scenarios against soft targEts – APPRAISE: the future for preventing and providing security for soft targets. In R. N. A. Fernandes, & P. Machado (Coord.). 40 anos das Ciências Policiais em Portugal (pp. 277-285), ICPOL.

Morgado, S. M. A., & Felgueiras, S. (2021). Big data in policing: Profiling, patterns, and out of the box thinking. In Rocha, A., Adeli, H., Dzemyda, G., Moreira, F., & Ramalho Correia, A. M. (Eds.), *Trends and Applications in Information Systems and Technologies. WorldCIST 2021. Advances in Intelligent Systems and Computing* (Vol. 1365, pp. 217–226). Springer., DOI: 10.1007/978-3-030-72657-7_21

Morgado, S. M. A., & Felgueiras, S. (2022). Technological policing: Big data versus real data. Politeia. *Revista Portuguesa de Ciências Policiais*, (XIX), 139–151. DOI: 10.57776/hkcb-br21

Morozov, E. (2018). *The net delusion: The dark side of Internet freedom.* PublicAffairs.

Morshed, M. B., Dye, M., Ahmed, S. I., & Kumar, N. (2017). When the Internet Goes Down in Bangladesh. In *Proceedings of the 2017 ACM Conference on Computer Supported Cooperative Work and Social Computing* (pp. 1591–1604). DOI: 10.1145/2998181.2998237

Mueller, R. S., III. (2019, March). Report on the investigation into Russian interference in the 2016 presidential election: Volume I of II. U.S. Department of Justice. https://www.justice.gov/storage/report.pdf

Mueller, M. L. (2020). Against Sovereignty in Cyberspace. *International Studies Review, 22*(4), 779–801. DOI: 10.1093/isr/viz044

Mugari, I., & Obioha, E. E. (2021). Predictive policing and crime control in the United States of America and Europe: Trends in a decade of research and the future of predictive policing. *Social Sciences (Basel, Switzerland), 10*(6), 1–14. DOI: 10.3390/socsci10060234

Munger, K. (2021). All the news that's fit to click: The economics of clickbait. *Journal of Media Economics.*

Murthy, D. (2023, April 17). "They're coming to take over our country": Researching global circuits of racist misinformation. MediaWell, Social Science Research Council. https://mediawell.ssrc.org/articles/theyre-coming-to-take-over-our-country-researching-global-circuits-of-racist-misinformation/

Napoli, P. M. (2019). *Social media and the public interest: Media regulation in the disinformation age*. Columbia University Press. DOI: 10.7312/napo18454

NATO. (2002). NATO open source intelligence reader.

New Age. (2025, April 12). 1,581 killed in mass uprising: students. New Age. https://www.newagebd.net/post/country/246450/1581-killed-in-mass-uprising-students

Newsweek. (2022, May 16). The Great Replacement theory has inspired several terror attacks in recent years. https://www.newsweek.com/great-replacement-theory-inspired-terror-attacks-recent-years-1706953

NoBias. (2024). NoBIAS: Artificial Intelligence without Bias. https://nobias-project.eu

Nolan, J., Plageman, G., Abrams, J. J., Thé, D., & Fisher, C. (Executive Producers). (2011-2016). Person of interest [TV series]. Killer Films; Bad Robot; Bonanza Productions; Warner Bros. Television.

Nye, J. S. (2004). *Soft power: The means to success in world politics*. PublicAffairs.

OECD Guidelines on the Protection of Privacy and Transborder Flows of Personal Data. (2013). Organisation for Economic Co-operation and Development.

Olaoye, F., & Egon, A. (2024). Predictive policing and crime prevention. https://easychair.org/publications/preprint/lQ2r/open

Onyeji, I., Bazilian, M., & Bronk, C. (2014). Cyber Security and Critical Energy Infrastructure. *The Electricity Journal*, *27*(2), 52–60. DOI: 10.1016/j.tej.2014.01.011

Oxford Analytica. (2024). *Socio-economic cost of internet shutdowns is rising*. Emerald Expert Briefings., DOI: 10.1108/OXAN-DB287653

Padmanabhan, R., Filastò, A., Xynou, M., Raman, R. S., Middleton, K., Zhang, M., Madory, D., Roberts, M., & Dainotti, A. (2021). A multi-perspective view of internet censorship in Myanmar. In *ACM SIGCOMM 2021 Workshop on Free and Open Communications on the Internet* (pp. 27–36). DOI: 10.1145/3473604.3474562

Palacín, V. (2021). *Practical threat intelligence and data-driven threat hunting: A hands-on guide to threat hunting with the ATT&CK™ framework and open source tools*. Packt Publishing.

Panguluri, S., Philips, W., & Cusimano, J. (2011). Protecting water and wastewater infrastructure from cyber attacks. *Frontiers of Earth Science*, *5*(4), 406–413. DOI: 10.1007/s11707-011-0199-5

Panini (1897) The Ashtadhyayi (S C Vasu, Trans) Benares, Panini Office

Pariser, E. (2011). *The filter bubble: What the Internet is hiding from you*. Penguin Press.

Parliament and Council. (2024). Regulation (EU) 2024/1689 of the European Parliament and of the Council of 13 June 2024 establishing the interoperability between information systems in the area of justice and home affairs and amending Regulations (EU) 2018/1726, (EU) 2019/816 and (EU) 2019/818. Official Journal of the European Union, L, 2024/1689, 13.6.2024.

Pasquale, F. (2015). *The black box society: The secret algorithms that control money and information*. Harvard University Press. DOI: 10.4159/harvard.9780674736061

PBS NewsHour. (2022, May 4). How the Telegram app became a hub for hate crime and radical extremists. PBS. https://www.pbs.org/newshour/show/how-the-telegram-app-became-a-hub-for-hate-crime-and-radical-extremists

Perkowitz, S. (2021). The bias in the machine: Facial recognition technology and racial disparities. https://mit-serc.pubpub.org/pub/bias-in-machine/release/1?readingCollection=34db8026

Pernik, P. (2018, Octobcr). Thc Early Days of Cyberattacks: The Cases of Estonia, Georgia and Ukraine. In N. Popescu & S. Secrieru (Eds.), *Hacks, Leaks and Disruptions: Russian Cyber Strategies* (pp. 53-64). Chaillot Paper No. 148, European Union Institute for Security Studies.

Perry, W L, McInnis, B, Price, C C, Smith, S C, & Hollywood, J S (2013) Predictive policing: The role of crime forecasting in law enforcement operations RAND Corporation

Perry, W. L., McInnis, B., Price, A. R., Smith, S., & Hollywood, J. S. (2013). *Predictive policing: The role of crime forecasting in law enforcement operations.* RAND Corporation. DOI: 10.7249/RR233

Personal Information Protection Law of the People's Republic of China. (2021).

Pesotskiy, A. A. (2023). The Economic Shock from the Introduction of the Sanctions Regime in the Regional Context. *Collection of Scientific Papers*, 118–128. DOI: 10.52897/978-5-7310-6226-8-2023-51-118-128

Peterson, D., & Hoffman, S. (2022). *Geopolitical implications of AI and digital surveillance adoption.* Brookings Institution.

Petersons, E. (2024, February 12). Cybersecurity challenges in the era of digitalization. DOI: 10.2139/ssrn.4723047

Pew Research Center. (2024, November 13). Mobile fact sheet. https://www.pewresearch.org/internet/fact-sheet/mobile/

Pilipenko, Z. A. (2019). Shock theory. In *Practice, progress, and proficiency in sustainability* (pp. 150–174). DOI: 10.4018/978-1-7998-1033-9.ch008

Piper, D. L. A. (n.d.). *Data protection laws of the world.* DLA Piper. Retrieved June 29, 2025, from https://www.dlapiperdataprotection.com

Plėta, T., Tvaronavičienė, M., Casa, S. D., & Agafonov, K. (2020). Cyber-attacks to critical energy infrastructure and management issues: Overview of selected cases. *Insights into Regional Development*, *2*(3), 703–715. DOI: 10.9770/IRD.2020.2.3(7)

Plumer, B. (2021, May 13). Pipeline Hack Points to Growing Cybersecurity Risk for Energy System. *The New York Times.* https://www.nytimes.com/2021/05/13/climate/pipeline-ransomware-hack-energy-grid.html

Pomerantsev, P. (2019). *This is not propaganda: Adventures in the war against reality*. Faber & Faber.

Prepare Prevent Resist. (2023, December 14). *Home - Prepare Prevent resist.* Prepare Prevent Resist -. https://preparepreventresist.org/wp-content/uploads/2022/12/Bangladesh-Summary-Report.pdf

Prier, J. (2017). Commanding the trend: Social media as information warfare. Strategic Studies Quarterly, 11(4), 50–85. https://www.jstor.org/stable/26271634

Prothomalo. (2024, July 15). *Chhatra League ready to respond to audacity on campus: Obaidul Quader.* Prothomalo. https://en.prothomalo.com/bangladesh/bi054q9uaz

Purdon, L., Ashraf, A., & Wagner, B. (2014). Security v Access: The impact of mobile network shutdowns, Case Study Telenor Pakistan. *Internet Policy Observatory.* https://core.ac.uk/download/pdf/76396194.pdf

Qadir, S., & Dar, A. A. (2021). How internet shutdowns affects the entrepreneurs in Jammu and Kashmir. *International Journal of Asian Business and Information Management, 12*(3), 109–116. DOI: 10.4018/IJABIM.20210701.oa7

Rademacher, T. (2020). Artificial intelligence and law enforcement. In Wischmeyer, T., & Rademacher, T. (Eds.), *Regulating Artificial Intelligence* (pp. 225–254). Springer., DOI: 10.1007/978-3-030-32361-5_10

Radvanovsky, R. (2006). *Critical Infrastructure: Homeland Security and Emergency Preparedness.* CRC/Taylor & Francis. DOI: 10.1201/9781420007428

Rahman, A. L. M. A. (2009). Quota Intervention in Civil Service: A Critical Review And Recommendations. *NDC E-JOURNAL, 8(1)*, 1-17. https://ndcjournal.ndc.gov.bd/ndcj/index.php/ndcj/article/view/64

Rahman, K. N. (2024, July 29). Quota movement: How will education system recover? *Bdnews24.* https://bdnews24.com/education/abed7e6b5262

RAND Corporation. (n.d.). International Fact-Checking Network (IFCN) codes and principles. https://www.rand.org/research/projects/truth-decay/fighting-disinformation/search/items/international-fact-checking-network-ifcn-codes-and.html

Rass, S., Schauer, S., König, S., & Zhu, Q. (2020). *Cyber-Security in Critical Infrastructures: A Game-Theoretic Approach.* Springer International Publishing. DOI: 10.1007/978-3-030-46908-5

Reed, J. (2025, January 10). Is the water safe? The state of critical infrastructure cybersecurity. *IBM.* https://www.ibm.com/think/insights/is-the-water-safe-state-of-critical-infrastructure-cybersecurity

Regulation - EU - 2018/1725 - EN - EUR-Lex

Regulation (EU) 2016/399 of the European Parliament and of the Council of 9 March 2016 on a Union Code on the rules governing the movement of persons across borders (Schengen Borders Code). (2016). *Official Journal of the European Union*, L 77, 1–52. https://eur-lex.europa.eu/legal-content/EN/TXT/?uri=CELEX:32016R0399

Regulation (EU) 2018/1725 of the European Parliament and of the Council of 23 October 2018 on the protection of natural persons by the Union institutions regarding processing of personal data. (2018). *Official Journal of the European Union*, L 295, 39–98.

Reporter, S. (2024, December 5). SG banks see over 1,800 cyberattacks weekly in past six months. *Asian Banking & Finance*. https://asianbankingandfinance.net/banking-technology/news/sg-banks-see-over-1800-cyberattacks-weekly-in-past-six-months

Reuters. (2024, December 6). Musk spent over quarter billion dollars to help elect Trump. Reuters. https://www.reuters.com/world/us/musk-spent-over-quarter-billion-dollars-help-elect-trump-2024-12-06/

Reuters. (2024, December 6). Why does the US want to ban TikTok? The allegations against it. https://www.reuters.com/technology/why-does-us-want-ban-tiktok-allegations-against-it-2024-12-06/

Reuters. (2024, July 18). Why are Bangladesh students protesting government job quotas? *Voice of America*. https://www.voanews.com/a/why-are-bangladesh-students-protesting-government-job-quotas-/7703253.html

Reza, Md. S., & Khan, M. M. H. (2011). Impact of global financial crisis on the economy of Bangladesh. *Bangladesh Journal of Political Economy, 27(1 & 2)*, 61–83. https://bea-bd.org/assets/articlesPhoto/VolNo_20230301155239.pdf

Ribeiro, A. (2023, December 18). Iranian petrol stations hit by cyber attack allegedly linked to Israeli hacker group. *Industrial Cyber*. https://industrialcyber.co/critical-infrastructure/iranian-petrol-stations-hit-by-cyber-attack-allegedly-linked-to-israeli-hacker-group/

Ribeiro, M. H., Ottoni, R., West, R., Almeida, V. A., & Meira, W., Jr. (2020). Auditing radicalization pathways on YouTube. In *Proceedings of the 2020 FAT* Conference.

Richardson, R., Schultz, J., & Crawford, K. (2019) Dirty data, bad predictions: How civil rights violations impact police data, predictive policing systems, and justice. New York University Law Review https://nyulawreview.org/wp-content/uploads/2019/04/NYULawReview-94-Richardson_etal-FIN.pdf

Richardson, R. (2021). Racial segregation and the data-driven society: How our failure to reckon with root causes perpetuates separate and unequal realities. *Berkeley Technology Law Journal*, *36*(3), 1051. DOI: 10.15779/Z38PN8XG3V

Richardson, R., Schultz, J. M., & Crawford, K. (2019). Dirty data, bad predictions: How civil rights violations impact police data, predictive policing systems, and justice. *NYUL Rev. Online*, *94*, 15.

Rid, T. (2012, February). Cyber War Will Not Take Place. *The Journal of Strategic Studies*, *35*(1), 5–32. DOI: 10.1080/01402390.2011.608939

Rid, T. (2020). *Active measures: The secret history of disinformation and political warfare*. Farrar, Straus and Giroux.

Roksandić, S., Protrka, N., & Engelhart, M. (2022, May). Trustworthy Artificial Intelligence and its use by Law Enforcement Authorities: where do we stand? In 2022 45th Jubilee International Convention on Information, Communication and Electronic Technology (MIPRO) (pp. 1225-1232). IEEE. Opatija, Croatia. DOI: 10.23919/MIPRO55190.2022.9803606

Rosenzweig, P. (2013). *Cyber Warfare: How Conflicts in Cyberspace Are Challenging America and Changing the World*. Bloomsbury Publishing USA. DOI: 10.5040/9798400636493

Roshanaei, M. (2021). Resilience at the Core: Critical Infrastructure Protection Challenges, Priorities and Cybersecurity Assessment Strategies. *Journal of Computer and Communications*, *9*(8), 80–102. DOI: 10.4236/jcc.2021.98006

Ross, T., Paun, C., & Popoviciu, A. (2024, December 6). Romanian court cancels presidential election amid Russian influence fears. Politico. https://www.politico.eu/article/romania-court-cancels-presidential-election-runoff-tiktok-russian-influence-calin-georgescu/

Rouse, W B (2011) Translational systems science: From discovery to application Wiley

Rowley, J. (2007). The wisdom hierarchy: Representations of the DIKW hierarchy. *Journal of Information Science*, *33*(2), 163–180. DOI: 10.1177/0165551506070706

Roy, G. (2024). Quota reform movement, internet shutdown and economic shock: Bangladesh. *SSRN*, Preprint. https://papers.ssrn.com/sol3/papers.cfm?abstract_id=4911644

Rudner, M. (2013). Cyber-Threats to Critical National Infrastructure: An Intelligence Challenge. *International Journal of Intelligence and CounterIntelligence, 26*(3), 453–481. DOI: 10.1080/08850607.2013.780552

Salminen, M., & Hossain, K. (2018). Digitalisation and human security dimensions in cybersecurity: An appraisal for the European High North. *The Polar Record, 54*(2), 108–118. DOI: 10.1017/S0032247418000268

Sandywell, B. (2006). Monsters in cyberspace: Cyberphobia and cultural panic in the information age. *Information Communication and Society, 9*(1), 39–61. DOI: 10.1080/13691180500519407

Sankin, A., & Mattu, S. (2023) Predictive Policing Software Terrible At Predicting Crimes https://themarkup.org/prediction-bias/2023/10/02/predictive-policing-software-terrible-at-predicting-crimes

Schuetz, P. N. (2021). Fly in the Face of Bias: Algorithmic Bias in Law Enforcement's Facial Recognition Technology and the Need for an Adaptive Legal Framework. *Minnesota Journal of Law & Inequality, 39*(1), 221–254. DOI: 10.24926/25730037.626

Seattle University. (n.d.). The European Union's Digital Services Act: A new era for the internet. Seattle University – Albers School of Business and Economics. https://www.seattleu.edu/business/news-events/pov/ethics-matter/posts/the-european-unions-digital-services-act-a-new-era-for-the-internet.php

Seemma, P. S., Nandhini, S., & Sowmiya, M. (2018, November). Overview of Cyber Security. *International Journal of Advanced Research in Computer and Communication Engineering, 7*(11), 125–128. DOI: 10.17148/IJARCCE.2018.71127

Selbst, A. D. (2017). Disparate Impact in Big Data Policing. *SSRN, 52*(1), 109–195. DOI: 10.2139/ssrn.2819182

SentinelOne. (2024, September 23). Cyber Security in Finance: Key Threats and Strategies. https://www.sentinelone.com/cybersecurity-101/cybersecurity/cyber-security-in-finance/

Shah, M. G., & Junaid-Ul-Shafi, N. (2024). COVID-19, Internet and Education: Loss of a generation. *Peace Review, 36*(3), 443–454. DOI: 10.1080/10402659.2024.2352411

Shahrezaye, M., Stier, S., & Neubaum, G. (2024). Designing algorithms to increase exposure to counter-attitudinal content. In de León, A., Esser, A., & Friemel, N. (Eds.), *The Routledge companion to media disinformation and populism* (pp. 265–278). Springer., DOI: 10.1007/978-3-031-78554-2_16

Sha, L., Gopalakrishnan, S., Liu, X., & Wang, Q. (2009). Cyber-Physical Systems: A New Frontier. In Tsai, J. J. P., & Yu, P. S. (Eds.), *Machine Learning in Cyber Trust: Security, Privacy, and Reliability* (pp. 1–13). Springer International Publishing. DOI: 10.1007/978-0-387-88735-7_1

Sharma, V., Oo, P. P., Hollaender, J., & Scott, J. (2021). COVID-19 and a coup: Blockage of internet and social media access further exacerbate gender-based violence risks for women in Myanmar. *BMJ Global Health*, *6*(6), e006564. DOI: 10.1136/bmjgh-2021-006564 PMID: 34193476

Shea, T., Gaycken, S., & Martellini, M. (2013). Cyber Security for Nuclear Power Plants. In Martellini, M. (Ed.), *Cyber Security: Deterrence and IT Protection for Critical Infrastructures* (pp. 25–35). Springer International Publishing. DOI: 10.1007/978-3-319-02279-6_3

Shirin, B. (2023, December 3). Internet ban lifted in violence-hit Manipur, restrictions in border areas till Dec 18. *India Today*. https://www.indiatoday.in/india/story/manipur-violence-internet-services-restored-border-areas-exception-meiteis-kukis-2471548-2023-12-04

Simon, D., Colesberry, R. F., & Noble, N. K. (Executive Producers). (2002-2008). The wire [TV series]. Blown Deadline Productions, HBO Entertainment. HBO.

Singer, P. W. (2015). Stuxnet and Its Hidden Lessons on the Ethics of Cyberweapons. *Case Western Reserve Journal of International Law*, *47*(1), 79–86. https://scholarlycommons.law.case.edu/jil/vol47/iss1/10

Sinha, S. K., Davis, C., Gardoni, P., Babbar-Sebens, M., Stuhr, M., Huston, D., Cauffman, S., Williams, W. D., Alanis, L. G., Anand, H., & Vishwakarma, A. (2023). Water sector infrastructure systems resilience: A social–ecological–technical system-of-systems and whole-life approach. *Cambridge Prisms*, *1*, 1–24. DOI: 10.1017/wat.2023.3

Slater, A. P. (2023). Social media intelligence (SOCMINT) investigative framework as a human trafficking deterrent tool (Master's thesis). American Military University.

Smith, D. C. (2021). Cybersecurity in the energy sector: Are we really prepared? *Journal of Energy & Natural Resources Law*, *39*(3), 265–270. DOI: 10.1080/02646811.2021.1943935

Smith, M., & Miller, S. (2021). *Biometric identification, law and ethics*. Springer Nature. DOI: 10.1007/978-3-030-90256-8

Smith, M., & Miller, S. (2022). The ethical application of biometric facial recognition technology. *AI & Society, 37*(1), 167–175. DOI: 10.1007/s00146-021-01199-9 PMID: 33867693

Söderholm, S. (2023). Fundamental rights control when implementing predictive policing–a European perspective. *Peking University Law Journal, 11*(1), 91–104. DOI: 10.1080/20517483.2023.2223850

Southern Poverty Law Center. (2017, August 12). Flags and other symbols used by far-right groups in Charlottesville. https://www.splcenter.org/resources/hatewatch/flags-and-other-symbols-used-far-right-groups-charlottesville/

Spielberg, S. (2002). Minory report [Movie]. 20th Century Fox, Dreamworks Pictures, Amblin Entertainment, Blue Tulip Productions; 20th Century Fox.

Stacy, E. (2017). *Human and algorithm facial recognition performance: Face in a crowd*. University of Technology Sydney.

Stankus, T. (2011). Our modern skulls house a stone age brain: An overview and annotated bibliography of evolutionary psychology, Part I. *Behavioral & Social Sciences Librarian, 30*(3), 131–150. DOI: 10.1080/01639269.2011.591276

Statista. (2023). Internet penetration rate worldwide in 2023, by country income level. https://www.statista.com/statistics/1361735/internet-penetration-rate-by-country-income-level/

Statista. (2024). Number of internet users worldwide from 2010 to 2024. https://www.statista.com/statistics/617136/digital-population-worldwide/

Steele, R. D. (2004). *Special Operations Forces Open Source Intelligence (OSINT) handbook*. OSS Inc.

Stevens, J. (2001, April 24-25). Defining intelligence-led policing. [Paper presented]. 2nd World Investigation of Crime Conference, Durban, South Africa.

Stevens, T. (2018). Cyberweapons: Power and the governance of the invisible. *International Politics, 55*(3-4), 482–502. DOI: 10.1057/s41311-017-0088-y

Stone, J. (2013). Cyber War Will Take Place! *The Journal of Strategic Studies, 36*(1), 101–108. DOI: 10.1080/01402390.2012.730485

Suler, J. (2004). The online disinhibition effect. *Cyberpsychology & Behavior, 7*(3), 321–326. DOI: 10.1089/1094931041291295

Sunstein, C. R. (2009). *Republic.com 2.0*. Princeton University Press.

Sunstein, C. R. (2018). *Republic: Divided democracy in the age of social media*. Princeton University Press.

Suroy, H. S. (2024, August 5). Bangladesh BPO sector faces $34Mn loss after internet shutdown. *Outsource Accelerator*. https://news.outsourceaccelerator.com/bangladesh-bpo-sector-faces-loss/

Tagat, A., Phokeer, A., & Kreitem, H. M. (2024). Net Loss: An econometric method to measure the impact of Internet shutdowns. *ACM Journal on Computing and Sustainable Societies*, *2*(2), 1–22. DOI: 10.1145/3659466

Tambini, D. (2017). *Fake news: Public policy responses. Media Policy Brief 20*. London School of Economics.

Tanner, J. (2024, July 22). *Bangladesh internet goes dark amid protest violence*. Developing Telecoms. https://developingtelecoms.com/telecom-business/telecom-regulation/17035-bangladesh-internet-goes-dark-amid-protest-violence.html

TASS. (2014a). *Number of requests for asylum by Ukrainians doubles in Krasnodar region* [Число обращений граждан Украины в ФМС в Краснодарском крае увеличилось на 100%]. *TASS Russian News Agency*, 26 March. http://itar-tass.com/obschestvo/1075504

TASS. (2014b). *Ukrainians request temporary asylum in Novgorod* [Граждане Украины просят временное убежище в Новгородской области]. *TASS Russian News Agency*, 26 March. http://itar-tass.com/spb-news/1076617

TASS. (2014c). *FMS: Over 245k Ukrainians ask for asylum in Russia* [ФМС: за временным убежищем в РФ обратились более 245 тыс. граждан Украины]. *TASS Russian News Agency*, 4 December. http://itar-tass.com/obschestvo/1616949

Tayebi, M. A., Glässer, U., & Skillicorn, D. B. (Eds.). (2020). *Open source intelligence and cyber crime: Social media analytics*. Springer. U.S. Army. 2016. Open source intelligence (OSINT) Analyst Manual. DOI: 10.1007/978-3-030-41251-7

The Business Standard. (2024, August 3). Bangladesh faces $10b setback, image crisis: Biz leaders. The Business Standard. https://www.tbsnews.net/economy/bangladesh-faces-10b-setback-image-crisis-biz-leaders-905336

The Business Standard. (2024, July 31). Internet, FB shutdown: Digital commerce loses Tk1,700cr in 13 days. *The Business Standard*. https://www.tbsnews.net/economy/e-cab-leaders-seek-govt-assistance-reviving-e-commerce-sector-amid-ongoing-crisis-907356

The Daily Star. (2024, August 1). E-commerce sector lost TK 1,700 crore for internet shutdown, violence: e-CAB. The Daily Star. https://www.thedailystar.net/business/news/e-commerce-sector-lost-tk-1700-crore-internet-shutdown-violence-e-cab-3667231

The Daily Star. (2024, August 10). Ledger of losses. The Daily Star. https://www.thedailystar.net/business/news/ledger-losses-3673416

The Daily Star. (2024, August 5). Mobile internet, social media blocked again. *The Daily Star*. https://www.thedailystar.net/news/bangladesh/news/mobile-internet-social-media-blocked-again-3669681

The Daily Star. (2024, September 13). At least 875 killed in July mass uprising. The Daily Star. https://www.thedailystar.net/news/bangladesh/crime-justice/news/least-875-killed-july-mass-uprising-3702451

The Economist. (2018, April 21). Protests in Bangladesh put an end to a corrupt quota system. The Economist. https://www.economist.com/asia/2018/04/21/protests-in-bangladesh-put-an-end-to-a-corrupt-quota-system

The Economist. (2022, August 17). How Democrats and Republicans see each other. https://www.economist.com/graphic-detail/2022/08/17/how-democrats-and-republicans-see-each-other

The Guardian. (2013, July 4). Brazilian protesters use Twitter, Microsoft data shows. https://www.theguardian.com/news/datablog/2013/jul/04/brazilian-protesters-twitter-microsoft

The Guardian. (2024). Elon Musk's Super Pac spent $200m to help elect Donald Trump https://www.theguardian.com

The Independent. (2019, August 24). Revered as a saint by online extremists: How Christchurch shooter inspired copycat terrorists around the world. https://www.independent.co.uk/news/world/australasia/brenton-tarrant-christchurch-shooter-attack-el-paso-norway-poway-a9076926.html

The Loop – ECPR. (2024, April 8). How Călin Georgescu's TikTok tactics rewired Romanian politics. https://theloop.ecpr.eu/how-calin-georgescus-tiktok-tactics-rewired-romanian-politics/

The New York Times. (2018, December 4). SWAT leader demoted after wearing QAnon patch while meeting Vice President Pence. https://www.nytimes.com/2018/12/04/us/swat-leader-qanon-patch.html

The New York Times. (2021, January 6). Protesters storm Capitol Hill building. https://www.nytimes.com/2021/01/06/us/politics/protesters-storm-capitol-hill-building.html

The New York Times. (2022, May 16). Buffalo shooting: What we know about the attack. https://www.nytimes.com/2022/05/16/nyregion/buffalo-shooting-attack.html

The Washington Post. (2021, January 15). Far-right symbols seen at the U.S. Capitol riot: What they mean and where they come from. https://www.washingtonpost.com/nation/interactive/2021/far-right-symbols-capitol-riot/

Thomi, L. B. (2021). *The impact of biometric systems at EU outside borders on the human rights of irregular migrating women* (Master's thesis). Gender, Conflict and Humanitarian Study.

Tiirmaa-Klaar, H. (2016). Building national cyber resilience and protecting critical information infrastructure. *Journal of Cyber Policy*, *1*(1), 94–106. DOI: 10.1080/23738871.2016.1165716

Tucek, A. (2015) Constraining Big Brother: The Legal Deficiencies Surrounding Chicago's Use of the Strategic Subject List https://legal-forum.uchicago.edu/print-archive/constraining-big-brother-legal-deficiencies-surrounding-chicagos-use-strategic

Tucker, J. A., Theocharis, Y., Roberts, M. E., & Barberá, P. (2017). From liberation to turmoil: Social media and democracy. *Journal of Democracy*, *28*(4), 46–59. DOI: 10.1353/jod.2017.0064

Tufekci, Z. (2018). YouTube, the great radicalizer. *The New York Times*.

Tufekci, Z. (2015). *Algorithmic harms beyond Facebook and Google: Emergent challenges of computational agency*. Colorado Technology Law Journal.

Tufekci, Z. (2017). *Twitter and tear gas: The power and fragility of networked protest*. Yale University Press.

Twitter. (2016, August 18). An update on our efforts to combat violent extremism. https://blog.x.com/en_us/a/2016/an-update-on-our-efforts-to-combat-violent-extremism

Uddin, H., Ali, H., & Hassan, M. K. (2020). Cybersecurity hazards and fnancial system vulnerability: A synthesis of literatüre. *Risk Management*, *22*(4), 239–309. DOI: 10.1057/s41283-020-00063-2

Uddin, M. M., & Chowdhury, M. J. A. (2016). Quota reservations in civil service: Arguments for a class based preference system. *Chittagong University Journal of Law*, *21*, 1–22.

Udoh, E. S. (2020, September). Is the data fair? An assessment of the data quality of algorithmic policing systems. In *Proceedings of the 13th International Conference on Theory and Practice of Electronic Governance* (pp. 1-7). DOI: 10.1145/3428502.3428503

United Nations. Human Rights. (2025). Fact-Finding: Report Human Rights Violations and Abuses related to the Protests of July and August 2024 in Bangladesh. In *UN Office of the High Commissioner for Human Rights (OHCHR)*. https://www.ohchr.org/sites/default/files/documents/countries/bangladesh/ohchr-fftb-hr-violations-bd.pdf

Vaidhyanathan, S. (2018). *Antisocial media: How Facebook disconnects us and undermines democracy*. Oxford University Press.

Van Brakel, R. (2020). Rethinking predictive policing: Towards a holistic framework of democratic algorithmic surveillance. In Schuilenbur, M., & Peeters, R. (Eds.), *The Algorithmic Society* (pp. 104–118). Routledge. DOI: 10.4324/9780429261404-9

Van Dijck, J. (2013). *The culture of connectivity: A critical history of social media*. Oxford University Press. DOI: 10.1093/acprof:oso/9780199970773.001.0001

Van Dijck, J. (2014). Datafication, dataism and dataveillance: Big data between scientific paradigm and ideology. *Surveillance & Society*, *12*(2), 197–208. DOI: 10.24908/ss.v12i2.4776

Van Dijck, J., & Poell, T. (2013). Understanding social media logic. *Media and Communication*, *1*(1), 2–14. DOI: 10.17645/mac.v1i1.70

Van Dijck, J., Poell, T., & de Waal, M. (2018). *The platform society: Public values in a connective world*. Oxford University Press. DOI: 10.1093/oso/9780190889760.001.0001

Van Prooijen, J.-W., Krouwel, A. P. M., & Pollet, T. V. (2015). Political extremism predicts belief in conspiracy theories. *Social Psychological & Personality Science*, *6*(5), 570–578. DOI: 10.1177/1948550614567356

Vavoula, N. (2022). *Frontex and the EU Commission quietly expand biometric data collection on migrants under PeDRA, risking discriminatory criminalization*. Queen Mary University of London. Web.: https://left.eu/frontex-europol-collusion-in-targeting-migrants

Venkatachary, S. K., Prasad, J., & Samikannu, R. (2017). Economic Impacts of Cyber Security in Energy Sector: A Review. *International Journal of Energy Economics and Policy*, *7*(5), 250–262. http://hdl.handle.net/11159/1315

Viner, K. (2016, July 12). How technology disrupted the truth. The Guardian. https://www.theguardian.com/media/2016/jul/12/how-technology-disrupted-the-truth

Virginia Consumer Data Protection Act (VCDPA), Va. Code Ann. § 59.1-575 et seq. (2021).

Voltmer, K. (2006). *Mass media and political communication in new democracies*. Psychology Press.

Wagner, B. (2018, September 18). *Authoritarian Practices in the Digital Age| Understanding Internet Shutdowns: A Case Study from Pakistan*. Wagner | International Journal of Communication. https://ijoc.org/index.php/ijoc/article/view/8545/2465

Wagner-Egger, P. (2007). Conditional reasoning and the Wason selection task: Biconditional interpretation instead of reasoning bias. *Thinking & Reasoning*, *13*(4), 484–505. DOI: 10.1080/13546780701415979

Walker, J. (2013). *The United States of paranoia: A conspiracy theory*. Harper.

Walsh, T. (2024). TikTok as a site of social protest in Iran's Gen-Z uprising. *Discourse & Society*, *35*(5), 625–650. DOI: 10.1177/09579265241234351

Wan, J. (2015). Fast and furious 7 [Movie]. MRC, Original Film, One Race Films, China Film Co., Ltd.; Universal Pictures.

Warner, M. (2002). Wanted: A Definition of "Intelligence". *Studies in Intelligence*, *46*(3), 15–22.

Washington, A. L. (2019). How to argue with an algorithm: Lessons from the COMPAS ProPublica Debate. The Colorado Technology Law Journal, 17(1), 1-37. https://ssrn.com/abstract=3357874

Weenink, A. W. (2022). Mental health and terrorism: A review of the literature. *Journal of Psychiatric Research*, *146*, 141–149. DOI: 10.1016/j.jpsychires.2021.12.057

Weiss, M., & Biermann, F. (2021). Cyberspace and the protection of critical national infrastructure. *Journal of Economic Policy Reform*, *26*(3), 250–267. DOI: 10.1080/17487870.2021.1905530

Wells, G. (2019, October 23). Islamic State's TikTok posts include beheading videos. The Wall Street Journal. https://www.wsj.com/articles/islamic-states-tiktok-posts-include-beheading-videos-11571855833

Wiil, U. K. (Ed.). (2011). *Counterterrorism and open source intelligence*. Springer., DOI: 10.1007/978-3-7091-0388-3

Willet, M. (2022). The Cyber Dimension of the Russia–Ukraine War. *Survival. Survival, 64*(5), 7–26. DOI: 10.1080/00396338.2022.2126193

Winner, L. (1980). Do artifacts have politics? *Daedalus, 109*(1), 121–136.

WIRED. (2016, March 8). Why ISIS is winning the social media war—and how to beat it. https://www.wired.com/2016/03/isis-winning-social-media-war-heres-beat/

WIVB News 4. (2022, May 16). Racist screed linked to Buffalo mass shooter plagiarized manifesto portions from Christchurch mosque shooter, Great Replacement theory. https://www.wivb.com/news/buffalo-supermarket-mass-shooting-tops/racist-screed-linked-to-buffalo-mass-shooter-plagiarized-manifesto-portions-from-christchurch-mosque-shooter-great-replacement-theory/

Woolf, S. H. (2008). The meaning of translational research and why it matters. *Journal of the American Medical Association, 299*(2), 211–213.

World Trade Organization. (2022). Digital connectivity, e-commerce and sustainable trade. In *Aid for Trade Global Review 2022* (pp. 86–127). Aid for Trade Global Review., DOI: 10.30875/9789287072085c006

Yasmin, N. (2010). Quota system in Bangladesh Civil Service: an appraisal [MA thesis], BRAC University. https://dspace.bracu.ac.bd/xmlui/bitstream/handle/10361/2085/Quota%20System%20in%20Bangladesh%20Civil%20Service%20An.pdf?isAllowed=y&sequence=1

Zangana, H. M., Omar, M., & Mohammed, D. (2025). Introduction to Artificial Intelligence in Cybersecurity and Forensic Science. In Omar, M., Zangana, H. M., & Mohammed, D. (Eds.), *Integrating Artificial Intelligence in Cybersecurity and Forensic Practices* (pp. 1–24). IGI Global Scientific Publishing., DOI: 10.4018/979-8-3373-0588-2.ch001

Zeng, J., Stevens, T., & Chen, Y. (2017). China's solution to global cyber governance: Unpacking the domestic discourse of "internet sovereignty". *Politics & Policy, 45*(3), 432–464. DOI: 10.1111/polp.12202

Ziosi, M., & Pruss, D. (2024, June). Evidence of what, for whom? The socially contested role of algorithmic bias in a predictive policing tool. In The 2024 ACM Conference on Fairness, Accountability, and Transparency (pp. 1596-1608). DOI: 10.1145/3630106.3658991

Zuboff, S. (2019). *The Age of Surveillance Capitalism: The Fight for a Human Future at the New Frontier of Power*. Profile Books / PublicAffairs.

Zuboff, S. (2019). *The age of surveillance capitalism: The fight for a human future at the new frontier of power*. PublicAffairs.

About the Contributors

Alp Cenk Arslan is an assistant professor specializing in security and intelligence studies at the Turkish National Police Academy. With a Ph.D. in Security Strategies and Management, his dissertation, The Construction of Security on the Basis of Techno-Politics: The Case of the United States, explores the evolving dynamics of security in the techno-political era. Dr. Arslan's research and teaching interests include the intersection of techno-politics, artificial intelligence governance, intelligence studies, and communication theories. His work examines the implications of emerging technologies on global security frameworks and intelligence methodologies. He is the author of Intelligence Analysis: Reproduction of Information, and his forthcoming book, Theory of the Techno-Political, expands on the theoretical underpinnings of his field. Dr. Arslan holds a double major in Political Science and Communications, a Master's degree in Intelligence Studies, and a Ph.D. in Security Strategies and Management from the Turkish National Police Academy. His scholarly work has been supported by numerous academic initiatives and is informed by his interdisciplinary approach to security and intelligence. He has delivered presentations and discussions on new types of terrorism, high-risk cybercriminal networks, radicalization, far-right and far-left extremism, and cult structures at summits and academic meetings organized under the auspices of the European Union CEPOL, the Council of Europe, and similar institutions.

Murat Tınas currently works at the Turkish National Police Academy as an Associate Professor Dr. His diverse career spans both academic and practical engagements, including his role as an academic adviser on various NATO and EU-sponsored projects since 2018. Dr. Tınas holds a Ph.D. in Area Studies from Middle East Technical University and complemented his graduate studies with intensive Arabic language training in Jordan. He also conducted research as an affiliate at the Center for Arab and Middle Eastern Studies at the American University of

Beirut, Lebanon. Dr. Tınas's current research focuses on Middle Eastern politics, radicalization, terrorism, and intelligence studies.

***

Md. Ashrafuzzaman is an Assistant Professor in the Department of Educational Technology and Engineering (EdTE) at the University of Frontier Technology, Bangladesh. Previously, he worked as a Research Coordinator in the EIA-DU-OU (UK) Research Collaboration Programme at the Institute of Education and Research (IER), University of Dhaka (DU). He has completed his BEd (Hons), MEd, and MPhil from IER, DU. He has fifteen years of experience in teaching and educational research, focusing on teachers' training programs, underprivileged children's education, English language education, classroom practice, teaching methods and techniques, assessment and feedback practice, ICT in education, online, blended and hybrid learning, AI in education and educational technology.

Yağız Atay holds a bachelor's degree in psychology with a minor in political science. He earned his master's degree in Intelligence Studies from the Turkish National Defence University, where he is currently pursuing a Ph.D. in Security Studies. His research focuses on radicalization, decision-making, and terrorism. He is particularly interested in the psychological and strategic dimensions of security-related issues.

Aurélie Banck is a data privacy expert with nearly 20 years of experience. She has implemented privacy programs for major organizations, including the French Ministry of the Interior and BNP Paribas, and spent three years at the French Data Protection Authority overseeing the banking and insurance sectors. Her combined experience as regulator and data controller allows her to align business operations with regulatory requirements. Aurélie is the author of 20 Data Protection Compliance Sheets (Gualino, 6th edition, 2025), a practical reference for professionals. She also shares her expertise as a part-time university lecturer in data protection.

Yusuf Dinçel got his bachelor's degree from International Relations department of Ankara University. He took his master's degree with his thesis "'Small Ally' in the Grip of Great Powers: Nestorians During and After the First World War" from International Relations department of TOBB University of Economics and Technology. Yusuf Dinçel completed his PhD in International Relations at Hacettepe University. He is currently working as an assistant professor in the field of International Security at the Turkish National Police Academy. His research areas focus on intelligence, history of intelligence, and Middle East.

Sérgio Ricardo Costa Felgueiras is now Superintendent and Deputy Chief in ISCPSI. Over recent years, has been distinguished for his role as the Director of Education at the ISCPSI, especially for his work in creating, coordinating, and accrediting study cycles in the field of police sciences, both in Portugal and Europe. With extensive experience in police education, Felgueiras is known for implementing a student-centred pedagogical policy, both in-person and online. The courses he has developed integrate various scientific areas, including Social and Political Sciences, Legal Sciences, and Police Sciences. In terms of teaching, his experience spans two decades across different fields of police sciences, having taught subjects like Armament, Ballistics, Police Strategy and Tactics, Security Technologies, Management and Direction of Security, and Public Order, among others. He is a Scientific Council and Pedagogical Council member at the Instituto Superior de Ciências Policiais e Segurança Interna. Felgueiras has specialized in distance learning pedagogy and is currently responsible for the digital transition in police higher education in Portugal. He participates in the Impulso 2025 project, representing ISCPSI in the consortium. Currently, he coordinates the Master's in Public Security and the Bachelor's in Police Sciences. Notably, he coordinated the European Joint Master Programme of the European Police College (2015-2019) and participated in the Higher Education Expert Group of CEPOL. His research journey is marked by consistency and an eclectic nature. Currently, he is an integrated member of ICPOL - Research Centre of the Instituto Superior de Ciências Policiais e Segurança Interna, where he coordinates the Police Work and Organization research line and collaborates with CAPP (Center for Administration and Public Policies) at the Instituto Superior de Ciências Sociais e Políticas (University of Lisbon). His research activity includes participation in 10 international projects and several national projects. Active research projects include APPRAISE, IMPROVE, SmartCFM (Smart Crowd and Flow Monitor), Police KPIs, and Security Technologies. He has published around 30 publications in various formats.

Mihaela Meresi is a researcher and innovator in Social Sciences, with a focus on advanced economic models based on green energy, social development, criminology and forensic psychology. A dedicated European public administrator since 2008, she managed important R&I projects and contributed to EU policies on Open Science, the European Open Science Cloud, Open Data and GDPR, in Brussels. Holding a Ph.D. in Sociology (2007) from "Al.I.Cuza" University of Iaşi, Romania, Dr. Meresi excels in international environments focused of policy design and implementation, integrating advanced research, innovation, development, diplomacy and international cooperation to drive transformative solutions.

Sónia Maria Aniceto Morgado, PhD, is a distinguished economist and researcher with a proven history of leadership and diverse experience across academia, public service, and specialized sectors. Currently a Head of Economics Department (since 2015), and Auxiliar Professor at the Instituto Superior de Ciências Policiais e Segurança Interna since 2012, she brings deep expertise in policing sciences. She is a Scientific Council and Pedagogical Council member at Instituto Superior de Ciências Policiais e Segurança Interna. Her professional journey includes significant roles as an auditor at the Court of Auditors, an economic and financial advisor, and a hospital administrator, demonstrating a unique breadth of experience and strong analytical capabilities derived from a robust academic foundation, including a PhD in Economics and Business Management. Dr. Morgado is at the forefront of critical research areas, coordinating the Work and Police Organization research line at ICPOL. Her involvement in key national and international projects, such as the EU-funded APPRAISE, IMPROVE, IMPRODOVA, Police KPI, highlights her impactful contributions to cutting-edge fields like AI in policing, security, and quality of life and economics. A registered economist with a strong publication record in international scientific journals, her expertise spans various economic domains and advanced research methodologies. Distinguished Fellow of the Portuguese Order of Economists, and recognized for her significant contributions and leadership in both academic and applied contexts, she is a highly versatile professional with a track record of driving impactful initiatives.

Efnan Gülşen Özkan graduated as the top student from the Department of Management Information Systems at Ankara Yıldırım Beyazıt University in 2023. Before graduating, she completed a front-end development internship at the Digital Transformation Office of the Presidency of the Republic of Türkiye and took part in several voluntary internships. Since October 2023, she has been working in the Business Development Department at Anadolu Agency. In 2024, she began her master's studies in the Intelligence Studies program at the Turkish National Police Academy. Her academic interests include perception management, information technologies, artificial intelligence, and international security, with a particular focus on how digital tools shape modern intelligence and strategic communication.

Gianina Anemona Radu is a Romanian professional with extensive experience in law enforcement, academia, and European Union affairs. Her background makes her a valuable contributor to forthcoming research. As of November 2024, Radu holds the position of Seconded National Expert at the European Border and Coast Guard Agency (Frontex) in Warsaw, Poland. Prior to this, Radu dedicated 21 years to academia at the Police Academy "Al. I. Cuza" in Bucharest, Romania (2003-October 2024), where she served as a Senior Lecturer PhD. She also held positions as an Associate Professor at Dunărea de Jos University in Gala i and an Assistant Professor at Danubius University in Gala i. Gianina Radu holds a Doctoral degree in Law and is the author of over 50 publications in the field of law and law enforcement. Her notable works include "Culegere de spe e în materie procesual-penală" (Collection of Cases in Criminal Procedural Law), "Drept procesual penal. Partea generală" (Criminal Procedural Law. General Part), and "Drept penal general" (General Criminal Law). She has also authored articles such as "Some Considerations Regarding the Use of Artificial Intelligence in Law Enforcement" and "The Investigation of Environmental Crimes – a Challenge with Significant Effects on our Approach". Her educational background includes a Bachelor's Degree in Law from "Al. I. Cuza" University, Iaşi, doctoral studies at Al.I. Cuza Police Academy, master's studies in Human Resources Management at Bucharest University of Economic Studies, and a postgraduate program in Criminal Law from the University of Bucharest. She has also obtained various certifications, including a Trainer Advanced Certificate and a Mediator Certificate

Md. Sanaullah is a Lecturer in History in the Department of General Education at the University of Frontier Technology, Bangladesh. He earned a Bachelor of Arts (Honors) in Islamic History and Culture and a Master of Arts in the Sociological History of Islam from the University of Dhaka. Prior to his current academic appointment, he served as a Lecturer in Islamic History and Culture at Barguna Government Mohila College, Bangladesh. With over four years of teaching experience, Mr. Sanaullah is dedicated to advancing historical scholarship and pedagogy. His research interests encompass socio-economic history, digital history, social science, and history education, reflecting a commitment to interdisciplinary and innovative approaches in historical inquiry.

Doğukan Tuncal holds a Bachelor of Laws degree from Bilkent University and a Master's Degree in Intelligence Studies (English) at the Turkish National Police Academy. He is currently a PhD candidate in the English-language International Security Doctoral Program at the same institution. He has professional experience in both private and public sectors. His scholarly interests cover counterintelligence, human intelligence (HUMINT), psychological operations, and the methodological foundations of intelligence studies.

Psychee Zaman is a postgraduate student at the Institute of Education and Research, University of Dhaka. She completed her Bachelor of Science in Educational Technology and Engineering from the University of Frontier Technology, Bangladesh. Her research focuses on educational technology, education and social sciences, with a particular focus on advancing innovative practices and evidence-based policies to enhance teaching and learning.

Index

A

B

C

D

E

F

G

H

I

L

M

N

P

Q

R

S

T

X